St
MILITARY FAMILY READINESS SYSTEM
for a Changing American Society

Committee on the Well-Being of Military Families

Kenneth W. Kizer and Suzanne Le Menestrel, *Editors*

Board on Children, Youth, and Families

Division of Behavioral and Social Sciences and Education

A Consensus Study Report of

The National Academies of
SCIENCES · ENGINEERING · MEDICINE

THE NATIONAL ACADEMIES PRESS
Washington, DC
www.nap.edu

THE NATIONAL ACADEMIES PRESS 500 Fifth Street, NW Washington, DC 20001

This activity was supported by a contract awarded to the National Academy of Sciences and funded by the U.S. Department of Defense through Basic Ordering Agreement No. HHSP233201400020B, Task Order No. HHSP23337071. Any opinions, findings, conclusions, or recommendations expressed in this publication do not necessarily reflect the views of any organization or agency that provided support for the project.

International Standard Book Number-13: 978-0-309-48953-9
International Standard Book Number-10: 0-309-48953-9
Library of Congress Control Number: 2019947790
Digital Object Identifier: https://doi.org/10.17226/25380

Additional copies of this publication are available for sale from the National Academies Press, 500 Fifth Street, NW, Keck 360, Washington, DC 20001; (800) 624-6242 or (202) 334-3313; http://www.nap.edu.

Printed in the United States of America

Suggested citation: National Academies of Sciences, Engineering, and Medicine. (2019). *Strengthening the Military Family Readiness System for a Changing American Society*. Washington, DC: The National Academies Press. https://doi.org/10.17226/25380.

The National Academies of
SCIENCES • ENGINEERING • MEDICINE

The **National Academy of Sciences** was established in 1863 by an Act of Congress, signed by President Lincoln, as a private, nongovernmental institution to advise the nation on issues related to science and technology. Members are elected by their peers for outstanding contributions to research. Dr. Marcia McNutt is president.

The **National Academy of Engineering** was established in 1964 under the charter of the National Academy of Sciences to bring the practices of engineering to advising the nation. Members are elected by their peers for extraordinary contributions to engineering. Dr. C. D. Mote, Jr., is president.

The **National Academy of Medicine** (formerly the Institute of Medicine) was established in 1970 under the charter of the National Academy of Sciences to advise the nation on medical and health issues. Members are elected by their peers for distinguished contributions to medicine and health. Dr. Victor J. Dzau is president.

The three Academies work together as the **National Academies of Sciences, Engineering, and Medicine** to provide independent, objective analysis and advice to the nation and conduct other activities to solve complex problems and inform public policy decisions. The National Academies also encourage education and research, recognize outstanding contributions to knowledge, and increase public understanding in matters of science, engineering, and medicine.

Learn more about the National Academies of Sciences, Engineering, and Medicine at **www.nationalacademies.org**.

The National Academies of
SCIENCES · ENGINEERING · MEDICINE

Consensus Study Reports published by the National Academies of Sciences, Engineering, and Medicine document the evidence-based consensus on the study's statement of task by an authoring committee of experts. Reports typically include findings, conclusions, and recommendations based on information gathered by the committee and the committee's deliberations. Each report has been subjected to a rigorous and independent peer-review process and it represents the position of the National Academies on the statement of task.

Proceedings published by the National Academies of Sciences, Engineering, and Medicine chronicle the presentations and discussions at a workshop, symposium, or other event convened by the National Academies. The statements and opinions contained in proceedings are those of the participants and are not endorsed by other participants, the planning committee, or the National Academies.

For information about other products and activities of the National Academies, please visit www.nationalacademies.org/about/whatwedo.

COMMITTEE ON THE WELL-BEING OF MILITARY FAMILIES

KENNETH W. KIZER, (*Chair*), School of Medicine, Betty Irene Moore School of Nursing, and Institute for Population Health Improvement, UC Davis Health, University of California, Davis
DAVID ALBRIGHT, The University of Alabama School of Social Work
STEPHEN J. COZZA, U.S. Army (*retired*), Uniformed Services University of the Health Sciences
ELLEN DEVOE, Boston University School of Social Work
ABIGAIL GEWIRTZ, Institute of Child Development and Institute for Translational Research in Children's Mental Health, University of Minnesota
MARY M. KELLER, Military Child Education Coalition
PATRICIA LESTER, University of California, Los Angeles, Semel Institute for Neuroscience and Human Behavior
SHELLEY MACDERMID WADSWORTH, Military Family Research Institute, Purdue University
LAURA L. MILLER, RAND Corporation
TRACY NEAL-WALDEN, U.S. Air Force (*retired*), Steven A. Cohen Military Family Clinic at Easterseals
DANIEL F. PERKINS, Clearinghouse for Military Family Readiness, The Pennsylvania State University
ASHISH S. VAZIRANI, Executive Director and Chief Executive Officer, National Military Family Association
IVAN C. A. WALKS, Ivan Walks & Associates

SUZANNE LE MENESTREL, *Study Director*
DAVID BUTLER, *Scholar, Director, Office of Military and Veterans Health*
SHEILA MOATS, *Program Officer (February–June 2018)*
PRIYANKA NALAMADA, *Associate Program Officer (July 2018–present)*
STACEY SMIT, *Senior Program Assistant*
JUDITH JONES, *Archer Fellow (May–August 2018)*
LAURA MINERO, *Christine Mirzayan Science and Technology Policy Graduate Fellow* (January–April 2019)
SUNDONIA WILLIAMS WONNUM, *Consultant, U.S. Air Force*

BOARD ON CHILDREN, YOUTH, AND FAMILIES

Acknowledgments

Supporting the well-being of military families is essential to ensuring the readiness of military personnel. Military families encompass a broad spectrum of American society and have diverse needs that have materially changed in recent years. In an effort to make sure its efforts to support military families are addressing their needs in a rapidly changing American society, the U.S. Department of Defense asked the National Academies of Sciences, Engineering, and Medicine to study the challenges and opportunities facing military families and what is known about effective strategies for supporting and protecting military children and families, as well as lessons to be learned from these experiences. The National Academies appointed the Committee on the Well-Being of Military Families in 2017 to address this charge. The committee thanks the sponsor of this study, the Office of Military Community and Family Policy, U.S. Department of Defense, for their support of the committee's activities.

This report would not have been possible without the contributions of many people. Special thanks go to the members of the committee who dedicated extensive time, expertise, and energy to the drafting of the report. The committee also thanks the members of the National Academies staff for their significant contributions to the report: Suzanne Le Menestrel, Priyanka Nalamada, David Butler, and Sheila Moats. Stacey Smit provided key administrative and logistical support and made sure that committee meetings ran smoothly.

The committee is also grateful to Anthony Bryant, Faye Hillman, and Lisa Alston for their administrative and financial assistance. From the Division of Behavioral and Social Sciences and Education Office of Reports and Communication, Kirsten Sampson Snyder, Viola Horek, Patricia L. Morison, Douglas Sprunger, and Yvonne Wise guided the report through the review and production process and assisted with its communication and dissemination. The committee also thanks the National Academies Press staff, Clair Woolley, Holly Sten, Autumn Rose, and Barbara Murphy for their assistance with the production of the final report; Daniel Bearss and Rebecca Morgan in the National Academies research library for their assistance with fact checking and literature searches; and the report's editor, Marc DeFrancis, for his expert editing. Finally, throughout the project, Natacha Blain, director of the Board on Children, Youth, and Families, together with Mary Ellen O'Connell and Monica Feit, provided helpful oversight.

Many individuals volunteered significant time and effort to address and educate the committee during our public information session. Their perspectives and personal experiences were essential to the committee's work. We thank Ashley Broadway-Mack, president, The American Military Partner Association; Karen Ruedisueli, government relations deputy director, National Military Family Association; Chaplain (COL) Jimmy Nichols, installation command chaplain, Fort Sill, Oklahoma; Edward Tyner, associate director, Office of Family Readiness/Office of Special Needs, U.S. Department of Defense; Kelly Hokanson, spouse of National Guard Bureau Vice Chief (LTG) Daniel R. Hokanson; Jill Marconi, director, Airman and Family Readiness, U.S. Air Force; Susan Lukas, director, Legislation & Military Policy, Reserve Officer's Association; Anthony A. Wickham, J1 program director, National Guard Bureau; Col. (Ret) Anthony Cox, Army, former manager, HQDA Family Advocacy Program; Ellyn Dunford, spouse of Gen. Joseph F. Dunford, chairman of the Joint Chiefs of Staff; Elka Franco-Giordano, Chief of Naval Operations OMBUDSMAN-at-Large and spouse of Master Chief Petty Officer of the Navy Steven S. Giordano; and Donald R. Neff, United States Special Operations Command.

The committee also appreciates the contributions of Sarah Beehler (University of Minnesota), David Chambers (National Cancer Institute), Schelomo Marmor (University of Minnesota), Lisa Militello (The Ohio State University), Nathaniel Mohatt (University of Colorado, Denver), Inbal Nahum-Shani (University of Michigan), Wynne Norton (National Cancer Institute), and Barbara Thompson (U.S. Department of Defense, retired) for their valuable commissioned papers, which informed our report. We would also like to extend our gratitude to our unpaid consultants, Diana Timba (University of Minnesota) and Sundonia Williams-Wonnum (U.S. Air Force) and our graduate fellows Laura Minero and Judith Jones. Many individuals also submitted memos for the committee's consideration; a listing of these individuals can be found in Appendix C in this report.

This Consensus Study Report was reviewed in draft form by individuals chosen for their diverse perspectives and technical expertise. The purpose of this independent review is to provide candid and critical comments that will assist the National Academies in making each published report as sound as possible and to ensure that it meets the institutional standards for quality, objectivity, evidence, and responsiveness to the study charge. The review comments and draft manuscript remain confidential to protect the integrity of the deliberative process.

We thank the following individuals for their review of this report: Nicholas J. Armstrong, Institute for Veterans and Military Families, Syracuse University; Ron Avi Astor, Suzanne Dworak-Peck School of Social Work, Rossier School of Education, University of Southern California; Kelly Blasko, Connected Health Branch, Defense Health Agency; Kenneth A. Dodge, Sanford School of Public Policy, Duke University; Richard Fabes, School of Social and Family Dynamics, Arizona State University; Eric M. Flake, Developmental Behavioral Pediatrician, Madigan Army Medical Center; Stacy A. Hawkins, Research Facilitation Laboratory, Army Analytics Group; Jay A. Mancini, Human Development and Family Science, The University of Georgia; Ann S. Masten, Institute of Child Development, University of Minnesota, Minneapolis; Sarah O. Meadows, Pardee RAND Graduate School, RAND Corporation; Lyndon A. Riviere, Center for Military Psychiatry and Neuroscience, Walter Reed Army Institute of Research; and Jonathan Woodson, Institute for Health System Innovation and Policy, Boston University.

Although the reviewers listed above provided many constructive comments and suggestions, they were not asked to endorse the conclusions or recommendations of this report nor did they see the final draft before its release. The review of this report was overseen by Dan G. Blazer, Duke University Medical Center, and Bradford H. Gray, The Urban Institute (retired). They were responsible for making certain that an independent examination of this report was carried out in accordance with the standards of the National Academies and that all review comments were carefully considered. Responsibility for the final content rests entirely with the authoring committee and the National Academies.

Kenneth W. Kizer, *Chair*

Contents

Boxes, Figures, and Tables

BOXES

FIGURES

TABLES

Summary

The U.S. military has been continuously engaged in foreign conflicts for almost two decades. The strains of these deployments, the associated increases in operational tempo, and the general challenges of military life affect not only service members but also the people who depend on them and who support them as they support the nation—their families. Family well-being is essential to the U.S. Department of Defense (DoD) for multiple reasons. Family members provide support to service members while they serve or when they have difficulties; family problems can interfere with the ability of service members to deploy or remain in theater; and family members are central influences on whether members continue to serve. Military families also raise a disproportionate number of future military service members, so the well-being of today's military family is important for future service members too.[1] In addition, service members' psychological or physical difficulties can reverberate within families, potentially generating costs for DoD. Years ago (Schneider and Martin, 1994, p. 5), the Army Science Board, an independent advisory group to the Secretary of the Army, concluded: "Recognition of the powerful impacts of the family on readiness, retention, morale and motivation must be instilled in every soldier from the soldier's date of entry-to-service through each succeeding promotion."

Widespread changes in societal norms and family structures have also occurred in the United States over the last few decades. The diversity and complexity of families have increased, and these shifts have multi-

[1] See https://www.rand.org/content/dam/rand/pubs/research_reports/RR200/RR247/RAND_RR247.pdf.

ple implications for DoD. First, individuals entering the military today may have experienced more family transitions as children, such as the divorce and remarriage of parents, than their predecessors. In addition, today's service members may create new families that are more diverse or complex than in the past. Therefore, fully understanding today's military families and their needs may require greater attention to family diversity and complexity. This rising diversity and complexity also could likely increase the difficulty of creating military policies, programs, and practices that adequately support families in the performance of service members' military duties.

DOD ACTIONS TO IMPROVE LIVES OF MILITARY MEMBERS AND THEIR FAMILIES

In response to these circumstances, DoD has taken several actions intended to improve the lives of military members and their families. Its Family Readiness Policy was overhauled in 2012, and policy makers have made major revisions to the military retirement, compensation, and benefits system. Other significant reorganization efforts include a consolidation of social support services under the Defense Health System. More recently, the John S. McCain National Defense Authorization Act for Fiscal Year 2019 (Public Law 115-232) calls for enhancing the readiness of the all-volunteer force, with an emphasis on the importance of supporting service members and their families. (Box S-1 provides definitions for key terms that are used in this report related to "family well-being," "family resilience," and "family readiness.")

STUDY CHARGE

Given the extent of these changes and priorities for ensuring the readiness of the force, DoD determined that now is an opportune time to review key issues central to the well-being of service members and their families so that programs and policies can be strengthened for the future. It asked the National Academies of Sciences, Engineering, and Medicine to provide insights to help prioritize its efforts and ensure that program and policy design aligns with its goals.

This report was prepared at the request of the Military Community and Family Policy (MC&FP) office, an organization within the Office of the Under Secretary of Defense (OUSD) for Personnel and Readiness. The National Academies Committee on the Well-Being of Military Families was formed to study the challenges and opportunities facing military families and what is known about effective strategies for supporting and

BOX S-1
Definitions of Key Terms Used in the Report

***Family Well-Being*:** There is no universal definition of family well-being in the research literature or across national or global organizations. The committee identified the following as key components:

- *Objective well-being* refers to having resources considered necessary for adequate quality of life, such as sufficient economic and educational resources, housing, health, safety, environmental quality, and social connections.
- *Subjective well-being* is the result of how individuals think and feel about their circumstances.
- *Functional well-being* focuses on the degree to which families and their members can and do successfully perform their core functions, such as caring for, supporting, and nurturing family members.

***Family Readiness*:** The *potential* capacity of families as dynamic [human] systems to adapt successfully to disturbances that threaten the function, survival, or development of these systems.

***Family Resilience* (or *resilient outcomes*):** Positive adjustment in the aftermath of adversity. Also: "the *manifested* capacity of families as dynamic [human] systems to adapt successfully to disturbances that threaten the function, survival, or development of these systems."

***Resilience Processes* (or *mechanisms*):** Refers to the dynamics that produce or impede resilience.

***Resilience Factors*:** Refers to the events, characteristics, or circumstances that shape resilience processes or outcomes. Resilience factors may be personal (e.g., hardiness), social (e.g., robust informal support networks), or environmental (e.g., stable community infrastructures).

SOURCE: Definitions of *family readiness* and *family resilience* adapted from Masten (2015, p. 187).

protecting military children and families, as well as lessons to be learned from these experiences. The committee's work was accomplished over a 24-month period that began in October 2017. The committee members represent expertise in psychology, psychiatry, sociology, human development, family science, education, prevention and implementation science, traumatology, public policy, medicine, public health, social work, delivery of services to military populations, and community health services. Six members of the committee are military veterans and several members were or are currently part of a military family.[2] The committee examined the evidence pertaining to both the positive experiences and the challenges presented by military life and the mechanisms by which resilience can be fostered. It used a developmental perspective to understand the threats to and ways to promote the well-being of military families. The committee also developed recommendations for DoD regarding what is needed to strengthen the support system for military families.

DoD asked the committee to focus on the active and reserve components in DoD, which includes the Army, Army National Guard, and Army Reserve; the Navy and Navy Reserve; the Marine Corps and Marine Corps Reserve; and the Air Force, Air National Guard, and Air Force Reserve.[3] The committee was asked to consider not only the well-being of single and married military personnel and their military dependents, but also the broad network of people who surround them. Thus, the committee referred to the definition used in military policy found in Chapter 1 but was directed heavily by research conducted with the general population that suggests greater diversity in family forms than is encoded in the military definition. As a result, the committee was guided by the more inclusive definition of family that appears in Chapter 2.

Six principles guided the committee's work:

(1) The focus is on the lived experience of military families.
(2) Families are systems. Members of the family are interdependent and they influence each other as individuals, as well as in relationships between other members.
(3) Families are embedded in larger contexts.
(4) The duration and timing of military service and experiences must be considered as they impact the family system.
(5) Military family readiness is directly linked to mission readiness.
(6) Implementation support is critical for a sustained and robust Military Family Readiness System (MFRS).

The MFRS is defined by the DoD as "the network of agencies, programs, services and people, and the collaboration among them, that facilitates and actively promotes the readiness and quality of life of Service

[2]The National Academies' policy states that no individual can serve on a committee used in the development of reports if the individual has a conflict of interest that is relevant to the functions to be performed. While neither active nor reserve component members served on this committee, their input was solicited at all phases of the study and played a great role in the committee's considerations.

[3]The Coast Guard is not included in the committee's report because it belongs to the Department of Homeland Security rather than to DoD.

members and their families."[4] The MFRS serves both active duty and reserve component service members and their families, and includes community partners to meet the needs of geographically separated military families, who are not near a military installation. The policies and programs that comprise the MFRS fall under the purview of the Under Secretary of Defense for Personnel and Readiness (USD P&R),[5] but they are governed by separate Assistant Secretaries of Defense (ASDs). The vast majority of services and activities are delivered by the individual military services. This division of labor and responsibilities has had some salutary effect on achieving a baseline level of delivery across the system to meet military families' expectations as they traverse the military lifestyle, but has also impeded coordination between and among the agencies that are delivering services to individual Service members and their families.

Understanding and supporting the well-being of military families is critical for a sustained and robust MFRS and requires consideration of people's characteristics and experiences, the processes that operate within people and families, and the ways these shift over time. Given the expansion of family diversity and changes in family stability and complexity over time, DoD's policies, programs, services, resources, and practices are more likely to be effective if they are attuned to different families' particular needs and characteristics. The committee thus concludes that **due to the widespread changes in societal norms and family structures that have occurred in the United States, understanding and addressing military families' needs today requires greater attention to family diversity and stability.**[6]

WHO ARE MILITARY SERVICE MEMBERS AND THEIR FAMILIES?

The demographic composition of military personnel is shaped by DoD and service policies and strategies for recruitment and retention in the all-volunteer force. Nearly one-half of the 2.1 million U.S. active and Selected Reserve service members are in the Army. The Marine Corps, which falls under the Department of the Navy, is the smallest service. In addition, the force is relatively young by design and, as such, 61 percent are age 30 or younger. Thus, most service members are either in the process of transitioning to adulthood or are in early adulthood.

In 2017, the majority (71%) of service members reported themselves as White and 17 percent as Black. Racial and ethnic minorities are not evenly distributed across the force. For example, in the active component, 67 percent of enlisted personnel are White and 19 percent are Black, but

---

[4]See https://public.militaryonesource.mil/footer?content_id=282320.
[5]See https://prhome.defense.gov.
[6]Conclusion 2-2, Chapter 2.

among officers 77 percent are White and 9 percent are Black. The Navy has the most racially diverse active component, while the Marine Corps has the least. According to DoD personnel administrative data files, in 2017, 14 percent of military personnel identified themselves as Hispanic or Latino.

DoD administrative personnel datasets track gender, but not gender identity. With regard to gender, the majority of military personnel are men. In 2017, approximately 18 percent of service members were women. About one-half of military personnel are married, and 39 percent have children. Single parents make up about 6 percent of the force; although this is a small percentage, it represents 126,268 personnel. About 5 percent of personnel are in dual-military marriages, meaning both members of the couple are U.S. service members. DoD's most recent published demographics report from 2017 does not provide statistics for the number of registered same-sex marriages among military personnel, and other estimates were not readily available. **The DoD's existing data on military families are insufficient for understanding the degree to which societal shifts in family structure are reflected in today's measurements of the military community population. Existing data lack information on long-term nonmarital partners, parents, ex-spouses and ex-partners, and others who play a significant role in the care of military children and service members. As a result, current military statistics could mislead policy makers and program managers, potentially resulting in some types of families being underserved by the MFRS.**[7]

WHAT ARE SOME OF THE OPPORTUNITIES AND CHALLENGES OF MILITARY LIFE?

Military personnel and their families encounter opportunities and challenges in life, just as any family does. In many ways, the life course of military families can be similar to the life course of their civilian counterparts. However, some experiences are specific to military life or are experienced differently because of the military context in which they occur. Moreover, there is great variability in military experiences across individuals and families. Events specifically related to military life include deployments, sea duty, and other temporary duty away from home; combat exposure; service-related mental and physical injuries and death; the receipt of pay and in-kind benefits such as housing and health care; permanent change of station moves; assignments to installations in other countries; lack or disruption of career progression; and separation from military service and transition to civilian life.

[7] Conclusion 3-1, Chapter 3.

Service members and their families may find some aspects of military life beneficial and attractive, such as the opportunities to develop one's skills or the steady pay and benefits. However, a great deal of recent research has paid particular attention to potential acute stressors associated with military life, such as combat exposure and family separations. There are also the daily and chronic stressors that can take a toll on individual and family well-being. Some aspects of military life may be fairly common, but service member and family responses to those experiences can vary widely. The impact of these events can relate to their timing and duration, how individuals interpret them, as well as the degree of perceived associated benefits or work-family conflict. The benefits and challenges of military life affect not only service members, spouses, and children, but also others such as nonmarital partners, parents, siblings, and grandparents.

National Guard and Reserve service members and their families experience many of the same opportunities and challenges as active-duty service members; however, there are certain experiences particular to the reserve component. Unlike active component personnel, National Guard and Reserve personnel do not face frequent, mandatory geographic relocation. There is evidence that for military children, friendships with other military children and participation in military-sponsored activities can be beneficial for their well-being. National Guard and Reserve children, as well as active-component children who live far from base, may have few opportunities for face-to-face interactions with others who would have a basic shared understanding of life as a military dependent.

HOW DO STRESSORS IMPACT MILITARY FAMILIES AND CHILDREN?

Certain military family challenges create levels of stress and burden that, predictably, overwhelm some families, if only temporarily. When these challenges exceed the capacity of individuals and families to manage them, they can undermine healthy processes that support family functioning, leading to cascading risk and reduction in well-being. The committee reviewed what is known about the effects on military families of duty-related illness, injury, and death. Physical injury and psychological traumatic stress serve as defining events that can complicate military family well-being, leading to problems within the family, affecting marital and parenting relationship functioning, and in turn undermining adult and child individual well-being.

For children, the early years represent a particularly vulnerable developmental stage for stress, and characteristics of the caregiving or parenting environment are key in the development of their stress regulatory capacities. More than 70 percent of children in military families are younger than age 11 and 38 percent are age 5 or younger. In addition, the committee also reviewed the impact of stress on development as well as childhood resilience. Severe stressors, such as maltreatment, parental psychopathology, violence, and institutional rearing can have profound effects on children's development. In addition, there is as yet relatively little evidence suggesting that separations due to military deployments have such profound effects. The effects on children of deployments and related military family transitions, such as extended occupationally related separations and relocations, are more likely mediated through their impact on parents and the caregiving system.

CHILDREN'S RESILIENCE

Systematic, theory-driven research on children's resilience has been ongoing since the 1970s and has accelerated with recent advances in prevention and intervention science, as well as in genetics and neurobiology.[8] The processes involved in childhood resilience operate across multiple domains both within and beyond the child. As such, there is no single resiliency trait. In parallel, then, there is no single measure of child resilience. Childhood resilience is multidimensional, and its measurement requires an understanding of the developmental context.

Key correlates and predictors of childhood resilience include sensitive, responsive, loving, predictable, and protective parents and caregivers; self-regulation, or the ability to monitor and regulate one's behavior, attention, thoughts, and emotions; mastery-motivation skills, the adaptational system associated with the development of self-efficacy and motivating persistence; strong cognitive abilities; and hope, or a positive outlook, and meaning-making.

Military families can be adversely affected by some aspects of military life, such as deployments, illnesses, and injuries, due to their undermining of healthy intrafamilial resilience processes that support family well-being and readiness. Family resilience processes (e.g., effective communication strategies, emotion regulation, problem solving, and competent parenting) serve as opportunities for promotion, prevention, and intervention in the wake of stress and trauma.[9]

EVIDENCE-BASED AND EVIDENCE-INFORMED INTERVENTIONS

Of high relevance to military service systems are consistent findings that the effects of severe stressors can be prevented and ameliorated

[8]For a review of the literature, see, for example, Masten (2018).
[9]Conclusion 6-1, Chapter 6.

with evidence-based and evidence-informed interventions focused on strengthening family relationships, caregiving/parenting, and family environment.[10] In addition, family-based prevention programs targeting risk events have crossover effects. For example, evidence-based parenting programs both improve parenting practices and also strengthen child adjustment and parent well-being. As shown in Box S-2, the committee identified 10 family strengthening goals to promote family resilience and well-being. These goals are all part of family strengthening programs that are critical to a public health approach to supporting wellness.

HOW CAN DOD IMPROVE THE SYSTEMS THAT ALREADY EXIST?

Military families play a critical role in the strength and readiness of our nation's military. The readiness and resilience of military families to thrive with the expected and unexpected challenges and opportunities of military life directly impacts the individual service members' readiness and attentiveness to the mission. DoD developed the MFRS to include a plethora of policies, programs, services, resources, and practices to support and promote family readiness and resilience.

The aim of the MFRS is to be a support infrastructure that promotes family well-being and thereby fosters family readiness, which in turn increases service members' readiness. The MFRS offers a high level of support, which is appropriate given the demands of military service and the reliance on volunteers to serve. This level of support compares favorably to what is offered by large employers in the civilian sector, with the DoD child care system being a well-known example. In addition, many installations offer their own services, which may or may not coordinate directly with their branch or DoD counterparts. These may be quite extensive and diverse, depending on the size of the garrison, the extent to which it is feasible for families to accompany service members to their posting, and the interests of garrison leadership. For instance, smaller and more isolated posts may have only modest services geared toward recreation opportuni-

[10] *Evidence-based* describes a service, program, strategy, component, practice, and/or process that demonstrates impact on outcomes of interest through application of rigorous scientific research methods (i.e., experimental and quasi-experimental designs) that allows for causal inference. *Evidence-informed* describes a service, program, strategy, component, practice, and/or process that (1) is developed or drawn from an integration of scientific theory, practitioner experience and expertise and stakeholder input with the best available external evidence from systematic research and a body of empirical literature; and (2) demonstrates impact on outcomes of interest through application of scientific research methods that do not allow for causal inference.

BOX S-2
Family-Strengthening Goals to Promote Family Resilience and Well-Being

1. ***Maintain a physically safe and structured environment,*** protecting against interpersonal aggression, and ensuring that children have adequate structure and support, have consistency in routines and rules, and are effectively monitored.
2. ***Engage required resources,*** accessing instrumental and social support within and outside the family, and teaching family members how to effectively use their support opportunities (friends, extended family, teachers, coaches, faith-based communities, etc.).
3. ***Develop and share knowledge within and outside of the family,*** building shared understanding about stressors, including service members' injury or illness, as well as modeling and teaching effective communication strategies.
4. ***Build a positive, emotionally safe, and warm family environment,*** including effective stress reduction and emotional regulation strategies for parents to engage in and model for children, as well as engaging in activities that are calming and enjoyable for all.
5. ***Master and model important interpersonal skills,*** including problem solving and conflict resolution and incorporating evidence-based strategies.
6. ***Maintain a vision of hope and future optimism for the family,*** engendering positive expectations and creating a hope-filled family narrative.
7. ***Utilize competent and authoritative parenting,*** encouraging consequence-based strategies that promote mastery and minimizing harsh disciplinary practices.
8. ***Incorporate trauma-informed approaches to care,*** recognizing that families faced with stress and adversity are likely to be affected by trauma and loss experiences that uniquely impact adults and children within families, their relationships, and their development.
9. ***Promote security among adults and children,*** strengthening parent-child relationships that are known to contribute to individual and relational wellness for both adults and children, and focusing on effective conflict resolution between spouses or partners.
10. ***Highlight the unique developmental needs of family members,*** helping parents and other engaged adults in the family recognize and respond to their family members' needs effectively at each developmental stage.

SOURCE: Goal 5 is based on the work of Dausch and Saliman (2009) and Gewirtz et al. (2018b). Goal 6 is based on the work of Saltzman et al. (2011).

ties for service members. Finally, nonprofit organizations operating across branches (for example, the National Military Family Association[11] and the United Service Organizations or USO[12]) as well as those focused on specific branches[13] supplement all of the military's resources with their own sources of help and links to providers.[14]

It is apparent that there are many sources of support and information about support for military families. What is unclear, though, is the extent to which service providers at the various levels of organization (DoD-wide, service branch, installation-based, and military-focused nonprofit) are aware of one another or can or do coordinate service provision. The committee concludes that **the current MFRS is siloed, with a diffusion in its division of labor and responsibility, and its delivery of services is fragmented in some instances. The system lacks a comprehensive, coordinated framework to support individual and population well-being, resilience, and readiness among military families. Addressing this deficit could improve quality, encourage innovation, and support effective response capabilities.**[15]

The current system lacks the processes and structures necessary to support ongoing population-level monitoring and mapping of family well-being, including a grounding in the continuum of promotion, prevention, treatment, and maintenance dimensions and integrated information infrastructures, accompanied by validated and appropriate assessments, necessary to support ongoing population-level monitoring and mapping of family well-being. **Utilizing a dynamic complex adaptive support-system approach**[16] **would improve the ability of the MFRS to respond to the needs of military families. Evidence-based and/or evidence-informed practices, resources, services, programs, and policies are foundational to a complex adaptive system. A continuous quality monitoring system that utilizes**

---

[11]See https://www.militaryfamily.org.

[12]See USO; https://www.uso.org.

[13]For example, Army Emergency Relief [https://www.aerhq.org]; Navy-Marine Corps Relief Society [http://www.nmcrs.org]; Air Force Aid Society [https://www.afas.org].

[14]DoD funds academic centers including the Purdue University Military Family Research Institute [www.mfri.purdue.edu] and the Penn State Clearinghouse for Military Family Readiness [www.militaryfamilies.psu.edu] to perform outreach, training, and support of service providers, and research on the effective delivery of services. These entities partner with DoD and the branches to help improve the quality of services and promote evidence-based decision making. While the centers are oriented toward practitioners and research, their websites include information and links useful to military families, making them yet another source of support and information.

[15]Conclusion 7-2, Chapter 7.

[16]A complex adaptive system is a structure with many dynamic, interacting relationships among components that are greater than the sum of its parts (Ellis and Herbert, 2010; Holland, 1996; Spivey, 2018).

solid measurements is needed to ensure a complex adaptive system that continues to progress in its effectiveness and relevance.[17] The premise of ongoing monitoring is not to find fault or blame, but to promote a *culture of learning* in the system through data-driven feedback loops that support continuous quality improvement.

In addition, the MFRS can learn from community engagement and participation examples in order to adapt strategies and tailor prevention and intervention efforts to ensure their continuous alignment, relevance, and effectiveness. Community engagement involves identifying and collaborating with key stakeholders, including military family members, service members, and veterans, all layers of military leadership across the services, and community leaders and providers. **Community engagement and meaningful collaboration with key stakeholders are critical from the beginning and throughout the implementation process to identify relevant targets for the continuum of support (i.e., promotion, prevention, and intervention efforts), ensure program alignment with diverse family needs and constellations, assure family engagement and program participation, and build community capacity to support military family well-being and readiness.**[18]

HOW CAN A LEARNING SYSTEM BE DEVELOPED AND SUSTAINED?

Many of the challenges faced by the MFRS within DoD in developing, implementing, evaluating, and improving military family readiness policies, programs, services, practices, and resources are similar to those found in civilian communities. These challenges are amplified by the limitations of existing research on military child and family resilience and well-being, as well as by a complex and dynamic landscape of military contexts, services, and policies. The committee recommends that **DoD should enable military family support providers, civilian or in uniform, who work for military systems, and consumers to access effective, evidence-based, and evidence-informed family strengthening programs, resources, and services.**[19]

The committee also recommends that **to support high-quality implementation, adaptation, and sustainability of policies, programs, practices, and services that are informed by a continuous quality improvement pro-**

[17]Conclusion 7-3, Chapter 7.
[18]Conclusion 7-4, Chapter 7.
[19]Recommendation 7, Chapter 9.

cess, DoD should develop, adopt, and sustain a dynamic learning system as part of its MFRS.[20] Such a dynamic learning system requires a process of tailoring and decision making grounded in a sufficient level of evidence about approaches to understanding and strengthening family well-being. By instituting ongoing accountability for system effectiveness, a high-functioning MFRS framework will incorporate assessments and the results of existing efforts, improve response capabilities, and point to the development of future resilience and readiness strategies for military families.

To enhance the effectiveness and efficiency of the MFRS, DoD should investigate innovations in big data and predictive analytics to improve the accessibility, engagement, personalization, and effectiveness of policies, programs, practices, and services for military families.[21] The increasing utility and acceptability of mobile platforms for the delivery of health and mental health services can be adapted to provide a special opportunity for DoD to strengthen individual and family well-being through screening and program delivery across the spectrum of coordinated support of the MFRS. Mobile and wireless devices allow for more accessible and cost-effective interventions because their widespread use, acceptability, and convenience can help reduce certain societal and structural barriers; and they offer strong capability for scalability across geographic locations, including within resource-limited, hard-to-reach, and deployed settings.

Finally, **to facilitate the consistency and continuation of its policies regarding military family readiness and well-being across political administrations and changes of senior military leadership, DoD should update and promulgate its existing instruction that operationalizes the importance of military family well-being by incorporating the conclusions and recommendations contained in this report.**[22] This directive would help withstand changes in political administrations and senior military leadership that could otherwise result in fluctuating support for military family readiness and well-being, especially when making tough budgetary decisions. Box S-3 provides a listing of the committee's recommendations, which have been excerpted for brevity.

---

[20]Recommendation 8, Chapter 9.
[21]Recommendation 10, Chapter 9.
[22]Recommendation 11, Chapter 9.

BOX S-3
Committee Recommendations

RECOMMENDATION 1: To facilitate synthesis and comparison of information across administrative and survey datasets and research studies, and to support evaluations of the effectiveness of service member and family support programs, the Department of Defense should develop and implement a standardized, military-specific definition of "family well-being."

RECOMMENDATION 2: To establish policies, procedures, and programs that will better support military family readiness, the Department of Defense should (i) take immediate steps to gain a more comprehensive understanding of the diversity of today's military families and their needs, well-being, and readiness to support service members; and (ii) develop policies and procedures to continuously improve and strengthen the information it collects, analyzes, and publicly reports about service members and their families to keep pace with societal, organizational, and operational changes.

RECOMMENDATION 3: The Department of Defense should more fully identify, analyze, and integrate existing data to longitudinally track population-based military child risk and adversity, while also ensuring the privacy of individual family member information.

RECOMMENDATION 4: The Department of Defense should review its current policies, programs, services, resources, and practices for supporting military families—as service members define families—to ensure that they recognize the wide diversity of today's military families and address the special circumstances of military life, especially with regard to major transitions, such as entering military service, moving to new duty stations, deploying, shifting between active duty and reserve status, and transitioning to veteran status.

RECOMMENDATION 5: To help military leaders and nonmilitary service providers in civilian communities better understand and prioritize issues specific to their local communities, the Department of Defense should provide guidance for military leaders and service providers on how to readily and reliably access and utilize information about the surrounding communities in which their personnel are situated.

RECOMMENDATION 6: The Department of Defense should build its capacity to support service members and families by promoting better civilian understanding of the strengths and needs of military-connected individuals. These efforts should particularly address misinformation, negative stereotypes, and lack of knowledge.

RECOMMENDATION 7: The Department of Defense should enable military family support providers, civilian or in uniform, who work for military systems, and consumers to access effective, evidence-based and evidence-informed family strengthening programs, resources, and services.

RECOMMENDATION 8: To support high-quality implementation, adaptation, and sustainability of policies, programs, practices, and services that are informed by a continuous quality improvement process, the Department of Defense should develop, adopt, and sustain a dynamic learning system as part of its Military Family Readiness System.

RECOMMENDATION 9: The Department of Defense should continually assess the availability and effectiveness of specialized family-centered policies, programs, services, resources, and practices to support the evolving and unexpected needs of families facing exceptionally high stressors (e.g., military service related injury, illness or death), in order to implement programs targeting emerging threats to military family well-being.

RECOMMENDATION 10: To enhance the effectiveness and efficiency of the Military Family Readiness System, the Department of Defense should investigate innovations in big data and predictive analytics to improve the accessibility, engagement, personalization, and effectiveness of policies, programs, practices, and services for military families.

RECOMMENDATION 11: To facilitate the consistency and continuation of its policies regarding military family readiness and well-being across political administrations and changes of senior military leadership, the Department of Defense should update and promulgate its existing instruction that operationalizes the importance of military family well-being by incorporating the conclusions and recommendations contained in this report.

REFERENCES

Dausch, B. M., and Saliman, S. (2009). Use of family focused therapy in rehabilitation for veterans with traumatic brain injury. *Rehabilitation Psychology, 54*, 279–287.

Ellis, B. S. and Herbert, S. (2010). Complex adaptive systems (CAS): An overview of key elements, characteristics and application to management theory. *Journal of Innovation in Health Informatics, 19*(1), 33–37.

Holland, J. H. (1996). *Hidden Order: How Adaptation Builds Complexity*. Boston, MA: Addison Wesley.

Gewirtz, A. H., DeGarmo, D. S., and Zamir, O. (2018). Testing a military family stress model. *Family Process 57*, 415–431.

Masten, A. S. (2015). Pathways to integrated resilience science. *Psychological Inquiry, 26*(2), 187–196.

Masten, A. S. (2018). Resilience theory and research on children and families: Past, present, and promise. *Journal of Family Theory and Review, 10*, 12–31.

Saltzman, W. R., Lester, P., Beardslee, W. R., Layne, C.M., Woodward, K., and Nash, W. P. (2011). Mechanisms of risk and resilience in military families: Theoretical and empirical basis of a family-focused resilience enhancement program. *Clinical Child and Family Psychology Review, 14*(3), 213–230.

Schneider, R. J., and Martin, J. A. (1994). Military families and combat readiness. In L. B. Davis, C. Mathews Quick, and S. E. Siegel (Eds.), *Military Psychiatry: Preparing in Peace for War* (pp. 19–30). Washington, DC: TMM.

Spivey, M. J. (2018). Discovery in complex adaptive systems. *Cognitive Systems Research, 51*, 40–55.

1

Introduction

In response to changes in the composition of the all-volunteer force, the U.S. labor market, and the demands and consequences of military operations, U.S. military programs and policies designed to support service members and their families have changed significantly in recent years. In 2012, the U.S. Department of Defense's (DoD's) Family Readiness Policy[1] was overhauled, and since then policy makers have made major revisions to the military retirement, compensation, and benefits system, including the new Blended Retirement System and "Forever GI Bill." The past decade has also seen major fluctuations in military budgets, a decline in the size of the force, and a significant reduction in the extent of operations in Iraq and Afghanistan, even though we remain, after 17 years of engagement in those countries, a nation at war.

Furthermore, dramatic personnel policy shifts now allow gay and lesbian service members to serve openly and women to serve in combat occupations and positions. Significant reorganization efforts include the consolidation of services under the Defense Health System. Most recently, the National Defense Authorization Act for FY 2019 calls for enhancing the readiness of the all-volunteer force, with an emphasis on the importance of supporting service members and their families.

Given the extent of these changes and priorities for ensuring the readiness of the force, this is an opportune time to review key issues central to the well-being of service members and their families so that programs and policies can be strengthened for future mission-readiness.

[1]See https://www.esd.whs.mil/Portals/54/Documents/DD/issuances/dodi/134222p.pdf.

Military life brings a diverse set of opportunities, including opportunities for career training and growth, opportunities to see new places and have new experiences, a sense of community, pride, and prestige in serving the nation, and access to many benefits, including health care, high-quality child care, and housing. The capacity of military families to be resilient—to adapt effectively to the unique challenges that military life can present—has been recognized and studied. Unlike many other positive social-emotional attributes, resilience is defined by the adversity in which it develops (Masten, 2001), so the experience of military families has special importance. For instance, young people may take on new roles and responsibilities while their parent is deployed, which may be a source of strength and an opportunity, rather than a challenge (Easterbrooks et al., 2013). In addition, DoD has established policies, programs, services, resources, and practices designed to strengthen families; for example, it has been an innovator in high-quality child care systems. These types of family support systems may increase the likelihood of fostering resilience and preparing parents and children for disruptions in family life due to the military context. Box 1-1 provides key terms related to resilience, readiness, and family well-being used throughout this report. (See Chapter 2 for more detailed descriptions of these terms.)

At the same time, military-connected families and children have a diverse and consistent set of challenges associated with their military affiliation. Most military personnel spend only a limited number of years in the service, but its effects on them and their families, both positive and negative, may persist for many years. Especially for those serving on active duty, frequent moves are an expected aspect of a military career. As a result of the military mission and training requirements, children may be separated from their military parent with some frequency, separations that may last for brief periods or for extended amounts of time. Children of all ages may experience developmental challenges. Further, school-age military-connected children have the additional experience of family relocations that involve school transitions. For military spouses, frequent moves make finding employment and sustaining their careers difficult, and some military families struggle financially. Families of members of the Reserves and National Guard experience the additional dilemma of having to deal with separations due to mobilizations and deployments away from the resources and comradery offered by military installations and their surrounding communities. In addition, there is a military-civilian gap associated, in part, with the fact that in the all-volunteer era only 1 percent of the population serves, which has resulted in a steep decline in the proportion of members of Congress with prior military experience and fewer family connections to the military.[2] Research by the nonpartisan Pew

[2]See https://www.pewresearch.org/fact-tank/2017/11/10/the-changing-face-of-americas-veteran-population and https://www.pewsocialtrends.org/2011/11/23/the-military-civilian-gap-fewer-family-connections.

BOX 1-1
Definitions of Key Terms Used in the Report

Family Well-Being: There is no universal definition of family well-being in the research literature or across national or global organizations. The committee identified the following as key components:

- *Objective well-being* refers to having resources considered necessary for adequate quality of life, such as sufficient economic and educational resources, housing, health, safety, environmental quality, and social connections.
- *Subjective well-being* is the result of how individuals think and feel about their circumstances.
- *Functional well-being* focuses on the degree to which families and their members can and do successfully perform their core functions, such as caring for, supporting, and nurturing family members.

Family Readiness: The *potential* capacity of families as dynamic [human] systems to adapt successfully to disturbances that threaten the function, survival, or development of these systems.

***Family Resilience* (or *resilient outcomes*)**: Positive adjustment in the aftermath of adversity. Also: "the *manifested* capacity of families as dynamic [human] systems to adapt successfully to disturbances that threaten the function, survival, or development of these systems."

***Resilience Processes* (or *mechanisms*)**: Refers to the dynamics that produce or impede resilience.

Resilience Factors: Refers to the events, characteristics, or circumstances that shape resilience processes or outcomes. Resilience factors may be personal (e.g., hardiness), social (e.g., robust informal support networks), or environmental (e.g., stable community infrastructures).

SOURCE: Definitions of *family readiness* and *family resilience* adapted from Masten (2015, p. 187).

Research Center indicates that individuals with military family connections have different attitudes toward the military than those who do not have family connections. This gap may create more stress for those who are in military families. All of these stressors can bring problems to military families, including anxiety, depression, abuse and neglect, behavioral and academic problems for children, and problems with substance use for young people and their parents.

CONTEXT FOR THE STUDY

This report was prepared at the request of the Military Community Family Policy (MC&FP) office, an organization within the Office of the Under Secretary of Defense (OUSD) for Personnel and Readiness. As of late 2018, its mission statement states that MC&FP

> . . . is directly responsible for programs and policies establishing and supporting community quality of life programs for active-duty, National Guard and reserve service members, their families and survivors worldwide. The office also serves as the resource for coordination of quality of life issues within the Department of Defense.[3]

MC&FP responsibilities span the life course of the service member's military career, from entry into the military through the transition to civilian life, and all of the stages in between including family life. Examples of support programs overseen by MC&FP include the Casualty Assistance Program; Children and Youth programs; the Family Advocacy Program; Family Assistance Centers; Military and Family Support Centers; Military OneSource; Morale, Welfare, and Recreation programs; nonmedical counseling programs; the Spouse Education and Career Opportunities Program; and programs to provide support for deployments and relocations. As such, the OUSD MC&FP asked the National Academies of Sciences, Engineering, and Medicine to provide insights to help the office prioritize its efforts and ensure that program and policy design aligns with its goals of supporting the well-being and readiness of service members and their families.

STUDY CHARGE

Recognizing the importance of supporting service members and their families to promote readiness and resilience, the OUSD MC&FP asked the National Academies to undertake a study to examine the challenges and opportunities facing military families and ways to protect them. The full statement of task for the committee is presented in Box 1-2. This study builds on previous National Academies reports that offered conclusions and recommendations regarding such issues as healthy community development, social support, mental health supports, the effects of multiple deployments on military families, cohesive responses to deployment-related health effects, and ways to address substance use disorders in the military (IOM, 2013a,b; NASEM, 2016, 2018).

[3]For more information see https://prhome.defense.gov/M-RA/Inside-M-RA/MCFP/How-We-Support.

BOX 1-2
Statement of Task

The National Academies of Sciences, Engineering, and Medicine will convene an ad hoc committee to study the challenges and opportunities facing military families and what is known about effective strategies for supporting and protecting military children and families, as well as lessons to be learned from these experiences. The committee will review available data and research on military children and families, including those who have left the military, with attention to differences by race, ethnicity, and other factors. The committee will also review related literature on childhood resilience and adversity. Specific topics may include

1. What can be learned from the positive experiences military families have and the protection conferred on them through supports provided by the Department of Defense and service branches, with attention to specific interventions that have been effective and how they might be used at broader scales and in nonmilitary contexts.
2. How the challenges presented by military life, such as frequent moves, exposure to trauma, and economic and other stresses to parents, influence children's social-emotional, physical, biochemical, and psychological development, and how those effects may vary across racial, ethnic, and other characteristics.
3. The mechanisms by which resilience can be fostered in military children and families, with attention to the broader literatures on human development, stress exposure, and resilience as well as available research from other countries.
4. What is needed to strengthen the support system for military families, with attention to consistency of the current system of services and resources across population subgroups, service branches, and military status (including families who have left the military).

STUDY APPROACH

The committee's work was accomplished over a 24-month period that began in October 2017. The committee members represented expertise in psychology, psychiatry, sociology, human development, family science, education, prevention and implementation science, traumatology, public policy, medicine, public health, social work, delivery of services to military populations, and community health services. Six members of the committee are military veterans and several members were or are currently part of a military family (see Appendix A for biographical sketches of the committee members and staff).[4] The committee met six times to deliberate in person, and it conducted additional deliberations by teleconference, web meetings, and electronic communications.

Information Gathering

The committee used a variety of sources to gather information. Public information-gathering sessions were held in conjunction with the committee's first and second meetings. The first session was held with the study sponsor. The second session provided the committee the opportunity to hear from representatives of service members, their families, and service member organizations who offered their perspectives on topics germane to this study (see Appendix B for the agenda of the second open session). Material from these open sessions is referenced in this report where relevant.

The committee reviewed literature and other documents from a range of disciplines and sources. An extensive review of the scientific literature pertaining to the questions raised in its statement of task was conducted. The literature searches included peer-reviewed scientific journal articles, books and reports, as well as papers and reports produced by government offices and other organizations. The committee also requested brief memos from experts from academia as well as a variety of different organizations that serve military service members and their families. A listing of the memos that the committee received appears in Appendix C.

The committee benefited from earlier reports by the National Academies based on studies conducted within the Institute of Medicine (now known as the Health and Medicine Division). In addition, the committee commissioned papers on diverse topics, including digital interventions, big data analytics, community engagement programs, implementation science, and success factors for effective systems of support for military families.

Scope

The study's sponsor, the OUSD MC&FP, asked the committee to focus on the active and reserve components in DoD, which include

- Army, Army National Guard, Army Reserve;
- Navy, Navy Reserve;

[4]The National Academies' policy states that no individual can serve on a committee used in the development of reports if the individual has a conflict of interest that is relevant to the functions to be performed. While neither active nor reserve component members served on this committee, their input was solicited at all phases of the study and played a great role in the committee's considerations. In addition, six members of the committee are military veterans.

- Marine Corps, Marine Corps Reserve; and
- Air Force, Air National Guard, and Air Force Reserve.

For the reserve component, the committee focused on the Selected Reserves, which refers to the prioritized reserve personnel who typically drill and train 1 weekend a month and 2 additional weeks each year to prepare to support military operations. Other reserve elements, which are not maintained at this level of readiness but could potentially be tapped for critical needs in a crisis, are the Individual Ready Reserves, Inactive National Guard, Standby Reserves, and Retired Reserves. The Coast Guard was excluded. Although Coast Guard members may at times serve in missions under the authority of the Department of the Navy, the Coast Guard belongs to the Department of Homeland Security rather than DoD.

The sponsor asked the committee to consider the well-being of single and married military personnel and their military dependents and also to consider more broadly the network of people who support them. The committee considered the definition of "military family" documented in DoD's Military Family Readiness Policy which focuses on dependents, yet it also allows for the possible inclusion of individuals who do not meet the legal status of a military dependent:

> *Military family.* A group composed of one Service member and spouse; Service member, spouse and such Service member's dependents; two married Service members; or two married Service members and such Service members' dependents. To the extent authorized by law and in accordance with Service implementing guidance, the term may also include other nondependent family members of a Service member (DoDI 1342.22, 2012) (U.S. Department of Defense, 2012, p. 32).

The committee also considered the legal definition of a *military dependent* as specified in Title 37 U.S.C. Section 401 (see Box 1-3) as it prepared its report.

While the committee referred to the definition used in military policy above, it was directed heavily by research conducted with the general population that suggests greater diversity in family forms than is encoded in the military definition. As a result, the committee was guided by the more inclusive definition of family that appears in Chapter 2.

Note, too, that the study charge asked the committee to consider military families that have recently left the military. Veterans who have completed their military service may be a joint responsibility of DoD and the Department of Veterans Affairs, depending upon their health status and years of service. The Department of Veterans Affairs also provides assistance to some family members, primarily spouses and dependents of disabled or deceased veterans.[5]

[5]See https://www.va.gov/HEALTHBENEFITS/apply/family_members.asp for more details about health benefits for veterans' family members.

BOX 1-3
U.S. Code, Title 37, Section 401:
Definition of Family Dependent

(a) DEPENDENT DEFINED.—In this chapter, the term "dependent", with respect to a member of a uniformed service, means the following persons:
(1) The spouse of the member.
(2) An unmarried child of the member who—
 (A) is under 21 years of age;
 (B) is incapable of self-support because of mental or physical incapacity is in fact dependent on the member for more than one half of the child's support; or
 (C) is under 23 years of age, is enrolled in a full-time course of study in an institution of higher education approved by the Secretary concerned for purposes of this subparagraph, is in fact dependent on the member for more than one-half of the child's support.
(3) A parent of the member if—
 (A) the parent is in fact dependent on the member for more than one-half of the parent's support;
 (B) the parent has been so dependent for a period prescribed by the Secretary concerned or became so dependent due to a change of circumstances arising after the member entered on active duty;
 (C) the dependency of the parent on the member is determined on the basis of an affidavit submitted by the parent any other evidence required under regulations prescribed by the Secretary concerned.
(b) OTHER DEFINITIONS.—For purposes of subsection (a):
(1) The term "child" includes—
 (A) a stepchild of the member (except that such term does not include a stepchild after the divorce of the member from the stepchild's parent by blood);
 (B) an adopted child of the member, including a child placed in the home of the member by a placement agency (recognized by the Secretary of Defense) in anticipation of the legal adoption of the child by the member;
 (C) an illegitimate child of the member if the member's parentage of the child is established in accordance with criteria prescribed in regulations by the Secretary concerned.
(2) The term "parent" means—
 (A) a natural parent of the member;
 (B) a stepparent of the member;
 (C) a parent of the member by adoption;
 (D) a parent, stepparent, or adopted parent of the spouse of the member;
 (E) any other person, including a former stepparent, who has stood in loco parentis to the member at any time for a continuous period of at least five years before the member became 21 years of age.

SOURCE: *Pay and Allowances of the Uniformed Services, 37* U.S.C. § 401 (1962).

The committee uses the terms *evidence-based* and *evidence-informed* to describe and review programs, practices, and policies (see Chapters 7 and 8). The term *evidence-based* describes a service, program, strategy, component, practice, and/or process that demonstrates impact on outcomes of interest through application of rigorous scientific research methods, namely experimental and quasi-experimental designs that allow for causal inference (Centre for Effective Services, 2011; Glasgow and Chambers, 2012; Gottfredson et al., 2015; Graczyk et al., 2003; Howse et al., 2013; Kvernbekk, 2016; Schwandt, 2014). Evidence-informed describes a service, program, strategy, component, practice, and/or process that (i) is developed by or drawn from an integration of scientific theory, practitioner experience and expertise, and stakeholder input with the best available external evidence from systematic research and a body of empirical literature; and (ii) demonstrates impact on outcomes of interest through the application of scientific research methods that do *not* allow for causal inference (Centre for Effective Services, 2011; Glasgow and Chambers, 2012; Howse et al., 2013; Kvernbekk, 2016; Schwandt, 2014). The committee notes later in this report (in Chapters 7 and 8) that some researchers have proposed a paradigm shift in how evidence-based interventions are applied, expanded, and disseminated.

The study charge required the committee to examine the evidence regarding the impact of military life on children and families. The committee notes that the vast majority of extant research on military children and families has provided correlational rather than causal evidence, such as from surveys that gathered data from individuals at a single point in time. These data provide important information about relationships (e.g., among risk factors) but are limited insofar as they are subject to shared method variance (reporter bias) and cannot provide information about directionality (what influences what). The committee relied on the most robust data available (longitudinal, randomized controlled trial, multiple-method, and multiple-informant data). Where no military study data were available, the committee reports on the relevant research from civilian populations.

Where applicable, the committee notes that there are additional contexts, systems, and entities that impact military families. These can include, for example, the formal pre-kindergarten to grade 12 public education system, youth-serving organizations such as the Y and 4-H, and other community-based and faith-based organizations. The committee acknowledges their relevance and importance to military families while noting, at the same time, that these organizations are outside the purview of MC&FP and thus outside the committee's charge.

BOX 1-4
Guiding Principles for the Report

(1) The focus is on the lived experience of military families.
(2) Families are systems.
(3) Families are embedded in larger contexts.
(4) The duration and timing of military service and experiences must be considered as they impact the family system.
(5) Military family readiness is directly linked to mission readiness.
(6) Implementation support is critical for a sustained and robust Military Family Readiness System.

GUIDING PRINCIPLES

This report is guided by six guiding principles, as shown in Box 1-4. These guiding principles were identified by the committee and are based on the research evidence on family systems and the unique experiences of military families.

Guiding Principle 1: Lived Experience

First, the committee focuses on the lived experience of military families, meaning that rather than relying upon policy definitions used to determine eligibility for specific military benefits, we consider how families may self-define (Meyer and Carlson, 2014). By recognizing families' lived experience, the committee aims to show a fundamental respect for families as unique and personal systems and recognize and appreciate the range of families' capacities to learn and adapt over time. As families learn and negotiate through their individual and collective life course, they evolve in their perspectives as well. Lived experiences can contribute in essential and complex ways to deepened understanding, problem-solving capabilities, discernment about connections, and the maturity in family function. This strategy helps us assess whether DoD's definitions and priorities leave gaps in the support system for military families.

Guiding Principle 2: Families Are Systems

Second, we understand families to be systems, meaning that families comprise not only individuals but also subgroups or subsystems, such as marital or parent-child subsystems (see Figure 1-1). Interactions among family members, both within and across subsystems, form patterns that go beyond

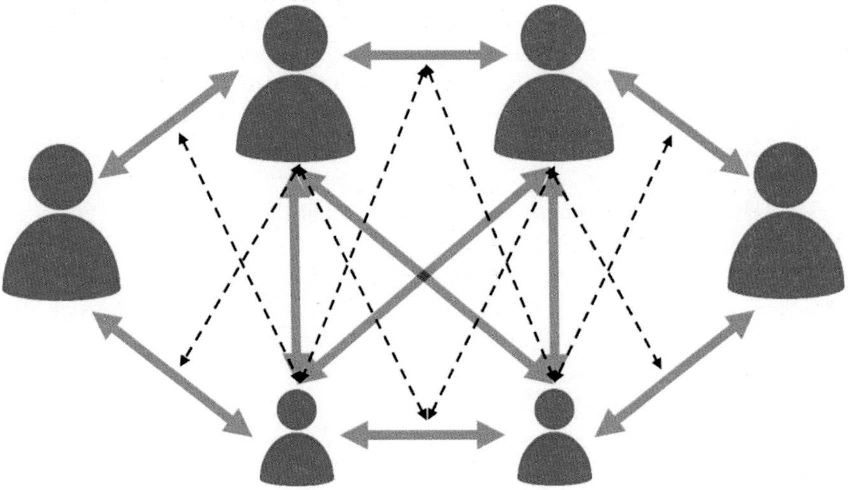

FIGURE 1-1 All family relationships are interdependent.

individual characteristics in shaping well-being and responses to adversity for all family members (Cox and Paley, 2003; Repetti et al., 2002). Individuals and subsystems within families are interdependent: The actions of one person can affect not only other individuals in the family but also other subsystems, such as mothers' actions affecting fathers' relationships with children. Family systems are dynamic, repeatedly adapting and reorganizing in response to both internal and external conditions (the systems principle of feedback loops; Cox and Paley, 2003). Family systems are diverse in organization, but families commonly work to sustain and re-establish familiar patterns (the systems principle of homeostasis). At the same time, changes in one part of the system can prompt systemwide change, offering multiple entry points for intervention (the systems principle of equifinality). Among the implications for family support systems, such as policies, programs, services, resources, and practices, is that changing the behavior of individuals may need to involve multiple family members, and vice versa, that changing the behavior of an individual may have cascading effects on other family members. Another implication is that there may be multiple pathways to successful outcomes.

Guiding Principle 3: Families Are Embedded in Larger Contexts

Third, as described in more detail in Chapter 2, we understand families to be embedded in larger contexts that both shape and are shaped by families (Bronfenbrenner et al., 1984; Cramm et al., 2018; Lubens and

Bruckner, 2018; Segal et al., 2015). These include physical contexts, such as military installations, neighborhoods, and communities; systems of services or care, such as infrastructures for food or safety and health care or economic systems; and social or cultural settings, such as religious institutions and societal or military values (Bronfenbrenner et al., 1984). Contexts can be thought of as layers surrounding families, some of them quite proximal "microsystem" settings in which family members participate actively, such as workplaces, and other, much more distal "macrosystem" settings in which families do not participate directly but by which they are nonetheless strongly affected, such as government organizations (Bronfenbrenner and Morris, 2007; Segal et al., 2015).

The levels and types of resources and support available in settings have significant implications for both physical and mental well-being, as acknowledged in the U.S. Department of Health and Human Services' Healthy People 2020 initiative.[6] Resources and support can include not only formal policies and programs, but also informal practices that can filter or augment their well-being, such as by limiting or expanding access. Most military families rely on a complex array of formal and informal supports and services provided through their personal networks or by military and civilian organizations. Together, these form a complex interwoven and dynamic system.

For example, most members of active component military families live in civilian communities and many may work or attend school there as well, but they also may have access to military supports and services on or near installations. Reserve component families have regular access to some military supports but intermittent access to others (as we will discuss further in Chapter 4).

Guiding Principle 4: Duration and Timing of Service Must Be Considered

Duration and timing of military service must be considered in relation to military family well-being (Bowen and Martin, 2011; Masten, 2015; Wilmoth and London, 2013). Duration refers to the length of military service or military experiences such as deployments. Timing refers to when events or experiences occur in the lives of individuals, in the family's history, and in the political or historical context. Exposures to adversity early in life, for example, may have especially serious consequences. Duration is important because short-term events or exposure may have different effects from protracted ones. Chapters 4 and 5 provide more in-depth discussion of duration and timing.

---

[6]For more information see https://www.healthypeople.gov/2020/topics-objectives/topic/social-determinants-of-health.

BOX 1-5
Characteristics, Strengths, and Challenges of the All-Volunteer Force

The contemporary all-volunteer force was initiated in 1973 with the close of the Vietnam draft. The initial success of the all-volunteer force largely resulted from significant increases in the recruitment of women and African Americans into the military (Kelty and Segal, 2013). Through the 1980s and 1990s, in response to the fall of the Soviet Union, the structure of the all-volunteer force shifted to a "blended force" model with heavy reliance on the reserve component (Carter et al., 2017). Post-Cold War Base Realignment and Closures (BRAC) resulted in the closure of more than 350 bases and the rollout of a new joint-base configuration hosting two or more components at one location.

Recruitment patterns also have shifted over the nearly five decades of the all-volunteer force. For instance, the 1990s economic boom made it difficult for the Department of Defense to recruit and retain qualified service members, a pattern that continues today with strong competition in the civilian sector, particularly in the cyber and high-tech arenas.

In addition, there have been many calls throughout the period of the all-volunteer force to smooth and ease the transition between military service and civilian status, which is particularly abrupt for family members (DoD Taskforce on Mental Health, 2007; National Child Traumatic Stress Network, 2018); hence we pay special attention in this report to issues related to transition. (See Box 1-5 for more details about the all-volunteer force.)

Guiding Principle 5: Military Family Readiness Linked to Mission Readiness

The fifth guiding principle is that military family readiness is directly linked to mission readiness. In 2002, the Deputy Assistant Secretary of Defense released a report describing a "new social compact" (U.S. Department of Defense, 2002, p. 6), which outlined a mutually beneficial partnership between DoD, service members, and their families. According to this report,

> the partnership between the American people and the noble warfighters and their families is built on a tacit agreement that families as well as the service member contribute immeasurably to the readiness and strength of the American military. Efforts toward improved quality of life, while made out of genuine respect and concern for service members and families' needs, also have a pragmatic goal: a United States that is militarily strong.

DoD's social compact philosophy is undergirded by the notion that "we're all in this together" in order to have a successful military and defend the security of our nation. As such, the committee used this philosophy as well as the long history of evidence that shows that families are important for military readiness as a backdrop for its conclusions and recommendations in this report. This guiding principle is described in more depth in Chapter 2 and elsewhere throughout the report.

Guiding Principle 6: Implementation Support Is Critical

The final principle that the committee used to guide its report is that implementation support is critical for a sustained and robust Military Family Readiness System (MFRS). The MFRS is defined by DoD as "the network of agencies, programs, services and people, and the collaboration among them, that facilitates and actively promotes the readiness and quality of life of Service members and their families."[7] The MFRS serves both active and reserve component service members and their families, and includes community partners to meet the needs of geographically separated military families, who are not near a military installation.

The policies and programs that comprise the MFRS fall under the purview of the Under Secretary of Defense for Personnel and Readiness USD (P&R),[8] but they are governed by separate Assistant Secretaries of Defense (ASDs). The vast majority of services and activities are delivered by the individual military services. This division of labor and responsibilities has had some salutary effect on achieving a baseline level of delivery across the system to meet military families' expectations as they traverse the military lifestyle but has also impeded coordination between and among all of the agencies who are delivering services to the individual service members and their families.

The concept of the MFRS was introduced in the Department of Defense Instruction (DoDI) 1342.22, "Military Family Readiness" in July 2012 under the signature of the then serving Under Secretary of Defense for Personnel and Readiness. This updated instruction introduced the concept of the MFRS that outlines diverse options for accessing a network of integrated services to help families easily find the support they need for everyday life in the military. According to a 2011 Request for Applications DoD's goal is to "implement a Military Family Readiness System (MFRS) that is a high quality, effective and efficient DoD-standard, joint-Service training resource (with supporting materials) that prepares Family Center/Family Readiness program staff (management and front line employees)

[7]See https://public.militaryonesource.mil/footer?content_id=282320.
[8]See https://prhome.defense.gov.

to implement individual programs within the context of a 'social service delivery system' model."[9]

As further delineated in Chapters 7 and 8, implementation processes are critical to ensuring that programs, services, and resources are delivered with quality and with an appropriate balance of fidelity and adaptation and are efficient in terms of return on investment. Specifically, there is a translation gap between evidence and practice that is likely intensified within the dynamic military context (see Chapter 8 for a detailed discussion). The committee does not have sufficient information to estimate the costs of the MFRS however the recommended MFRS as a learning system (as described in Chapter 7) will lead to cost savings by avoiding spending money on ineffective programs, better targeting of services, and better learning about what is working and what is not.

ORGANIZATION OF THE REPORT

This report is organized into nine chapters. Chapter 2 describes what is meant by "family" in the military context and introduces the concept of family well-being. Chapter 2 also attends to the broader literatures on human development, stress exposure, and resilience. Chapter 3 describes the demographic and military service characteristics of military families, including the sources and current state of these data. In Chapter 4, the committee highlights opportunities, stressors, and challenges that military life poses. Chapter 5 focuses on resilience and the impact of stress and trauma on the development of the children of service members. This includes an examination of children's social-emotional, physical, neurobiological, and psychological development. Chapter 6 examines what is known about the impact of highly stressful or traumatic challenges on the family system. In Chapter 7, the committee presents a framework as a method to build a more coherent, comprehensive approach to military family well-being and readiness and to transform the current MFRS into a coherent, comprehensive, complex adaptive system. Chapter 8 presents the research and components needed to develop a learning community system to support military family well-being. Chapter 9 presents the committee's recommendations to DoD. Appendix A includes biographical sketches of the committee and project staff. Appendix B includes the agenda for the public information-gathering session. Appendix C lists the individuals and organizations that submitted memos to the committee. Appendix D provides a glossary of terms and an acronyms list.

---

[9] See https://nifa.usda.gov/sites/default/files/rfa/11_military_readiness.pdf.

REFERENCES

Bowen, G. L., and Martin, J. A. (2011). The resiliency model of role performance for service members, veterans, and their families: A focus on social connections and individual assets. *Journal of Human Behavior in the Social Environment, 21*(2), 162–178.

Bronfenbrenner, U., Moen, P., and Garbarino, J. (1984). Child, family, community. In R. D. Parke (Ed.), *Review of Child Development Research* (vol. 7, pp. 283–328). Chicago: University of Chicago Press.

Bronfenbrenner, U., and Morris, P. A. (2007). The bioecological model of human development. In W. Damon and R. Lerner (Eds.), *Handbook of Child Psychology* (6th ed., vol. 1, pp. 793–828). Hoboken, NJ: John Wiley & Sons, Inc.

Carter, P., Kidder, K., Schafer, A., and Swick, A. (2017). *Working Paper, AVF 4.0: The Future of the All-Volunteer Force*. Washington, DC: Center for New American Security.

Centre for Effective Services. (2011). *The What Works Process: Evidence-Informed Improvement for Child and Family Services*. Dublin, Ireland: Centre for Effective Services.

Cox, M. J. and Paley, B. (2003). Understanding families as systems. *Current Directions in Psychological Science, 12*, 193–196.

Cramm, H., Norris, D., Venedam, S., and Tam-Seto, L. (2018). Toward a model of military family resiliency: A narrative review. *Journal of Family Theory & Review, 10*(3), 620–640.

DoD Task Force on Mental Health. (2007). *The Department of Defense Plan to Achieve the Vision of the DoD Task Force on Mental Health: Report to Congress*. Washington, DC: U.S. Department of Defense. Available: file:///N:/BOCYF%20Projects%20-%20Current/Military%20Families/Relevant%20Literature/91907DoDTaskForceMentalHealth.pdf.

Easterbrooks, M. A., Ginsburg, K., and Lerner, R. M. (2013). Resilience among military youth. *The Future of Children, 23*(2), 99–120.

Glasgow, R. E., and Chambers, D. (2012). Developing robust, sustainable, implementation systems using rigorous, rapid and relevant science. *Clinical and Translational Science, 5*(1), 48–55.

Gottfredson, D. C., Cook, T. D., Gardner, F. E., Gorman-Smith, D., Howe, G. W., Sandler, I. N., and Zafft, K. M. (2015). Standards of evidence for efficacy, effectiveness, and scale-up research in prevention science: Next generation. *Prevention Science, 16*(7), 893–926.

Graczyk, P. A., Domitrovich, C. E., and Zins, J. E. (2003). Facilitating the implementation of evidence-based prevention and mental health promotion efforts in schools. In *Handbook of School Mental Health Advancing Practice and Research* (pp. 301–318). Boston: Springer.

Howse, R. B., Trivette, C. M., Shindelar, L., Dunst, C. J., and The North Carolina Partnership for Children, Inc. (2013). *The Smart Start Resource Guide of Evidence-Based and Evidence-Informed Programs and Practices: A Summary of Research Evidence*. Raleigh, NC: The North Carolina Partnership for Children, Inc.

Institute of Medicine. (IOM) (2013a). *Returning Home from Iraq and Afghanistan: Assessment of Readjustment Needs of Veterans, Service Members, and Their Families*. Washington, DC: The National Academies Press.

________. (2013b). *Substance Use Disorders in the U.S. Armed Forces*. Washington, DC: The National Academies Press.

Kelty, R., and Segal, D. R. (2013). The military as a transforming influence: Integration into or isolation from normal adult roles? In J. M. Wilmoth and A. S. London (Eds.), *Life Course Perspectives on Military Service* (pp. 19–47). New York, NY: Routledge.

Kvernbekk, T. (2016). *Evidence-based Practice in Education: Functions of Evidence and Causal Presuppositions*. New York, NY: Routledge.

Lubens, P., and Bruckner, T. A. (2018). A review of military health research using a social-ecological framework. *American Journal of Health Promotion, 32*(4), 1078–1090.

Masten, A. (2001). Ordinary magic: Resilience processes in development. *American Psychologist, 56*(3), 227–238.

_______. (2015). Pathways to integrated resilience science. *Psychological Inquiry*, *26*(2), 187–196.

Meyer, D. R., and Carlson, M. J. (2014). Family complexity: Implications for policy research. *ANNALS of the American Academy of Political Social Sciences, 654*(1), 259–276.

National Academies of Sciences, Engineering, and Medicine (NASEM). (2016). *Gulf War Health: Volume 10: Update of Health Effects of Serving in the Gulf War, 2016*. Washington, DC: The National Academies Press.

_______. (2018). *Evaluation of the Department of Veterans Affairs Mental Health Services*. Washington, DC: The National Academies Press.

National Child Traumatic Stress Network. (2018). *After Service: Veteran Families in Transition*. Retrieved from https://www.nctsn.org/sites/default/files/resources//after_service_veteran_families_in_transition.pdf.

Repetti, R. L., Taylor, S. E., and Seeman, T. E. (2002). Risky families: Family social environments and the mental physical health of offspring. *Psychological Bulletin*, *12*(8), 330–366.

Schwandt, T. A. (2014). Credible evidence of effectiveness: Necessary but not sufficient. In S. I. Dondalson, C. A. Christie, and M. M. Mark (Eds.), *Credible and Actionable Evidence: The Foundation for Rigorous and Influential Evaluations* (2nd ed., pp. 259–273). Los Angeles, CA: Sage.

Segal, M. W., Lane, M. D., and Fisher, A. G. (2015). Conceptual model of military career, family life course events, intersections, and effects on well-being. *Military Behavioral Health*, *3*(2), 95–107.

U.S. Department of Defense. (2002). *A New Social Compact: A Reciprocal Partnership Between the Department of Defense, Service Members, and Families*. Washington, DC. Retrieved from http://download.militaryonesource.mil/12038/MOS/Reports/A%20New%20Social%20Compact.pdf.

_______. (2012). *Department of Defense Instruction: Military Family Readiness*. Washington, DC. Retrieved from http://www.esd.whs.mil/Portals/54/Documents/DD/issuances/dodi/134222p.pdf.

Wilmoth, J. M., and London, A. S. (2013). *Life Course Perspectives on Military Service*. New York, NY: Routledge.

2

Family Well-Being, Readiness, and Resilience

In this chapter, the committee lays the foundation for subsequent chapters by establishing the importance to the U.S. Department of Defense's (DoD's) mission of the well-being, readiness, and resilience of military families, including the service members in them. After reviewing the evidence concerning family well-being, the committee lays out its approach to this subject from objective, subjective, and functional perspectives. This is followed by a discussion of the ways various dimensions of family well-being within the military context are illuminated by developmental science, bioecological models of individual and family development, and life course theory. Equal importance is placed on reviewing the concepts of family readiness and resilience within the military context. The chapter concludes with a discussion of the measurement of family resilience, which finds that while there are no comprehensive measures, there are still well-established measures that can be used to assess many of the major components of resilience and readiness.

The well-being of military families is essential to DoD for multiple reasons. First, family well-being is an important consideration to individuals who are deciding whether to enter or remain in military service (Keller et al., 2018; Meyers, 2018). The resources that DoD provides to support family well-being can help to make military service more attractive than civilian employment. Second, family difficulties can be costly to DoD due to the expenses incurred in response to legal, medical, mental health, or financial problems (Institute of Medicine [IOM], 2013; Lubens and Bruckner, 2018). Service members' psychological or physical difficulties can reverberate within families, potentially generating costs for DoD (IOM, 2013). Years ago, the Army Science Board (an independent advisory group to the Secretary of the Army) concluded: "Recognition of the powerful impacts of the family on readiness, retention, morale and motivation must be instilled in every soldier from the soldier's date of entry-to-service through each succeeding promotion" (Schneider and Martin, 1994, p. 25).

Third, family difficulties can detract from a service member's readiness for and focus on the military mission. Family members provide support to service members while they serve and when they have difficulties; family problems can interfere with the ability of service members to deploy or remain in theater; and family members are central influences on whether members continue to serve (Keller et al., 2018; Meyers, 2018; Schneider and Martin, 1994; Shiffer et al., 2017; Sims et al., 2017).

Finally, and perhaps most importantly, service members' families support the military mission by supporting them while they serve, making it possible for service members to leave home to train and deploy, and providing significant care for service members when they are wounded, ill, or injured (IOM, 2013). Service members must rely even more on their families during and following the transition from military service to civilian life, when access to DoD resources shrinks. Given that most family members cannot receive services from the Veterans Administration (VA), this time of transition may be especially challenging.

LINKAGES BETWEEN FAMILY ISSUES AND MILITARY READINESS

Most of the evidence regarding links between family issues and military readiness assumes or ignores the positive contributions of families to military service. An exception is the literature related to choosing military service, which shows that parents appear to be important influencers of youths' decisions to enlist and to take tangible steps toward doing so (Gibson et al., 2007; Legree et al., 2000). In addition, family structure while growing up is related to propensity to serve. For example, the large, National Longitudinal Study of Adolescent to Adult Health or Add Health study found that youth raised in families by stepparents or social (i.e., non-biological) parents were approximately twice as likely to enlist rather than go to college as youth from families with two biological parents, even after controlling for socioeconomic status (Spence et al., 2013).

Family-related factors are associated with job performance during military service. In the 2011 Health-Related Behaviors Survey (Barlas et al., 2013), service members reported that conflicts between military and family/personal responsibilities and separation from family or friends were among the top three stressors of military life (see Table 5-2). In a large study at Fort Jackson, male service members with a marital status of separated, divorced, or widowed were at an increased risk of medical discharge from basic training (Swedler et al., 2011). In data from the 2002 DoD Health-Related Behaviors Survey of Active Duty Personnel, occupational stress, which was significantly related to both mental health problems and work performance, was highest among married service members living away from their spouses (Hourani et al., 2006).

Family factors also have implications for the performance of military members during deployments. In one small but dyadic study, Carter and colleagues (2015) found that communication between partners was robustly related to deployed male soldiers' reports of being able to focus on their jobs. Data from the 2010 Joint Mental Health Advisory Team 7 (2011), gathered in the Middle East from deployed soldiers and Marines, indicated that between 11 and 16.7 percent of married service members, and between 6.4 and 8.5 percent of single service members, perceived that stress or tension related to their families was producing preoccupation or lack of concentration or making it hard to do their military jobs. Family issues were comparable to combat experiences in their relationship to sleep quality and visits to behavioral health care providers.

Specifically regarding military readiness, Schumm and colleagues (2001) tabulated results from multiple samples of Army soldiers showing that family-related factors were significantly related to multiple indicators of soldier readiness. Data from more than 4,500 Army participants in the 1992 DoD Survey of Officers and Enlisted Personnel indicated that soldiers' perceptions of spouses' satisfaction with soldier family time and soldiers' satisfaction with the environment for families both were significantly related to satisfaction with military life and their military job, after controlling for years of service, unit morale, and unit readiness. In the 1991–1992 Survey of Total Army Personnel, soldiers' self-ratings of readiness and satisfaction with military life were significantly related to how often Army responsibilities created problems for their families, as well as stress in their personal or family lives (Schumm et al., 2001).

There is a long history of evidence that families are important for military retention. Rosen and Durand (1995) summarized some of this literature, citing studies from multiple branches showing that service members were more committed to military service if they were married and that spouses' attitudes were implicated in service members' retention decisions. Analyzing longitudinal data they collected from more than 1,200 Army spouses (776 spouses participated in the follow-up survey 1 year after deployment) of enlisted service members deployed for Operation Desert Storm, they found that after controlling for rank, years of service, and spouses' expectations, the key predictors of attrition for junior spouses were marital problems and the number of years as a military spouse. The single largest predictor of intentions to leave service was the degree to which spouses perceived it as compatible with family life. Among midlevel noncommissioned officer (NCO) spouses, the strongest predictors of attrition were marital problems and spouses' wishes; these also were significant predictors of intentions to leave service (Rosen and Durand, 1995). During the Operation Iraqi Freedom/Operation Enduring Freedom (OIF/OEF) conflict, married enlisted members in the Neurocognition Deployment Health Study (n = 740) were almost twice as likely as others to remain in military service 12 months following return from deployment (Vasterling et al., 2015), with the role of marital status being similar in magnitude to those of unit support, pay grade, and age. By comparison, military occupational type, stressful war zone events, and mental health problems were not significantly related to retention.

Lancaster and colleagues studied retention among more than 400 National Guard service members of a brigade combat team deployed in 2006 (Lancaster et al., 2013). Surveys were administered immediately prior to and 2 to 3 months following deployment. Social support during deployment from military leaders and unit members was significantly and positively related to intentions to reenlist for both men and women, while predeployment concerns about family disruption were not. Postdeployment stressors, which included job loss, divorces, financial stressors, and other family-related experiences, were significantly and negatively related to intentions to reenlist. Among 282 participants in a later data collection, actual enlistment behavior was closely related to their earlier intentions.

There is some evidence that family-related issues may be even more important to the retention of female than male service members. In a recent small qualitative study of women veterans, most reported leaving military service before they planned or wished to, primarily because of personal health problems or responsibilities for children (Dichter and True, 2015). These findings echo the results of earlier longitudinal research by Pierce (1998), which showed that Air Force women who became mothers in the 2 years following the launch of Operation Desert Storm were twice as likely to leave military service as women who did not have children. Across the full sample, there were five reasons for leaving that were each reported by more than 20 percent of the respondents. Separation from family and friends and work-family conflict were comparable in prevalence to dissatisfaction with work conditions and somewhat less common than concerns about lack of promotion/recognition and deployment.

More recently, Kelley et al., (2001) studied 154 mothers serving in the Navy, who were divided into a nondeploying group and a group that deployed just prior to 2001. About 80 percent of their children were ages 3 or younger. Two interviews were conducted prior to and following deployment. For both groups, reenlistment intentions at the second interview were significantly related to military benefits and to work-family concerns, which were identified by one-third of the mothers as reasons for planning to leave service. Experiencing deployment was associated with a greater sense of integration into the Navy, which in turn was positively related to intentions to reenlist.

Family issues are also implicated in the mental health of service members. In a study of previously deployed Canadian military personnel (n = 14,624), the relationship between combat exposure and mental health problems was stronger among married than unmarried personnel, possibly due to the interpersonal challenges of marriage (Watkins et al., 2017). Another study, which examined the records associated with over 700 cases of death by suicide among Army National Guard members between 2007 and 2014 (Griffith and Bryan, 2017), found that parent-family relationship issues were among the top five most common factors, implicated in 27.5 percent of the cases, along with military performance problems (36.4%), substance use (27.3%), and income difficulties (22%). Divorce or separation were present in 15 percent of the cases. Among soldiers who died by suicide within 365 days of return from deployment, parent-family problems were the most common factor—tied with transition problems and substance use during the first 120 days, and more than 8 percentage points more common than the next most common factors during the remainder of the first year.

Family issues are often thought of as potential problems for military service, despite evidence that families appear to be positive influences on joining or remaining in the military, on perceiving oneself as well-prepared for military duties or performing them well, and on the receipt of support and assistance while serving. The importance of families for DoD was reaffirmed by Chairman of the Joint Chiefs Admiral Michael Mullen when the Total Force Fitness directive was crafted in 2010. A resilience-based framework, Total Force Fitness recognizes families as "central to the total force fitness equation" (Land, 2010, p. 3). An article summarizing the evidence base for Total Force Fitness asserts that "social and family fitness are essential to total force fitness and impact performance from such disparate areas as the rate of wound healing to overall unit functioning" (Jonas et al., 2010, p. 12).

DEFINING FAMILY

There is no universal definition of *family*, and little evidence of a "best" family form, as family structures have changed continuously throughout history. In the United States, for example, the nuclear family form became prominent following World War II; households prior to that time were much more likely to include nonrelatives (Furstenberg, 2014). At any given time, multiple "official" definitions are operating across and even within government agencies, DoD included (IOM, 2013). The ability to understand increases in family diversity and complexity is limited by how families are defined for the purposes of tabulation. The U.S. Census Bureau currently uses the following definition:

> A family is a group of two people or more (one of whom is the householder) related by birth, marriage, or adoption and residing together; all such people (including related subfamily members) are considered as members of one family. Beginning with the 1980 Current Population Survey, unrelated subfamilies (referred to in the past as secondary families) are no longer included in the count of families, nor are the members of unrelated subfamilies included in the count of family members.[1]

Groups of individuals who do not conform to this definition are *not* counted by the Census Bureau as families, obscuring knowledge about actual families—those who do not live together and couples who are unmarried, to take two examples. The rise of family diversity and complexity has increased the difficulty of assigning individual families to a single category in a standardized list (Cherlin and Seltzer, 2014). Meyer and Carlson (2014) suggest that it may be necessary in the future to categorize families along several dimensions, including such variables as the presence of children, social versus biological parents or siblings, and nonresidential children or parents. In Canada, the Vanier Institute of the Family has begun to intentionally refer to families according to their functional roles rather than their structure, referring for example to "solo," "lead," or "co-" parents rather than to single or married parents, accommodating the reality that partners, grandparents, or even nonrelatives may play these roles (Spinks, 2018).

For the purposes of this report, the committee considers the following as *family*:

(1) People to whom service members are related by blood, marriage, or adoption, which could include spouses, children, and service members' parents or siblings.
(2) People for whom service members have—or have assumed—a responsibility to provide care, which could include unmarried partners and their children, dependent elders, or others.
(3) People who provide significant care for service members.

DEFINING FAMILY WELL-BEING

There is no universal definition of family well-being in the research literature or across national and global organizations. With regard to well-

[1]See https://www.census.gov/programs-surveys/cps/technical-documentation/subject-definitions.html#family.

being among individuals, the World Health Organization (WHO) pivoted away from a purely medical perspective in an earlier conceptualization, arguing that individual "health is a state of complete physical, mental and social well-being and not merely the absence of disease or infirmity" (WHO, 1948, p. 1). The Healthy People 2020 (HP2020) Framework for individual well-being[2] asserts that health and well-being are determined not only by individual-level health behaviors but also by broad social-structural influences such as the characteristics and functioning of families and communities. Because individual health and well-being depend on social determinants, the well-being of individuals is tightly connected with that of families.

The committee considered family well-being from three perspectives: objective, subjective, and functional (Centers for Disease Control and Prevention [CDC], 2018; Organisation for Economic Co-operation and Development [OECD], 2017; Skomorovsky, 2018). *Objective* well-being refers to resources considered necessary for adequate quality of life, such as sufficient economic and educational resources, housing, health, safety, environmental quality, and social connections (OECD, 2017). One example of an objective standard is budgets created to identify the minimum income necessary for family self-sufficiency.[3] For military families, the ability to meet such budgets depends on several conditions: whether service members and their partners have adequate employment opportunities, pay, and benefits (Mason, 2018; Military Officers Association of America, 2018); whether families are able to afford adequate housing in safe neighborhoods; whether the environments where families live and work are free of significant threats to health and safety and offer opportunities and support infrastructures that are available, accessible, and affordable; and whether families have adequate networks of informal support.

Subjective well-being is the result of how individuals think and feel about their circumstances, and family well-being is higher when multiple family members experience high subjective well-being. Feelings of happiness and pleasure are the focus of the "hedonic" perspective on well-being (OECD, 2017; Ryan and Deci, 2001), while the "eudaimonic" perspective emphasizes self-actualization (Keyes, 2006). The latter perspective focuses on the cultivation of a meaningful life, one in which a person is able to exercise personal choice, gain a sense of competence and mastery, cultivate healthy relationships, and find meaning and purpose in life. Good health, particularly mental health, comprises high hedonic *and* eudaimonic well-being.

[2]This is an initiative of the Office of Disease Prevention and Health Promotion, U.S. Department of Health and Human Services, which was launched in 2010 to provide an agenda for the nation's health. See https://www.healthypeople.gov/2020/About-Healthy-People.

[3]For more information, see http://www.selfsufficiencystandard.org.

Third and finally, well-being may also be viewed from a *functional* perspective, which focuses on the degree to which families and their members can and do successfully perform their core functions, such as caring for, supporting, and nurturing family members. Although positive family functioning involves skills and abilities that are common and perhaps often thought to be "natural," many of them can be taught and strengthened with education. A variety of standardized instruments exist to assess aspects of family functioning, such as the quality of communication between spouses or partners, parenting and co-parenting, and also general family functioning. Although there is no single consensus definition of functional family well-being, a recent Australian report (Pezzullo et al., 2010, p. 6) defines positive family functioning as

> characterised by emotional closeness, warmth, support and security; well-communicated and consistently applied age-appropriate expectations; stimulating and educational interactions; the cultivation and modelling of physical health promotion strategies; high quality relationships between all family members; and involvement of family members in community activities.

Though they are not synonymous, these three different types of well-being are interrelated: if one is rated as high, the other two are more likely to be rated high as well, and if one is rated as low, likewise the other two are more likely to be rated low. In general, however, it is important to note that more is known about the indicators and determinants of individual than family well-being.

MILITARY-FOCUSED DEFINITIONS OF WELL-BEING

DoD does not have an agreed-upon definition of family well-being. Although the Defense Center of Excellence for Psychological Health and Traumatic Brain Injury (2011) referred to "core components" of well-being as happiness and life satisfaction, consistent with subjective well-being, objective and functional well-being also have operational relevance for DoD. The significance of subjective well-being stems from the way it is linked with service members' and family members' willingness to continue serving. Objective family well-being is essential, given that DoD must successfully compete with private employers for workers and thus needs to provide compensation, benefits, and support for an adequate quality of life. Functional well-being is important as well, because DoD relies on families to support service members' ability to perform their missions, care for them when wounded, ill, or injured, and support transitions to civilian life.

Data currently gathered or monitored by DoD, for example through the Status of Forces Surveys (see Chapter 3), provide information about some aspects of family well-being. But this information primarily concerns subjective well-being, while information about objective and functional well-being is limited or lacking.

TRENDS IN FAMILY LIFE

In most Western societies, including the United States, industrialization over the past 150 years has been accompanied by significant changes in the work and family behavior of both men and women, especially mothers (Furstenberg, 2014). In the United States since World War II, family structures have become substantially more diverse as connections among partnering, marriage, and childbearing have weakened (Cherlin and Selzer, 2014). Cohabiting is now as common as marriage, which occurs later in life, if at all. Moreover, 40 percent of children are now born to parents who are not married, although the percentage of parents with partners has not changed (Cherlin, 2010). There also have been substantial declines in the average number of births per woman (Cherlin, 2010; OECD, 2011). Other trends contributing to family diversity include increases in the prevalence of shared custody of children following divorce and in the number of couples who do not live together, same-sex couples, and mixed-immigration-status families.

Young adults today are likely to have accumulated more family transitions, such as marriage, divorce, or changes in household composition, than their predecessors, and their own children are likely to share this characteristic. For example, the proportion of young adults now occupying more than one parental role (e.g., having not only residential biological children but also residential "social" children[4] or nonresidential biological children) prior to age 30 has risen by close to 50 percent (Berger and Bzostek, 2014). The percentage of children not living with both biological parents increased in the 1970s and 1980s, but largely stabilized in the 1990s at about 40 percent (Manning et al., 2014). The proportion of children living in three-generation households has risen, increasing the involvement of grandparents in some children's lives (Dunifon et al., 2014). Children in families today are more likely to have ties to parents or siblings in multiple households than in the past (Cherlin and Seltzer, 2014).

In addition, some individuals, traditionally women, may find themselves "sandwiched" between simultaneous caregiving roles and responsibilities. The Pew Research Center estimates that there are more than

---

[4]*Social children* are those who are not biological, step, or adopted, such as when an unmarried partner brings his or her biological children to a cohabiting relationship. Those children are social children for the partner—there is no legal status, but the partner may function as a parent.

40 million unpaid caregivers of adults age 65 and older (Pew Research Center, 2015). The committee notes that for military families, there are two possible roles in which caregivers and/or spouses may be sandwiched: (i) an adult child caring for an older parent; or (ii) a younger adult, such as a wounded service member, being cared for by a spouse, adult sibling, or parent. A recent systematic review of the literature on veterans' informal caregivers found that there was limited relevant research with regard to informal caregiving of individuals with disabilities, and there were few studies conducted on protective factors for caregivers of both older (over age 55) and younger family members (Smith-Osborne and Felderhoff, 2014). However, as discussed in more detail in Chapter 3, less than 1 percent of active component dependents (0.6%) and less than one-half of a percent of reserve component dependents are adult dependents who are not the spouses or children of service members.

Some scholars view these increasingly diverse family forms as a continuation of longstanding trends (Biblarz and Stacey, 2010), but others express concern, particularly about a specific form of family diversity labeled *family complexity*, which is tied to multipartner fertility (i.e., where one person has children with multiple partners). This latter pattern tends to produce families that are unstable, because the structure of the family or the household (or both) changes frequently, increasing the risk of negative consequences for family members. The prevalence of multipartner fertility among parents with at least two children is estimated to range from 23 percent of fathers ages 40–44 and 28 percent of mothers ages 41–49 (Guzzo, 2014).

Multipartner fertility and the family instability that often accompanies it may have negative implications for children. Evidence from a large national sample indicates that children who live with single or cohabiting parents receive less total caregiving time than children living in married-couple or three-generation households (Kalil et al., 2014). Children living apart from a biological parent receive less caregiving from that parent, benefit less from that parent's earnings, experience more transitions in living arrangements, and are at increased risk of maltreatment at the hands of social parents (i.e., an unmarried partner of the parent with whom children live; Sawhill, 2014). Thus, rising family *instability*, or frequent changes in the composition of families or households, in the United States is a potentially problematic development.

In the United States, multipartner fertility is more common among low-resource populations. Recent decades have seen a widening educational divide in family structure, such that college-educated individuals are more likely to get married, stay married, and have children while married than individuals with only a high school education (Furstenberg, 2014; Manning et al., 2014). Furstenberg (2014) links these trends to rising economic inequality and the ongoing transformation of roles within families. He points out that limited economic resources can make individuals hesitant to make marital commitments and make it difficult to obtain birth control and to develop the skills necessary to sustain family relationships, with negative implications for family well-being and functioning. In addition, a recent report from the World Family Indicators Family Map Project indicates that growth in cohabiting (as opposed to single-parent families) predicts growth in family instability (Social Trends Institute, 2017). In summary, both family diversity and family complexity are rising, but it is family complexity that is associated with family instability.

IMPLICATIONS FOR THE DEPARTMENT OF DEFENSE

There may be a large and rising number of families that are invisible because they are neither tabulated nor targeted in family readiness efforts (Hawkins et al., 2018; Meyers, 2018). Examples of invisible families may include same-sex-headed households and families as well as co-parenting but unmarried families. Given that half of the military force is unmarried—a portion of which is certainly in committed relationships—this risk could be substantial. Consequently, to the extent that family forms continue to become more diverse, DoD policies, programs, services, resources, and practices could become increasingly misaligned with actual family structures. Because the prevalence of invisible families is by definition not regularly documented, knowledge is further limited about recent trends related to military family diversity, complexity, and stability.

Across DoD, the term "military family" typically refers to service members and their spouses and/or children, consistent with eligibility rules for military benefits (see Chapter 1). These eligibility conditions are in part bounded by lawmakers who allocate funding to DoD. For example, Congress determines who can be considered "military dependents" for the purposes of benefits through U.S. law.[5] Most military dependents are spouses or children of service members, but other individuals, such as parents, also may qualify under certain circumstances, as the definitions provided in Chapter 1 indicate. In practice, however, rules and practices governing eligibility of family members vary across programs and services. For example, while they would not normally be classified as military dependents, service members' parents, unmarried partners, and others are sometimes invited to participate in deployment briefings, permitted to participate in some activities, or allowed to use facilities on military installations (Thompson, 2018). Other rules are less inclusive, such as those that restrict the eligibility

[5]U.S. Code, Title 37 ("Pay and Allowances of the Uniformed Services"), Chapter 7 ("Allowances"), Section 401 ("Definitions"). See https://www.gpo.gov/fdsys/pkg/USCODE-2010-title37/html/USCODE-2010-title37-chap7-sec401.htm for more information.

of single parents or applicants with two dependents for military service (see DoD Instruction 1304.26).[6]

Because military service has lengthened in the all-volunteer era, service members are now older and more likely to have partners and children; the population of spouses and children alone exceeds the population of service members (U.S. Department of Defense [DoD], 2017a). Because family eligibility for programs and supports is necessary for family members to be able to perform important functions that support military missions, this eligibility requirement is especially challenging for service members who are unmarried or childless. Considerable evidence indicates that service members' well-being is closely connected to the well-being of family members (IOM, 2013). Family members are also important for military retention, especially for women (Keller et al., 2018). DoD acknowledged some of these themes in its articulation of a "social compact" with service members and their families in 2002, which remains relevant today (DoD, 2017b; Office of Deputy Assistant Secretary of Defense for Military Community and Family Policy, 2002).

Historically, DoD has relied on marriage as a gateway to a variety of resources, such as access to military housing or housing allowances, and the ability to take partners on accompanied tours of duty. This marriage-focused stance has been credited with positive consequences, such as reducing racial disparities in marriage and divorce relative to the general population and producing higher rates of marriage as opposed to cohabiting (IOM, 2013), which in turn may help to minimize the flux experienced by children, particularly children of male service members (Hawkins et al., 2018). Some evidence also suggests, however, that military members have high rates of early marriage, increasing the prevalence of divorce and remarriage in this population (Adler-Baeder et al., 2006).

The *accumulation* of family transitions, which is generally not captured by snapshot assessments at any single point in time, may have implications for later individual well-being and family functioning. Individuals who currently have the same marital status, for example, may have quite different family responsibilities because of differences in their respective histories of family transitions and family instability. The focus on marriage and legal dependents in military policy also means that far more is known about certain kinds of military families—service members (mostly male) with civilian spouses, and their custodial children—than others, such as unmarried partners, or service members' parents and siblings, who are functionally invisible to DoD.

[6]For example, for those interested in applying for admission to the United States Military Academy West Point, the FAQ page states, "You must not be married, pregnant, or have a legal obligation to support a child or children." See https://westpoint.edu/admissions/apply-now.

Over time, marital status is becoming less useful as an indicator of family structure because connections are weakening between when or with whom individuals form relationships, and whether or when they marry, share households, or have children. It also is important to recognize that almost all service members, including those who are unmarried, are part of some form of family, and many receive assistance from informal support systems while they perform military duties, when they deploy, or when they become injured (Polusny et al., 2014). Although there have so far been few studies documenting the support systems of unpartnered service members, the largest one conducted to date found that more than 60 percent of parents in the sample reported daily or almost daily communication with their service member children, regardless of their partner status. Parents' concerns about their military child's deployment proved protective for service members' post deployment symptoms of posttraumatic stress disorder (PTSD) and depression (Polusny et al., 2014). DoD's stance regarding privileging certain family forms may be related to the degree to which individuals are willing to choose military service over civilian employment, and service members' informal systems of support are well prepared to facilitate fulfillment of military duties with minimal negative consequences.

Rising family diversity and complexity have several implications for DoD (Gribble et al., 2018). First, individuals entering the military today may have experienced more family transitions as children than their predecessors. Second, today's service members may create new families that are more diverse or complex than those their predecessors created (Adler-Baeder et al., 2006). Third, fully understanding military families and their needs may require greater attention to family diversity and complexity. Fourth, the rising diversity and complexity may increase the difficulty of creating military policies, programs, services, resources, and practices that adequately support families in the performance of military duties.

ECOLOGICAL AND LIFE COURSE MODELS OF MILITARY FAMILY WELL-BEING

To understand the dimensions of military family well-being, we apply the principles of developmental science (Lerner, 2007), bioecological models of individual and family development (Bronfenbrenner, 1979; Bronfenbrenner and Morris, 2007), and life course theory (Wilmoth and London, 2013). Central to all three of these multilayered models are two principles: that development over the lifespan is a dynamic, transactional, and relational process that unfolds, affects, and is influenced by social contexts; and that individuals are "active ingredients" in their own development, from infancy through old age (Lerner, 2007; Sameroff, 2010).

According to developmental systems theory, there is tremendous diversity both within individuals, who have the potential for multiple developmental outcomes, and among individuals and groups. As the actors, people shape their experiences and well-being by responding to and evoking a variety of responses from the environment and within social and family relationships (Darling, 2007). As proposed by Masten (2013), the well-being of military-connected family members and their children may be understood within developmental systems theory as "the idea that a person's adaptation and development over the life course is shaped by interactions among many systems, from the level of genes or neurons to the level of family, peers, school, community, and the larger society" (Masten, 2013, p. 199).

The concept of *purposive development* further explains that as individuals move through the life course, they have the capacity to be intentional in shaping their lives, through decision-making and choices (Aldwin, 2014). Individual growth and development for service members, partners and spouses, and children unfold in relationship to the opportunities, context, and confines of military life and structure, throughout the family's service and beyond. Segal and colleagues' (2015) military life course model highlights service members' stress points, such as deployment or injury, as well as family life events, whether specific to military life or not (e.g., birth of child), that affect all members of the family system simultaneously (Segal and Lane, 2016; Segal et al., 2015).

Centering the Family

Bronfenbrenner and Morris's (2007) bioecological model of multilayered systems includes the *microsystem* at the center and expands through the *mesosystem, exosystem, macrosystem,* and *chronosystem* (see Figure 2-1).

What is critical in applying this model to military family well-being is the question of *who is centered* within the microsystem. From DoD's perspective, the service member has historically been the key focus, while Military Community and Family Policy (MC&FP) centers the military family system, the military child, partners, spouses and caregivers, as well as the individual service member, depending upon the program or service. Military culture, command structure, mission, rank, component, and DoD policies operate throughout the service member and military family systems. Arguably, the characteristics of the micro- and mesosystems for service members and family members are distinct although they share characteristics and interact. For example, the level of acculturation to the military context may be uneven across service members and their family members, and it will be influenced by the family's location, such as whether it is near or on an installation or in a civilian community, and by the density of the

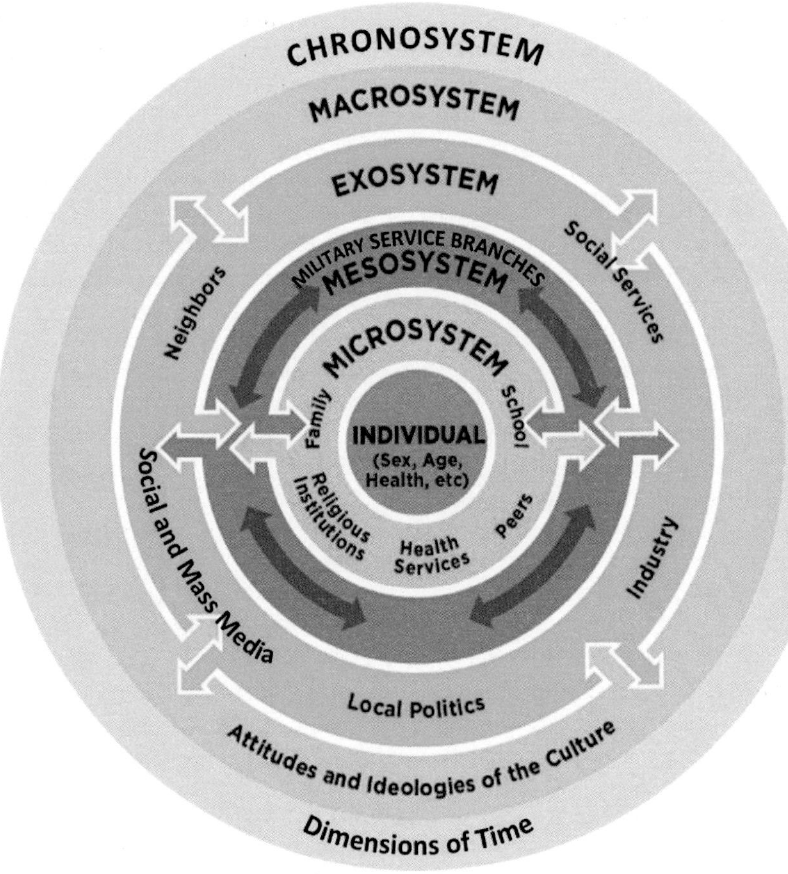

FIGURE 2-1 Bronfenbrenner's ecological theory of development.
SOURCE: Adapted from Small et al. (2013).

local military population. Acculturation will also be influenced by component, by the individual family member's history of service, that is, whether he or she is new to the military or earlier generations have served, and by demographic characteristics, such as first language and racial, ethnic, and cultural background. Theories of acculturation are also helpful in understanding specific transitional experiences of military service members returning to the United States after deployment and in understanding the transition/reintegration challenges that may accompany the shift to civilian or other post-service life (Demers, 2011).

In this framework, a service member's *microsystem* is the most immediate environment in which he or she lives. It includes individual or intrapersonal characteristics, such as temperament, emotion regulation, and behavior, relational processes with family and friends, and interactions with the immediate military context. The last includes his or her military role and mission, relationships with unit and leadership, and ability to function within a strict command structure. Service member agency is especially visible during important transition points across a military career, such as the decision to join, choice of friends and significant others (e.g., "linked lives") during service, and the timing of life course transitions such as intimate partner commitment and parenthood. The concept of "linked lives," which is borrowed from the family life-course literatures and consistent with bioecological theory, describes the interconnectedness and intergenerational nature of family relationships, such as couple and parent-child relationships. Elder and colleagues (2003) discuss the term and theoretical framework to explain that each member of a family will influence and also will be affected by the other members of the family system. In the context of military families, this concept is useful in considering how the life course trajectories of service members' partners and children, in particular, are directly linked to the service member's career moves, deployments, and required trainings.

Elder and colleagues' research, which the examined life-course trajectories of World War II veterans, suggests that the timing of these critical decisions will have a significant impact on the service member's developmental trajectory and life course (Elder et al., 2009). For instance, the decision to enlist has the potential to function as a "recasting experience" for young male service members who join at an early age. Wilmoth and London (2013) discuss "cumulative exposure" and early life disadvantage and hypothesize "that participation in the military can exacerbate, ameliorate, or have no moderating effect on early life disadvantages" (p. 9). Thus, the formation of the service member's military identity occurs in tandem with the transition to adulthood.

The next outer ring of the ecological framework includes the *mesosystem*, which encompasses the linkages between and among the service member and the everyday microsystems in which he or she lives, such as work, interactions with unit and leadership, school, training, and family. For the service member, this setting is centrally defined by the service branch to which the service member has committed. Relatedly, the culture and structure of each service branch are variable and include housing and residence, the persons whom the service member lives with and interacts with socially, work and training environments, and neighborhood communities. Service members must move back and forth between deployment settings, work or training contexts, and their home life—and each of these requires vastly different coping strategies and skills. More distal influences on military families include events that indirectly impact the family's immediate environment (Bronfenbrenner, 1993) as well as local cultural attitudes about the military, its personnel, and U.S. involvement in foreign wars.

For example, there is variation across regions of the United States in the density of military personnel and the degree of political support for the military. In addition, ever since the end of the draft, there has been a pattern of underrepresentation of service members from the Midwest and the northeastern corridor, relative to the southern states (Maley and Hawkins, 2018). Finally, military families must adapt to local contexts, which vary in terms of acceptance of LGBT persons and support for same-sex marriage, attitudes toward immigrant families, and the quality of race relations. Broader elements of the *exosystem* include economic trends and political systems, military and federal policy, social services, education, the mass media and social media (see Box 2-1).

The next ring in the model is the *macrosystem*, which encompasses cultural systems. This is where military culture meets and intersects with dominant beliefs, assumptions, and worldviews, as well as ideologies in society.

BOX 2-1
The Rise of Digital Technology and Its Impact on Service Member Privacy and Security

The global rise of digital technology in the 2000s has fundamentally altered human communication and culture, as well as global connectedness. In North America, Internet penetration is estimated to be approximately 95 percent, with social media usage at 70 percent (Kemp, 2019). For military families, the availability of multiple social media platforms (e.g., Facebook, Instagram, Snapchat, Twitter), streaming services, video-calling apps (e.g., Skype, Facetime, WhatsApp), and mobile technologies (e.g., smartphones) has vastly influenced not only everyday communication but also the ability to stay connected through the transitions and separations inherent to military life. For military-connected youth, social media and mobile apps can provide connection to peer groups and support during transitions to new communities and schools.

The digital revolution has introduced complexity for DoD in relation to service members' privacy and security issues (e.g., geotagging, location, and identification), operational safety, and appropriate use of technology.[a] Indeed, service branches have developed guidelines, policies, and resources for service personnel and their families as they navigate the digital world. On balance, the digital revolution also offers new opportunities for engagement, education, and intervention in support of family readiness.

---

[a]For service branch-specific policies, see, for example, https://www.army.mil/socialmedia/, https://www.navy.mil/socialmediadocs/NavySocialMediaHandbook.pdf, https://www.navy.mil/ah_online/opsec/docs/Policy/Marines-Social-Media-Handbook.pdf, and https://static.e-publishing.af.mil/production/1/saf_pa/publication/afi35-107/afi35-107.pdf.

Societal-level influences are the large, macro-level factors that influence well-being, such as gender inequities, income inequality, societal norms, policies, and regulations, which are also at play within the military system.

A significant dynamic in the post-9/11 era is a growing disconnection between the military and the U.S. civilian population it serves. Specifically, Carter and colleagues (2017), as well as others (Fleming, 2010; McFadden, 2017), raise concerns regarding a growing military-civilian divide, including diverging cultures, the separation of communities (e.g., military bases viewed as "gated communities"), the lack of geographic representation, and civilian disconnection from military operations. Importantly, for service members and military families, macrosystem influences extend to U.S. military policy; to DoD assumptions about what constitutes a ready force; to military personnel's and political leadership's decision making regarding national security; and to the nature and characteristics of contemporary warfare and missions (Carter et al., 2017).

Finally, in this framework the temporal dimensions—the *chronosystem*—are critical to understanding the timing of developmental and life-course milestones and events, such as accession or transition to parenthood, as well as socio-historical conditions and their implications for the future force. At the individual level, military events such as deployments may be more or less disruptive for the service member, depending on what life stage that member has reached (Wilmoth and London, 2013). In addition, interventions are often effective at point-of-life transitions, since they can function as opportunities for change from negative to more positive life pathways or the reverse (Institute of Medicine and National Research Council, 2013). The changing nature of warfare and contemporary service in the post-9/11 era is another critical aspect of timing for service members and families.

When the military family is placed at the center, the salient elements and interactions between and among these multilevel layers shift. Both the military and the family, as institutions, have been described as "greedy," in that each demands commitment, time, and loyalty without regard for work-life-family balance (Segal, 1986). The demands of military life are dictated by military needs, service member readiness, and mission, although they do come with guaranteed employment and wages and with a clear path for advancement (Kleykamp, 2013). By contrast, family members and children are yoked to service member careers and have little control over or decision-making power regarding the timing or location of change of station and deployment.

The concept of tied migration is applicable in the military context and predominately affects women who are partnered with service members and children in military families (Segal et al., 2015). The tied migrant is an individual within a family who moves, as with frequent military "permanent changes of station" (PCSs), but who may not want to move or may move against her own or her children's best interests (Cooke, 2013). For military spouses and partners, this pattern of moving interferes with educational attainment, labor participation and earnings, and career development (Hosek et al., 2002; Kleykamp, 2013). For children and adolescents, frequent moving and parental deployment have important and often negative implications for school and peer functioning (Meadows et al., 2016). Burrell and colleagues (2006) also identify work- and duty-related demands as current military-specific stressors, as well as "pressures for military families to conform to accepted standards of behavior, and the masculine nature of the organization" (p. 44).

Relevance of a Multilevel, Ecological Systems Framework for Prevention and Intervention

Ecological or multilevel frameworks are useful in highlighting the differing experiences and accumulation of risk and adversity among service members and families, as well as the social and other environmental influences, including military policies, that can support individual and family readiness and resilience—and they can likewise help in identifying barriers to individual and family well-being (Chmitorz et al., 2018). Moreover, applying a multilevel conceptualization suggests diverse and multiple potential ports of entry for prevention, intervention, and capacity-building in support of service member and family well-being. To be effective, military family support and prevention strategies should consider risk and protective processes across multiple determinants of health and well-being. In this context, the influences at the individual level are processes of personal risk or protection that increase or decrease the likelihood of military children or other family members encountering problematic outcomes.

Ecological and multilevel frameworks are also helpful when considering the diversity of military families and their experiences. While resources have already been allocated to address special needs associated with the families of junior enlisted or Special Operations members as well as families containing members with exceptional needs, additional dimensions of diversity may combine to create other "ecological niches" that also merit consideration. In sum, because multilevel ecological frameworks are useful in highlighting differential accumulation of risk and adversity they are also important in tailoring approaches to distinctive subgroups.

Prevention effects at the individual level, such as student mentoring, aim to change individual-level risk factors. Family stress models (Conger and Conger, 2002; Gewirtz et al., 2018; Simons et al., 2016), which posit that contextual stressors mediate individual, relationship, and family process outcomes, point to family-level intervention efforts. Interpersonal- or relationship-level influences are factors that increase risk or are protective and that can be attributed to interactions with family, partners, and peers. Prevention strategies that address these influences include the promotion of good communication skills in marital relationships and strengthening parents' ability to teach children using positive parenting skills.

Community-level influences are factors that increase risk or protection based on formal and informal organizations or social environments, such as schools, recreation, and family support communities. The institutional level for military family well-being includes DoD itself, as well as state and community systems and institutions that issue specific instructions, policies, and regulations (such as the Veterans Health Administration [VHA], veteran serving organizations, and community mental health programs). Community norms concerning where service members and their families live or return to can also shape the risk and protective factors that affect military family well-being.

Overall, multilevel conceptualization indicates that to support the well-being of service members and their families, one needs to recognize diverse and multiple potential ports of entry for prevention, intervention, and capacity-building.

RESILIENCE AND READINESS

Family readiness and resilience are as important for DoD as family well-being, because they are rooted in families' need to be prepared for and adjust to the inevitable challenges of military life. The concept of resilience has emerged from studies of individuals, families, and communities experiencing stressors like natural disasters, war, isolation, and abuse. Resilience is related to but distinct from well-being, because positive adjustment by itself is not evidence of resilience. In contrast to approaches that prioritize preventing psychopathology, resilience-based approaches emphasize building on a person's strengths and coping ability (Meadows et al., 2016; Meredith et al., 2011). Resilience is commonly defined as positive adjustment in the aftermath of adversity, and thus cannot be observed in the absence of exposure to adverse experiences (Chmitorz et al., 2018; Meadows et al., 2016). For the purposes of this report and as noted in Chapter 1, we are guided by Masten's (2015) definition:

> the potential or manifested capacity of a dynamic [human] system to adapt successfully to disturbances that threaten the function, survival, or development of the system (p. 187).

This definition is designed to acknowledge that individuals, families, units, and communities are also systems. Like Meadows and colleagues

(2016), we differentiate between potential and manifested resilience. As stated in Chapter 1, we equate potential resilience with *readiness,* which is similar to the way the DoD Instruction on Family Readiness describes readiness, specifically as "the state of being prepared to effectively navigate the challenges of daily living experienced in the unique context of military service" (DoD, 2012). This latter definition encompasses but is broader than an individual service member's military operational readiness, stating that it is DoD policy that "the role of personal and family life shall be incorporated into organizational goals related to the recruitment, retention, morale and operational readiness of the military force" (DoD, 2012, p. 2). Thus, for military families, *readiness* connotes preparation for specific challenges that they may encounter.

The term *resilience* has been used in many different ways (Bonanno et al., 2015, p. 139), with distinctions sometimes—but not consistently—made between this term and *resiliency.* For clarity, and similar to Kalisch and colleagues (2015), we use the term *resilience* to refer to the display of resilient outcomes, *resilience processes* (or *mechanisms*) to refer to the dynamics that produce or impede resilience, and *resilience factors* to refer to the events, characteristics, or circumstances that shape resilience processes or outcomes. Resilience factors may be personal (e.g., hardiness), social (e.g., robust informal support networks), or environmental (e.g., stable community infrastructures) (Chmitorz et al., 2018). Box 2-2 lists seven key principles supported by existing research about resilience among children, youth, adults, and families more generally (not limited to military families).

The committee also examined the key factors in the production of resilience. These are summarized in Table 2-1.

Decades of research have identified common characteristics among children, youth, adults, families, and communities that display resilience, although more is known about resilience in individuals than in families or communities (Bonanno et al., 2015, p. 141). Nevertheless, separating resilience factors and resilience outcomes can be difficult. Positive family functioning, for example, could be construed as either a factor or an outcome—or both. Because family readiness focuses on preparation for adversity with the goal of maximizing resilient outcomes, it may be especially important to focus on the knowledge, skills, and abilities of family members as key resilience factors aimed at improving readiness, and to focus on family well-being when considering resilience outcomes.

Meadows et al. (2016), Walsh (2016) and others (Hawkins et al., 2018; Masten, 2018; Masten and Obradović, 2006) have suggested the following groups of factors as associated with resilience outcomes in families:

- *Belief systems*—Family members share their confidence that the family can persist and thrive in the face of adversity, feel optimistic

BOX 2-2
Key Resilience Principles

Principle 1: Resilience is not rare. Most families respond to most adversities with resilience, when normal adaptive processes can operate without impairment (Masten, 2001; Perkins et al., 2018).

Principle 2: Resilience does not equate to invulnerability (Masten and Obradović, 2006), and resilience training is not a "vaccination" against distress following adverse experiences. Some evidence suggests that individuals who ultimately experience posttraumatic growth experience above-average distress following adversity, before regaining positive adjustment (Bonanno et al, 2015, p. 145).

Principle 3: Understanding resilience requires paying attention not only to the nature of the response to adversity but also to the nature of the adversity itself, which may comprise acute events (e.g., death, natural disaster) or chronic experiences (e.g., abuse, minority stress, lengthy separations), and also can vary in scope or scale (e.g., affecting many people or a single family). Individuals also may vary in the degree to which they are either exposed to or protected from adverse experiences (Bonanno et al., 2015; Masten, 2015; Masten and Narayan, 2012). Thus, individuals' experiences may vary widely, even in conditions that may appear to be similar.

Principle 4: Resilience is a function of the characteristics of both individuals and environments (Masten and Obradović, 2006). Individuals' past experiences are also relevant, such as their family history, their developmental status, and prior exposures to adversity (Bonanno et al., 2015; Masten, 2015), all of which can affect physiological processes in the brain that condition the potential for resilience

and able to control their circumstances, and have a sense of meaning about adversity or a worldview that transcends immediate challenges (Henry et al., 2015; Masten and Monn, 2015; Saltzman et al., 2011). Saltzman and colleagues (2011), for example, describe how lack of a shared belief in the service member's mission can interfere with children's coping and adaptation. Helping families to build a shared sense of confidence and hope is a strengths-based strategy that supports resilience in this context. Masten and Monn (2015) identify family routines and cultural traditions as important for maintaining a sense of meaning.

- *Organizational patterns*—Family members spend time together in constructive activities, the family is organized to provide effective support to its members with a good balance of flexibility and connectedness, family members play appropriate roles, and the family has adequate social and economic resources that it

(Bonanno et al., 2015, p. 144). In the case of military families, family resilience models must incorporate attention to structural forces—such as organizational or government policies; socioeconomic status; and factors that define social location, such as gender, race, or sexual orientation—that influence service members and family resources, strengths, and vulnerabilities. Each individual and family experiences a unique configuration of risk and resilience factors (Cox, 2018; Lerner, 2018).

Principle 5: While some innate characteristics are associated with resilience, such as cognitive ability or hardiness, resilience is not a single, stable personality trait (Chmitorz et al., 2018; Escolas et al., 2013). Rather, personality is one of many factors that may make resilience more or less likely following adversity (Masten and Obradović, 2006). Resilience is dynamic across time and circumstances—individuals may respond with resilience to some circumstances at certain times but not to others (Chmitorz et al., 2018; Meadows et al., 2016).

Principle 6: Adjustment after exposure to adversity may over time follow multiple pathways that vary in terms of whether and when declines in adjustment and recovery occur. In some cases post-traumatic growth occurs, while in others there is little evidence of any relationship between adversity and adjustment (Bonanno and Diminich, 2013; Chmitorz et al., 2018; Masten and Narayan, 2012, Fig. 1).

Principle 7: The characteristics of resilient families are related to but distinct from the characteristics of resilient individuals (Bonanno et al., 2015; Meadows et al., 2016); one neither guarantees nor completely prevents the other. However, far more is known about resilience in individuals than about resilience in families (Bonanno et al., 2015, p. 141; Cramm et al., 2018).

manages adequately (Masten, 2014; Saltzman et al., 2011). For example, coercive family interactions, inconsistent discipline, and poor coordination between parents can impair functioning in military families. Improving parents' abilities to teach their children and to co-parent effectively can counteract this threat to resilience (Gewirtz and Zamir, 2014; Saltzman et al., 2011). During times of transition, family organizational patterns often shift, creating both risks and opportunities. For example, they can also increase opportunities for young people to increase their sense of meaning and purpose by helping with family tasks in developmentally appropriate ways (National Research Council and Institute of Medicine 2002; Villarruel et al., 2003).

- *Communication/problem solving*—Family members communicate openly, clearly, and constructively with each other, respond sensitively to one another's emotions, show interest in one another's

TABLE 2-1 Key Factors in the Production of Resilience

Factor	Description	Variations
Risk and Vulnerability Factors	Challenges that can threaten or disturb adjustment (Masten and Narayan, 2012)	*Exposures* are the degree to which individuals or families come into contact with risks (Masten and Narayan, 2012). Exposures vary systematically in relation to factors, including gender, age, race, sexual orientation, and socioeconomic status. *Dosage* is the level of exposure to risk, which can be a factor of severity, accumulation, proximity, or breadth of the risk (Masten and Narayan, 2012). *Risk* factors are operational at all times, while vulnerability factors become operational only in high-risk environments.
Assets	Factors that enhance adaptive capacity	*Promotive* factors are associated with better outcomes regardless of the presence of risk factors (Masten and Narayan, 2012). *Protective* factors are associated with better outcomes particularly in the presence of risk factors (Masten and Narayan, 2012).
Cascades	A reverberation of positive or negative effects across developmental domains within a person, across persons, and across generations and families (Doty et al., 2017; Masten and Cicchetti, 2010; Masten, 2016; Masten and Narayan, 2012; Trail et al., 2017).	Skills or difficulties developed in one domain may generalize to affect others, such as when improvements in parenting lead to improvements in parent and child well-being and in turn reductions in substance use (Patterson et al., 2010). Regardless of levels of support or preparation, some levels of adversity are so high that they exceed the capacity of most systems (individuals, families, or communities) to adapt.

problems, and work together to solve problems. Walsh (2003), for example, described how inappropriate withholding of information, suppression of emotions, or ineffective problem solving can heighten anxiety, promote tension, intensify conflict, and impede family members' ability to provide emotional support to one another. Hawkins and colleagues' (2018) review of research related to military families indicated that supportiveness among family members was associated with better mental health for all family members (p. 189).

- *Physical and psychological health of individual family members*—Families members enjoy good emotional, behavioral, and physical health; they possess mastery and hardiness (Meadows et al., 2016). Although physical and psychological health are technically properties of individuals, health problems reverberate beyond individuals and can challenge family resilience (IOM, 2013; Saltzman et al., 2011). Similar to Meadows and colleagues' (2016) recognition of the importance of hardiness, Masten (2014) identified individual characteristics and skills such as self-efficacy, self-control, emotion regulation, and motivation to succeed as factors associated with resilience. (See Chapter 5 for more detail about individual resilience.)
- *Family support system*—There is a robust network of informal support from family members and others, such as community members, neighbors, and coworkers. Support systems important to resilience comprise both informal supports that come from social relationships, such as those with family, friends, neighbors, coworkers, and others; and formal supports in the form of resources, programs, and services (Hawkins et al., 2018; Masten, 2014) that provide emotional, instrumental, and other forms of support. Henry and colleagues (2015) refer to the "family maintenance system" as the ability of families to secure sufficient resources to meet their needs, including financial resources, food, shelter, clothing, and education. In their comprehensive review of research related to the resilience of military families, Hawkins and colleagues (2018) observed that the employment challenges and pay gaps experienced by military spouses—especially wives—represent significant challenges to resilience, and also highlight accessibility as an important factor in the adequacy of support systems.

While some might consider it frustrating that no single predictor has emerged as a holy grail for predicting resilience (Bonanno et al., 2015, p. 150), a positive interpretation is that the family systems principle of equifinality means there can be multiple pathways to resilience.

RESILIENCE IN THE MILITARY CONTEXT

DoD has placed considerable emphasis in recent years on the resilience of service members and their families. This includes the Total Force Fitness initiative launched by the chairman of the Joint Chiefs of Staff in 2013 (Joint Chiefs of Staff, 2013; Jonas et al., 2010), which grew out of the Comprehensive Soldier Fitness effort begun in 2008 by the Army (Cornum et al., 2011). Grounded in principles of positive psychology and resilience, the initiative acknowledges eight domains of fitness—physical, environmental, medical/dental, nutritional, spiritual, psychological, behavioral, and social—and references not only service members but also family members, units, and communities. Its aim is to promote both well-being (primarily subjective well-being, that is feeling good) and resilience (functioning well despite adversity). Linked with this, significant infrastructure has been built in both the Army (Department of the Army, 2014) and the Air Force (Secretary of the Air Force, 2014), particularly regarding physical, medical, and nutritional fitness, to require service members to periodically complete assessments and training to promote fitness across the domains.

Although the Total Force Fitness model incorporates family fitness, and family members are encouraged to participate in resilience assessments, most of the focus has been on service members and units.[7] In 2015, at the request of the Defense Center of Excellence for Psychological Health and Traumatic Brain Injury, Meadows and colleagues (2016) conducted a comprehensive review of more than 4,000 documents related to the resilience of military families. They found no standard definitions of family resilience across DoD, although they identified 26 relevant policies, noting that almost all were limited to particular parts of DoD (i.e., branches, components, or program areas) rather than being inclusive.

The Family Readiness Department of Defense Instruction (DoDI) targets three specific areas of readiness for which service members and family members are considered primarily responsible: (i) mobilization and deployment readiness, (ii) mobility and financial readiness, and (iii) personal and family readiness. In the Total Force Fitness[8] model, the view of family fitness is more expansive, defining fitness as the ability of a family to use physical, psychological, social, and spiritual resources to prepare for, adapt to, and grow from the demands of military life (Westphal and Woodward, 2010). Bowles at al. (2015) elaborate:

---

[7]For more information see http://readyandresilient.army.mil/index.html.

[8]For more information see https://www.jcs.mil/Portals/36/Documents/Library/Instructions/3405_01.pdf?ver=2016-02-05-175032-517.

> Fit, or "ready," families are knowledgeable about potential challenges and equipped with the necessary skills to competently face those challenges. They are aware of and able to use resources available to them. Fit families function successfully in supportive environments that allow for healthy individual development and well-being. Being fit does not make families immune to the daily struggles and hassles of life. This prepares families to respond effectively to difficulties, access support/resources as needed, and develop a better capacity to become resilient when adverse or traumatic situation occur for the family. A key assumption of the MFFM [Military Family Fitness Model][9] is that characteristics of fit families can be learned. Therefore, identifying both adaptive and maladaptive responses to familial stress is important. This concept is analogous to preparing for athletic competition—successful practice improves real-life performance (p. 248).

MEASURING FAMILY READINESS AND RESILIENCE

No gold standard instrument exists inside or outside DoD for assessing resilience in individuals (Windle et al., 2011), and measures of resilience in families lag even further behind (Chmitorz et al., 2018, p. 79). Because definitions of resilience vary widely, measures address a wide variety of constructs, some treating resilience as a stable trait, some ignoring the presence or absence of exposure to adversity (Chmitorz et al., 2018; Wright et al., 2013), some equating resilience with positive adjustment (Wright et al., 2013) and still others conflating resilience factors or mechanisms with outcomes (Windle et al., 2011).

The distinction between readiness and resilience is to some extent arbitrary, because positive adjustment could simultaneously be evidence of resilience following earlier adversity, *and* evidence of readiness or potential resilience for adversity yet to come. In order to assist military families in being "ready" for adversity, there is a need to focus programs, services, and resources, as well as assessments, on the knowledge, skills, and abilities needed for positive adjustment—or their functional well-being—following adversity. Subjective well-being may be especially important when assessing resilience or positive adjustment in the aftermath of adversity.

Some scholars question whether developing a single instrument to assess a construct as multifaceted and dynamic as family resilience is possible, particularly in the military context. Development of measurement instruments is challenging, because resilience in each family can comprise a different

[9]A comprehensive model aimed at enhancing family fitness and resilience across the life span. This model is intended for use by service members, their families, leaders, and health care providers, but it also has broader applications for all families. The MFFM has three core components: (1) family demands, (2) resources (including individual resources, family resources, and external resources), and (3) family outcomes (including related metrics) (Bowles et al., 2015, p. 246).

mix of characteristics, skills, and resources. Another challenge is measuring constructs at the family level—neither scientific consensus nor statistical tools are yet available to guide appropriate consideration of family dynamics and the vantage points of multiple family members at once (Bonanno et al., 2015; Meadows et al., 2016). Although statistical techniques like multilevel and structural equation modeling make it possible to incorporate the perspectives of multiple family members in statistical analyses, no standard has been established for what the results of such models should show in order to draw conclusions about family readiness or resilience.

Because resilience unfolds in diverse patterns, sometimes over long periods of time, assessments ideally will track change over time. Bonanno and colleagues (2015) suggest that observational measures of family interactions may have the greatest validity (e.g., the Beavers Interactional Competence Scale; Family Interaction Tasks). Such methods are usually too expensive and burdensome for use in widespread screening or monitoring, though less expensive proxies such as "KidVid"—short video vignettes that family members react to (DeGarmo and Forgatch, 2004) or the Five Minute Speech Sample (Narayan et al., 2012)—may be just as reliable and valid in predicting family interactions.

In two recent efforts to build tools for assessing family resilience, Finley and colleagues (2016) and Duncan Lane and colleagues (2017) each developed item pools based on Walsh's theory of family resilience, which goes beyond seeing individual family members as resources for individual resilience to focus on risk and resilience in the family as a functional unit (Walsh, 2003). In these two studies, the researchers subjected the item pools to pilot testing or expert review, and then administered the trimmed item pools to small convenience samples of individuals in the military (Finley et al., 2016) or general populations (Duncan Lane et al., 2017). The study of military individuals used 40 items administered to 151 individuals, and the general population study used 29 items administered to 113 women with breast cancer. Psychometric properties of both instruments were generally promising. Both efforts were limited, however, by the absence of assessments of adversity, and even more importantly, by the failure to administer the instruments to other family members. Thus, these measures can best be considered preliminary but promising efforts to assess perceptions of the resilience of families.

Measurement of resilience also requires attention to adversity. Family readiness and resilience may be supported by increasing the presence of resilience factors, facilitating the operation of resilience mechanisms, *and* by reducing exposure to adversity. Separation and relocation are relatively well understood as stressors, but at the present time, DoD does not monitor *accumulations* of adversity by military families, beyond attempts to track cumulative deployments by service members via the PERSTEMPO system[10] (or Individual Exposure Record). As indicated earlier, accumulations of family transitions can increase the risk of negative outcomes for both children and adults, and robust evidence has emerged that adverse experiences in childhood have far-reaching implications for health during adulthood (Shonkoff et al., 2012).

While there are not yet any comprehensive measures of family resilience that are considered to be "gold standards" by scientists, there are measures with well-established psychometric properties that can be used to assess many of the major components of resilience and readiness. A 2014 National Academy of Sciences report to DoD made specific recommendations regarding strategies and measures that could be fruitfully used to assess prevention efforts; most of these recommendations have yet to be implemented (IOM, 2014, Chapter 5).

Scientific evidence indicates that when adaptive systems in families are functioning well, resilience is the likely result (Masten, 2014). The readiness and resilience of military families are important for service members' recruitment, retention, performance, satisfaction, well-being, and functioning when they are wounded, ill, or injured. Developing agreed-upon definitions of family readiness and resilience will allow DoD to declare its most relevant indicators, which in turn will make it possible to identify the resilience factors most likely to produce those outcomes, and thus which knowledge, skills, and abilities are most important to promote through military family readiness activities. Some relevant information is undoubtedly already available from the Status of Forces surveys, program record data, and other sources. In the future, monitoring exposures to adversity and tracking levels of preparation and training will be required so that the implications for subsequent resilience can be discerned.

CONCLUSIONS

CONCLUSION 2-1: The Department of Defense lacks an agreed-upon definition of family well-being. Subjective, objective, and functional components of family well-being are all relevant to military recruitment, retention, and performance.

CONCLUSION 2-2: Due to the widespread changes in societal norms and family structures that have occurred in the United States, under-

---

[10]PERSTEMPO is a "congressionally mandated program, directed by the Office of the Secretary of Defense (OSD). It is the Army's method to track and manage individual rates of deployment (time away from home), unit training events, special operations/exercises and mission support TDYs." For more information, see the U.S. Army Human Resources Command Frequently Asked Questions at https://www.hrc.army.mil/content/PERSTEMPO%20FAQs.

standing and addressing military families' needs today requires greater attention to family diversity and stability.

CONCLUSION 2-3: Service members' well-being is typically connected to the well-being of their families, and both relate to military recruitment, performance, readiness, and retention. Every service member, including those who are unmarried, is part of some form of family, and all require assistance from informal support systems in order to perform military duties.

CONCLUSION 2-4: The Department of Defense does not have a consistent definition of a family nor does it have a consistent definition and indicators of family readiness and resilience necessary to track relevance, effectiveness, and improvements of programs, services, resources, policies, and practices.

REFERENCES

Adler-Baeder, F., Pittman, J. F., and Taylor, L. (2006). The prevalence of marital transitions in military families. *Journal of Divorce and Remarriage, 44*(1–2), 91–106.

Aldwin, C. M. (2014). Rethinking developmental science. *Research in Human Development, 11*(4), 247–254.

Barlas, F. M., Higgins, W. B., Pflieger, J. C., and Diecker, K. (2013). *2011 Department of Defense Health Related Behaviors Survey of Active Duty Military Personnel.* Fairfax, VA: ICF International.

Berger, L. M., and Bzostek, S. H. (2014). Young adults' roles as partners and parents in the context of family complexity. *The ANNALS of the American Academy of Political and Social Science, 654*(1), 87–109.

Biblarz, T. J., and Stacey, J. (2010). How does the gender of parents matter? *Journal of Marriage and Family, 72*(1), 3–22.

Bonanno, G. A., and Diminich, E. D. (2013). Annual research review: Positive adjustment to adversity—trajectories of minimal-impact resilience and emergent resilience. *Journal of Child Psychology and Psychiatry, 54*(4), 378–401.

Bonanno, G. A., Romero, S. A., and Klein, S. I. (2015). The temporal elements of psychological resilience: An integrative framework for the study of individuals, families, and communities. *Psychological Inquiry, 26*(2), 139–169.

Bowles, S. V., Pollock, L. D., Moore, M., Wadsworth, S. M., Cato, C., Dekle, J.W., Meyer, S. W., Shriver, A., Mueller, B., and Stephens, M. (2015). Total Force Fitness: The military family fitness model. *Military Medicine, 180*(3), 246–258.

Bronfenbrenner, U. (1979). *The Ecology of Human Development: Experiments by Design and Nature.* Cambridge, MA: Harvard University Press.

________. (1993). The ecology of cognitive development: Research models and fugitive findings. In R. H. Wozniak and K. Fischer (Eds.), *Development in Context: Acting and Thinking in Specific Environments* (pp. 3–46). Hillsdale, NJ: Erlbaum.

Bronfenbrenner, U., and Morris, P. A. (2007). The bioecological model of human development. In W. Damon and R. Lerner (Eds.), *Handbook of Child Psychology* (6th ed., vol. 1, pp. 793–828). Hoboken, NJ: John Wiley & Sons, Inc.

Burrell, L. M., Adams, G. A., Durand, D. B., and Castro, C. A. (2006). The impact of military lifestyle demands on well-being, Army, and family outcomes. *Armed Forces and Society, 33*(1), 43–58.

Carter, P., Kidder, K., Schafer, A., and Swick, A. (2017). Working Paper, AVF 4.0: The Future of the All-Volunteer Force. Washington, DC: Center for New American Security.

Carter, S. P., Loew, B., Allen, E. S., Osborne, L., Stanley, S. M., and Markman, H. J. (2015). Distraction during deployment: marital relationship associations with spillover for deployed Army soldiers. *Military Psychology, 27*(2), 108–114.

Centers for Disease Control and Prevention (2018). *Well-Being Concepts*. Retrieved from https://www.cdc.gov/hrqol/wellbeing.htm#three.

Cherlin, A. (2010). Demographic trends in the United States: A review of research in the 2000s. *Journal of Marriage and Family, 72*(3), 403–419.

Cherlin, A. J., and Seltzer, J. A. (2014). Family complexity, the family safety net, and public policy. *The ANNALS of the American Academy of Political and Social Science, 654*(1), 231–239.

Chmitorz, A., Kunzler, A., Helmreich, I., Tüscher, O., Kalisch, R., Kubiak, T., Wessa, M., and Lieb, K. (2018). Intervention studies to foster resilience—A systematic review and proposal for a resilience framework in future intervention studies. *Clinical Psychology Review, 59*, 78–100.

Conger, R. D., and Conger, K. J. (2002). Resilience in Midwestern families: Selected findings from the first decade of a prospective, longitudinal study. *Journal of Marriage and Family, 64*(2), 361–373.

Cooke, T. J. (2013). All tied up: Tied staying and tied migration within the United States, 1997 to 2007. *Demographic Research, 29*(30), 817–836.

Cornum, R., Matthews, M. D., and Seligman, M. E. P. (2011). Comprehensive Soldier Fitness: Building resilience in a challenging institutional context. *American Psychologist, 66*(1), 4–9.

Cox, A. L. (2018). *Invited Comments for the Committee on the Well-Being of Military Families*. Presented at a public information-gathering session of the National Academies of Sciences, Engineering, and Medicine, Washington, DC, April 24.

Cramm, H., Norris, D., Venedam, S., and Tam-Seto, L. (2018). Toward a model of military family resiliency: A narrative review. *Journal of Family Theory and Review, 10*, 620–640.

Darling, N. (2007). Ecological systems theory: The person in the center of the circles. *Research in Human Development, 4*(3-4), 203–217.

Defense Center of Excellence for Psychological Health and Traumatic Brain Injury. (2011). *Measuring Military Family Well-Being: A Renewed Focus on Military Family Well-Being*. Retrieved from http://www.moaa.org/uploadedFiles/MOAA_Main/Main_Menu/Access_Member_Benefits/Professionalism/Symposia/May2011_dcoe.pdf.

DeGarmo, D. S., and Forgatch, M. S. (2004, May). Assessing the external and predictive validity of the KIDVID. Paper presented at the "Innovation in Observation Methods for Prevention Science" symposium at the annual meeting of the Society for Prevention Research, Quebec City, Canada.

Demers, A. (2011). When veterans return: The role of community in reintegration. *Journal of Loss and Trauma, 16*(2), 160–179.

Department of the Army. (2014). *Comprehensive Soldier and Family Fitness*. Washington, DC. Retrieved from https://www.army.mil/e2/downloads/rv7/r2/policydocs/r350_53.pdf.

Dichter, M. E., and True, G. (2015). This is the story of why my military career ended before it should have: Premature separation from military service among U.S. women veterans. *Journal of Women and Social Work, 30*(2), 187–199.

Doty, J., Davis, L., and Arditti, J. A. (2017). Cascading resilience: Leverage points in promoting parent and child well-being. *Journal of Family Theory & Review, 9*, 111–126.

Duncan Lane, C., Meszaros, P. S., and Savla, J. (2017). Measuring Walsh's family resilience framework: Reliability and validity of the family resilience assessment among women with a history of breast cancer. *Marriage and Family Review, 53*(7), 667–682.

Dunifon, R. E., Ziol-Guest, K. M., and Kopko, K. (2014). Grandparent coresidence and family well-being: Implications for research and policy. *The ANNALS of the American Academy of Political and Social Science, 654*(1), 110–126.

Elder Jr., G. H., Johnson, M. K., and Crosnoe, R. (2003). The Emergence and Development of Life Course Theory. In J. T. Mortimer, M. J. Shanahan (Eds.), *Handbook of the Life Course. Handbooks of Sociology and Social Research* (pp. 3-19). Boston, MA: Springer.

Elder Jr., G. H., Clipp, E. C., Brown, J. S., Martin, L. R., and Friedman, H.S. (2009). The lifelong mortality risks of World War II experiences. *Research on Aging, 31*(4), 391–412.

Escolas, S. M., Pitts, B. L., Safer, M. A., and Bartone, P. T. (2013). The protective value of hardiness on military posttraumatic stress symptoms. *Military Psychology, 25*(2), 116–123.

Finley, E. P., Pugh, M. J., and Palmer, R. F. (2016). Validation of a measure of family resilience among Iraq and Afghanistan veterans. *Military Behavioral Health, 4*(3), 205–219.

Fleming, B. E. (2010). *Bridging the Military-Civilian Divide: What Each Side Needs to Know About the Other, and About Itself.* Washington, DC: Potomac Books, Inc.

Furstenberg, F. F. (2014). Fifty years of family change: From consensus to complexity. *The Annals of the American Academy of Political and Social Science, 654*(1), 12–30.

Gewirtz, A. H., and Zamir, O. (2014). The impact of parental deployment to war on children: The crucial role of parenting. *Advances in Child Development and Behavior, 46*, 89–112.

Gewirtz, A. H., DeGarmo, D. S., and Zamir, O. (2018). Testing a military family stress model. *Family Process, 57*, 415–431.

Gibson, J. L., Griepentrog, B. K., and Marsh, S. M. (2007). Parental influence on youth propensity to join the military. *Journal of Vocational Behavior, 70*, 525–541.

Gribble, R., Mahar, A., Godfrey, K., Muir, S., Albright, D., Daraganova, G., Spinks, N., Fear, N., and Cramm, H. (2018). *What Does the Term "Military Family" Mean? A Comparison Across Four Countries.* Canadian Institute for Military and Veteran Health Research, Queen's University, Ontario, Canada. Retrieved from https://cimvhr.ca/documents/Military-families-definitions.pdf.

Griffith, J., and Bryan, C. J. (2017). Soldier background and postinvestigative events associated with timing of suicide following deployment of U.S. Army National Guard soldiers. *Military Psychology, 29*(3), 202–215,

Guzzo, K. B. (2014). New partners, more kids: Multiple-partner fertility in the United States. *The Annals of the American Academy of Political and Social Science, 654*(1), 66–86.

Hawkins, S. A., Condon, A., Hawkins, J. N., Liu, K., Melendrez Ramirez, Y., Nihill, M. M., and Tolins, J. (2018). *What We Know About Military Family Readiness: Evidence from 2007-2017.* Monterey, CA: Office of the Deputy Under Secretary of the Army. Retrieved from https://apps.dtic.mil/dtic/tr/fulltext/u2/1050341.pdf.

Henry, C. S., Sheffield Morris, A., and Harrist, A. W. (2015). Family resilience: Moving into the third wave. *Family Relations, 64*(1), 22–43.

Hosek, J., Asch, B. J., Fair, C. C., Martin, C., and Mattock, M. G. (2002). *Married to the Military: The Employment and Earnings of Military Wives Compared with Those of Civilian Wives.* MR-1565-OSD. Santa Monica, CA: RAND Corporation.

Hourani, L. L., Williams, T. V., and Kress, A. M. (2006). Stress, mental health, and job performance among active duty military personnel: Findings from the 2002 Department of Defense Health-Related Behaviors Survey. *Military Medicine, 171*(9), 849-856.

Institute of Medicine (IOM). (2013). *Returning Home From Iraq and Afghanistan: Assessment of Readjustment Needs of Veterans, Service Members, and Their Families.* Washington, DC: The National Academies Press.

________. (2014). *Preventing Psychological Disorders in Service Members and Their Families: An Assessment of Programs*. Washington, DC: The National Academies Press.

Institute of Medicine and National Research Council. (2013). *Improving the Health, Safety, and Well-Being of Young Adults: Workshop Summary*. Washington, DC: The National Academies Press.

Joint Chiefs of Staff. (2013). *Chairman of the Joint Chiefs of Staff Instruction: Chairman's Total Force Fitness Framework*. Retrieved from https://www.jcs.mil/Portals/36/Documents/Library/Instructions/3405_01.pdf?ver=2016-02-05-175032-517.

Joint Mental Health Advisory Team 7. (2011). *Joint Mental Health Advisory Team 7 (J-MHAT 7) Operation Enduring Freedom 2010 Afghanistan*. Washington, DC: Author.

Jonas, W., O'Connor, F., Deuster, P., Peck, J., Shake, C., and Frost, S. S. (2010). Why Total Force Fitness? *Military Medicine*, 175(8), 6-13.

Kalil, A., Ryan, R., and Chor, E. (2014). Time investments in children across family structures. *The ANNALS of the American Academy of Political and Social Science*, *654*(1), 150–168.

Kalisch, R., Müller, M. B., and Tüscher, O. (2015). A conceptual framework for the neurobiological study of resilience. *Behavioral and Brain Sciences*, *38*(92), 1–79.

Keller, K. M., Hall, K. C., Matthews, M., Payne, L. A., Saum-Manning, L., Yeung, D., Schulker, D., Zavislan, S., and Lim, N. (2018). *Addressing Barriers to Female Officer Retention in the Air Force*. Santa Monica, CA: RAND Corporation.

Kelley, M. L., Hock, E., Bonney, J. F., Jarvis, M. S., Smith, K. M., and Gaffney, M. A. (2001) Navy mothers experiencing and not experiencing deployment: Reasons for staying in or leaving the military. *Military Psychology, 13* (1), 55–71.

Kemp, S. (2019). *Digital 2019: Global Internet Use Accelerates*. Retrieved from https://wearesocial.com/blog/2019/01/digital-2019-global-internet-use-accelerates.

Keyes, C. L. (2006). Mental health in adolescence: Is America's youth flourishing? *American Journal of Orthopsychiatry*, *76*(3), 395–402.

Kleykamp, M. (2013). Labor market outcomes among veterans and military spouses. In J. M. Wilmoth and A. S. London (Eds.), *Life Course Perspectives on Military Service* (pp. 144–164). New York, NY: Routledge.

Lancaster, S. L., Erbes, C. R., Kumpula, M. J., Ferrier-Auerbach, A., Arbisi, P. A., and Polusny, M. A. (2013). Longitudinal predictors of desire to re-enlist in the military among male and female National Guard soldiers. *Military Medicine*, *178*, 267–273.

Land, B. C. (2010). Current Department of Defense guidance for Total Force Fitness. *Military Medicine*, *175*(8), 3–5.

Legree, P. J., Gade, P. A., Martin, D. E., and Fischl, M. A. (2000). Military enlistment and family dynamics: Youth and parental perspectives. *Military Psychology*, *12*(1), 31–49.

Lerner, R. M. (2007). Developmental science, developmental systems, and contemporary theories of human development. In W. Damon and R. Lerner (Eds.), *Handbook of Child Psychology* (6th ed., vol. 1, pp. 1–17). Hoboken, NJ: John Wiley & Sons, Inc.

________. (2018). *Theoretical and Methodological Innovations in Understanding Resilience Among Military Children*. Memo prepared for the Committee on the Well-Being of Military Families. Medford, MA: Tufts University.

Lubens, P., and Bruckner, T. A. (2018). A review of military health research using a social–ecological framework. *American Journal of Health Promotion*, *32*(4), 1078–1090.

Maley, A. J., and Hawkins, D. N. (2018). The southern military tradition: Sociodemographic factors, cultural legacy, and US Army enlistments. *Armed Forces and Society*, *44*(2), 195–218.

Manning, W. D., Brown, S. L., and Stykes, J. B. (2014). Family complexity among children in the United States. *The ANNALS of the American Academy of Political and Social Science*, *654*(1), 48–65.

Mason, R. (2018). *Memo prepared for the Committee on the Well-Being of Military Families.* Washington, DC: Army Emergency Relief.

Masten, A. S. (2001). Ordinary magic: Resilience processes in development. *American Psychologist, 56*(3), 227–238.

_______. (2013). Afterword: What we can learn from military children and families. *The Future of Children, 23*(2), 199–212.

_______. (2014). *Ordinary Magic: Resilience in Development.* New York, NY: Guilford Press.

_______. (2015). Pathways to integrated resilience science. *Psychological Inquiry, 26*(2), 187–196.

_______. (2016). Resilience in developing systems: The promise of integrated approaches. *European Journal of Developmental Psychology, 13*(3), 297–312.

_______. (2018). Resilience theory and research on children and families: Past, present, and promise. *Journal of Family Theory and Review, 10*, 12–31.

Masten, A. S., and Cicchetti, D. (2010). Developmental cascades. *Development and Psychopathology, 22*(3), 491–495.

Masten, A. S., and Monn, A. R. (2015). Child and family resilience: A call for integrated science, practice, and professional training. *Family Relations, 64*(1), 5–21.

Masten, A. S. and Narayan, A. J. (2012). Child development in the context of disaster, war, and terrorism: Pathways of risk and resilience. *Annual Review of Psychology, 63.*

Masten, A. S., and Obradović, J. (2006). Competence and resilience in development. *Annals of the New York Academy of Sciences, 1094*(1), 13–27.

McFadden, M. S. (2017). *Civil and Military Relations Gap: America's Disconnect with Its Military.* Syracuse, NY: Syracuse University Institute for National Security and Counterterrorism.

Meadows, S. O., Beckett, M. K., Bowling, K., Golinelli, D., Fisher, M. P., Martin, L. T., Meredith, L. S., and Osilla, K. C. (2016). Family resilience in the military: Definitions, models, and policies. *RAND Health Quarterly, 5*(3), 12.

Meredith, L. S., Sherbourne, C. D., Gaillot, S. J., Hansell, L., Ritschard, H. V., Parker, A. M., and Wrenn, G. (2011). *Promoting psychological resilience in the US military.* Santa Monica, CA: RAND Corporation.

Meyers, J. (2018, August). *Memo prepared for the Committee on the Well-Being of Military Families.* Washington, DC: Defense Advisory Committee on Women in the Services.

Meyer, D. R., and Carlson, M. J. (2014). Family complexity: Implications for policy and research. *The ANNALS of the American Academy of Political and Social Science, 654*(1), 259–276.

Military Officers Association of America. (2018, August). *Memo prepared for the Committee on the Well-Being of Military Families.* Arlington, VA: Author.

Narayan, A. J., Herbers, J. E., Plowman, E. J., Gewirtz, A. H., and Masten, A. S. (2012). Expressed emotion in homeless families: A methodological study of the Five-Minute Speech Sample. *Journal of Family Psychology, 26*(4), 648–653.

National Research Council and Institute of Medicine. (2002). *Community Programs to Promote Youth Development.* Washington, DC: The National Academies Press.

Office of the Deputy Assistant Secretary of Defense for Military Community and Family Policy. (2002). *A New Social Compact: A Reciprocal Partnership Between the Department of Defense, Service Members and Families.* U.S. Department of Defense. Retrieved from http://download.militaryonesource.mil/12038/MOS/Reports/A%20New%20Social%20Compact.pdf.

Organisation for Economic Co-operation and Development (OECD). (2011). *Doing Better for Families.* Paper no. 1283130769. Paris.

_______. (2017). *How's Life? 2017: Measuring Well-being.* Paris. Retrieved from https://www.oecd-ilibrary.org/economics/how-s-life-2017_how_life-2017-en.

Patterson, G. R., Forgatch, M. S., and DeGarmo, D. S. (2010). Cascading effects following intervention. *Development and Psychopathology*, 22(4), 949–970.

Perkins, D. F., Caldwell, L. L., and Witt, P. A. (2018). Resiliency, protective processes, promotion, and community youth development. In P.A. Witt and L. L. Caldwell (Eds.), *Youth Development: Principles and Practices in Out-of-School Time Settings* (pp. 173-192). Urbana, IL: Sagamore-Venture Publishing.

Pew Research Center (2015). *5 Facts About Family Caregivers*. Retrieved from https://www.pewresearch.org/fact-tank/2015/11/18/5-facts-about-family-caregivers/.

Pezzullo, L., Taylor, P., Mitchell, S., Pejoski, L., Le, K., and Bilgrami, A. (2010). *Positive Family Functioning*. Sydney, Australia: Access Economics. Retrieved from https://www.dss.gov.au/sites/default/files/documents/positive_family_functioning.pdf.

Pierce, P. F. (1998). Retention of Air Force women serving during Desert Shield and Desert Storm. *Military Psychology, 10*(3), 195–213.

Polusny, M. A., Erbes, C. R., Campbell, E. H., Fairman, H., Kramer, M., and Johnson, A. K. (2014). Pre-deployment well-being among single and partnered National Guard soldiers: The role of their parents, social support, and stressors. In S. MacDermid Wadsworth and D.S. Riggs (Eds.), *Military Deployment and its Consequences for Families, Risk and Resilience in Military and Veteran Families* (pp. 152–172). New York: Springer.

Rosen, L. N., and Durand, D. B. (1995). The family factor and retention among married soldiers deployed in Operation Desert Storm. *Military Psychology,* 7(4), 221–234.

Ryan, R. M., and Deci, E. L. (2001). On happiness and human potentials: A review of research on hedonic and eudaimonic well-being. *Annual Review of Psychology*, *52*(1), 141–166.

Saltzman, W. R., Lester, P., Beardslee, W. R., Layne, C.M., Woodward, K., and Nash, W. P. (2011). Mechanisms of risk and resilience in military families: Theoretical and empirical basis of a family-focused resilience enhancement program. *Clinical Child and Family Psychology Review, 14*(3), 213–230.

Sameroff, A. (2010). A unified theory of development: A dialectic integration of nature and nurture. *Child Development, 81*(1), 6–22.

Sawhill, I. (2014). Family complexity: Is it a problem, and if so, what should we do? *The ANNALS of the American Academy of Political and Social Science, 654*(1), 240–244.

Schneider, R. J., and Martin, J. A. (1994). Military families and combat readiness. In L. B. Davis, C. Mathews Quick, and S. E. Siegel (Eds.), *Military Psychiatry: Preparing in Peace for War* (pp. 19-30). Washington, DC: TMM.

Schumm, W. R., Bell, D. B., and Resnick, G. (2001). Recent research on family factors and readiness: Implications for military leaders. *Psychological Reports, 89*, 153–165.

Secretary of the Air Force. (2014). Air Force Instruction 90-506. Washington, DC. Retrieved from https://www.ramstein.af.mil/Portals/6/documents/DTC/AFD-151216-016.pdf?ver=2016-04-14-155129-117.

Segal, M. W. (1986). The military and the family as greedy institutions. *Armed Forces and Society, 13*(1), 9–38.

Segal, M. W., and Lane, M. D. (2016). Conceptual model of military women's life events and well-being. *Military Medicine, 181*(1), 12–19.

Segal, M. W., Lane, M. D., and Fisher, A. G. (2015). Conceptual model of military career and family life course events, intersections, and effects on well-being. *Military Behavioral Health, 3*(2), 95–107.

Shiffer, C. O., Maury, R. V., Sonethavilay, H., Hurwitz, J. L., Lee, H. C., Linsner, R. K., and Mehta, M. S. (2017). *2017 Blue Star Families Military Family Lifestyle Survey.* Encinitas, CA: Blue Star Families. Available: https://www.secome.org/MFLS-ComprehensiveReport17-FINAL.pdf.

Shonkoff, J. P., Garner, A. S., Committee on Psychosocial Aspects of Child and Family Health, Committee on Early Childhood, Adoption, and Dependent Care, and Section on Developmental and Behavioral Pediatrics. (2012). The lifelong effects of early childhood adversity and toxic stress. *Pediatrics, 129*(1), e232-e246.

Simons, L. G., Wickrama, K. A. S., Lee, T. K., Landers-Potts, M., Cutrona, C., and Conger, R. D. (2016). Testing family stress and family investment explanations for conduct problems among African American adolescents. *Journal of Marriage and Family, 78*(2), 498–515.

Sims, C. S., Trail, T. E., Chen, E. K., and Miller, L. L. (2017). *Today's Soldier: Assessing the Needs of Soldiers and Their Families*. Santa Monica, CA: RAND Corporation. Retrieved from https://www.rand.org/pubs/research_reports/RR1893.html.

Skomorovsky, A. (Ed.) (2018). *Impact of Military Life on Children from Military Families*. Ottawa, Ontario: North Atlantic Treaty Organization.

Small, N., Raghavan, R., and Pawson, N. (2013). An ecological approach to seeking and utilizing the views of young people with intellectual disabilities in transition planning. *Journal of Intellectual Disabilities, 17*(4), 283–300.

Smith-Osborne, A. M., and Felderhoff, B. J. (2014). Veterans' informal caregivers in the "sandwich generation": A systematic review toward a resilience model. *Journal of Gerontological Social Work, 57* (6–7), 556–584.

Social Trends Institute. (2017). *World Family Map 2017: Mapping Family Change and Child Well-Being Outcomes*. New York. Retrieved from https://worldfamilymap.ifstudies.org/2017/files/WFM-2017-FullReport.pdf.

Spence, N. J., Henderson, K. A., and Elder, G. H. (2013). Does adolescent family structure predict military enlistment? A comparison of post-high school activities. *Journal of Family Issues, 34*(9), 1194–1216.

Spinks, N. (2018, November). *What, So What, Now What?* Plenary address at the annual meeting of the National Council on Family Relations, San Diego, CA.

Swedler, D. I., Knapik, J. J., Williams, K. W., Grier, T. L., and Jones, B. H. (2011). Risk factors for medical discharge from United States Army basic combat training. *Military Medicine, 176*, 1104–1110.

Thompson, B. (2018). *Department of Defense Military Family Readiness System: Supporting Military Family Well-Being*. Paper commissioned by the Committee on the Well-Being of Military Families. Washington, DC: The National Academies of Sciences, Engineering, and Medicine.

Trail, T. E., Meadows, S. O., Miles, J. N., and Karney, B. R. (2017). Patterns of vulnerabilities and resources in US military families. *Journal of Family Issues, 38*(15), 2128–2149.

United States Department of Defense. (2012). *Department of Defense Instruction 1342.22: Military Family Readiness*. Washington, DC. Retrieved from http://www.esd.whs.mil/Portals/54/Documents/DD/issuances/dodi/134222p.pdf.

________. (2017a). *2017 Demographics: Profile of the Military Community*. Washington, DC. Retrieved from http://download.militaryonesource.mil/12038/MOS/Reports/2017-demographics-report.pdf.

________. (2017b). *The Third Quadrennial Quality of Life Review*. Washington, DC. Retrieved from http://download.militaryonesource.mil/12038/MOS/Reports/QQLR2017.pdf.

Vasterling, J. J., Proctor, S. P., Aslan, M., Ko, J., Jakupcak, M., Harte, C. B., Marx, B. P., and Concato, J. (2015). Military, demographic, and psychosocial predictors of military retention in enlisted Army soldiers 12 months after deployment to Iraq. *Military Medicine, 180*, 524–532.

Villarruel, F. A., Perkins, D. F., Borden, L. M., and Keith, J. G. (Eds.) (2003). *Community Youth Development: Programs, Policies, and Practices*. Thousand Oaks, CA: Sage.

Walsh, F. (2003). Family resilience: A framework for clinical practice. *Family Process, 42*(1), 1–18.

________. (2016). *Strengthening Family Resilience, Third Edition*. New York: The Guilford Press.

Watkins, K., Lee, J. E. C., and Zamorski, M. A. (2017). Moderating effect of marital status on the association between combat exposure and post-deployment mental health in Canadian military personnel. *Military Psychology*, *29*(3), 177–188.

Westphal, R. J., and Woodward, K. R. (2010). Family fitness. *Military Medicine*, *175*(suppl_8), 97–102.

Wilmoth, J. M., and London, A. S. (Eds.). (2013). *Life Course Perspectives on Military Service*. New York, NY: Routledge.

Windle, G., Bennett, K. M., and Noyes, J. (2011). A methodological review of resilience measurement scales. *Health and Quality of Life Outcomes*, *9*(8), 1–18.

World Health Organization (WHO). (1948). *Constitution of the World Health Organization*. Retrieved from http://apps.who.int/gb/bd/PDF/bd47/EN/constitution-en.pdf?ua=1.

Wright, K. M., Riviere, L. A., Merrill, J. C., and Cabrera, O. A. (2013). Resilience in military families: A review of programs and empirical evidence. In R. R. Sinclair and T. W. Britt (Eds.), *Building Psychological Resilience in Military Personnel: Theory and Practice* (pp. 167–191). Washington, DC: American Psychological Association.

3

Demographic and Military Service Characteristics of Military Families

In this chapter, we present an overview of military families' key demographic and military service characteristics in an effort to better understand these families and the extent to which the U.S. Department of Defense (DoD) is meeting their needs. After first laying out the sources of this information that are available to DoD, including those both internal and external to DoD, we highlight statistics corresponding to organizational and individual characteristics of service members and their dependents. In this overview, the committee points out how DoD may be using or interpreting these statistics in assessing military family needs, and how attention to intersectionality can aid DoD in identifying any gaps or undetected patterns in these needs. Based on this overview, the committee identifies additional demographic and military service data collection and analyses that would help DoD understand how well a wider range of military families is faring and whether new or revised programs and policies are required to meet their needs. This additional input should assist DoD in meeting its obligations regarding the care of service members and their families and the readiness of the all-volunteer force.

As described in Chapter 1, the focus of this report is active and reserve component service members and their families, both while they are in the military and as they transition out of it.[1] This population is heterogeneous

[1]For the reserve component, the committee focuses on the Selected Reserve, which refers to the prioritized reserve personnel who typically drill and train 1 weekend a month and 2 additional weeks each year to prepare to support military operations. Other reserve elements that are not maintained at this level of readiness but could potentially be tapped for critical needs or in a crisis are the Individual Ready Reserve, Inactive National Guard, Standby Reserve, and Retired Reserve.

in ways that other chapters in this report show are relevant for understanding their experiences, their responses to those experiences, and possible strategies to help them meet their needs. Additionally, the statement of task for this study specifically requested that the committee be attentive to population subgroups and named race, ethnicity, service branch, and military status as examples. Thus, this chapter serves as a reference for the relative size of different types of key subgroups discussed throughout this report.

Because DoD's primary family-related responsibility is to "dependent" family members (as defined in Title 37, Section 401, of the U.S. Code),[2] and because most of the available information about military families concerns service members and their military dependents, that was also the primary, although not exclusive, focus of this committee. As noted in Chapter 1, a dependent family member may be

- a spouse;
- an unmarried child who is either under age 21, incapable of self-support, or under age 23 and a full-time student;
- a parent; or
- an unmarried person in the legal custody of the service member.

A *child* may be a child by blood, by marriage, or by adoption. A *parent* may be a natural parent, a step-parent, or an "in loco parentis" parent. A spouse is considered a military dependent regardless of his or her own earnings. With all of this in mind, it is important to note that there are more military dependents than there are military personnel. In 2017, there were 2,103,415 active component and Selected Reserve service members, with 2,667,909 dependents (U.S. Department of Defense [DoD], 2017, p. vi).

The committee considers the demographic information and military service characteristics presented in this chapter to be relevant for understanding

- individual and family well-being and resilience;
- how service members' and military families' experiences and their attitudes toward military life may vary by subgroup, service branch, military status, and other factors;
- the extent to which current DoD programs and policies are designed to meet the various needs of the full range of military families; and
- the degree to which DoD has the information it needs to understand majority and minority subgroups within this population.

---

[2] *Pay and Allowances of the Uniformed Services*, United States Code, 2006 Edition, Supplement 5, Title 37.

Reviewing all potentially relevant demographic and military service characteristics here is not feasible; therefore, the absence of discussion of any particular characteristics should not be construed as an indication that it is irrelevant.

INFORMATION SOURCES: WITHIN DOD

Identifying sources of information about military families is critical for understanding the availability and quality of data that DoD has at its disposal. DoD gathers and maintains certain types of demographic and military service data on service members and military dependents to assist with the organizational management of personnel (e.g., to determine their pay and make assignments), the administration of programs and benefits (e.g., for health care, housing, and tuition assistance), and statistical research (e.g., to understand reenlistment trends). DoD also routinely sponsors surveys to gather insights on the attitudes and experiences of service members and spouses, such as the perceived impact of deployments, satisfaction with military programs and services, and attitudes toward continued military service. These surveys also typically gather demographic and military service data, some of which are used to weight the analytic sample.

The surveys include the recurring active and reserve component versions of the Status of Forces surveys of service members and spouse surveys. They also include the Millennium Cohort Study and Millennium Cohort Family Study, which are longitudinal epidemiological studies of cohorts of military personnel and family members. The latter two studies focus on health and well-being, health behaviors, health conditions and symptoms, exposures (e.g., to combat, chemicals, sexual assault), aspects of military life (e.g., deployment, moves), and aspects of life in general (e.g., stressful events, self-mastery). Additionally, the family study covers issues such as family functioning and children's behaviors and health conditions. The Department of Veterans Affairs Office of Research and Development also conducts the Million Veteran Program, a national voluntary research program that collects information from veterans to build a database of genetic, lifestyle, and health information as well as information on the military experience.[3]

A strength of DoD efforts is their visibility on many characteristics of the entire population of service members and contact information that can be used to solicit participation in research. Although the administrative personnel datasets will contain some missing, erroneous, or outdated information, DoD possesses much more information about this population than most organizations or scientific studies are able to access for any given population. However, DoD has much less information about dependents

[3]For more information, see https://www.research.va.gov/MVP/veterans.cfm.

than about service members; in fact, dependents are often studied by making use of their related service members' characteristics. DoD routinely publishes online[4] aggregate reports of certain demographic and military service characteristics, such as the annual demographics reports sponsored by Military Community and Family Policy (MC&FP) (e.g., DoD, 2017).

This committee considered whether there are additional characteristics that DoD should be collecting information about, or additional ways MC&FP should be analyzing or sponsoring analyses of the data DoD is already collecting.

Parameters

Although DoD maintains a wealth of data, understanding the legal boundaries within which it is required to operate is essential. DoD policy and practices regarding information systems such as these must comply with the U.S. law known as the Privacy Act of 1974.[5] Consequently, it is DoD policy that

> a. An individual's privacy is a fundamental legal right that must be respected and protected.
>
> (1) The DoD's need to collect, use, maintain, or disseminate (also known and referred to in this directive as "maintain") personally identifiable information (PII) about individuals for purposes of discharging its statutory responsibilities will be balanced against their right to be protected against unwarranted privacy invasions . . .
>
> . . .
>
> k. PII collected, used, maintained, or disseminated will be:
>
> (1) Relevant and necessary to accomplish a lawful DoD purpose required by statute or Executive order. (DoD, 2014, pp. 2–3).

Federal law known as the Paperwork Reduction Act of 1980[6] was enacted to reduce the burden on the public of government information collection. Under Title 10—Section 1782 (a), Survey of Military Families—DoD is permitted to survey service members, family members, and survivors of personnel who died while on active duty or while retired from military service "in order to determine the effectiveness of Federal programs relating to military families and the need for new programs . . ." DoD surveys of the

[4]Published on the Military OneSource website at https://www.militaryonesource.mil/reports-and-surveys.

[5]Privacy Act of 1974, 5 U.S.C. § 552a (1974). For related DoD policies, see DoD (2007a, 2014).

[6]Paperwork Reduction Act of 1980, 44 U.S.C. §§ 3501–3521 (1980).

general public, to include military contractors, require an application to the Office of Management and Budget (OMB) (DoD, 2015a), which falls under the executive branch of the government, and an approval process that may take a year or more to complete.

Consequently, although there are certainly exceptions, most available DoD data focus on service members and dependents, who as beneficiaries fall clearly within the above legal parameters. However, as the evidence in Chapter 2 demonstrates, DoD could benefit from learning more about military family members who are not dependents, such as the intimate partners of unmarried service members. Legal review may be necessary to determine whether OMB approval is necessary for primary data collection on other family members, but even if OMB review is required, an exploratory effort to solicit direct input from other family members could be illuminating in practical and policy-relevant ways.

Individual health records are maintained separately from personnel records, and the Health Insurance Portability and Accountability Act of 1996[7] limits the sharing of certain health information. It is possible to obtain permission to link health and personnel records for research purposes, as was done for the Army Study to Assess Risk and Resilience in Servicemembers (Kessler et al., 2013), but approvals and data safeguards must be in place, and these datasets are complex and not simple to analyze.

INFORMATION SOURCES: EXTERNAL TO DOD

External scholars and organizations are additional sources of information that can supplement official DoD data. Sources of information that focus on military personnel or family members include academic scholars in universities and research institutions (e.g., Pew Research Center, RAND Corporation), associations (e.g., Blue Star Families), and news organizations (e.g., *Military Times*). Additionally, broader data collection by the government, such as the Census's American Community Survey, can include indicators of military service or military spouse status. As another example, the 2015 National Survey on Drug Use and Health added questions to determine whether respondents had any military family association; the survey asked respondents whether they had immediate family members who were serving in the U.S. military and to specify their relationship to the service member (Lipari et al., 2016).

These data collection efforts and studies have been particularly helpful for understanding characteristics not (or not yet) collected by DoD, such as sexual orientation (e.g., Moradi and Miller, 2010), gender identity

[7]Health Insurance Portability and Accountability Act of 1996, P.L. 104-191, 110 Stat. (1996).

(e.g., Gates and Herman, 2014), and the prevalence of traumatic brain injury and posttraumatic stress disorder (PTSD) (Tanielian and Jaycox, 2008). Without access to DoD databases, it can be challenging for scholars to determine how representative some of these findings are, because DoD data are necessary for obtaining contact information to construct probability samples and to assist in weighting data and in analyzing results for nonresponse bias. However, obtaining exact percentages is less important than understanding key patterns across populations, or even demonstrating whether certain subgroups exist, for example whether gay and lesbian service members were actually serving and serving openly when open service was prohibited.

ORGANIZATIONAL AND INDIVIDUAL CHARACTERISTICS

Drawing from multiple sources within and outside of DoD, in this section we describe selected key demographic and military service characteristics of military families.

Characteristics of Service Members

The demographic composition of military personnel is shaped by DoD and Service policies and strategies for recruitment and retention in the all-volunteer force. Applicants must be deemed fit for military service and fit for their particular occupation. Overarching qualification standards are outlined in DoD policy (DoD, 2015b). Waivers for certain requirements may be considered for particularly strong candidates or in times of great need. Accessions criteria may also change to meet DoD's needs for personnel, such as during wartime, to respond to congressional mandates, or to adapt to societal or technological changes.

The courts have repeatedly deferred to congressional authority regarding military personnel law and policy related to national security interests. For example, in *Rostker* v. *Goldberg*,[8] the U.S. Supreme Court determined that it was not unconstitutional to require only men to register for the draft, and that "Congress was entitled, in the exercise of its constitutional powers, to focus on the question of military need, rather than 'equity.'" Thus, the military has not been subject to the same employment standards as civilian society. Age, gender, medical conditions, physical ability, mental ability, and other criteria are used to screen for suitability for military service or for specific occupations or positions within it, as defined by Congress, DoD, or the Services. What defines fitness for or compatibility with military service has been the crux of debates, such as whether military women should

[8] *Rostker* v. *Goldberg* [453 U.S. 57 (1981)].

serve in certain occupations or units (e.g., in the infantry, in special operations, or onboard submarines), whether openly gay and lesbian individuals should serve, and whether transgender individuals should serve.

Service and Component

Nearly half of the 2,103,415 active and Selected Reserve service members are in the Army, as is shown in Figure 3-1. The Marine Corps, which falls under the Department of the Navy, is the smallest service. Reserve component personnel can also serve on active duty (e.g., when mobilized for a deployment), but in this figure they are grouped according to their National Guard or Reserve organizational affiliation in the reserve component, rather than with the active component. Army National Guard and Air National Guard members work for their states (under Title 32), unless they are mobilized to work under the federal government (under Title 10),

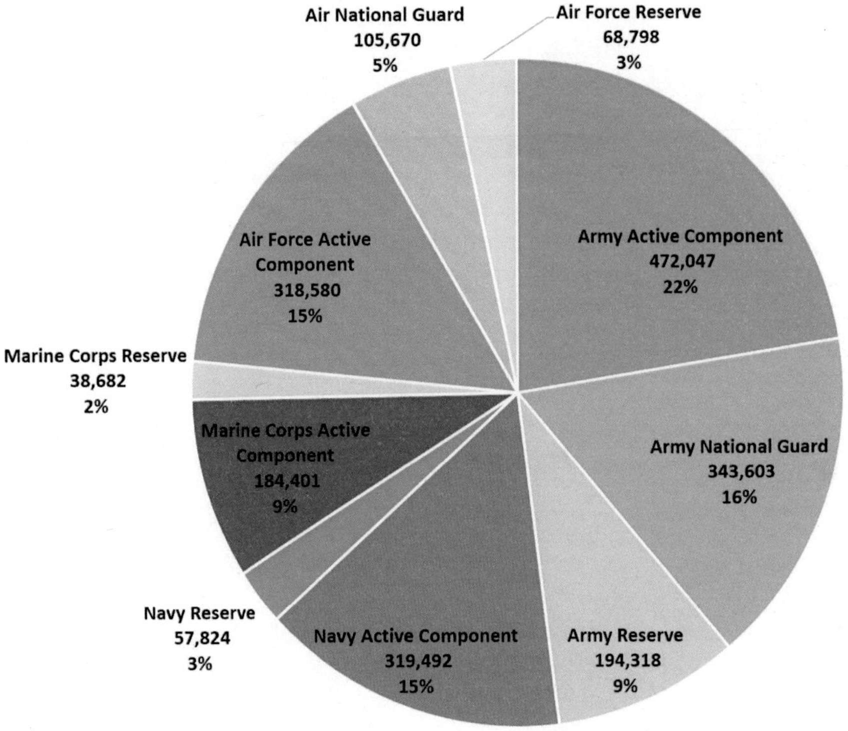

FIGURE 3-1 Distribution of service members, by service and component.
SOURCE: DoD (2017, pp. iii–iv).
NOTE: Percentages may not total to 100 due to rounding.

as they would be for an overseas military deployment. Their job requirements, eligibility for programs and services, health care system, and more can vary depending upon whether their current orders fall under Title 32 or Title 10. Reservists work for the federal government only, but like National Guard members they traditionally train 1 weekend a month and 2 weeks in the summer, although they may also be called to full-time active-duty service. Chapter 4 describes further how National Guard, reserve, and active component service context can vary.

Assigned Geographical Location

One major difference between active and reserve component service members is that the Services typically assign active component members to installations in the United States and abroad for tours that tend to last 2 to 3 years, whereas reserve component service members can generally maintain a continuous affiliation with a unit in the National Guard or Reserves. There are exceptions, of course: Some active members can have extended tours in one location, and members of the reserve component may choose to move, for example if they wish to relocate or pursue a particular position in another guard or reserve unit, or they may need to move as units close or change in composition.

In both cases, the majority of service members (88 percent active component, 99 percent reserve component) are based in the United States or its territories (DoD, 2017, pp. 31, 89). In 2017, approximately 5 percent of active component service members (70,236) were stationed in East Asia, particularly Japan and South Korea, and approximately 5 percent (65,855) were stationed in Europe, particularly Germany (DoD, 2017, p. 31).[9] Approximately 1 percent of active component service members were stationed in other overseas locations or serving on ships afloat (DoD, 2017, p. 33).

Within the United States, 67 percent of active component service members are stationed in just 10 states: California, Colorado, Florida, Georgia, Hawaii, North Carolina, South Carolina, Texas, Virginia, and Washington (DoD, 2017, p. iv). Among reserve component personnel (in the National Guard or the Reserves), a slightly different set of top 10 states are home to 43 percent of personnel: California, Florida, Georgia, Illinois, New York, North Carolina, Ohio, Pennsylvania, Texas, and Virginia (DoD, 2017, p. v).

Some installations are designated as "remote and isolated" by the Services (DoD, 2009a). By DoD policy, this designation allows certain morale,

[9]Countries highlighted were selected from the December 2016 data reported by the DoD's Defense Manpower Data Center under the Military and Civilian Personnel by Service/Agency by State/Country, see https://www.dmdc.osd.mil/appj/dwp/dwp_reports.jsp.

welfare, and recreational activities to receive a greater level of appropriated funds rather than relying as heavily upon income to cover their operating costs. It may be useful to consider how many service members and their families are living in this type of location, far from urban centers and main transportation hubs, because it may be more challenging for friends and family to visit them and vice versa, and they may have greater challenges finding activities or community resources to help them with their problems. Although DoD does not appear to publish aggregated statistics on how many service members are assigned to the officially designated remote and isolated locations, it does report for each U.S. installation the number of miles to the nearest metro city (DoD, 2017, pp. 176–185). Specific locations that have received this "remote and isolated" status are named in policy: In addition to many overseas locations, examples within the United States include the Naval Ordnance Test Unit in Cape Canaveral, Florida; Naval Outlying Field San Nicolas Island, California; Marine Corps Air Station, Yuma, Arizona; Marine Corps Recruit Depot, Parris Island, South Carolina; the Army's Fort Wainwright near Fairbanks, Alaska; the Army's White Sands Missile Range, New Mexico; Minot Air Force Base, North Dakota; and Vance Air Force Base, Oklahoma (Commander Navy Installations Command, 2014, pp. 6–7; Department of the Navy, 2007, pp. 1–25; Headquarters Department of the Army, 2010, pp. 21–22; Department of the Air Force, 2009, p. 14).

In contrast to such remote and isolated locations, some military installations are in or near large urban areas. San Diego, California; San Antonio, Texas; and Norfolk, Virginia, are examples of large urban areas with large concentrations of military personnel and dependents (DoD, 2017, pp. 176–177, 183–184). Most notably, there are a number of military installations in the nation's capital region just north and south of Washington, D.C., such as the Pentagon, Fort Meade, Fort Belvoir, Joint Base Andrews, Marine Corps Base Quantico, and the Walter Reed National Military Medical Center. Additionally, the U.S. Naval Academy is located just over an hour east of the capital. Military families in this region are surrounded by a vast array of military and nonmilitary service providers, a great concentration of other current and former military families, multiple options for neighborhoods and forms of transportation, many education and employment opportunities, and endless opportunities for indoor and outdoor recreation and fitness activities for family members of all ages.

Age

Given the physical requirements and stressors of many military occupations and assignments, the force is relatively young by design. Recruitment strategies for enlisted personnel, who comprise approximately 83 percent

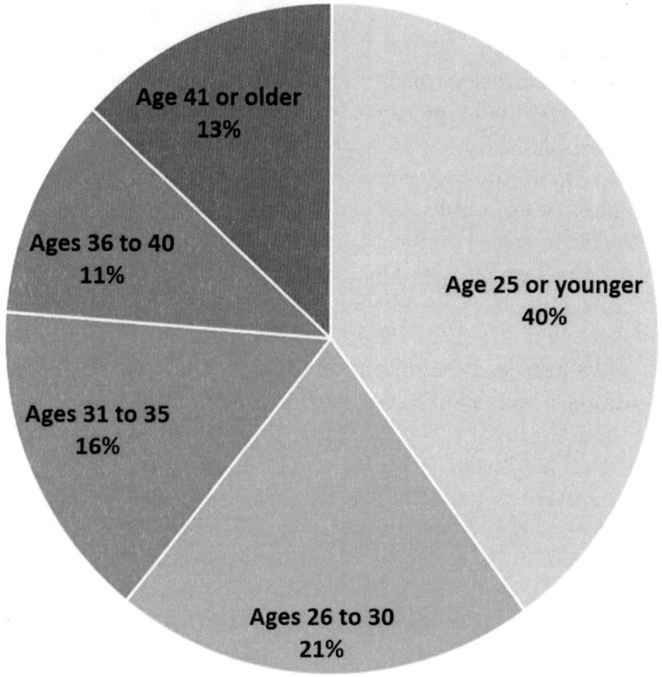

FIGURE 3-2 Service members' age (percent distribution).
SOURCE: Adapted from DoD (2017, p. 8).
NOTE: Percentages may not total to 100, due to rounding.

of the force (DoD, 2017, p. 6), target recent high school graduates, so most new recruits are under the age of 25. Officer entrants are slightly older, on average, than enlisted recruits, since they typically must hold a bachelor's degree to be commissioned as a military officer.[10] The minimum age for initial entrance into the military is 17 and the maximum age allowed by law is 42, although the maximum age varies by Service and over time. For example, in 2014 the Air Force raised the maximum age from 27 to 39, while the other Services' age limits remained at 35 years (Army), 34 years (Navy), and 28 years (Marine Corps) (Carroll, 2014). Service members become eligible for retirement after 20 years of service, so individuals who join immediately after high school may retire before the age of 40 and may seek post-service careers.

---

[10]Warrant officers (in all Services but the Air Force) and the Navy's Limited Duty Officers may not need a bachelor's degree, but in most cases they are older because they come from the enlisted force (Army warrant officer helicopter pilots being a notable exception, as prior service is not required).

As a result of these policies and recruitment strategies, as shown in Figure 3-2, 40 percent of service members are age 25 or younger, and 61 percent are age 30 or younger (DoD, 2017, p. 8). Thus, most service members are either in the process of transitioning to adulthood or are in early adulthood. This is a life stage in which many service members attempt to or begin to form families and raise children. These are also the primary childbearing ages for women. Therefore, age is a highly relevant characteristic for any study of service member and family well-being.

Education

Overall, 66 percent of military personnel have a high school diploma, General Equivalency Diploma [GED], or some college (but no degree) as their highest level of educational attainment: only 1 percent have no high school diploma or GED (DoD, 2017, p. 9). The remainder have an associate's degree (8%), bachelor's degree (15%), or advanced degree (8%) as their highest level of education (DoD, 2017, p. 9). As noted in the previous section, military officers must hold at least a bachelor's degree in order to receive a military commission, however some enlisted have college degrees as well. Indeed, 11 percent of active component and 8 percent of reserve component enlisted personnel hold an associate's degree as their highest level of education, and 8 percent of active component and 12 percent of reserve component enlisted have earned a bachelor's or higher degree (DoD, 2017, pp. iv, 199).

Race, Ethnicity, and Citizenship

DoD adheres to the requirements for federal program language and classification of race and ethnicity outlined in OMB's 1997 *Revisions to the Standards for the Classification of Federal Data on Race and Ethnicity* (OMB, 1997). These standards are designed to produce uniform and comparable statistics across federal agencies. Revisions to OMB's standards have been recently considered with the aim of gathering more complete and accurate data, and a few changes are expected for the 2020 Census, so OMB standards could be revised in the future (OMB, 2017; U.S. Census Bureau, 2017; U.S. Census Bureau, 2018). Nevertheless, in this section our terminology reflects the limitations of OMB race and ethnicity categories and naming conventions that DoD uses for its data collection and reporting.

Currently the only information DoD gathers on ethnicity, as defined by OMB, is whether service members are Hispanic or Latino. According to DoD personnel administrative data files, in 2017, 14 percent of military personnel identified themselves as Hispanic or Latino (DoD, 2017, p. 8). In accordance with OMB directives, DoD does not treat Hispanic or Latino as a minority race designation (DoD, 2017, p. iv), and reports race as a separate category. Of course, the Hispanic or Latino population in the military is racially diverse. For example, in 2017 this population made up 57 percent of active component personnel listed as having an "other" or "unknown" race, 22 percent of American Indian or Alaska Native personnel, 17 percent of White personnel, 15 percent of those who identified as multiracial, 10 percent of Native Hawaiian or Other Pacific Islander personnel, 5 percent of Black or African American personnel, and 4 percent of Asian personnel (DoD, 2017, p. 25).

In terms of race, as defined by OMB, 71 percent of service members reported themselves as White, and 17 percent as Black or African American (DoD, 2017, p. 7). As shown in Figure 3-3, all other races, individuals

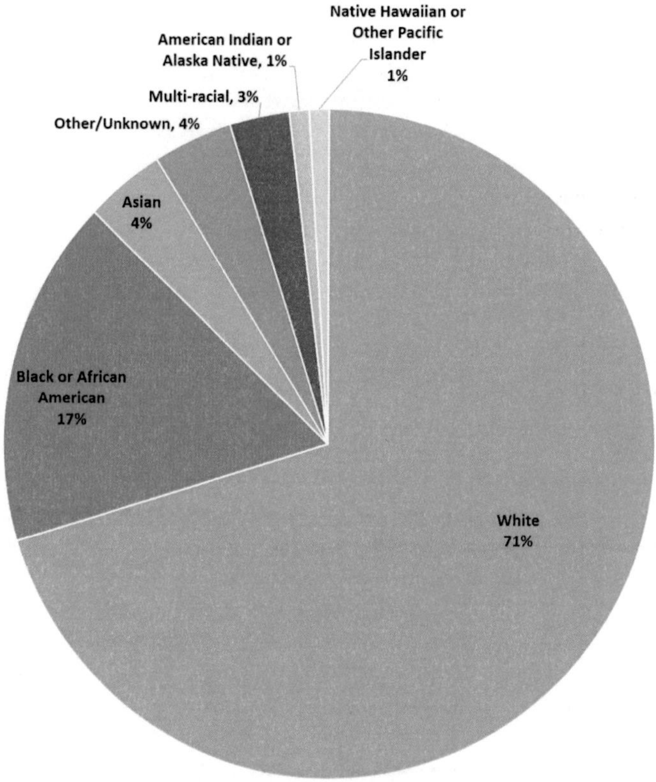

FIGURE 3-3 Service members' race (percent distribution).
SOURCE: Adapted from DoD (2017, p. 7).
NOTES: The Army and the Army Reserve do not report "multiracial." Percentages may not total to 100, due to rounding.

who indicate they are multiracial, and those for whom race information is unavailable make up the remaining 13 percent (DoD, 2017, p. 7).

Racial and ethnic minorities are not evenly distributed throughout the military hierarchy or across the force. For example, in the active component, 67 percent of enlisted personnel are White and 19 percent are Black or African American, but among officers 77 percent are White and 9 percent are Black or African American (DoD, 2017, pp. 24–25). Although corresponding statistics for ethnicity were not reported in DoD's 2017 profile of the military community, from other sources we learn that approximately 18 percent of active component personnel are Hispanic or Latino, but only about 8 percent of officers are (Kamarck, 2019, p. 20). The Navy has the most racially diverse active component, while the Marine Corps has the least (DoD, 2017, p. 30). The Navy Reserve is the most racially diverse reserve component, while the least is the Air National Guard (DoD, 2017, p. 83). In the active component, the Marine Corps has the highest percentage of Hispanic or Latino personnel—21 percent—while the other three services are about 14 to 15 percent Hispanic or Latino (DoD, 2017, p. 26). There is greater variation across the reserve component, ranging from 22 percent (Marine Corps Reserve) to 6 percent (Air Force Reserve) Hispanic or Latino (DoD, 2017, p. 80).

Military service has long been a path to U.S. citizenship for immigrants; indeed, it streamlines and can expedite the naturalization process (U.S. Citizenship and Immigration Services [USCIS], 2018a). Since October 1, 2001, more than 125,000 immigrant service members have become naturalized citizens (USCIS, 2018b). However, because security clearances are limited to U.S. citizens and some occupations require security clearances, not all enlisted occupations are open to immigrants who are noncitizens, and availability varies by service (McIntosh et al., 2011). Additionally, regardless of race, ethnicity, country of origin, or citizenship, English proficiency is a requirement for service in the U.S. armed forces (McIntosh et al., 2011).

Although military officers and warrant officers must be U.S. citizens, DoD stated in 2015 that each year about 5,000 legal permanent resident aliens join the enlisted force (DoD, 2015c). Through Title 10 (Section 504), Congress gives the Secretary of Defense the authority to enlist individuals who are not citizens or permanent residents "if the Secretary determines that such enlistment is vital to the national interest" (p. 221 of Title 10[11]). In November 2008, the Military Accessions Vital to the National Interest program was approved to broaden recruitment beyond citizens and permanent residents to meet the need for particularly hard-to-fill medical, language, and cultural skills. Although approximately 10,000 immigrant

[11]For access to Title 10 Section 504, see https://www.govinfo.gov/content/pkg/CPRT-112HPRT67342/pdf/CPRT-112HPRT67342.pdf.

military personnel earned citizenship through this program, DoD suspended it in 2016 and its future is uncertain (Copp, 2018).

Religion

DoD routinely collects data on the religious preferences of military personnel for practical reasons, although statistics are not commonly made publicly available. Military life can interfere with service members' access to their religious leaders, communities, places of worship, and rituals (a good example being the last rites in Catholicism in preparation for death). Military commanders are responsible for protecting their personnel's free exercise of religion and for preventing religious discrimination (Joint Chiefs of Staff, 2018). On that basis, the military includes a chaplain corps, places of worship in military camps and installations, community partnerships with off-base providers of religious and spiritual care, and, depending on the circumstances, accommodation of religious practices.[12] Under the First Amendment to the U.S. Constitution, the U.S. military, as a part of the federal government, cannot endorse or promote any particular religion. How the military should balance national security concerns with the religious freedoms of its members has been the subject of numerous debates throughout its history.[13]

The religious affiliations of U.S. military personnel today reflect a trend in the broader society, namely that of a rising proportion of adults, and young in adults in particular, who claim no religious affiliation (Hunter and Smith, 2012). DoD administrative data from 2009 showed that 20 percent reported no religious preference (Military Leadership Diversity Commission, 2010, p. 2). Some of those individuals, however, may have had preferences they were uncomfortable reporting to DoD. The majority of military personnel were recorded as affiliated with a Christian faith (69%), with the most common denominational preferences being Catholic (20%) and Baptist (14%) (Military Leadership Diversity Commission, 2010, p. 2). In 2009, non-Christian reported affiliations that made up 1 percent or more of the force were Humanist (4%), Pagan (1%), and Jewish (1%) (Military Leadership Diversity Commission, 2010).

More recent DoD administrative data focused on active duty personnel show that as of January 2019, approximately 70 percent were recorded as Christian (about 32% no denomination, 20% Catholic, 18% Protestant, 1%

---

[12]For policy on religious accommodation, see DoD (2009b).

[13]For example, *United States v. Seeger* and *Gillette v. United States* address the tension between the draft and conscientious objector status. *Goldman v. Weinberger* (10 USC 774) and *Singh v. Carter* address accommodations for religious clothing, accessories, or symbols while in uniform. For differing perspectives on policies and practices related to religion in the military, see the collection of essays in Section I of Parco and Levy, 2010.

Mormon), 2 percent as Atheist or Agnostic, 1 percent as affiliated with an Eastern religion, 0.4 percent each as Jewish or Muslim, and the remainder (about 24%) were reported as "other/unclassified/unknown" (Kamarck, 2019, pp. 46–47).

Following years of organized efforts by service members and others acting on their behalf to obtain stronger protections and support for religious diversity, in 2017 DoD nearly doubled the length of its list of faith and belief codes used to track service members' preferences.[14] DoD expects this expanded list to help it obtain and provide more accurate data, better plan for religious support to the force, and better assess the capabilities and requirements of the chaplain corps. Today's faith and belief group codes include Agnostic, Atheist, Druid, Heathen, Magick, Pagan, Shaman, Spiritualist, and Wiccan. Changes also include more specific affiliations for existing groups, such as Orthodox Judaism, Conservative Judaism, and Reform Judaism, rather than simply Judaism.[15]

Gender

The majority of military personnel are men. In 2017, approximately 18 percent of service members (370,085) were women (DoD, 2017, p. 6). The proportion who are women varies by military affiliation (see Figure 3-4). For example, in 2017 enlisted personnel in the Marine Corps Reserve had the smallest percentage of women (about 4%) while the greatest percentage was found among officers in the Air Force Reserve (27%) (DoD, 2017, p. 72). Additionally, the percentage of women in the reserve component (20%) is higher than in the active component (16%) (DoD, 2017, p. vii).

However, the gender composition of service members' work units and those with whom they interact may not reflect those ratios. Infantry and Special Forces units, for example, may consist entirely of men and rarely interact with service members who are women, whereas medical, administration, and supply units may have a large percentage of women service members. In fiscal year 2016, 25 percent of active component enlisted military women worked in administrative careers and nearly 15 percent were in health care, while less than 5 percent held an occupational specialty in the category of infantry, gun crews, or seamanship specialists (Office of the Under Secretary of Defense for Personnel and Readiness [OUSD P&R], 2018, p. 52). In contrast, more than 20 percent of active component enlisted men served in electrical and mechanical equipment repair, and more than 15 percent worked in infantry, gun crews, and seamanship careers (OUSD P&R, 2018, p. 52).

---

[14]For more information, see http://forumonthemilitarychaplaincy.org/wp-content/uploads/2017/04/Faith-and-Belief-Codes-for-Reporting-Personnel-Data-of-Service-Members.pdf.

[15]For a complete list, see: http://forumonthemilitarychaplaincy.org/wp-content/uploads/2017/04/Faith-and-Belief-Codes-for-Reporting-Personnel-Data-of-Service-Members.pdf.

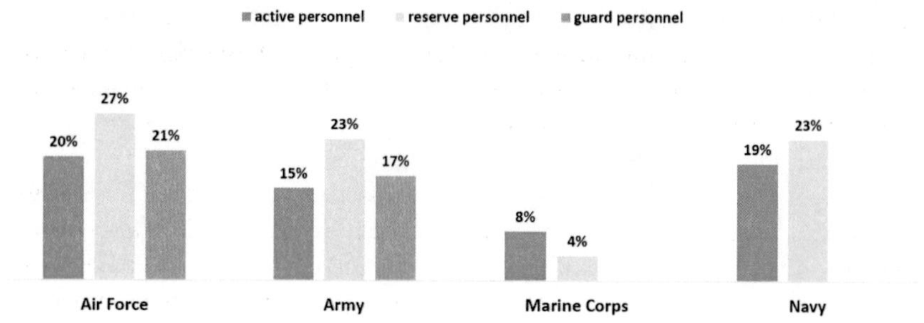

FIGURE 3-4 Service members who are women, by service and component.
SOURCE: Information from DoD (2017, pp. 20, 72).

Gender Identity

Gender identity refers to individuals' own sense of their gender, not individuals' anatomy and not how others perceive them. The term *cisgender* refers to those whose gender identity aligns with the sex (male or female) they were assigned at birth. *Transgender* individuals have a gender expression or identity that does not match or is not limited to the sex they were assigned at birth. They may identify with the opposite sex, or may adopt a gender identity such as bigender, gender-fluid, third gender, or agender (genderless).[16] Gender identity is independent of sexual orientation, which is a matter of which gender one is attracted to romantically and/or sexually.

In the past, DoD policy treated transgender identity as a disorder that is medically disqualifying for military service (Schaefer et al., 2016). However, in July 2015 Secretary of Defense Ashton Carter initiated a review of the policy and readiness implications of allowing transgender personnel to enter and remain in the military. He moved the authority to discharge based on gender identity up to the Under Secretary of Defense for Personnel and Readiness (DoD, 2015d). In October 2016, the Secretary of Defense ended the ban on transgender service (DoD, 2016a). Moreover, the Secretary announced that DoD would begin providing medical care and treatment for medically necessary gender transitions, and further stated that after transition transgender personnel must meet the military standards associated with

[16]This is also distinct from *intersex* individuals, those whose genitalia at birth did not fit into either of the standard binary as male or female. According to DoD policy, "History of major abnormalities or defects of the genitalia, such as hermaphroditism, pseudohermaphroditism, or pure gonadal dysgenesis" is a disqualifying medical condition" (DoD, 2018a, p. 24). It is possible that some individuals whose genitalia was surgically modified entered the military with this history undetected.

their chosen gender (e.g., regarding the uniform) and use the corresponding berthing, bathroom, and shower facilities, and that DoD would treat discrimination based on gender identity as sex discrimination to be addressed through equal opportunity channels (DoD, 2016b).

Following the U.S. presidential transition in January 2017, there has been uncertainty regarding transgender service policies. Although training and other preparations were in place to begin accepting new transgender recruits as of July 1, 2017, the new Secretary of Defense, James Mattis, announced in a June 30, 2017, memo a delay to this change to allow for further evaluation of the potential impact (Kamarck, 2019, p. 41). Then the President announced his intention to revert to the pre-2016 policy and prohibit transgender service. These actions were met with legal challenges, and federal judges reviewing the cases issued injunctions against reinstating a ban (Phillips, 2018). In September 2017, the Secretary of Defense issued interim guidance that stated that the existing policies would remain in force until DoD could consult with a panel of experts and prepare new policy recommendations that would respond to the presidential memorandum (Mattis, 2017).

The Secretary's subsequent recommendations to the President in February 2018 called for disqualification of self-identified transgender individuals, with certain exemptions for those service members who had already received a diagnosis of gender dysphoria after the ban on transgender service was lifted (DoD, 2018c). At that time, DoD reported that 937 current active-duty service members had been diagnosed with gender dysphoria since June 30, 2016 (DoD, 2018c, p. 32). Note that this figure captures only the subset of transgender personnel who revealed their transgender status to a military medical provider and who, as part of the diagnostic criteria for gender dysphoria, had also experienced distress or functional impairment because of the incongruity between their gender identity and their biological sex. In January 2019, the Supreme Court lifted the lower courts' injunctions blocking new military policies while the legal challenges continue, meaning DoD was free to move forward with policy restricting the military service of transgender individuals (Kamarck, 2019). As of the time of this writing, it remains to be seen whether Congress will enact any legislation to support or oppose the policy, whether the policy will withstand the legal challenges, and whether the administration or DoD will modify the policy to relax or tighten the restrictions. Nevertheless, there are transgender personnel serving in the U.S. military today.

DoD administrative personnel datasets track gender, but they do not track gender identity. An analysis comparing individuals' recorded gender over time could serve as one way to estimate the open transgender population; however, some transgender personnel may not have had their records updated or they may feel uncomfortable self-reporting their gender identity to DoD. Additionally, changes could merely reflect data errors. Recent DoD surveys have been used to estimate how many military personnel are transgender. The 2015 DoD Health Related Behaviors Survey of active component personnel (administered November 2015–April 2016) found that

> 0.6 percent of service members described themselves as transgender. This is the same as the percentage of U.S. adults who describe themselves in this manner (Flores et al., 2016). Less than one percent of respondents (0.4 percent) declined to answer the transgender question. If all non-responders were in fact transgender, the overall transgender percentage would be 1.1 percent. (Meadows, et al., 2018, p. xxx).

In a weighted sample of the 151,010 participants in the 2016 Workplace and Gender Relations Survey of Active Duty Members (administered as the transgender ban was being lifted, from July to October 2016), 1 percent of men and 1 percent of women identified as transgender, 1 percent of men and 1 percent of women were unsure, and 5 percent of men and 3 percent of women preferred not to respond to this question (Davis et al., 2017, p. 356). Thus, DoD estimates that approximately 1 percent of the force, or 8,980 service members, identify as transgender (DoD, 2018c, p. 7). The reserve component version of this survey was administered from August to October 2017, after the President had announced his intention to reinstate the transgender ban, and did not include a question on transgender identity (Grifka et al., 2018, Appendix D).

Using the size of DoD forces for the year 2014, one study applied a range of previous estimates of transgender prevalence derived from multiple sources (Schaefer et al., 2016). The new calculations estimated that there were between 1,320 and 6,630 transgender active component service members and between 830 and 4,160 transgender reserve component service members (Schaefer et al., 2016, pp. x–xi). Midrange estimates for the size of the transgender military population in 2014 were about 2,450 in the active component and 1,510 in the reserve component (Schaefer et al., 2016, p. xi).

Sexual Orientation

DoD does not track sexual orientation in its administrative personnel databases and thus does not publish such statistics in its annual demographics reports. However, measures were included in two recent DoD surveys on topics for which sexual orientation can be relevant.

In the 2015 DoD Health Related Behaviors Survey, nearly 6 percent of the 16,699 active component respondents identified as gay, lesbian, or bisexual (Meadows et al., 2018, p. 213). More specifically, 2 percent of men and 7 percent of women identified as gay or lesbian, and 2 percent of men and 9 percent of women identified as bisexual (Meadows et al., 2018, p. 213). Reserve component personnel were not included in this survey. The sample was weighted along other key demographic and military service characteristics.

These survey results suggest that there may be service differences as well. For example, 5 percent of Navy men identified as gay, compared to 2 percent of Air Force men, 1 percent of Army men, and less than 1 percent of Marine Corps men (Meadows et al., 2018, p. 214). There were no service differences in the proportion of men who identified as bisexual. Among women, 10 percent of Marine Corps women identified as lesbian, compared to 8 percent of Army women, 7 percent of Navy women, and 5 percent of Air Force women (Meadows et al., 2018, p. 214). Service differences were even greater for women who identified as bisexual: 19 percent of Marine Corps women, 10 percent of Navy women, and 8 percent of both Air Force and Army women (Meadows, et al., 2018, p. 214).

Another estimate comes from a weighted sample of the 151,010 participants in the 2016 Workplace and Gender Relations Survey of Active Duty Members. Overall, 5 percent identified as lesbian, gay, bisexual, or transgender (LGBT), which represented 3 percent of men and 12 percent of women (Davis et al., 2017, p. xxii). Specifically:

- 90 percent of men and 79 percent of women identified as heterosexual or straight;
- 1 percent of men and 6 percent of women identified as gay or lesbian;
- 1 percent of men and 5 percent of women identified as bisexual;
- 1 percent of men and 2 percent of women identified as other (e.g., questioning, asexual, undecided); and
- 6 percent of men and 8 percent of women preferred not to indicate sexual orientation on the DoD survey (Davis et al., 2017, p. 356).

Even though the 2016 survey of active component members found that personnel who identify as LGBT were more likely than those who did not identify as LGBT to report experiencing sexual assault, sexual harassment, and gender discrimination (Davis et al., 2017, p. xxii), the 2017 Workplace and Gender Relations Survey of Reserve Component Members did not collect data on sexual orientation (Grifka et al., 2018). Thus, LGBT estimates based on the 41,099 respondents in the National Guard and Reserves in 2017 (Grifka et al., 2018, p. iv) were not reported.

Using another approach to estimate the size of the lesbian, gay, and bisexual (LGB) population in the military, data from the 2008 General Social Survey and 2008 American Community Survey were used to estimate that less than 1 percent of men and 3 percent of women in the active component (about 1 percent of active component personnel overall) were LGB, but among members of the National Guard and Reserves 2 percent of men and 9 percent of women were LGB (about 3 percent overall in the reserve component) (Gates, 2010, p. 2). This would equate to about 70,781 LGB military personnel in 2008 (Gates, 2010, p. 1).

Drawing upon these survey results, if 3 to 5 percent of active and Selected Reserve service members in 2016 were sexual minorities, this would equate to between approximately 63,000 and 105,000 service members. The number of sexual minority partners, spouses, dependent teenagers, and young adults in the military family population is unknown, but comprise an even larger potential pool of people who may need assistance with and provider-sensitivity to issues related to stigma, harassment, or discrimination based on sexual orientation. These surveys also suggest that relative to military men, a disproportionate number of military women are sexual minorities.

Family Status

The family status of service members, as tracked and reported by DoD, is shown in Figure 3-5 (DoD, 2017, p. 124). Overall, about 50 percent of military personnel are married, and 39 percent have children. Single parents make up about 6 percent of the force; although this is a small percentage, it represents 126,268 personnel (DoD, 2017, pp. 134, 158). About 5 percent of personnel are in *dual-military marriages*, meaning both members of the couple are U.S. service members (DoD, 2017, p. 124). These couples can request assignment to the same or nearby installations, although the military cannot guarantee such co-location. Similarly, they may try to manage their deployment schedules, but the needs of the military take precedence.

Family status differences by component are noteworthy, as Figure 3-6 shows (DoD, 2017, pp. 132, 155). A greater percentage of active component members (53%) are married compared to reserve component members (44%) (DoD, 2017, p. iv, 103). More specifically (and not shown in the figure), a greater percentage of men than women in the military are married: 54 percent vs. 45 percent, respectively, in the active component and 47 percent vs. 35 percent, respectively, in the reserve component (DoD, 2017, pp. 48, 105).

Figure 3-6 also shows that a greater percentage of members in the active component are in dual-military marriages (nearly 7%) than is the case in the reserve component (nearly 3%) (DoD, 2017, p. iv, vi). Gender differences by component are particularly noteworthy: Although not shown in the figure, approximately 20 percent of active component women and 8 percent of reserve component women are in dual-military marriages, while 4 percent of active component men and 1 percent of reserve component men are (DoD, 2017, pp. 50, 108). If the scope is narrowed to married

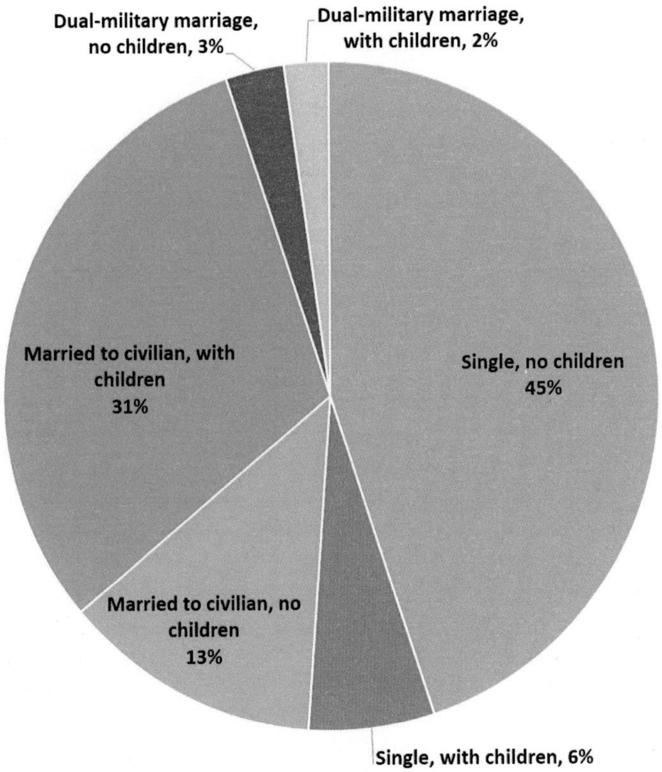

FIGURE 3-5 Family status of all service members (percent distribution).
SOURCE: Data from DoD (2017, pp. 134, 158).
NOTES: *Single* includes annulled, divorced, and widowed. *Married* includes remarried. *Children* include minor dependents age 20 or younger and dependents age 22 or younger enrolled as full-time students. Percentages may not total to 100 due to rounding.

personnel, the gender and component differences are even starker: 44 percent of married active component women and 11 percent of married reserve component women are in dual-military marriages, while 7 percent of married active component men and 5 percent of married reserve component men are (DoD, 2017, pp. 51, 108).

To provide further detail on the single service member, 43 percent of active component personnel have never been married and 5 percent are unmarried but divorced (DoD, 2017, p. 46). Among reservists, 49 percent have never been married and 7 percent are unmarried but divorced (DoD, 2017, p. 103).

In demographic and survey reports, DoD typically groups divorced personnel who have remarried with other married personnel, so no overall

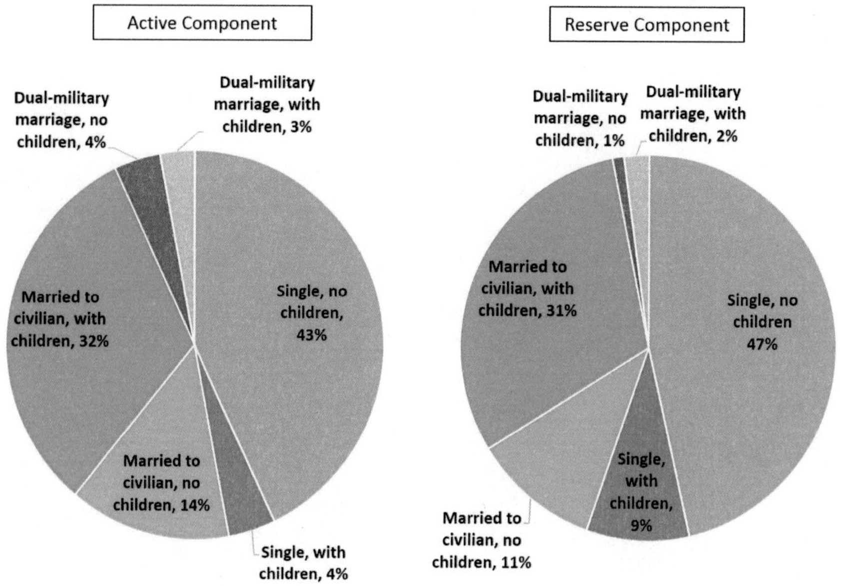

FIGURE 3-6 Family status of active and reserve component service members (percent distribution).
SOURCE: Data for the lefthand figure from DoD (2017, p. 132), and for the righthand figure from DoD (2017, p. 158).
NOTES: See Figure 3-5 concerning definitions of *single, married,* and *children.* Percentages may not total to 100, due to rounding.

statistic showing how many service members have *ever* gone through a divorce is readily available. The estimated percentage of married personnel who divorced in a single year (2017) was 3 percent of married active component members and 3 percent of married reserve component members (DoD, 2017, pp. 51, 109).

Unreported in DoD's demographics profiles is how many unmarried service members are in long-term relationships and/or cohabiting with a significant other (e.g., a fiancé(e), boyfriend, or girlfriend). Although the 2015 DoD Health Related Behaviors Survey of active component personnel did include "cohabitating (living with fiancé(e), boyfriend, or girlfriend but not married)" among the marital status categories, the size of the cohabiting population was not provided separately in the survey report (Meadows, et al., 2018, pp. 30-31, 284). Through direct correspondence with the authors, however, this committee learned that 3 percent of respondents self-reported as cohabiting. The 2015 version of the National Survey on Drug Use and Health included questions to determine whether respondents had any military family association, including whether they were an unmarried partner,

TABLE 3-1 Total Number of Exceptional Family Members in 2016, by Military Service

Service	Total
Army	43,109
Air Force	34,885
Navy	17,553
Marine Corps	9,150
Total	104,697

SOURCE: Adapted from U.S. Government Accountability Office (2018, p. 12).

but it is not readily apparent from available reports how many individuals indicated they were partners (Lipari et al., 2016).

The weighted 2017 Status of Forces survey results indicate that while 57 percent of active component and 49 percent of reserve component personnel reported being married or separated, nearly 10 percent of active component and 17 percent of reserve component personnel indicated they had been in a relationship with a significant other for a year or longer (DoD, 2018b). If those survey responses are representative of the broader population, in 2017 there would have been approximately 266,964 individuals who for a year or longer had been the unmarried partner of a service member.[17]

Special Needs Dependents

The Exceptional Family Member Program (EFMP) provides support to military families with adult or child dependents who have special medical or educational needs (or both), including coordination support documenting family members' special needs for personnel agencies to consider before finalizing personnel reassignments that would require relocation. Table 3-1 lists the total number of enrolled exceptional family members recorded in 2016 according to Service. As of February 2018, more than 132,500 family members are enrolled (U.S. Government Accountability Office [GAO], 2018, p. 1). Data on enrollment by age group or family relationship may be available internally, but they were not published in a 2018 GAO report on the EFMP or in the DoD's 2017 demographics profile, nor did the 2017 Status of Forces surveys or spouse surveys include questions regarding special needs among family members. However, recently a publication by members of MC&FP indicated that about two-thirds of enrollees are military children (Whitestone and Thompson, 2016, p. 294).

[17]Based on an active component population of 1,294,520 and a reserve component population of 808,895 (DoD, 2017, pp. iii, iv).

A recent survey of 160 EFMP family support providers found that the disabilities encountered by the largest percentage of providers were autism, attention-deficit hyperactivity disorder (ADHD), emotional/behavioral disorders, speech and language disorders, developmental delays, asthma, and mental health problems (Aronson et al., 2016, p. 426).

Characteristics of Spouses and Partners

DoD administrative personnel files contain more demographic information about the service members who are employed by DoD than they do concerning their dependent family members. Still, DoD does routinely administer surveys of military spouses, which provide supplementary demographic information. DoD does not gather demographic data for its personnel files on family members who are not dependents (i.e., not beneficiaries), but some insights are available through surveys of service members or spouses that are designed to inform DoD policies, programs, and services. Recall that in DoD policy, the "dependent" status applies to all military spouses and is therefore unrelated to whether they are financially dependent upon the service member.

Across all of DoD, there are 977,954 spouses who were not military personnel themselves (DoD, 2017, p. 123).

Age

Military spouses' ages span different life stages. As shown in Figure 3-7, 19 percent are 25 years old or younger, and 20 percent are 41 years or older (DoD, 2017, p. 125). Thus, the population will include those in the early stages of adulthood, parenthood, education, and career development as well as those with established careers and children who are adults. The average age of active component spouses is 32, while the average age of reserve component spouses is 36 (DoD, 2017, pp. 137, 161).

Race, Ethnicity, and Citizenship

DoD survey data provide sources of information about the race and ethnicity of spouses and use the same race and ethnicity categories asked of service members. A weighted sample of participants in the 2017 Survey of Active Duty Spouses shows that 61 percent were non-Hispanic White and 38 percent were Hispanic and/or of other races (DoD, 2018b). More specifically, 11 percent were non-Hispanic Black and 15 percent were Hispanic (DoD, 2018b). Similarly, in a longitudinal survey of active component military spouses administered in 2010, 2011, and 2012, 70 percent were non-Hispanic White and 30 percent were minority race/ethnicity (DMDC, 2015, p. 10).

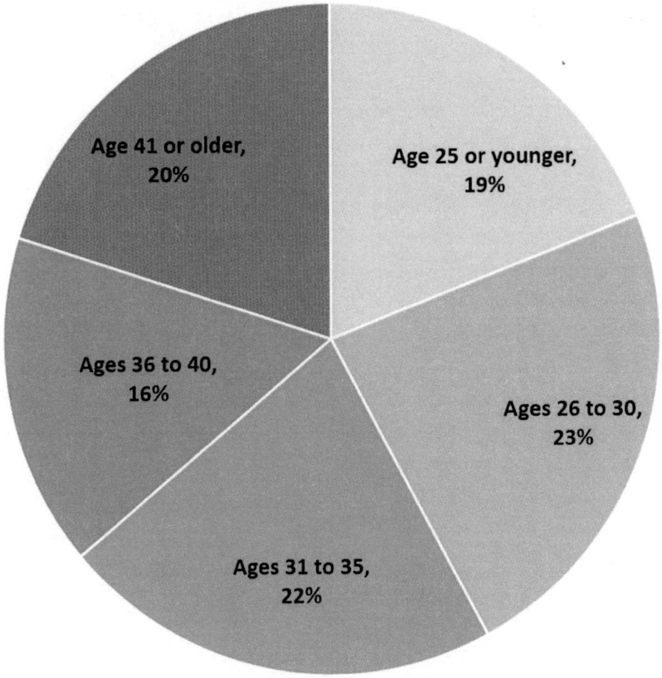

FIGURE 3-7 Ages of military spouses (percent distribution).
SOURCE: Adapted from DoD (2017, p. 125).
NOTE: Percentages may not total to 100, due to rounding.

A weighted sample of participants in the 2017 Survey of Reserve Component Spouses shows that 71 percent were non-Hispanic White, and 29 percent were Hispanic and/or of other races (DoD, 2018b). More specifically, 9 percent were non-Hispanic Black and 12 percent were Hispanic (DoD, 2018b). If the spouse survey results are representative of the spouse population at large, a greater percentage of active component spouses are racial or ethnic minorities compared to reserve component spouses.

Unfortunately, the committee is unaware of any published statistics on the citizenship status of spouses extracted from administrative records, and DoD's recurring spouse surveys do not currently ask spouses about their citizenship. Spouses of U.S. service members who are not U.S. citizens may be eligible for expedited or overseas naturalization, and service members' children may also be eligible for overseas naturalization (Stock, 2013; USCIS, 2018c). U.S. Citizenship and Immigration Services reports that in the approximately 10 years since fiscal year 2008, 2,925 military spouses have been naturalized in ceremonies overseas in more than 35 countries

(USCIS, 2017). Those countries are quite diverse and include Afghanistan, Australia, Chile, China, Germany, India, Norway, Oman, Panama, Philippines, Poland, Tanzania, and Turkey (USCIS, 2017).

It appears that the last time the spouse surveys asked about citizenship was in 2006. At that time, 7 percent of the 11,953 active component spouse respondents to that question (n = 781) reported not being a U.S. citizen, and 6 percent (n = 669) reported being a U.S. citizen by naturalization (DMDC, 2007a, p. H-12). In the same 2006 survey, 13 percent of active component spouse participants (n = 1,520) indicated that English was a second language for them (DMDC, 2007a, p. H-493). Although citizenship and English as a second language questions were included in the 2006 reserve component spouse survey, the results were not included in the results report (DMDC, 2007b, App., p. 2). Thus, this important information may not be visible to leaders or program managers or nonmilitary organizations who might rely upon published demographic reports or surveys to help them understand and prioritize the potential needs of the military spouse population.

Religion

The committee is unaware of any statistics on the religious affiliation of military spouses or partners.

Gender

The vast majority of military spouses are women: 92 percent of active component spouses and 87 percent of reserve component spouses are women (DoD, 2017, pp. 136, 160). Although their presence may seem small when expressed as a percentage, military spouses who are men are nevertheless large in number (100,723) (DoD, 2017, pp. 136, 160).

Sexual Orientation

Currently married gay and lesbian service members and their same-sex spouses are technically eligible for the same military benefits as their heterosexual counterparts, including health care for spouses and the higher "with dependents" basic allowance for housing. This equality also extends to benefits from the Department of Veterans Affairs (VA). However, we caution that eligibility does not mean that same-sex spouses are equally comfortable self-identifying or applying for DoD or VA benefits or that they are treated equitably or to the same standard of care as their heterosexual counterparts. Indeed, even in the broader U.S. society, stigma, fear of discrimination from providers, and provider knowledge about and attitudes toward sexual minorities can present barriers to equitable health care and associated detriments to overall well-being (Institute of Medicine, 2011).

DoD's most recent published demographics report (DoD, 2017) does not provide statistics for the number of registered same-sex marriages among military personnel, and other estimates were not readily available.

Education, Employment, and Earnings

Among spouse participants in the 2017 Survey of Active Duty Spouses, 10 percent of the weighted sample reported having no college, while 44 percent reported having some college or a vocational diploma, 30 percent reported having a 4-year degree, and 15 percent reported having a graduate or professional degree (DoD, 2018b). The 2017 DoD Survey of Reserve Component Spouses measured education level slightly differently: 46 percent of the weighted sample reported having no college or some college, 33 percent a 4-year degree, and 21 percent a graduate or professional degree (DoD, 2018b).

These spouse surveys suggest that active component spouses are less likely than their reserve component counterparts to be employed (53% compared to 73%, as seen in Figure 3-8). At the time of the survey, 13 percent of

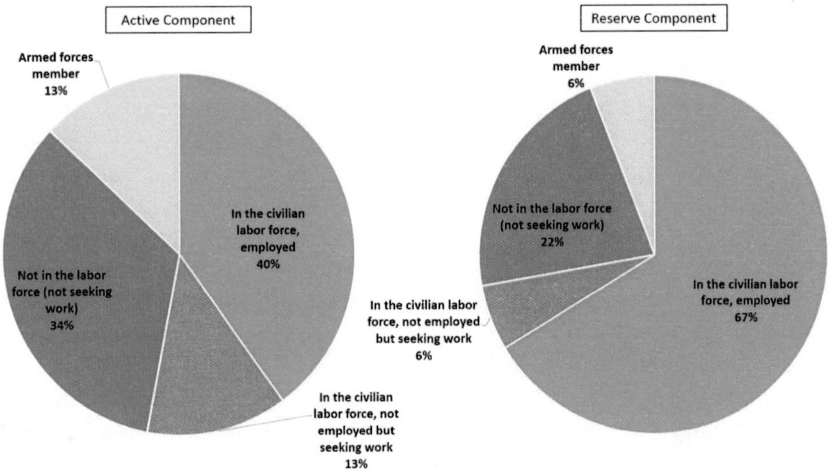

FIGURE 3-8 Employment status of active and reserve component spouses (percent distribution).
SOURCE: DoD (2018b).
NOTE: Categories are constructed from multiple 2017 spouse survey items to conform to the Bureau of Labor Statistics' standards using Current Population Survey labor force items. Percentages may not total to 100, due to rounding.

active component spouses were not employed but seeking work, compared to 6 percent of reserve component spouses. Since unemployment rates exclude those who are not in the labor force (i.e., not working and not seeking work), the unemployment rate among the active component spouse respondents was 19 percent, compared to 7 percent for reserve component spouse respondents. Note that 34 percent of active component spouses and 22 percent of reserve component spouses were not working nor seeking work.

One recent study using DoD administrative data and Social Security Administration earnings data for civilian spouses of active component military members between 2000 and 2012 found that, on average, 67 percent of military spouses were working (defined as having any earnings in a given year) (Burke and Miller, 2018, p. 1269). Average annual earnings across all of these military spouses was $15,301, and across working military spouses it was $22,812 (Burke and Miller, 2018, p. 1269). The average annual earnings for the service members of these spouses in this same period was $55,367 (Burke and Miller, 2018, p. 1269). A military move was associated with a $2,100, or 14 percent, decline in average spousal earnings during the year of the move (Burke and Miller, 2018, p. 1261).

Children

The total number of children who are identified as military dependents is 1,678,778 (DoD, 2017, p. 124). Across DoD, 40 percent of all service members (831,870) have children who are minor dependents age 20 or younger, or up to age 22 if enrolled as a full-time student (DoD, 2017, p. 124). In the active component, the Marine Corps has the lowest percentage of service members with children (26%), while the Army has the highest (44%) (DoD, 2017, p. 140). In the reserve component, the Marine Corps Reserve stands out as having the lowest percentage of service members with children (20%), while between 38 and 50 percent of personnel in the other Selected Reserve components have children (DoD, 2017, p. 164).

DoD routinely publishes a few other characteristics of parents as well. About 60 percent of active component children and reserve component children have military parents who are NCOs (paygrades E-5 to E-9) (DoD, 2017, pp. 140, 164). Service members' average age at the birth of their first child is 26 in the active component and 28 in the reserve component (DoD, 2017, pp. 140, 165).

Age of Children

Reflecting the relatively young age of military personnel, the majority of military children have not yet reached their teens, as seen in Figure 3-9. Though not shown in the figure, a greater percentage of active component

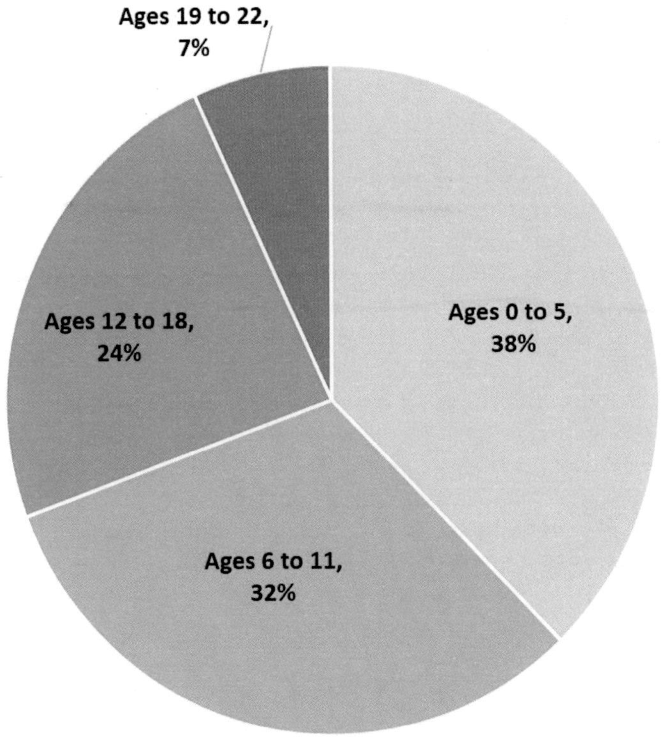

FIGURE 3-9 Ages of children in military families (percent distribution).
SOURCE: Adapted from DoD (2017, p. 125).
NOTE: Children ages 21 to 22 must be enrolled as full-time students in order to qualify as dependents. Data are presented for the total DoD military force; therefore, DHS Coast Guard Active Duty and DHS Coast Guard Reserve are not included. Percentages may not total to 100, due to rounding.

children are ages 5 or younger compared to children in the reserve component (42% and 31%, respectively) (DoD, 2017, pp. 143, 167). While this youngest age group is also the largest age group among active component children, reserve component children ages 6 to 11 make up 32 percent, or about the same percentage as those who are ages 5 or younger (31%) (DoD, 2017, pp. 143, 167). DoD includes "children" ages 19 to 22 in these statistics because, as noted in Chapter 1, by law (Title 37 U.S.C. Section 401) adult children retain eligibility to be military dependents until age 21, or until age 23 if enrolled fulltime at an approved institution of higher learning (or longer if they are disabled, and then they become "adult dependents"). Thus, service members' children can benefit from the support of access to military health care and many other resources as they work on their own transitions to adulthood (e.g., internship, entry-level job, college, starting a business).

Education

Out of the 1.68 million military children today, about 56 percent (more than 933,000) fall into the K–12 education range of 6–18 years of age (DoD, 2017, p. 125). Approximately 60 percent of the children in active-duty military families residing in the United States are school age, and the majority of them (nearly 80 percent) attend public schools (U.S. Department of Defense Education Activity [DoDEA], 2019a). A majority of the more than 443,000 children of National Guard and Reserve members also attend public schools (DoDEA, 2019a). Additionally, more than 71,000 military-connected children attend one of the 164 accredited DoD schools (including one virtual school) run by the U.S. Department of Defense Education Activity (DoDEA), which are located across 11 foreign countries, 7 states, Guam, and Puerto Rico (DoDEA, 2019b). (See Box 3-1 for more information on the recognition of military connected students in public schools.)

Other Child Demographics

Even though children represent such a significant number and proportion of the military community, unfortunately several key demographics with relevance for the potential needs of military children are missing from DoD's demographic profiles of the military community. These include the race and ethnicity of military children, which the committee's statement of task specifically asked us to consider. Because of adoption, blended families, and interracial coupling, parents' race and ethnicity cannot be presumed to be proxies for their children's. The demographics profiles also do not make readily available statistics on children's school status (DoD, public, private, homeschool), EFMP status, whether they live on- or off-base, whether they live in the United States or not, whether they live with the service member or not, and so on.

Other Family Members, Friends, and Neighbors

Other family members, such as parents, siblings, grandparents—and even friends and neighbors whom service members self-define as "family"—can be an important part of a military family's support network, and the converse may be true as well: These people may depend on military personnel for financial or other support. Service members may still have co-parenting relationships with former spouses or partners as well. Additionally, some of the individuals in a service member's primary network may be military personnel themselves.

BOX 3-1
Military Student Identifier Reporting

The Every Student Succeeds Act (ESSA), signed into law in 2015, is the latest reauthorization of the Elementary and Secondary Education Act (ESEA), requiring states to collect and report assessment data on vulnerable students who are at greater risk for academic failure. Given the number of school transitions that children of service members often make and the potential impact on their academic performance, ESSA recognized military-connected students as a distinct subgroup of students and set into motion the requirement for all states to implement a Military Student Identifier (MSI). The provision requires public schools to include the MSI question, for example in their student enrollment procedure, which identifies students who have a parent who is a member of the Army, Navy, Air Force, Marine Corps, or Coast Guard on active duty, including full-time National Guard duty.[a] The provision does not include students with a parent who serves in the National Guard or Reserve unless that parent serves fulltime. In addition, ESSA requires each state or public school system to determine additional collection and reporting requirements related to their pupil management systems, policies, and processes. The MSI reporting can help to identify the unique challenges that military-connected students face in making academic progress, so educators, families, and policy makers are better equipped to support their needs (Zinskie and Rea, 2016; Military Child Education Coalition [MCEC], 2019a,b).

Prior to ESSA, approximately 20 states had already established MSI reporting, relying on Common Education Data Standards[b] as a guide to help them determine how to collect, code, and organize data about military-connected students. However, ESSA's MSI provision creates consistencies in collecting and reporting this data nationally for policy making and practice. While ESSA directed implementation of the MSI provision for the 2017–2018 school year, as of September 2018 most school districts were still in the early stages of implementation and state education agencies were working on how to incorporate the MSI into their data systems (Mesecar and Soifer, 2018; MCEC, 2017). Arkansas was early to adopt MSI reporting, beginning with the 2013–2014 school year; the state includes all military-connected student populations regardless of a parent's full-time status. Although it does not have a large military installation, Arkansas has made significant steps in disaggregating data on military-connected students down to the level of service branch for both active-duty and reserve status service members. Arkansas offers this information at the district and even the campus level and makes it easily accessible through the Arkansas Department of Education (ADE) Data Center.[c]

---

[a]Every Student Succeeds Act of 2015, Pub. L. No. 114–95 § 114 Stat. 1177 (2015–16) Section 1111(h)(1)(C)(ii)).

[b]For more information, see https://ceds.ed.gov/element/001576.

[c]For more information on Arkansas' ESS MSI reporting, see https://adedata.arkansas.gov/.

TABLE 3-2 2013 Characteristics of Caregivers of Military Personnel and Veterans Who Served Post-9/11

Relation to Care Recipient	Percentage
Spouses, Partners, or Significant Others	33
Parents	25
Friends or Neighbors	23
Child	6
Other Family	10

SOURCE: Adapted from Ramchand et al. (2014, p. 34).

Other family members besides spouses or partners may provide support to service members. For example, individuals may be caregivers to service members who have a disabling physical or mental wound, injury, or illness. Table 3-2 summarizes one recent effort to understand the hidden population of caregivers through a probability-based survey in 2013 of caregivers of military personnel and veterans who served post-9/11 (after September 11, 2001). The 2007 DoD Task Force on Mental Health recommended that DoD improve coordination of care by facilitating access to military installations for those caregivers who do not have military identification cards but are caring either for military children during a parent's deployment or for wounded service members (U.S. DoD Task Force on Mental Health, 2007, pp. 36–37).

Family members are involved in supporting military families in numerous other ways: providing emotional and social support, attending graduation from basic training or promotion or retirement ceremonies, sending letters and care packages, serving as an emergency contact, providing the "home" that service members and their families visit while on leave, holding power of attorney during deployments, storing property or caring for pets or children during deployments, providing child care even when service members are not deployed, helping during emergencies (e.g., after flood or fire), and so on.

Others may also depend on military families for support. Adults who hold the status of military dependents could include grown children, former spouses, siblings, parents, grandparents, or others in the legal custody of a service member. In 2017, there were 8,988 adult dependents of active component service members and 1,591 adult dependents of DoD reserve component members (10,579 adult dependents) (DoD, 2017, p. 145; 2019b). Less than 1 percent of active component dependents (0.6 percent) and less than one-half of a percent of reserve component dependents are adult dependents who are not the spouses or children of service members (DoD, 2017, pp. vii, 130, 151; 2019b). The age distribution of adult dependents suggests that National Guard and Reserve families with adult dependents are most likely to be caring for parents or grandparents, given that 57 percent of them are age 63 or older. By contrast, active component families with adult dependents are most likely to be caring for grown children, siblings, or former spouses, since only 33 percent of these dependents are age 63 or older (DoD, 2017, p. 145; 2019b).

Military families may also be providing financial or social support to friends and family. They may be helping out during others' deployments, when they have serious health problems, or during natural disasters or other times of need by assisting with child care, temporary housing, managing the household (e.g., repairs, yardwork), or organizing food or clothing drives, among other things. Other friends and family members may also be seriously impacted by what happens to military families, such as when a family member is assigned or deployed far away from them, seriously injured, sexually assaulted, killed, or has taken their own life. These relationships remain unidentified in official reports.

Thus, the military families and others that service members support and rely upon extend beyond spouses, partners, and children, even though by far the most is known about the size and characteristics of spouses and children. If every service member had just three individuals they considered to be close relatives or friends—parents, step-parents, parents-in-law, aunts, uncles, grandparents, siblings, friends, etc.—then the size of this population would be 6,310,245. These individuals may find it challenging to connect with others in their same situation and to learn which, if any, military-sponsored activities or resources might be open to them to help them better support military families.

CHARACTERISTICS THAT CHANGE OVER TIME

It is important to track trends in characteristics like these, as they may vary over time. To illustrate very simply, we highlight a few examples of how active component characteristics at the end of the Cold War, in 1990, differ from those reported in 2017. Keep in mind that demographics can fluctuate over time, so differences between two points in time cannot be assumed to represent a steady, gradual change in the same direction from year to year. Also, some demographics may remain relatively stable, such as average age (about age 24 for enlisted personnel and age 35 for officers (DoD, 2007b, p. 25; 2017, p. 40).

- Education: In 1990, less than 3 percent of the enlisted active duty force held a bachelor's or advanced degree; by 2017 that was true for about 8 percent (DoD, 2007b, p. 28; 2017, p. iv).
- Race and ethnicity: Changes to the way race and ethnicity data have been collected and reported present some challenges to long-term

comparisons. Nevertheless, in 1990, racial minorities (not coded to include White Hispanics) were about 25 percent of the active component, compared to 31 percent in 2017 (DoD, 2007b, p. 19; 2017, p. iii). Hispanic representation, which per U.S. Office of Personnel Management (OPM) guidance has been treated as its own separate ethnicity category since 2003, rose from 9 percent in 2004 to 16 percent in 2017 (DoD, 2004, p. 13; 2017, p. iv).
- Gender: The proportion who are women has been gradually increasing. In 1990, 11 percent of active-duty enlisted personnel and 12 percent of officers were women, compared with 16 percent and 18 percent, respectively, in 2017 (DoD, 2007b, p. 13; 2017, p. iii).
- Family Status: In 1990, 57 percent of active-duty personnel were married, compared with 53 percent in 2017 (DoD, 2007b, p. 35; 2017, pp. 45–46). In 1990, 39 percent of personnel were married with children, while in 2017, 34 percent were, although the percent of single parents was the same in both years (4%) (DoD, 2007b, p. 45; 2017, p. vi).

Much to its credit, DoD does indeed track and report overall trends on broad categories like these, and sometimes breaks out trends for one characteristic by another (e.g., by service or gender).

ATTENTION TO INTERSECTIONALITY

To better understand military personnel and their families, it is important to remember that the characteristics described throughout this chapter intersect with one another and countless other statuses not mentioned here (e.g., religion/spirituality, native language). In other words, *intersectionality* refers to the observation that characteristics are interrelated and interact with one another. No one's experiences are defined by a single characteristic, such as gender, and the relevance of a characteristic may vary depending on the time, place, context, and other characteristics. For example, the experiences of Black women are not necessarily similar to those of White women or Black men: Examining survey results or health statistics only by gender or by race may miss important patterns, such as varying risk factors for negative outcomes. No subgroup is monolithic, so Black women's experiences will vary as well, and they will interact with other statuses and contexts—such as being a naval officer, being a pilot, having a Marine husband, having no children, being stationed on an aircraft carrier, or being 30 years old. Likewise, an individual can hold majority and minority statuses at the same time (e.g., being heterosexual and Hispanic) and can belong to a subgroup that is a numerical majority (e.g., being enlisted) without necessarily being in a position of privilege or power.

As an illustrative example of an intersectional approach with implications for well-being, one sociological study using a survey of a nationally representative sample of U.S. adults examined whether the intersections of race, ethnicity, foreign- or U.S.-born status, gender, and socioeconomic status were associated with individuals' perceived need for mental health care (Villatoro et al., 2018). The analyses included not only the total sample but subsamples of respondents who did and did not appear to meet diagnostic criteria for a psychiatric disorder. The researchers found that "men are less likely than women to have a perceived need [for mental health care], but only among non-Latino whites and African Americans. Foreign-born immigrants have lower perceived need than U.S.-born persons, but only among Asian Americans" (Villatoro et al., 2018 p. 1).

From a programmatic perspective, the significance of a greater appreciation of the complexity of the population is that "identifying the statuses and mechanisms that lead to differential self-labeling [as having a need for treatment for mental health-related problems] is essential to explaining why disparities in mental health care utilization exist (Villatoro et al., 2018 p. 20)." Of course, it is important to explore other potential explanations for differences in utilization of mental health care as well, such as language or cultural barriers, lack of awareness of service options, differing perceptions of or experiences with mental health care providers, and so on.

Paying greater attention to intersectionality could help DoD look for gaps and previously undetected patterns that might call for differing approaches to outreach or intervention and also help DoD affirm its commitment to a diverse range of military personnel and families. It may also help support recruitment and retention goals by promoting better attention to the varied interests, strengths, disadvantages, and needs of the myriad populations that could or do serve in the military.

This chapter has contained examples of how demographic characteristics vary by other characteristics, such as how the gender composition of service members varies by branch and occupational specialty. Many possibilities for detailed subgroup statistics exist within DoD personnel databases but are not routinely published. For example, statistics on race/ethnicity by gender by rank are not currently available. Compiling a complete cross-listing of *all* characteristics that DoD tracks would itself be a monumental task, beyond the scope of this study, and would be costly and impractical for DoD to produce. However, DoD can focus on the intersections that the literature shows are relevant for individual and family well-being and resilience, and for retention and readiness, or for which there is evidence or plausible reason to believe there could be important differences.

One of the purposes of this study is to help DoD think about how service member and family well-being and appropriate interventions can vary by demographic and military service characteristics. In this report, the committee has highlighted certain intersections as they relate to well-being, but there are other important intersections beyond those specifically named that could matter as well.

VETERAN POPULATION

Although the primary focus of this study is military personnel and their families, the study's sponsor asked the committee to be mindful of those who have left the military as well. Thus, we next briefly discuss some key characteristics of the veteran population.

In 2016, veterans were 8 percent of the U.S. adult population. According to the VA's Veteran Population Projection Model 2016,[18] the overall veteran population of 20.0 million in 2017 is expected to decline to 13.6 million in 2037 (U.S. Department of Veterans Affairs [VA], 2016a,b). By generation, Baby Boomers (born between 1946 and 1964), were the largest generation represented among veterans in 2017, but estimates project that the Baby Boomer veteran population will decline and the Millennial veteran population (born between 1977 and 1995) will grow, to the extent that by 2037 these cohorts will be similarly sized. Due primarily to a decline in the number of White veterans, the proportion of minority veterans is expected to grow from 23 percent in 2017 to 33 percent in 2037.

Half of veterans reside in just 10 states: California, Florida, Georgia, Illinois, New York, North Carolina, Ohio, Pennsylvania, Texas, and Virginia (VA, 2016b). Those are the same 10 states that have the largest numbers of reserve component members, and they include 6 of the top 10 states for active component members (DoD, 2017, pp. 91, 35). During the period 2011–2015, about 5 million veterans (24%) lived in areas the U.S. Census Bureau classifies as rural (Holder, 2017); however, a smaller percentage of veterans who served since 2001 live in rural areas (about 18%). Regardless, rural residence can present challenges to accessing VA or other resources that tend to be concentrated in urban areas.

The veteran population is relevant and valuable to the current military population in many ways. Veterans can be spouses or other family members of current military personnel. Many civilian employees who work for DoD or the Services are veterans. Veterans may also be a part of the military community surrounding military bases and thus interact with military families as neighbors, coworkers, fellow students, caretakers, and the like. Retirees may be eligible for and use some of the services provided on military bases

[18]For more information, see https://catalog.data.gov/dataset/vetpop2016.

to promote individual and family well-being. Veterans may also influence their or others' children's decisions to join the military, either directly by encouraging (or dissuading) service, or indirectly by their own example.

Yet our understanding of post-9/11 veterans is extremely limited, and the lack of research on veterans' transition experiences has been noted as a key gap in the literature (Mattox and Pollard, 2016). This lack of empirical information means a dearth of understanding about the concerns that are most relevant to veterans at the time of military separation. Moreover, it has been difficult to determine how veterans' needs change over time, because the vast majority of studies of veterans are cross-sectional (Mattox and Pollard, 2016; Vogt et al., 2018). A number of large-scale longitudinal studies have been done to examine the effects of war-zone deployments on the health and health-related quality of life among U.S., UK, and Canadian veterans (Chesbrough et al., 2002; Mattox and Pollard, 2016; Pinder et al., 2011; Thompson et al., 2013). However, none of these studies has examined how veterans' needs change throughout the period immediately following their transition from service, none has examined how veterans are functioning in terms of employment and finances, and none provides information about the veterans' children or families. A recently longitudinal study, The Veterans Metrics Initiative, attempts to address these shortcomings by becoming the first longitudinal study of the military-to-civilian transition process within a national sample of post-9/11 U.S. veterans (Vogt et al., 2018). Data from this study may provide important information about veterans' well-being, given that this study specifically investigates the well-being of these veterans in four domains: vocational, health, financial, and social.

CONCLUSIONS

Any effort to understand the experiences, attitudes, and needs of U.S. military personnel and their families and what might be needed to best support them must first appreciate the great size of this population and the diversity of its demographic and military service characteristics. As subsequent chapters will show, throughout the committee's work we were ever mindful of the challenges in understanding and supporting diverse individuals and families, dispersed across diverse organizations, locations, and cultures, and all experiencing unique combinations of life events, despite some commonly shared experiences. Indeed, the study's statement of task asked that the committee attend to differences and needs across various population subgroups, to include race, ethnicity, service branches, and other factors. Thus, this chapter provided high-level descriptive statistics on demographic and military service characteristics both as frame of reference for future chapters and to highlight the types of information likely relevant for well-being that DoD does and does not appear to be routinely tracking and types of information it does and does not appear to be making available to others.

To its credit, DoD routinely gathers, stores, and analyzes an extensive amount of administrative and survey data on the demographic and military service characteristics of service members and, to a lesser extent, their spouses and children. These data can and do serve as a valuable resource for understanding variation in military family needs, well-being, and readiness. DoD's online publication of annual demographics profiles and descriptive statistics from major surveys provides context and background information freely accessible not only to military leaders and service providers, but also to military community members, community partners, congressional staffers, researchers, and nonprofit organizations that support service members, veterans, and their families.

Moreover, these data are also used by DoD analysts and other scholars for more sophisticated research related to the well-being of service members and their families. In this chapter, we have highlighted examples of where additional DoD data collection, analyses, or reporting could provide useful information for understanding and addressing the needs of military families.

Having reviewed DoD and non-DoD information on the demographic and military service characteristics of military families, and having considered the types of information that would be useful for understanding the well-being and readiness of military families, the committee draws the following overarching conclusions about the strengths and limitations of DoD's data.

CONCLUSION 3-1: The Department of Defense's existing data on military families are insufficient for understanding the degree to which societal shifts in family structure are reflected in today's measurements of the military community population. Existing data lack information on long-term nonmarital partners, parents, ex-spouses and ex-partners, and others who play a significant role in the care of military children and service members. As a result, current military statistics could mislead policy makers and program managers, potentially resulting in some types of families being underserved by the Military Family Readiness System.

CONCLUSION 3-2: The Department of Defense routinely gathers, stores, and analyzes an extensive amount of administrative and survey data on the demographic and military service characteristics of service members and, to a lesser extent, their spouses and children. These data serve as a valuable resource for understanding variation in military family needs, well-being, and readiness. Purposefully measuring addi-

tional characteristics, including sexual orientation, citizenship status, English as a second language, and Exceptional Family Member Program status by age or relationship to service member, will ensure that the Military Family Readiness System is able to address the variation in military family needs, well-being, and readiness.

REFERENCES

Aronson, K. R., Kyler, S. J., Moeller, J. D., and Perkins, D. F. (2016). Understanding military families who have dependents with special health care and/or educational needs. *Disability and Health Journal*, *9*(3), 423–430.

Burke, J., and Miller, A. R. (2018). The effects of job relocation on spousal careers: Evidence from military change of station moves. *Economic Inquiry*, *56*(2), 1261–1277.

Carroll, C. (2014). Air Force raises enlistee age limit from 27 to 39. *Stars and Stripes*. June 25. Retrieved from https://www.stripes.com/news/air-force/air-force-raises-enlistee-age-limit-from-27-to-39-1.290578.

Chesbrough, K. B., Ryan, M. A., Amoroso, P., Boyko, E. J., Gackstetter, G. D., Hooper, T. I., Riddle, J. R., Gray, G. C., and Millennium Cohort Study Group. (2002). The Millennium Cohort Study: A 21-year prospective cohort study of 140,000 military personnel. *Military Medicine*, *167*(6), 483–488.

Commander Navy Installations Command. (2014). *UFM Quick Reference Guide: A Guide to Uniform Funding Management Support for Fleet and Family Readiness Programs*. Millington, TN: Commander Navy Installations Command.

Copp, T. (2018). Here's the bottom line on the future of MAVNI: Many foreign-born recruits may soon be out. *Military Times*. July 6. Retrieved from https://www.militarytimes.com/news/your-military/2018/07/06/heres-the-bottom-line-on-the-future-of-mavni-many-foreign-born-recruits-may-soon-be-out.

Davis, L., Grifka, A., Williams, K., and Coffey, M. (Eds.). (2017). *2016 Workplace and Gender Relations Survey of Active Duty Members*. Alexandria, VA: U.S. Department of Defense, Office of People Analytics.

Defense Manpower Data Center (DMDC). (2007a). *2006 Survey of Active Duty Spouses: Administration, Datasets, and Codebook*. Arlington, VA: U.S. Department of Defense. Retrieved from https://www.esd.whs.mil/Portals/54/Documents/FOID/Reading%20Room/Personnel_Related/2006_ADSS_Codebook_and_Appendices_A-M-but_not_H.pdf.

_______. (2007b). *2006 Survey of Reserve Component Spouses*. Alexandria, VA: U.S. Department of Defense. Retrieved from http://www.dtic.mil/dtic/tr/fulltext/u2/a473485.pdf.

_______. (2015). *Military Family Life Project: Active Duty Spouse Study Longitudinal Analyses 2010-2012 Project Report*. Department of Defense, Office of the Deputy Assistant Secretary of Defense for Military Community and Family Policy. Retrieved from http://download.militaryonesource.mil/12038/MOS/Reports/MFLP-Longitudinal-Analyses-Report.pdf.

Department of the Air Force. (2009). *Appropriated Fund Support of Morale, Welfare and Recreation (MWR) and Nonappropriated Fund Instrumentalities (NAFIS). (Air Force Instruction 65-106)*. Washington, DC: Department of the Air Force. Retrieved from http://static.e-publishing.af.mil/production/1/saf_fm/publication/afi65-106/afi65-106.pdf.

Department of the Navy. (2007). *Marine Corps Community Services Policy Manual (Marine Corps Order P1700.27B)*. Washington, DC: Headquarters United States Marine Corps. Retrieved from https://www.marines.mil/Portals/59/MCO%20P1700.27B%20W%20CH%201.pdf.

Gates, G. J. (2010). *Lesbian, Gay, and Bisexual Men and Women in the U.S. Military: Updated Estimates*. Los Angeles, CA: The Williams Institute.

Gates, G. J., and Herman, J. L. (2014). *Transgender Military Service in the United States*. Los Angeles, CA: The Williams Institute. Retrieved from https://williamsinstitute.law.ucla.edu/wp-content/uploads/Transgender-Military-Service-May-2014.pdf.

Grifka, A., Davis, L., Klauberg, W., Peeples, H., Moore, A., Hylton, K., and Klahr, A. (2018). *2017 Workplace and Gender Relations Survey of Reserve Component Members: DoD Overview Report*. (No. 2018-026). Alexandria, VA: U.S. Department of Defense Office of People Analytics.

Headquarters Department of the Army. (2010). *Military Morale, Welfare, and Recreation Programs and Nonappropriated Fund Instrumentalities. (Army Regulation 215-1)*. Washington, DC: Headquarters of the Department of the Army. Retrieved from http://www.ssi.army.mil/ncoa/AGS_SLC_ALC_REGS/AR percent20215-1%202010.pdf.

Holder, K. A. (2017). *Veterans in Rural America: 2011–2015: American Community Survey Reports*. (No. ACS-36). Washington, DC: U.S. Census Bureau.

Hunter, C. E., and Smith, L. M. (2012). Exploring the management of religious diversity within the US military. In D. P. McDonald and K. M. Parks (Eds.), *Managing Diversity in the Military: The Value of Inclusion in a Culture of Uniformity* (pp. 188-218). New York: Routledge.

Institute of Medicine. (2011). *The Health of Lesbian, Gay, Bisexual, and Transgender People: Building a Foundation for Better Understanding*. Washington, DC: The National Academies Press.

Joint Chiefs of Staff. (2018). *Joint Guide 1-05 for Religious Affairs in Joint Operations*. Retrieved from http://www.jcs.mil/Portals/36/Documents/Doctrine/jdn_jg/jg1_05.pdf.

Kamarck, K. N. (2019). *Diversity, Inclusion, and Equal Opportunity in the Armed Services: Background and Issues for Congress*. Washington, DC: Congressional Research Service. Retrieved from https://fas.org/sgp/crs/natsec/R44321.pdf.

Kessler, R. C., Colpe, L. J., Fullerton, C. S., Gebler, N., Naifeh, J. A., Nock, M. K., Sampson, N. A., Schoenbaum, M., Zaslavsky, A. M., and Stein, M. B. (2013). Design of the Army Study to Assess Risk and Resilience in Servicemembers (Army STARRS). *International Journal of Methods in Psychiatric Research* 224(4), 267–275.

Lipari, R. N., Forsyth, B., Bose, J., Kroutil, L. A., and Lane, M. E. (2016). *Spouses and Children of US Military Personnel: Substance Use and Mental Health Profile from the 2015 National Survey on Drug Use and Health*. Substance Abuse and Mental Health Administration. Retrieved from https://www.samhsa.gov/data/sites/default/files/NSDUH-MilitaryFamily-2015/NSDUH-MilitaryFamily-2015.htm.

Mattis, J. (2017.) *Military Service by Transgender Individuals—Interim Guidance*. Washington, DC: Department of Defense.

Mattox, T., and Pollard, M. (2016). *Ongoing Survey Research on Post-9/11 Veterans*. Santa Monica, CA: RAND Corporation. Retrieved from https://www.rand.org/content/dam/rand/pubs/research_reports/RR1500/RR1532/RAND_RR1532.pdf.

McIntosh, M. F., Sayala, S., with Gregory, D. (2011). *Non-Citizens in the Enlisted U.S. Military*. Alexandria, VA: CNA.

Meadows, S. O., Engel, C. C., Collins, R. L., Beckman, R., Cefalu, M., Hawes-Dawson, J., Doyle, M., Kress, A. M., Sontag-Padilla, L., Ramchand, R., and Williams, K. M. (2018). *2015 Department of Defense Health Related Behaviors Survey (HRBS)*. Santa Monica, CA: RAND Corporation.

Military Leadership Diversity Commission. (2010). *Religious Diversity in the U.S. Military*. Issue Paper no. 22, Version 2. Arlington, VA: Military Leadership Diversity Commission.

Moradi, B., and Miller, L. (2010). Attitudes of Iraq and Afghanistan war veterans toward gay and lesbian service members. *Armed Forces & Society 36*(3), 397–419.

Office of Management and Budget (OMB). (1997). Revisions to the Standards for the Classification of Federal Data on Race and Ethnicity. *Federal Register 62*(210), 58782-58790. Retrieved from https://www.gpo.gov/fdsys/pkg/FR-1997-10-30/pdf/97-28653.pdf.

_______. (2017). Proposals from the Federal Interagency Working Group for Revision of the Standards for Maintaining, Collecting, and Presenting Federal Data on Race and Ethnicity. *Federal Register 82*(39), 12242-12247. Retrieved from https://www.gpo.gov/fdsys/pkg/FR-2017-03-01/pdf/2017-03973.pdf.

Office of the Under Secretary of Defense, Personnel and Readiness (OUSD P&R). (2018). *Population Representation in the Military Services: Fiscal Year 2016 Summary Report*. Retrieved from https://www.cna.org/pop-rep/2016/summary/summary.pdf.

Parco, J. E., and Levy, D. A. (2010). *Attitudes Aren't Free: Thinking Deeply about Diversity in the US Armed Forces*. Maxwell Air Force Base, AL: Air University Press.

Phillips, D. (2018). Ban was lifted, but transgender recruits still can't join up. *The New York Times*. July 5. Retrieved from https://www.nytimes.com/2018/07/05/us/military-transgender-recruits.html.

Pinder, R. J., Greenberg, N., Boyko, E. J., Gackstetter, G. D., Hooper, T. I., Murphy, D., Ryan, M. A., Smith, B., Smith, T. C., Wells, T. S., and Wessely, S. (2011). Profile of two cohorts: UK and US prospective studies of military health. *International Journal of Epidemiology 41*(5), 1272–1282.

Ramchand, R., Tanielian, T., Fisher, M. P., Vaughan, C. A., Trail, T. E., Epley, C., Voorhies, P., Robbins, M. W., Robinson, E., and Ghosh-Dastidar, B. (2014). *Hidden Heroes: America's Military Caregivers*. Santa Monica, CA: RAND Corporation.

Schaefer, A. G., Iyengar, R., Kadiyala, R., Kavanagh, J., Engel, C. C., Williams, K. M., and Kress, A. M. (2016). *Assessing the Implications of Allowing Transgender Personnel to Serve Openly*. Santa Monica, CA: RAND Corporation.

Stock, M. D. (2013). Hidden immigration benefits for military personnel. *GP Solo Magazine 30*(5).

Tanielian, T., and Jaycox, L. H. (Eds.). (2008). *Invisible Wounds of War: Psychological and Cognitive Injuries, Their Consequences, and Services to Assist Recovery*. Santa Monica, CA: RAND Corporation.

Thompson, J., Hopman, W., Sweet, J., VanTil, L., MacLean, M. B., VanDenKerkhof, E., Sudom, K., Poirier, A., and Pedlar, D. (2013). Health-related quality of life of Canadian Forces veterans after transition to civilian life. *Canadian Journal of Public Health 104*(1), 15–21.

U.S. Census Bureau. (2017). *2015 National Content Test—Race and Ethnicity Analysis Report: A New Design for the 21st Century*. Washington, DC: U.S. Census Bureau. Retrieved from https://assets.documentcloud.org/documents/4316468/2015nct-Race-Ethnicity-Analysis.pdf.

_______. (2018). *2020 Census Program Memorandum Series: 2018.02*. Washington, DC: U.S. Census Bureau. Retrieved from https://assets.documentcloud.org/documents/4360640/2020-Memo-2018-02.pdf.

U.S. Citizenship and Immigration Services (USCIS). (2017, May 19). *Naturalization Fact Sheet*. Retrieved from https://www.uscis.gov/news/fact-sheets/naturalization-fact-sheet.

_______. (2018a, January 8). *Naturalization Through Military Service*. Retrieved from https://www.uscis.gov/military/naturalization-through-military-service.

_______. (2018b, January 26). *Military Naturalization Statistics: Statistics through Fiscal Year 2017*. Retrieved from https://www.uscis.gov/military/military-naturalization-statistics.

_______. (2018c, July 6). *Citizenship for Family Members*. Retrieved from https://www.uscis.gov/military/citizenship-family-members.

U.S. Department of Defense (DoD). (2004). *Demographics 2004: Profile of the Military Community*. Washington, DC. Retrieved from http://download.militaryonesource.mil/12038/MOS/Reports/Combined%20Final%20Demographics%20Report.pdf.

_______. (2007a). *Department of Defense Privacy Program*. (DoD Regulation 5400.11-R). Washington, DC. Retrieved from http://www.esd.whs.mil/Portals/54/Documents/DD/issuances/dodm/540011r.pdf.

_______. (2007b). *Demographics 2007: Profile of the Military Community*. Washington, DC. Retrieved from http://download.militaryonesource.mil/12038/MOS/Reports/2007%20Demographics.pdf.

_______. (2009a). *Military Morale, Welfare, and Recreation (MWR) Programs*. (DoD Instruction 1015.10, Incorporating Change 1, May 6, 2011). Washington, DC. Retrieved from http://www.esd.whs.mil/Portals/54/Documents/DD/issuances/dodi/101510p.pdf.

_______. (2009b). *Accommodation of Religious Practices Within the Military Services*. (DoD Instruction 1300.17, Incorporating Change 1, January 22, 2014). Washington, DC. Retrieved from https://www.esd.whs.mil/Portals/54/Documents/DD/issuances/dodi/130017p.pdf.

_______. (2014). *DoD Privacy Program*. (DoD Directive 5400.11). Washington, DC. Retrieved from http://www.esd.whs.mil/Portals/54/Documents/DD/issuances/dodd/540011p.pdf.

_______. (2015a). *DoD Surveys*. (DoD Instruction 1100.13, Incorporating Change 1, Effective March 21, 2017). Washington, DC. Retrieved from http://www.esd.whs.mil/Portals/54/Documents/DD/issuances/dodi/110013p.pdf.

_______. (2015b). *Qualification Standards for Enlistment, Appointment, and Induction*. (DoD Instruction 1304.26, Incorporating Change 2, April 11, 2017). Washington, DC. Retrieved from http://www.esd.whs.mil/Portals/54/Documents/DD/issuances/dodi/130426p.pdf.

_______. (2015c). *Military Accessions Vital to National Interest (MAVNI) Recruitment Pilot Program*. Washington, DC. Retrieved from https://dod.defense.gov/news/mavni-fact-sheet.pdf.

_______. (2015d). *Memorandum for Secretaries of the Military Departments: Transgender Service Members*. U.S. Department of Defense. Retrieved from https://dod.defense.gov/Portals/1/features/2016/0616_policy/memo-transgender-service-directive-28-July-2015.pdf.

_______. (2016a). *Directive-type Memorandum (DTM) 16-005, "Military Service of Transgender Service Members."* U.S. Department of Defense. Retrieved from https://dod.defense.gov/Portals/1/features/2016/0616_policy/DTM-16-005.pdf.

_______. (2016b). *Transgender Service Member Policy Implementation Fact Sheet*. Washington, DC. Retrieved from https://dod.defense.gov/Portals/1/features/2016/0616_policy/Transgender-Implementation-Fact-Sheet.pdf.

_______. (2017). *2017 Demographics: Profile of the Military Community*. Washington, DC. Retrieved from http://download.militaryonesource.mil/12038/MOS/Reports/2017-demographics-report.pdf.

_______. (2018a). *Medical Standards for Appointment, Enlistment, or Induction into the Military Services (DoD Instruction 6130.03)*. Washington, DC. Retrieved from http://www.esd.whs.mil/Portals/54/Documents/DD/issuances/dodi/613003p.pdf.

_______. (2018b). *Personal Communication of 2017 Service Member and Spouse Survey Statistics to Supplement Statistics Reported in 2017 Demographics: Profile of the Military Community*. Washington, DC.

_______. (2018c). *Department of Defense Report and Recommendations on Military Service by Transgender Persons*. Washington, DC.

_______. (2019a). *Military Service by Transgender Persons and Persons with Gender Dysphoria*. Directive-type memorandum (DTM) 19-004. Washington, DC. Retrieved from https://www.esd.whs.mil/Portals/54/Documents/DD/issuances/dtm/DTM-19-004.pdf?ver=2019-03-13-103259-670.

_______. (2019b). *Personal Communication of 2017 DoD-only Reserve Component Administrative Statistics to Supplement Statistics Reported in 2017 Demographics: Profile of the Military Community*. Washington, DC.

U.S. Department of Defense Education Activity (DoDEA). (2019a). *DoDEA Educational Partnership: About Educational Partnership*. Retrieved from https://www.dodea.edu/Partnership/.

_______. (2019b). *About DoDEA—DoDEA Schools Worldwide*. Retrieved from https://www.dodea.edu/aboutDoDEA/today.cfm.

U.S. Department of Defense Task Force on Mental Health. (2007). *An Achievable Vision: Report of the Department of Defense Task Force on Mental Health*. Falls Church, VA: Defense Health Board. Retrieved from http://www.dtic.mil/dtic/tr/fulltext/u2/a469411.pdf.

U.S. Department of Veteran Affairs (VA). (2016a). *Supportive Services for Veteran Families (SSVF) FY 2016 Annual Report*. Washington, DC. Retrieved from https://www.va.gov/HOMELESS/ssvf/docs/SSVF_FY2016_Annual_Report_508c.pdf.

_______. (2016b). *National Center for Veterans Analysis and Statistics: Veteran Population Infographic*. Retrieved from https://www.va.gov/vetdata/docs/Demographics/New_Vetpop_Model/Vetpop_Infographic_Final31.pdf.

U.S. Government Accountability Office (GAO). (2018). *Military Personnel: DoD Should Improve Its Oversight of the Exceptional Family Member Program*. (No.18-348). Washington, DC.

Villatoro, A. P., Mays, V. M., Ponce, N. A., and Aneshensel, C. S. (2018). Perceived need for mental health care: The intersection of race, ethnicity, gender and socioeconomic status. *Society and Mental Health*, *8*(1), 1–24.

Vogt, D., Perkins, D. F., Copeland, L. A., Finley, E. P., Jamieson, C. S., Booth, B., Lederer, S., and Gilman, C. L. (2018). The Veterans Metrics Initiative study of US veterans' experiences during their transition from military service. *BMJ Open*, *8*(6), 1–10.

Whitestone, Y. K., and Thompson, B. A. (2016). How do military family policies influence parenting resources available to families? In A. H. Gewirtz and A. M. Youssef (Eds.), in *Parenting and Children's Resilience in Military Families* (pp. 283–297). Cham, Switzerland: Springer.

4

Military Life Opportunities and Challenges

To build a clearer picture of military families and gain insights into both their strengths and their needs, in this chapter we build on Chapter 3 by examining the real-life experiences of active and reserve component military personnel and their families. By highlighting the opportunities and challenges of military life at different stages of service and for different subgroups, this chapter offers insights into how major and minor life stressors accumulate and converge to wear down service members and their families, as well as insights into features that mitigate their impact or help provide a safety net, such as a sense of community and opportunities for personal and professional growth.

This chapter is not intended to be a complete listing of all of the major opportunities and challenges of military life. The sponsor of this study will be familiar with these general topics, since understanding what attracts individuals to military service, what supports or impedes performance and deployability, and why personnel leave the military are all key to managing the all-volunteer force. Nevertheless, the challenges highlighted here are likely experienced and managed quite differently by today's military families compared to those who served as recently as 2000.

Military families encounter opportunities and challenges in life, just like any family does, and the life-course of military families is similar to the life-course of their civilian counterparts. However, some experiences are particular to military life or are experienced differently because of the military context in which they occur. Moreover, there is great variability in military experiences across individuals and families.

An extensive body of research has emerged since the terrorist attacks of September 11, 2001 (9/11), which raises questions as to whether and how the experiences of service members and their families have changed with the times, and whether or how these experiences relate to family, such as well-being, resilience, readiness, and retention. Taken individually, the studies each face limitations such as: cross-sectional rather than longitudinal data, difficulties recruiting participations (particularly family members and junior enlisted personnel), relying on parents for insights about children, inability to weight samples to unknown characteristics, sample sizes that limit analyses of small subgroups, and restrictions on access to military populations, datasets, and findings not released to the public. As a body of research, however, considered alongside testimonials, news articles, and DoD-reported facts and figures, there are a number of prominent themes that emerge and questions they invite. The literature echoes most of the significant demands on military personnel and their families as well as influential societal trends that Segal (1986) described more than 30 years ago. However, in light of recent, rapid societal changes (discussed below) and ongoing military efforts to support service members and their families, we must continue to seek to understand how today's families experience and respond to military life.

Recent research has paid particular attention to acute stressors that can be associated with military life, such as combat exposure, traumatic brain injury, family separations during deployment, and post-deployment family reintegration (see Chapters 5 and 6). There are also the daily and chronic stressors that can take a toll on individual or family well-being when they are experienced by particularly vulnerable populations or when they become cumulative, either through the same stressor chronically recurring or through multiple stressors occurring simultaneously. Military families must manage a wide range of stressors, of course, not just those that are particular to military life. At the same time, one should not overlook the aspects of military life that service members and their families may find attractive and beneficial.

This chapter highlights broad categories of opportunities and challenges of military life for active or reserve component[1] military personnel and their families. Several overarching themes frequently appear across reports that convey input from service members and spouses, whether that input is qualitative or quantitative, based on large or small samples, based on opportunity or probabilistic samples, or originate from inside or outside

[1] As noted in Chapter 1, for the reserve component, the committee focuses on the Selected Reserves, which refers to the prioritized reserve personnel who typically drill and train one weekend a month and two additional weeks each year to prepare to support military operations.

of the Department of Defense (DoD). We chose to spotlight the following seven issue areas, which the chapter addresses in turn, because of their prominence and implications for family well-being:

1. Transition into the military
2. Pay and benefits
3. Geographic assignment and relocation
4. Deployments, sea duty, training away from home
5. National Guard and Reserve issues
6. Diversity and inclusion issues
7. Transition out of the military.

These issue areas are all interrelated: we call them out separately to better highlight their contributions or roles as military opportunities or stressors.

OPPORTUNITIES OR CHALLENGES?

In this chapter, the committee has not categorized events or features of military families' lives according to whether they are opportunities or challenges, nor does it presume that all challenges are stressors, for these reasons:

- Some experiences could be opportunities, challenges, *and* stressors—such as job promotion.
- Circumstances may influence how one individual appraises an experience. For example, someone may be eager for a permanent change of station (mandatory moves known as PCS) and to move away from one assignment or town, but then be reluctant to have to move away from another.
- Different individuals have different preferences. For example, some personnel may welcome the opportunity to deploy multiple times, while others may prefer never to deploy.

Nevertheless, some aspects of military life are generally positive, such as opportunities to develop one's skills and to receive steady pay and benefits; others may be generally negative, such as being passed over for promotion; and a few may be potentially catastrophic, such as a service-related permanent disability or the death of a loved one. Figure 4-1 depicts how challenges and opportunities, such as the examples discussed in this chapter, can contribute to or rely upon individual, family, and external resources, such as the ability to cope, social networks, and community organizations. That process can result in positive or negative well-being

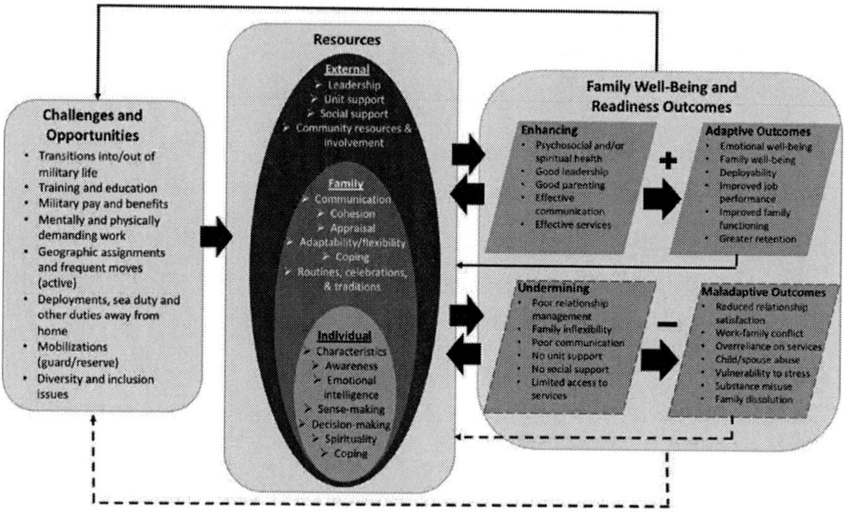

FIGURE 4-1 The military family well-being and readiness model and illustrative elements.
SOURCE: Adapted from in Bowles et al. (2015, Fig. 1).

and readiness outcomes. Managing challenges or opportunities can be an iterative process, one that involves multiple engagements with resources and potentially strengthens or drains resilience factors. These well-being and readiness outcomes can themselves contribute to new challenges or opportunities. This model builds upon a previously proposed Military Family Fitness model (discussed in detail in Bowles et al., 2015), and similarly provides illustrative examples rather than a complete listing in every category.

Military families, particularly those who choose to and are able to remain in the military, can be very adaptable and resilient and can develop healthy coping strategies for the stressors of military life such as moves and deployments (Easterbrooks et al., 2013; Meadows et al., 2016). Military families can develop their own norms and rhythms for the process of managing family separations or moves and for finding out about the right networks, programs, and services available for their particular needs. Children's responses to the opportunities and strains of military family life are likely to depend on parental and family maturity and the individual child's developmental stage, temperament, and social capacity. Based on individual differences within the same family, one child can thrive and another struggle.

The impact of the challenges and opportunities of military life can be shaped by the *duration* and *timing* of these events as well. For example, a deployment can be a short mission to transport equipment, supplies, or personnel overseas and back, or it can require service members to live and operate in a combat zone for a year or longer. On the positive side, longer deployments can offer greater opportunities to hone leadership and occupational skills, enhance the ability to compete for promotion or key assignments, and increase service-member income through special pays and tax benefits. However, longer duration deployments can also increase service members' exposure to hazardous environments (e.g., chemical, biological, climatic); present greater risk of war-related injury, death, or exposure to traumatic events; lengthen family separations; and cause service members to miss major milestones such as births and holidays. Individual family members are developing throughout their lives, and the timing of particular events relative to individual development may be consequential.

Early experiences can shape responses to later—sometimes much later—events (Wilmoth and London, 2013). For example, service members' exposure to adverse events such as abuse or violence prior to joining the military can affect their likelihood of later post-traumatic stress disorder (PTSD) or suicide (Carroll et al., 2017). Military service typically begins during the transition to adulthood, with the possibility of enhancing or disrupting the trajectories of individuals' later work and family lives. Service members' military experiences may alter the career trajectories of their spouses or partners (Kleykamp, 2013). An individual could become a military spouse or partner well before their own careers have been established, or long afterward. That timing could result in differing processes for managing the demands of military life, differing levels of resilience resources, and differing types of need for support. Timing is particularly salient in childhood, when development happens so rapidly. For example, children's experiences with relocations may affect later school performance (Lyle, 2006; Moeller et al., 2015). Effects of the content and timing of life experiences can cascade across developmental domains, such that early difficulties at school might lead to later difficulties in relationships with peers (Masten, 2013; Masten and Cicchetti, 2010).

These long-term effects of military experiences may be positive, as the "military-as-turning-point" perspective attests; they may be neutral; or they may be negative, as expressed in the "life-course disruption" perspective (Segal et al., 2015; Wilmoth and London, 2013). The impact of life events and transitions is conditioned by their characteristics, such as how expected, how abrupt, or how traumatic they are (Boss, 2002). In addition, both risks and resilience factors can accumulate to create mutually reinforcing 'caravans' that move together over time, accelerating positive or negative effects (Layne et al., 2014).

Timing also refers to the historical and social context of military service. MacLean and Elder (2007), for example, documented how the effects of military service varied substantially across conflicts during the 20th century, as societal perceptions of those conflicts shifted. Historical changes in military compensation and educational benefits can also shape both the attractiveness and the consequences of military service. Attitudes of the public toward service members and their families can be powerful influences on the consequences of military service, leading to both positive consequences, such as special efforts to employ veterans, and negative ones, such as society's failure to seek out military and veteran families as assets to their communities (MacLean and Elder, 2007).

THE CONTEXT OF MILITARY FAMILY LIFE: YESTERDAY VERSUS TODAY

The context of military service is dramatically different today from what it was when the all-volunteer force was designed. Today, U.S. forces increasingly serve in diverse missions, including combat, peacekeeping, disaster relief, public health and humanitarian efforts, and homeland security. Many missions, such as those that involve technology or long-term engagement with local populations overseas, require expert knowledge and advanced skills that take years to develop. Today's armed forces prepare for and carry out missions not only in the air, on the land, and on the sea, but through space and cyberspace. Unlike during the Cold War era, today the military is focused not on a single main adversary but on ever-changing threats from state and nonstate actors around the globe. In addition, the National Guard and the Reserves have been called up like never before in our nation's military history (Commission on the National Guard and Reserves, 2008).

As discussed in chapters 2 and 3, today's military personnel and military families are more diverse than ever (DoD, 2017a; Hawkins et al., 2018). The proportions of military personnel who are women, who are dual-military couples, and who are racial and ethnic minorities have all grown. As of 2011, gay, lesbian, and bisexual service members have been allowed to serve openly, and now dependent benefits extend to same-sex spouses. Occupations and units that had been closed to women have gradually opened, and by 2016 the policies that had excluded them from the remaining combat positions were lifted. Also, as discussed in Chapter 3, in 2016, the secretary of defense ended the ban on transgender service (DoD, 2015), which was reversed effective April 2019, with certain exemptions for those diagnosed with gender dysphoria after the ban was lifted (DoD, 2019). There is no ban on transgender military dependents, however, and these dependents have been increasingly seeking gender affirming care through the military health system since it became available in 2016 (Klein et al., 2019; Van Donge et al., 2019).

The number of military dependents continues to outnumber service members by increasingly large margins, and survey data suggest that there are also significant numbers of unmarried partners of personnel in long-term relationships (see Chapter 3) (DoD, 2018). The younger generations have grown up with smartphones, computer tablets, ubiquitous Internet access, GPS-based location and mapping services, online search engines, and the use of social media to create and share content with others (e.g., Facebook, Twitter, Instagram, Snapchat, Reddit, YouTube). Another important development is that today's military and veteran family populations are more likely than those of past wars to include individuals with physical and mental wounds and challenges, because service members who historically would have died of battlefield wounds, illnesses, or injuries have survived in recent wars due to advances in military medicine, in training, and in aeromedical evacuations.[2]

Geographic distribution has shifted as well. Today's military families do not necessarily live near other military families or installation-based support services. Instead, they live across communities that are more geographically dispersed, rather than being concentrated in specific neighborhoods, as the active component has shifted from living primarily on military installations to living primarily off-installation (DoD, 2017a). Some families do live in regions with a greater concentration than average of military and veteran families, as noted in Chapter 3. One way in which active component military personnel have become *less* diverse is that they are increasingly likely to have come from the South and least likely to come from the Northeast (Maley and Hawkins, 2018). Recent analyses find that these regional differences are largely explained by differences in demographic characteristics, such as race, education, and religious adherence (Maley and Hawkins, 2018). Nevertheless, the armed forces still bring together individuals from diverse communities across the United States who work and sometimes live together but who are also immersed in nonmilitary communities.

The structure of DoD's personnel system has important implications for service member and family retention and readiness. To compete with civilian job market opportunities and mitigate the impacts of the demands of military life, particularly post-9/11, support programs for military personnel and their families have grown enormously. However, decades of research continue to show that other one-size-fits-all legacy aspects of the military personnel system, such as the up-or-out policy of promotion, frequent relocation, lack of individual and family control over placements and timing, and the standardization of career pathways, can often negatively impact service members and their families; moreover, they can also increase the military's expenses and limit its ability to develop, assign, and retain the optimal staffing for its needs (Carter et al., 2017; Task Force on Defense

---

[2]For further details, see health.mil/Reference-Center/Publications/2016/09/01/Advances-in-Army-Medicine-since-9-11.

Personnel, 2017). Turnover is highest among women (DACOWITS, 2017) and among the junior ranks, where DoD has invested heavily in training and support but has not yet seen the yield of those costs (GAO, 2017).

The widespread access to the internet and the rise of social media and smartphone use can facilitate information sharing, communication with friends and loved ones, self-expression, education, access to services, social networking, mentoring, translation, job and housing searches, and staying in touch with "battle buddies" after moves and deployments. But these digital developments can also be new channels for deception, inappropriate content, misinformation, information overload, abuse and harassment (e.g., cyberbullying, revenge porn, trolling), and distractions from real-world obligations and face-to-face interactions. Additionally, for many members of the American public the news media is the primary or sole source of information about U.S. military members, veterans, and their families, and this in turn can contribute to stereotyping, both positive and negative (Kleykamp and Hipes, 2015; Parrott et al., 2018; Substance Abuse and Mental Health Services Administration, 2013).

The Pew Research Center estimates that U.S. internet use among adults has grown from 52 percent in 2000 to 89 percent in 2018 (Pew Research Center, 2018a). Social media use among adults has grown from 5 percent in 2005 (when Pew first began to collect estimates) to 69 percent in 2018 (Pew Research Center, 2018b). Smartphone ownership among adults rose from 35 percent in 2011 to 77 percent in 2018 (Pew Research Center, 2018c). Usage rates are even higher among younger adults; for example, 94 percent of those ages 18 to 29 had a smartphone in 2018, compared to 73 percent of adults ages 50 to 64 (Pew Research Center, 2018c).

Given these rapid changes over the past decade and a half—in military life, deployments, societal views, family arrangements, and digital access—to the extent possible we have relied in this study on the most recent literature, highlighting where there is still significant work to be done as well as where new developments may call for new strategies or new perspectives on perennial issues. We emphasize that many of the stressors of military life are not inevitable, inherent features, but policies that could be adapted to allow for greater flexibility for the preferences and needs of the diverse individuals and families DoD needs to attract and retain in order to meet the demands of the current and anticipated future national security environment.

TRANSITION INTO THE MILITARY

The military invests significant resources to attract quality recruits and transform them into disciplined and skilled military personnel. Most young Americans do not meet military recruitment standards because of their weight, drug or alcohol abuse, physical or mental health conditions, criminal record, or other such issues. Among youths ages 17 to 24, only about 29 percent (9.6 million) meet all the core eligibility requirements and would be able to enlist without a waiver (JAMRS, 2016, p. 5). Narrowed further to youths who are not enrolled in college and able to score average or better on the Armed Forces Qualification Test, the pool drops to 13 percent of youths (4.4 million) (JAMRS, 2016, p. 5). That figure does not account for individuals' interest in serving in the military or reflect that the military must compete with other organizations with similar employment criteria, such as law enforcement agencies, fire departments, and the Department of Homeland Security.

The estimated cost to recruit, screen, and train each new enlistee is approximately $75,000 (GAO, 2017). Rapid and successful adaptation to military life is key to military family readiness as well as to reducing attrition (failure to complete the first term of service) and increasing the retention of quality personnel beyond the first term of service. First terms of enlistment are typically 4 to 6 years long, but in fiscal year 2011 approximately 27 percent active component enlistees had separated from the military before they had completed 4 years of service, and close to 10 percent of new enlistees had attritted within just 6 months of service (GAO, 2017, p. 12). The recorded indicators of why service members attrite provide little insight, since the leading documented reason was the catch-all "unqualified for active duty, other" (GAO, 2017, p. 14).[3]

This section considers some of the benefits and challenges that new service members may encounter as they transition into the service and into their first duty stations. Prominent examples from the literature and other sources (e.g., testimonials) discussed here are summarized in Box 4-1. As noted earlier in this chapter, the committee does not sort issues into positive and negative categories, because characterization may depend upon the context and circumstances, the time at which they occur, individuals' own vulnerabilities and interpretations, and other factors. Also, even positive changes can serve as stressors, and both positive and negative experiences can result in individual growth and enhanced resilience. The issues discussed in this section apply to both active and reserve component individuals, and many of them extend throughout the military life course.

For most service members, transitioning from civilian life into military service is typically simultaneous with the transition to adulthood (Kelty et al., 2010). Some military spouses and partners are also experiencing this transition. As discussed in Chapter 3, 40 percent of service members and

---

[3]Less common reasons for attrition, in order of occurrence (specific numbers not provided), were drug abuse; disability, severance pay; failure to meet weight or body fat standards; character or behavior disorder; temporary disability retirement; pregnancy; permanent disability retirement; fraudulent entry; and alcoholism (GAO, 2017, p. 14).

BOX 4-1
Examples of Prominent Themes Associated with Transition into and Service in the Military

- Unfamiliar jargon, rules, regulations, culture, organization
- Training in life skills (e.g., discipline, health behaviors, teamwork, problem-solving, first aid, survival, financial management)
- Occupational training and skill mastery
- Opportunities for personal growth, career advancement, raises, awards, and continued education and training
- Development of physical strength, fitness, endurance, coordination
- Sense of community, belonging, camaraderie, esprit de corps
- Pride in serving the nation, prestige of military affiliation
- For many, entry coinciding with transition to adulthood
- Early-in-life opportunities for responsibility, power, authority
- Loss of privacy, restrictions on social relationships, greater intrusion into personal realm than experienced in most civilian jobs
- Subjection to military law enforcement and criminal justice system

19 percent of military spouses are age 25 or younger (DoD, 2017c, pp. 8, 125). Military service often begins with geographic separation from friends and family, as service and occupational entry-level training typically take even members of the National Guard and Reserves away from their hometowns. After initial entry training, reserve component personnel may return to their hometowns and be able to put down roots, but geographic separation from friends and family will be an ongoing feature of military life for many service members.

Especially for those not raised in a military family, entering service can require quite an adjustment to elements of military life. Military jargon, acronyms, organization, culture, and rules and regulations may present a steep learning curve. The loss of a certain degree of privacy—not just of physical space but also potentially loss of privacy of health records if deemed a military necessity—may also require an adjustment.

Military service can also provide a range of intangible benefits. Service members and families alike may greatly enjoy a sense of belonging, a sense of community, camaraderie and esprit de corps. Of course, not everyone who values those qualities feels valued and fully included in their military community. Being ostracized, socially excluded, or otherwise rejected in a tight-knit community can be physically and psychologically painful; DoD policy prohibits such treatment but only when it takes the form of retaliation for reporting crimes (McGraw, 2016; Williams, 2007). In such environments, members may consider the risks of exclusion, ostracization, or other retaliation when reporting misconduct or criminal behavior within the community, or revealing anything that may be stigmatized in that particular community.

New service members may be in a particularly vulnerable position in the organization given their relative unfamiliarity with the rules, regulations, and acceptable norms, and given the power imbalance between them and authority figures who have significant influence over their careers. This may put them at greater risk for abuse, such as sexual harassment or sexual assault (Davis et al., 2017) and hazing rituals (Office of Diversity Management and Equal Opportunity, 2017).

At the same time, it may not be long into a military career before a new service member gains the opportunity to hold a level of responsibility, authority, or power that someone their age and background might rarely experience in a civilian job. For example, recent college graduates (young military officers) can be sent to military operations or battlefields overseas, be held responsible for the lives of their charges, operate multimillion-dollar equipment, control weapons that could cause major loss of life and damage to infrastructure, and be expected to maintain the peace on the ground in an area of heightened tensions.

Related to the hierarchical structure of the organization and the stakes of military missions, the military forbids certain types of relationships. *Fraternization* refers to Service and DoD policies prohibiting certain relationships that can compromise or appear to compromise the chain of command. Although the term is often used to refer to romantic or sexual relationships, it can also refer to friendships, business partnerships, or other relationships that may indicate a supervisor or commander who is unable to be fair or impartial, who is using rank or position for personal gain or to take advantage of subordinates, or who would not have the ability to exert their authority properly. An example is officers who are too informal with and too often socialize with their subordinates outside of official settings and then find they cannot command effectively in military operations.

Military work can be challenging in both growth-enhancing and negative ways. Less desirable challenges include too-heavy work demands, particularly if they are seemingly relentless, are related to tasks that do not seem essential, or are perceived as being the consequence of poor leadership or organizational management. Examples might include long hours, understaffing, stressful work, or being frequently called away from home for temporary duty (TDY), training, unaccompanied tours, or deployments. As the next chapters will discuss further, traumatic military experiences can include participation in or exposure to combat or its aftermath, being taken a prisoner of war, and being physically or sexually abused, harassed, or assaulted by fellow DoD personnel or contractors.

Military service, awards, and promotions can become a source of pride. On the other end of the spectrum, disciplinary action can be a risk to well-being, and family members may feel the brunt of the consequences economically or by reputation if their service member is confined, docked pay, demoted, required to perform additional duties, denied reenlistment, or discharged.

Officer and enlisted transitions into the military are not equivalent. Officers obtain a college degree prior to obtaining their commission, and thus on average are older and have a higher level of education. Poorer family well-being has been consistently correlated with lower rank (Hawkins et al., 2018, Key Findings, p. ES-8). In addition, there is evidence that enlisted ranks may be at higher risk of developing or reporting post-traumatic stress disorder (PTSD) (Hawkins et al., 2018, p. 31; Lester et al., 2010). Service members in the lower enlisted ranks and their spouses experience more isolation than officers and their families, and officers' children have been reported to use more effective coping skills than those of lower-ranked parents (Hawkins et al., 2018, p. 4; Lucier-Greer et al., 2016). Not surprisingly, military families with lower incomes (such as those with members in the junior enlisted ranks) experience less financial stability and more strain than those with higher incomes. For married or partnered service members, unemployment or underemployment of nonmilitary spouses and disruption of their career progression are often by-products of aspects of the military lifestyle, and these consequences are further affected by a spouse's gender and by the service member's paygrade (Shiffer, et al., 2017).

PAY AND BENEFITS

Service members and their families can benefit from various levels of military pay, health care, housing or housing allowances, education and training (or financial assistance to support it), subsidized child care, and recreational activities, facilities, and discounts. Eligibility can vary by active and reserve component military status, as noted in the examples summarized in Box 4-2). More benefits are available to service members on active duty status, as they are full-time military personnel. Members of the active component and the Reserves always serve under federal control (Title 10), and that is true regardless of whether members of the Reserves are on active duty or reserve status. Members of the National Guard serve under federal control when they are called up for a federal mission, which could include being mobilized for war or providing domestic assistance during national emergencies. When not on Title 10 orders, however, National Guard members work for their states. Responding to natural disasters or accidents as well as homeland security missions could fall under either federal (Title 10) or state (Title 32) control.[4]

[4]For more information on National Guard domestic operations and authorities, see U.S. Departments of the Army and the Air Force (2008).

BOX 4-2
Examples of Prominent Themes Associated with Military Pays and Benefits

For active component and reserve component members when on Title 10 active duty:

- Stable military employment
- Standard military basic pay based on rank and time in service
- Paid leave
- Special and incentive pays (e.g., flight pay, critical language skills pay, enlistment or reenlistment bonuses for hard-to-fill occupations)
- Retirement plans
- Health care coverage (partners not covered, but in those households, the service member and child(ren) are covered)
- Housing or housing allowance
- Occupational training and professional military education
- Tuition assistance, college credits for military training and experience
- Post-9/11 GI Bill
- Quality subsidized child care (though often with limited capacity)
- Morale, welfare, and recreation programs and facilities

For reserve component members when not on Title 10 active duty:

- Stable military employment
- Reserve drill pay based on rank and time in service
- Retirement plans
- Special and incentive pays (akin to those noted above)
- Occupational training and professional military education
- Tuition assistance, college credits for military training and experience
- Post-9/11 GI Bill

NOTES: Pays and benefits subject to certain conditions. For detail on current pays and benefits, see https://militarypay.defense.gov/.

Because military service offers the promise of financial stability and upward mobility for many families, service members who come from lower socioeconomic backgrounds are over-represented in the forces (Kelty and Segal, 2013) and within the enlisted ranks, although they are by no means the only socioeconomic class of individuals to join the all-volunteer force. Military service offers opportunities for overcoming structural and cumulative disadvantage among those who have been raised in poorer families and communities and received low-quality education, including among racial and ethnic minority groups (Bennett and McDonald, 2013).

Youth from disadvantaged backgrounds often have relatively few options for accessing jobs that provide living wages and skill development or higher education. Thus, military service offers the potential for socioeconomic advancement through competitive wages, educational achievement, including a pathway to college, housing, and health benefits (Bennett and McDonald, 2013, p. 138). In addition, service members have the flexibility to use their service to acquire needed training and skills for later entry into the civilian labor market or may stay in the military through retirement. Military employment opportunities can appeal to the middle class as well, for reasons such as the cost of financing a college education or vocational training, alternative entry-level employment for American youths looking for benefits and on-the-job training, and employment opportunities during economic downturns such as the Great Recession of 2008.

Pay

Among the major benefits of military service are steady earnings and employment for service members. For active duty service, those earnings include paid leave and pay when sick or off-duty recovering from injuries. Some personnel will qualify for bonuses or special pays based on the military's need, their specialized skills, or their duty conditions (e.g., enlistment and re-enlistment bonuses, pays for critical skills, hazardous duty incentive pay, flight pay, family separation allowance, tax breaks).[5] Increases in active and reserve component base pay correspond to increasing rank and years of service, regardless of age, gender, race, ethnicity, or sexual orientation. However, there is not proportional representation across ranks and occupations by gender, race, or ethnicity. We cannot determine representation across ranks and occupations in terms of lesbian, gay, bisexual, or transgender (LGBT) service members due to limited systematic data. In the past, the military's pay structure has resulted in a significantly smaller, though still present, wage gap between African American and White service members (Booth and Segal, 2005).

Over time, there have been fluctuations in approved pay, incentives, and the design of the retirement system. One of the most significant recent changes is the new Blended Retirement System, which took effect January 1, 2018. This now provides options to the military's legacy system, which had previously allowed only personnel who had served 20 years or more to receive retirement benefits, and those were in the form of monthly payments. The new system includes a Thrift Savings Plan (similar to a 401(k) retirement savings plan), a pay bonus for those who continue beyond 12 years of service, and an annuity payment calculated with a

[5]For military pay charts, see https://www.dfas.mil/militarymembers/payentitlements/Pay-Tables.html.

2 percent multiplier (rather than 2.5% multiplier under the legacy system).[6] The preferences of service members and their families, and the impact of their choices (e.g., lump sum instead of monthly payout, Thrift Savings Plan option), remain to be seen.

In periods of downsizing, service members can be incentivized to leave voluntarily before their term of service ends, or involuntarily "let go" even if they have not done anything wrong. So a military term of service is not without uncertainties; however, such unexpected discharges tend to be less common than in the civilian sector. Service members serve under a contract or commitment for length of service: although some young adults might find it daunting to make a 4- to 6-year commitment to a job and an employer, especially not knowing what it will be like, where they will be serving, or what their boss or co-workers will be like, others may find the job security reassuring.

Financial Stress and Food Insecurity

Although service members receive steady pay and benefits, they may still struggle financially. Varied sources of data, including the 2013 Status of Forces Survey of Active Duty Members, indicate that junior enlisted families with children are the most vulnerable to experiencing food insecurity, although systematic data on the proportion or characteristics of military families who are food insecure is limited (GAO, 2016). Analyses of nationally representative data on veterans have found that veterans serving during the all-volunteer era have had significantly higher odds of food insecurity when compared to either veterans serving during the previous era or to civilian households (Miller et al., 2016). There are 18 federal programs for food assistance, such as the Supplemental Nutrition Assistance Program (SNAP), Temporary Assistance for Needy Families (TANF), Special Supplemental Nutrition Program for Women, Infants, and Children (WIC), and free and reduced-lunch programs, all of which have different eligibility criteria and access points (GAO, 2016). Military personnel are not ineligible for these programs. In 2015, 24 percent of children in Department of Defense Education Activity (DoDEA) schools qualified for reduced lunch, and another 21 percent qualified for free lunch (GAO, 2016).

Due to limited systematic data from these benefit providers, DoD does not have a comprehensive picture of the extent to which service members need or use food assistance programs (GAO, 2016, p. 13). Nevertheless, the use of SNAP among service members, while hard to measure exactly,

[6]For an overview of the new system in a reader-friendly format, see https://militarypay.defense.gov/Portals/3/Documents/BlendedRetirementDocuments/A%20Guide%20to%20the%20Uniformed%20Services%20BRS%20December%202017.pdf.

indicates that food insecurity is significant. According to estimates from a 2013 Census Bureau survey, approximately 23,000 active duty service members utilized SNAP in the previous 12 months (GAO, 2016). London and Heflin (2015) examined SNAP use by active duty, veteran, and reservist participants in the American Community Survey from 2008 to 2012 and reported that use was low but "non-trivial" among the active duty respondents (2.2%), while use was 9 percent among surveyed reservists, and about 7 percent among veterans. More recently, service members on active duty spent over $21 million in food stamp benefits at military commissaries from September 2014 through August 2015 (GAO, 2016).

As is the case for people struggling financially in the civilian sector, service members and their families face both logistical challenges and stigma in seeking food assistance (GAO, 2016, p. 21). Specifically, military families may have limited awareness of assistance programs and may assume that they do not qualify or may fear being stigmatized for using the services.

Health Care

Particularly relevant to the well-being of military families is free military health care, a benefit that extends to service members and their legal dependents. The military health care system covers preventive care, maternity care, hospitalization, outpatient procedures, mental health care, prescription medications, catastrophic illnesses, and preexisting conditions. This system is discussed more thoroughly in subsequent chapters, but it may be worth noting here that critiques of it include long wait times, poor care quality, limited access to specialists, and limited access for members of the National Guard and Reserves who are not serving on Title 10 active duty orders.

Supplemental to the military mental health care system are confidential, short-term nonmedical counseling options, akin to employee assistance program offerings, that help families with issues such as coping with a loss, stress management, work-life balance, managing deployment issues, and parenting and relationship challenges. These options, available through Military OneSource and the Military and Family Life Counseling Program, have been positively rated by most participants; however, these limited sessions alone are not likely to be able to resolve complex or severe problems, and awareness of this benefit may be limited among military families (Trail et al., 2017).

Housing

For active component personnel, military service includes on-installation housing or a housing allowance adjusted to the local housing market and intended to cover the cost of housing in the local economy.

Military housing varies from installation to installation in terms of modernization, configuration, and location relative to other buildings, but regardless of this, housing options will vary based on personnel's rank group and dependent status. DoD sets minimum configuration and privacy standards for housing, so that higher-ranking personnel have more space and more privacy than lower-ranking personnel. For example, all senior noncommissioned officers (NCOs) (pay grades E-7 to E-9), warrant officers, and commissioned officers unaccompanied by military dependents must have a private housing unit with a private bedroom, bathroom, kitchen, and living room; junior NCOs (pay grades E-5 to E-6) may live in a shared unit, but must have at least a private bedroom and a bathroom shared with not more than one other person; and junior enlisted personnel (E-1 to E-4) may live in a shared unit with a bedroom and bathroom shared with one other person (DoD, 2010, p. 25). Thus, junior enlisted and junior NCO housing may resemble shared college dormitory or shared apartment living, but even the most junior officers without dependents will have private housing.

Family housing on installations accommodates service members accompanied by dependents, and families are not required to share a unit with another family. DoD guidance is for commanders to make reasonable attempts, based on the inventory and need, to provide family housing that will allow each dependent to have a bedroom, or at least share it with no more than one other "unless the installation commander determines the bedroom is large enough to accommodate more" (DoD, 2010, p. 14). Generally, family housing is separate from unaccompanied housing, and unaccompanied housing units are grouped by whether they house junior enlisted members, NCOs, or officers.

Over the last several decades, there has been a major shift among active component personnel and their spouses and children, from living primarily on installations to living primarily off of them and not necessarily even living close to their assigned installations. This shift in residence offers benefits to service members, including greater privacy, greater opportunities for single service members to meet potential partners, opportunities to live with nonmarital partners or others of one's choosing, more control over the choice of neighborhood and housing, and more choice over how the home is kept and decorated.

The downsides of this shift include a more dispersed military community, neighbors who may know little about the military or even be hostile to it, additional time taken out of every work day to commute and get through the morning line at the gate to the installation (and potentially the need for a car where one otherwise would not have existed), the possibility of choosing housing that is more expensive than one can responsibly afford, and greater challenges for leadership and service providers in identifying families that are isolated or in trouble.

Education and Training

In addition to entry-level, on-the-job, and more advanced occupational training, the military can support other types of service member education. The military service academies are highly competitive colleges that provide a full-time, 4-year college degree, plus room and board, educational expenses, and military and other training opportunities at no expense to the students or their families, in exchange for a minimum service commitment once the graduate is commissioned as a military officer. Under competitive Reserve Officer Training Corps (ROTC) scholarships, students receive full or partial scholarships for tuition, books, and fees at a civilian university, along with military training, in exchange for a minimum service commitment (also as an officer). Enlisted personnel are also able to compete to attend the academies or receive an ROTC scholarship.

The military also sponsors relevant graduate degrees for selected officers. Graduate degrees may help officers prepare for military careers. For example, the Uniformed Services University of the Health Sciences provides a tuition-free medical school education plus a salary of $64,000 or more for selected service members to pursue their degree and obtain leadership training, in exchange for an additional service commitment after graduation.[7] Some officers may have opportunities to earn PhDs in graduate schooling sponsored by the military, but this is not the norm. More commonly, during the course of officers' careers there are often opportunities to obtain military-sponsored master's degrees at military graduate schools, such as the Air Force Institute of Technology, Marine Corps University, National Defense University, Naval Postgraduate School, and the U.S. Army War College, or occasionally at civilian institutions. Some families are geographically separated while officers attend graduate programs in-residence for a year, and then reunite through a permanent change of station (PCS) to the next duty station. For this reason, among others, graduate study can therefore be both an opportunity and a stressor.

As enlisted personnel move up the organizational hierarchy, professional military education helps prepare them for the leadership and management duties that noncommissioned officers must take on. As is the case for officers, these professional development opportunities for selected enlisted personnel will be paid for by the military. Enlisted personnel and officers alike may take advantage of Defense Voluntary Education benefits, including education counseling services, testing services, academic skills training, tuition assistance, and college credit exams. Through use of a Joint Services Transcript, they can also have their military training translated into

[7]See https://www.usuhs.edu/medschool/admissions.

equivalent civilian college credits. The 2008 Post-9/11 GI Bill[8] offers service members postsecondary education tuition assistance, a living allowance, and related expenses, and personnel with a minimum number of years of service can transfer some or all of these benefits to a spouse or child(ren). In less than a decade, more than one million service members and veterans and more than 200,000 dependents utilized this benefit (Wenger et.al., 2017, p. xii).

Service members may take college classes on their own time, and enlisted personnel may earn an associate's degree, bachelor's degree, or license or certificate beyond their military training. Some civilian colleges and universities even offer courses located on military installations, and of course many schools today offer courses online, which can provide opportunities for military families that lack the transportation or travel time to attend school on-campus.

Local installations typically offer classes to service members, and in some cases their families, for recreation, well-being, or self-improvement. Examples from the wide range of class subjects include stress management, anger management, communication, time management, financial management and budgeting, auto repair and maintenance, scuba, arts and crafts, yoga, nutrition, healthy cooking, smoking cessation, disease management (e.g., asthma, diabetes), parenting, job search skills, and English as a second language.

Child Care

A key benefit of active component military service is access to quality affordable child care. As outlined in Chapter 3, the military is a young force with many young families. Indeed, the average age of the active component force is 28 years old (DoD, 2017c, p. iv). More than one-half of all active component members are married, and 43 percent of spouses are age 30 or younger. Nearly 41 percent of active component personnel have children; almost 38 percent of these children are age 5 or younger, and 69 percent are age 11 or younger.

DoD is the provider of the nation's largest employer-sponsored child care system, serving approximately 180,000 children ranging in age from birth to age 12 (DoD, 2016a). More than 700 DoD child development centers and child care facilities are located across more than 230 installations worldwide (DoD 2017b, pp. 3–4).

In terms of both cost and quality, DoD's child development program is viewed as a model of child care for the nation. The quality of DoD child care is upheld through national accreditation standards; 97 percent of DoD

[8]Title 38 U.S.C., Chapter 33, Sections 3301 to 3324 – Post-9/11 Educational Assistance.

child development centers are accredited (DoD, 2017b). More broadly, one report notes that, "Nationally, only 11 percent of child care establishments are accredited by the National Association for the Education of the Young Child or the National Association for Family Child Care" (Schulte and Durana, 2016). The affordability of DoD's child development program for service members and their families is assured by appropriated funding. The National Defense Authorization Act (NDAA) of 1996 required that the amount appropriated by Congress for child development centers must equal or exceed what service members pay in fees. On average, these subsidies cover about 64 percent of the cost of military installation child care, which for each child includes 50 hours of care a week and two meals and two snacks per day, with all families paying some fees based on an income scale (Floyd and Phillips, 2013, p. 85). Free respite care provides a temporary break in caregiving to spouses whose service member is deployed overseas or to families with children with special needs.

However, civilian child care for infants and toddlers is costly, so demand for subsidized military child care for this age group is high and child care spaces are limited. In 2016, at 32 percent of installations the wait lists for child care exceeded 3 months—in particular, areas with large military populations and a high cost of living, such as San Diego (California), Hawaii, the Tidewater Region of Virginia, and the National Capitol Region (DoD, 2016b).

Limited access to child care and lengthy wait times are key concerns for many military families. In a 2017 Blue Star Families survey, 67 percent of military family respondents indicated they are not always able to obtain the childcare they need. The survey found that the top employment obstacles reported by military spouse respondents who wanted to be working but were not, were service member job demands (55%), child care (53%), and family commitments (43%), rather than lack of job skills or opportunities (Shiffer et al., 2017). Moreover, 67 percent of female service members and 33 percent of male service members reported they could not find child care that worked with their schedules (Shiffer et al., 2017). That finding was reinforced by focus groups that also emphasized the mismatch between the hours military child care is available and the needs of service women (DACOWITS, 2017). Although the survey and focus groups may not be representative samples, it is clear from these and numerous sources over recent decades that there is a high demand for more affordable, quality child care and that DoD's capacity still has not yet been able to fully meet the need (DACOWITS, 2017; Hawkins et al., 2018; Huffman et al., 2017; Zellman et al., 2009).

By DoD's own metrics, in fiscal year 2015 it was only able to meet 78 percent of the child care needs of military families, rather than its goal of 80 percent, and was reaching into the civilian community to expand child care, as well as building new child care facilities while repairing or replacing aging ones (DoD 2017b, p. 5). Additionally, as part of a secretary of defense initiative, in 2016 installations began offering extended child care hours to better align with service member schedules. Some child development centers faced hurdles in recruiting and hiring providers, however, which Congress addressed in the fiscal year 2018 NDAA by modifying the hiring authorities (Kamarck, 2018). Time will tell how much headway these reforms will be able to contribute toward better meeting the child care needs of military families with children. DoD may need to increase its goal for how much of the child care need it aims to meet, although not *all* eligible parents of military children needing child care services will likely wish to use DoD's.

Activities, Facilities, and Discounts

Other benefits of military service include free or low-cost recreational facilities, such as installation pools, fitness centers, movie theaters, golf courses and hobby shops; rental of outdoor equipment, such as kayaks, bikes, and camping gear; ticketing services for activities, such as concerts, festivals, amusement parks, and comedy shows; and free or discounted flight opportunities. Additionally, some businesses and organizations offer discounts to military personnel and their families, such as free or discounted admission to zoos, parks, and museums. Many of these benefits provide access to venues through which community and family bonds are built and reinforced, and the subsidies and discounts go far to keeping such activities affordable for military families.

DoD policy for Morale, Welfare and Recreation Programs specifically states that these offerings by DoD are an integral part of the military and benefits package, that they build healthy families and communities, and that their purpose is to maintain individual, family, and mission readiness (DoD, 2009). A 2018 GAO study, however, found that from 2012 to 2017 the Services had not been consistently meeting funding targets for some of these resources, and noted DoD recognition that, "extended engagement in overseas conflicts and constrained budgets have resulted in an operating environment that is substantially different from the peacetime setting in which the targets were first established" more than 20 years ago (GAO, 2018c, p. 13). Thus, the GAO concluded that we cannot be certain that even meeting those funding targets would be adequate for today's operating environment. DoD concurred with the GAO's recommendation to evaluate the funding targets and develop measurable goals and performance measures for these programs (GAO, 2018c).

BOX 4-3
Examples of Prominent Themes Associated with Geographic Assignment and Relocation

For active component service members:
- Being assigned to live in a remote and isolated area
- Living far from a military installation: community and resources
- Being assigned to live in a foreign country
- Frequent permanent change of station (PCS) moves (every 2 or 3 years)
- Logistics of PCS moves (e.g., packing and unpacking; delayed, damaged, missing household goods)
- Separation from friends and family, disruption of support networks due to assignments/PCS moves
- Family members living apart due to unaccompanied tour, short tour, dual-military couples assigned apart, so family member can finish education, or until spouse/partner can find work in new location
- Spouse/partner unemployment gaps, underemployment, wage penalties due to PCS moves and labor markets near military installations
- Unemployment Compensation eligibility for spouses who quit to follow their service member for a military move (some states include domestic partners or those about to be married)
- Disruption in continuity of health care due to PCS move
- Disruption of education due to PCS move
- Difficulty of establishing home ownership, building equity and thus family wealth

For reserve component service members when on Title 10 active duty:
- Being assigned to live in a remote and isolated area
- Living far from a military installation: community and resources
- Being assigned to live in a foreign country
- Family members living apart due to location of Title 10 assignment
- Unemployment Compensation eligibility for spouses who quit to follow their service member for a military move (some states include domestic partners or those about to be married)

For reserve component service members when not on Title 10 active duty:
- Living far from a military installation: community and resources

GEOGRAPHIC ASSIGNMENT AND RELOCATION

As shown in the summary in Box 4-3, many of the challenges related to military assignments and relocations are primarily associated with the active component, as reserve component members can typically choose where to live and are not required to keep moving to new locations throughout their military careers.

Location

Military families' geographic location can play a significant role in their satisfaction with military life, their ability to access military resources, and their ability to interact with other military families or their own family members. Families may prefer to live near other family members, in either rural or urban areas, or in particular climates or regions of the country. Life in remote and isolated areas can present difficulties, however even for families who otherwise enjoy rural or small-town life. For example, in such areas there may be few opportunities for civilian employment or education for members of the National Guard or Reserves or for military spouses or partners, and only limited opportunities for single service members to meet potential romantic partners. Remote areas also provide more limited access to specialists who can examine and treat those with particular medical needs. Because remote and isolated locations offer fewer local nonmilitary opportunities for socializing, fitness, and recreation, additional appropriated fund spending on morale, welfare, and recreation is permitted at installations in such locations (DoD, 2009).

Foreign assignments can present multiple advantages, such as the opportunity to experience new cultures and learn new languages, as well as an appreciation of taken-for-granted advantages back home. They can also introduce difficulties. Some service members or their family members may be uncomfortable venturing off of installations, spouses may face limited opportunities for employment, and the distance and differences in time zones can make communication and contact with family and friends at home particularly challenging. Those who have difficulty adapting to overseas assignments can experience poor mental and physical health as a result (Burrell et al., 2006).

Reactions to a foreign assignment may depend in part on timing. For example, a 2012 survey of 1,036 adolescents with at least one active-duty parent found differences between those living in the United States and those living in Europe (Lucier-Greer et al., 2016). Among adolescents ages 11 to 14, foreign residence was associated with being more likely to turn to their family as a means of coping along with lower levels of self-reliance/optimism, and among adolescents ages 15 to 18 it was associated with higher levels of self-reliance but more depressive symptoms (Lucier-Greer et al., 2016).

Relocation: PCS Moves

Active component personnel typically experience frequent PCS moves approximately every 2 to 3 years. These can be welcome opportunities to move to a more desirable area (with "desirable" being self-defined), to see other parts of the country or world, to take advantage of new career opportunities at another location, or to reunite with friends and family. However, PCS moves can be stressors even when desired, because of the process of packing, moving, finding a new home (for some, selling the current home), transferring schools, changing medical providers, and so on (Tong et al., 2018). PCS moves can be undesired as well, as they can disrupt social networks, children's education, spouses' employment and career and educational advancement, the families' ability to build home equity, and continuity of health care, especially for military families that include members with special needs. For LGBT service members and racial or ethnic minorities, PCS moves may create specific stressors when the new location offers fewer protections or is less welcoming within the local social and cultural contexts.

Moreover, PCS moves can split families, such as when dual-military couples cannot co-locate, when a family decides it is better for the spouse/partner or children to remain behind until the spouse can find a new job, or when a significant milestone passes, such as a newborn reaching a certain age, a child graduating, or a family member in a vulnerable state stabilizing or recovering. Unfortunately, the literature is lacking evidence on the extent to which families relocate together or in staggered fashion or remain separated, or the effect of the adopted strategy on PCS-related disruptions (Tong et al., 2018).

PCS Moves and Children

Mobility and geographic transitions were once considered a key benefit of military service. While that mobility continues to be an inducement for military service, PCS moves can have a harmful impact on the education of military children. On average, military children move and change schools six to nine times from the start of kindergarten to high school graduation, which is three times more often than their civilian peers. School-age military children are especially vulnerable to the stress related to frequent transitions, as they must simultaneously cope with normal developmental stressors, such as establishing peer relationships, conflict in parent/child relationships, and increased academic demands (Ruff and Keim, 2014). Although many PCS moves occur during the summer months, some families must move during the school year.

Frequent moves can cause military children to suffer academically, lose connections with others, and miss out on opportunities for extracurricular activities (because of the timing of the move) and, among children with special needs, experience gaps in services, continuity of care, and educational plans (Bronfenbrenner Center for Translational Research, 2013; Hawkins et al., 2018). These are issues that any child who moves may face, not just military children. Across various studies of military children, relocation has been associated with reduced grades, increased depression and anxiety symptoms, skipping class, violence and weapon carrying, gang membership, and early sexual activity, although the overall prevalence is quite low (Hawkins et al., 2018). Evidence is limited regarding the impact of single relocations vs. accumulations of relocations over time.

However, there is evidence suggesting that for some children, frequent relocations may promote resiliency and the development of coping behaviors, and PCS moves can become normative in some military families (Spencer et al., 2016). Having experienced a number of military moves, these children have a better sense of what is involved, and some look forward to the excitement of new opportunities in a new location.

The Interstate Compact on Educational Opportunity for Military Children aims to address what it identifies as the major challenges for children in public schools, including:

- Enrollment requirements for educational records and immunizations
- Waiver of course requirements for graduation if similar classes were completed
- Similar course placement (e.g., honors, vocational) and flexibility in waiving prerequisites
- Excusing absences so children can spend time with service members on leave from or immediately returned from a deployment
- Special education services
- Flexibility with application deadlines for extracurricular activities (Military Interstate Children's Compact Commission, 2018).

Families with children may also rely on social supports offered by the military and civilian communities in dealing with PCS moves (MCEC, 2009). DoD has stated their commitment to serve military children by providing youth programming for children ages 6 to 18 on installations and in communities where military families live. Part of this effort includes establishing approximately 140 youth and teen centers worldwide that serve more than 1 million school-age children of active duty and reserve component members annually. Centers provide educational and recreational programs designed around character and leadership development, career development, health and life skills, and the arts, among others (DoD, 2016a).

DoD has also recognized researchers' recommendations to align the formal supports of a military installation with the informal supports of the nonmilitary community to support families (Huebner et al., 2009). DoD has partnered and/or contracted with federal and nonfederal youth-serving organizations, such as Boys & Girls Clubs of America (BGCA), Big Brothers Big Sisters, 4-H, Young Men's Christian Association (YMCA), the Department of Labor summer employment program, and other local and national youth organizations to provide programming to military youth on and off installations. Programs that have resulted from partnerships with national youth serving organizations, such as the USA Girl Scouts Overseas[9] and BGCA-affiliated Youth Centers,[10] often identify their goal to positively influence well-being, resiliency, and academic success and provide a sense of security, stability, and continuity as families transition to new locations. DoD has stated its intention to continue to building "strong partnerships with national youth-serving organizations that augment and offer valued resources" (DoD, 2016, p. 5). Given that a significant proportion of the current military population comprises reserve component service members, the expansion of formal support systems to include agencies and organizations located outside of the military installations is key (Easterbrooks et al., 2013; Huebner et al., 2009).

PCS Moves and Family Financial Well-Being

PCS moves every 2 to 3 years can disrupt the pursuit by spouses and partners of higher education, as well as partner eligibility for in-state tuition. Moves can also disrupt their employment, leading to loss of seniority, employment gaps, and underemployment. All of these effects can hurt the financial well-being of a military family.

In a representative longitudinal DoD-wide survey of active component civilian spouses conducted by the Defense Manpower Data Center (DMDC), 6,412 spouses participated in all three waves of the 2010, 2011, and 2012 surveys. The study provided self-reported evidence that PCS moves had a negative impact on spouses' pursuit of higher education or training, on their employment, and on families' financial condition (DMDC, 2015). Another study of the earnings of active component spouses who were not in the active component themselves also found evidence of a family financial disruption associated with a PCS move. Based on an analysis of DoD administrative data and Social Security Administration earnings data between 2000 and 2012, it found that a PCS move was associated with a 14 percent decline in average spousal earnings during the year of the move (Burke and Miller, 2018, p. 1261).

The impact of these moves on the financial well-being and satisfaction of service member families is likely more widespread than has been estimated, given that in the 2017 Status of Forces surveys nearly 10 percent of active component and 17 percent of reserve component personnel indicated they are in a long-term relationship that has lasted a year or longer (DoD, 2018). Those unmarried partners of service members may also have experienced

[9]For more information, see http://www.usagso.org/en/our-council/who-we-are.html.

[10]For more information, see https://www.bgca.org/about-us/military.

a disruption to their education and earnings, but they would have been ineligible for assistance to spouses provided by DoD. For example, Military Community and Family Policy's (MC&FP's) Spouse Education and Career Opportunities Program offers career counseling and tuition assistance in the form of My Career Advancement Account [MyCAA] Scholarships for spouses of early-career service members to support occupationally focused education and training in portable career fields. Through these initiatives, DoD helps spouses select and prepare for portable careers likely to be in demand wherever their service member is stationed, so that the spouse's employment and earnings trajectory will be better able to weather frequent military moves. Unmarried partners are not eligible for this support, nor are they eligible for state benefits for military spouses negotiated by the DoD State Liaison Office, such as unemployment compensation eligibility after following their service member for a PCS move, or accommodations to support the portability of occupational licenses and credentials across state lines.[11]

TRAINING, SEA DUTY, AND DEPLOYMENTS

Deployments and sea duty[12] can provide service members with a number of desirable opportunities and benefits, such as

- Employing or developing their skills in real-world settings
- Making a difference in the world
- Developing strong bonds with others
- Earning financial bonuses through special pays and tax advantages, and
- Learning about other parts of the world.

Training and field exercises can also confer some of these advantages and help prepare service members to succeed in military operations.

Personnel tempo, commonly referred to as *perstempo*, refers to the amount of time individuals serve away from their home duty station, whether for deployments, sea duty, exercises, unit training, or individual training. Although a 2013 DoD policy is supposed to limit the amount of time service members spend away from home, a 2018 GAO assessment found that DoD perstempo data are incomplete and unreliable and that the Services do not have or do not enforce perstempo thresholds (GAO, 2018a). Thus, GAO found, DoD lacks the ability to gauge the amount of stress

---

[11]For more information, see https://statepolicy.militaryonesource.mil.

[12]*Sea duty* refers to Navy personnel assignments to ships or submarines. It contrasts with *shore duty*, or land-based assignments. For more information, see http://www.public.navy.mil/bupers-npc/reference/milpersman/1000/1300Assignment/Documents/1306-102.pdf.

perstempo rates place on the force and any associated impacts on military readiness (GAO, 2018a).

Much of the literature has focused on the stressors of these family separations, which can have a negative impact on individuals, relationships, and the family as a unit. Examples include service members worrying about their families while geographically separated and trying to manage family problems from afar; relationship problems (e.g., couples growing apart, infidelity, or the end of a relationship); and missing major life events (e.g., births, weddings, funerals, childhood "firsts," graduations, holidays, and family reunions). Other challenging life events associated with military separations include traumatic experiences, such as combat participation or exposure to dead bodies, violence, atrocities, or abhorrent living conditions (discussed further in subsequent chapters); family members' fear of death, injury, or illness (physical or psychological) of their service member serving in a hostile area; and post-absence readjustment/reintegration between/among family members, including the service member's adjustment to "routine" life upon returning. Family difficulties can be created or exacerbated due to communication challenges, such as connectivity problems, time zones, military-implemented blackouts (e.g., before a secret raid or after major casualties), and even the well-intentioned withholding of information among family members about problems or dangers (Carter and Renshaw, 2016). Box 4-4 provides a brief overview of examples of opportunities and challenges of these types of duties away from personnel's home duty station. As a reminder, these are not sorted into positive and negative categories, as that interpretation can depend on the context and timing, individuals' experiences, and other factors, and some can have both positive and negative aspects.

Deployments

More than two million military service members and their families have been impacted by deployments since the inception of combat operations in 2001, and some families have faced five or more such separations and reunions. The effects of combat deployments on military families can be complex (Cozza and Lerner, 2013). Combat deployments have been associated with increased rates of interpersonal conflict (Milliken et al., 2007), impaired parenting (Davis et al., 2015), and child maltreatment (Gibbs et al., 2007; McCarroll et al., 2008; Rentz et al., 2007). Military spouses have demonstrated increased distress (Lester et al., 2010) and utilization of mental health treatment (Mansfield et al., 2011) associated with deployments. Military children have similarly demonstrated negative deployment-related effects, including emotional and behavioral problems, increased mental health utilization, and suicidal behaviors (Chandra et al., 2010; Flake et al., 2009; Gilreath et al., 2015; Lester et al., 2010; Mansfield et al., 2011).

BOX 4-4
Examples of Prominent Themes Associated with Deployments, Sea Duty, and Training Exercises Away from Home

- Unpredictability, lack of information about who will go as well as when, where, and for how long
- Service member opportunity to see the world, employ skills in real-world setting
- Family adjustment (or lack thereof) to separation from service member
- Limited, unpredictable communication between family members
- Worry about safety of service member
- Service member risk of injury, illness, or death or of becoming a prisoner of war
- Harm to or death of service member's friends, unit members
- Special and incentive pays (e.g., hardship duty pay, hazardous duty incentive pay, family separation allowance)
- Savings Deposit Program while in combat zone*
- Service member's Civil Relief Act protections (e.g., termination of leases, protection from eviction, mortgage relief)*
- Service member combat exposure, occupational exposure to mass casualties (e.g., terrorist attack)
- Forging of strong bonds between service member and other unit members
- Service member missing major life events and family activities
- Spouse or partner functioning as head of household, single parent while service member is away
- Child custody or child care issues for single parents or when both parents in dual-military couple must be away at the same time
- Service member's and family's development of mastery, independence, and new responsibilities during deployment cycles
- Family's readjustment when service member returns
- Lack of sufficient service member "dwell time" between absences, lack of leave upon return
- Service member's deployment experience helping them to be competitive for promotion or choice assignment

NOTE: *Does not apply to reserve component not on Title 10 active duty.

Combat deployment is associated with increased anxiety in military children, which is highly associated with distress in both civilian and active duty parents (Lester et al., 2010). Additionally, deployment has a cumulative effect on children, which can continue even upon return of the deployed parent. Thus, effects in children may be sustained beyond the actual threat to the deployed service member's safety, potentially reflecting elevated anxiety and distress in highly deployed communities where children witness cycling deployments of adults in their lives. Importantly, children's anxiety reflects the broader distress within their parents and family as a whole.

Many of these studies involved cross-sectional designs to examine associations between deployment and effects within families and were limited by the lack of longer-term outcomes. The few longitudinal studies that have been conducted provide a more nuanced picture of deployment's impact on families (e.g., Balderrama-Durbin et al., 2015; Erbes et al., 2017; Gewirtz et al., 2010; Snyder et al., 2016). For example, one study using DoD data found that an increase in cumulative time deployed was associated with a greater risk of divorce and that this risk was greater for women service members, those who served on hostile deployments, and those who married before 9/11 (when there may have been less of an expectation of deployments as frequent events) (Negrusa et al., 2013). A similar study, focusing on Army soldiers, found that in addition to time spent in deployment, self-reported mental health symptoms consistent with PTSD further increased the risk of divorce (Negrusa and Negrusa, 2014).

The Deployment Life Study, conducted by the RAND Corporation (Meadows et al., 2016), assessed military family members at different times during the deployment cycle (before, during, and after deployment), focusing on the health of family, marital, and parental relationships, the physical and psychological health of adults and children within the family, and attitudes toward the military. The study found that changes in marital satisfaction across the deployment cycle were no different than those experienced by matched controls. However, service members' exposure to physical injury or psychological trauma (but not combat exposure) was associated with increased physical and psychological aggression after deployment, as reported by spouses. Any perceived negative effects of deployment on family satisfaction and parenting were confined to the deployment period, although the presence of psychological trauma and stress contributed to negative post-deployment consequences for families. The researchers found no long-term psychological or behavioral effects of deployment on service members or spouses, except when deployment trauma was experienced. Similarly, child and teen responses to deployment appeared to be contained within the deployment period, except when deployment-related trauma (e.g., injury or post-deployment mental health problems) was involved.[13] These findings resonate with results from other studies showing that a service member's psychological functioning as a result of combat exposure during deployments (i.e., PTSD, traumatic brain injury [TBI], and related symptoms) appears to influence family functioning more than the physical characteristics of the deployments, such as their length or number (Gewirtz et al., 2018).

Military deployments add an additional stress to military families in addition to frequent moves, changing schools, and the challenge of integrating

[13]For a summary of these findings, see Meadows et al. (2016).

into new communities. The deployment of a parent requires the child to manage stress related to separation from a loved one and the impending sense of danger that accompanies a deployment and combat operations. Spouses or partners who are parents can find themselves needing to function as single parents. These additional demands while their service member is away can present conflicts for those who are employed or seeking employment, and spouses or partners may need to scale back their hours or even give up their jobs if they cannot obtain work schedules allowing them to fulfill household and child responsibilities. This can in turn have a negative impact on the financial well-being of the family. Some spouses and partners are fortunate to live in communities that offer support to families of deployed personnel, such as help with lawn care, maintenance tasks, and transportation to appointments.

Research indicates that a caregiver's emotional well-being is related to the child's emotional well-being. In one study (Chandra et al., 2011), caregivers who reported poorer emotional well-being also reported that their children had greater emotional, social, and academic difficulties. Further, if a caregiver's emotional health difficulties persisted or increased on average over the study period, youth difficulties remained higher when compared with youth whose caregivers reported fewer emotional difficulties. In the same study, it was found that families that experienced more total months of parental deployment also reported more emotional difficulties among the youth, and these difficulties did not diminish over the study period. Families in the study with more months of deployment reported more problems both during deployment and during reintegration. Caregivers in the study with partners in the reserve component (National Guard or Reserves) reported having more challenges than their counterparts in the active component. In particular, National Guard and Reserve caregivers in the study reported more difficulties with emotional well-being, as well as more challenges during and after deployment (Chandra et al., 2011).

Deployments also take a toll on the psychological health of military children of all ages. Studies have shown that preschoolers with a deployed parent are more likely than other preschoolers to exhibit behavioral problems and that school-age children and adolescents with a deployed parent show moderately higher levels of emotional and behavioral distress (Chartrand et al., 2008). School-age children and adolescents with a deployed parent have also displayed increased problems with peer relationships, increased depression and suicidal thoughts, and higher use of mental health services. It has also been found that children with a deployed parent are more likely to be maltreated or neglected, especially in families with younger parents and young children (Lester and Flake, 2013). Again, although there may be increased risks for these negative outcomes, overall these effects are not the norm.

Research has also shown that a parent's deployment can affect how military children perform academically. Studies of military children, caregivers, and schools have shown that deployments have a modest negative effect on performance. Children with a deployed parent have shown falling grades, increased absence, and lower homework completion (Lester and Flake, 2013, p. 129). A recent study of military children in North Carolina and Washington State whose parents have deployed 19 months or more since 2001 demonstrates that they have modestly lower (and statistically different) achievement scores than those who have experienced less or no parental deployment. This last study suggests that rather than developing resilience, children appear to struggle more with more cumulative months of deployment. Further, the study found that some of the challenges observed by teachers and counselors are ones that stem from the high mobility of this population, which could be amplified during deployment (Moeller et al., 2015; Richardson et al., 2011).

Understanding the effects of deployments on children is challenging, in part because it is difficult to distinguish factors related to deployment and military service. Furthermore, it is difficult to know whether military and civilian children differ. There are currently no publicly available large-scale studies presenting well-controlled comparisons of military and civilian families regarding parenting beliefs or practices, or other family behavior. Well-controlled comparisons of child outcomes among military and civilian children also are rare. The largest source of information about how child outcomes might differ comes from the Youth Risk Behavior Survey program administered by the Centers for Disease Control and Prevention, through which all youth in selected middle and high schools in every state throughout the United States are asked to complete a mostly standard set of items. A few states have incorporated a military identifier, providing the best comparisons to date of military and civilian youth (for more detail, see Box 3-1 in Chapter 3). Due to slight variations in items across states, some of the data sets include children whose parents have left military service as well as those who continue to serve, some data sets include children whose siblings served, and some include children whose military parents have not deployed or who deployed several years ago rather than recently. As a result, it is possible to identify differences indexed by military service alone vs. military service and deployment, and whether it was a parent or sibling who served.

Across the available data, calculations suggest that children with family members who served but were not deployed were more likely to report higher levels of a variety of kinds of risky behaviors or adverse experiences than nonmilitary children, including more use of cigarettes or other substances, and more experiences of violence and harassment, carrying a knife or gun to school, or having suicidal thoughts. These differences were larger for children whose parents (vs. siblings) had served. Military and civilian children did *not* differ in rates of ever having used alcohol.

With regard to children whose military parents had deployed, reports of risky behaviors or adverse experiences were more common than among children whose parents had served but not deployed. Thus, military service and deployment *each* were associated with increments. For example, increments in the rate of ever having used alcohol were 9 percent each for military service and for deployment. Among military children whose parents had deployed, reports of suicidal thoughts were 34 percent higher and reports of having carried a knife or gun to school were about double those of children whose parents had not been deployed and about 80 percent higher than those of civilian children.

It is important to point out that these data come from self-reports by children, which may be subject to biases and memory errors. The differences for some of these experiences or activities, while large on a percentage basis, are small in terms of percentage points. Finally, patterns about exposures to violence may reflect mistreatment of military children as much as they do military children's behavior. The committee notes that the degree to which stresses faced by military families during combat deployments are attributable simply to family separations, sudden single parenthood, or fear regarding the safe return of the service member has not been disentangled.

There are positive aspects to deployments as well. Deployments can present opportunities for service members to apply their training, improve their skills, take pride in a sense of accomplishment from overcoming hardships and living in austere conditions, and derive satisfaction from feeling that their work makes a difference in the world. The last aspect may particularly hold true for humanitarian and disaster relief missions. Additionally, during military operations overseas, service members can forge close bonds with their unit members and form lasting friendships. Service members and families can financially benefit in significant ways, through tax benefits and additional pays associated with serving in a combat zone, re-enlisting while deployed, and family separation pays. These deployments can thus provide opportunities to pay off debt, invest in property, help relatives, or improve one's standard of living. Deployments can also help service members subsequently be competitive for promotion or choice assignments.

Several researchers have postulated resilient pathways for children facing combat deployments (e.g., Easterbrooks et al., 2013), including the seven C's model of positive development, where attributes such as competence, confidence, contribution, and control may all have relevance in providing positive opportunities for military children through such challenging experiences, resulting in pride and growth. However, the committee notes that these pathways of resilience have not been tested in military children.

NATIONAL GUARD AND RESERVE SERVICE

Although members of the National Guard and Reserves and their families experience many of the other opportunities and challenges described throughout this chapter, there are certain experiences particular to the reserve component. We consider those experiences here and summarize them in Box 4-5.

National Guard and Reserve service can be appealing to some families because of the geographic choice and residential stability affords. Unlike active component personnel, guard and reserve personnel do not face frequent, mandatory geographic relocation, and some move from the active component to the reserve component precisely for this reason. If National Guard members choose to move, they can request an interstate transfer. However, National Guard and Reserve members who do not live near their units are responsible for their own transportation expenses for travel to and from duty. Additionally, those who move may face challenges, in that the unit near their new home may not have a vacancy for their same occupation and pay grade.

There is evidence that for military children, friendships with other military children and participation in military-sponsored activities can be beneficial for their well-being (Bradshaw et al., 2010; Lucier-Greer et al., 2014). Children of members in the reserve component (as well as active component children who live far from military installations) may have few opportunities for face-to-face interactions with others who would have a basic shared understanding of life as a military dependent.

BOX 4-5
Examples of Prominent Themes Specific to Members of the National Guard and Reserves

- Geographic assignment not determined by the military, permanent change of station moves not required
- Unprecedented frequency of National Guard/Reserves mobilizations since 9/11
- Varying eligibility for benefits and programs based on military status (e.g., health care)
- Service member and family might live far from a military installation
- Service member and family may have no prior connection to the unit the service member is mobilizing to join
- Pay issues associated with changes in military status (e.g., when mobilized)
- Mobilization contributing to service members' unemployment or underemployment in the civilian sector, or being detrimental to their own business/self-employment

Because the National Guard and Reserves are both part of the "reserve component," clarifying what aspects of their service differ from service in the active component is critical to having a comprehensive picture of the military. National Guard members usually apply to enlist and work at the unit closest to their home, although they do not necessarily live close to that unit's headquarters or facilities. Recall that they work for their states (under Title 32), unless they are mobilized to work under the federal government (under Title 10), as they would be for an overseas military deployment. Moreover, for the National Guard and Reserves the job requirements, eligibility for programs and services, health care system, and more can vary depending on whether the member's current orders fall under Title 32 or Title 10. Reservists work for the federal government only, but like National Guard members they traditionally train one weekend a month and two weeks in the summer, although they may also be called to full-time active duty service. We are unaware of any tool that would assist National Guard and Reserve families in understanding what they are eligible for at any point based on their service member's current status or upcoming change in status.

Deployment for National Guard and Reserve personnel is typically preceded by mobilization and followed by demobilization, and thus can have deployment cycles that are lengthier than their active component counterparts. When they are mobilized for federal service, they are not necessarily mobilized with their National Guard or Reserve unit as a whole. Individuals may be called up to augment other units that could be located quite far from their homes. Thus, even for those who do live near their own unit, they and their family members may not be near the deploying unit and thus not have easy access to predeployment briefings, activities, or support groups, nor would they already be on the distribution list for unit or spouse network email announcements or newsletters. Similarly, those families may be distant from programs and services designed to aid with post-deployment family reintegration. During demobilization, National Guard and Reserve members usually return to their hometowns and civilian jobs, which may not be close to any fellow unit members or military resources that can assist them with their transition or post-deployment issues.

Mobilizations as Disruptions to Service Member and Spouse Employment

The Uniform Services Employment and Reemployment Rights Act of 1994[14] requires that civilian employers not discriminate against reservists in their hiring practices, allow reservists time away from work to fulfill their federal military duties, and hold their position for them until they

[14]For more information, see https://www.dol.gov/vets/programs/userra/userra_fs.htm.

return and at that time compensate them as though they had been working continuously the entire time (e.g., with regard to pay rate, position, and benefits terms and eligibility). This can present challenges to employers, and despite these legal protections, reservists may still face employers hesitant to hire them. Since 9/11, National Guard and Reserve members have been mobilized at unprecedented levels (Figinski, 2017; Werber et al., 2013). Due to the large numbers of reservists mobilized for long deployments to Iraq and Afghanistan, there were dramatic increases in the number of veterans receiving unemployment benefits, as more reservists were eligible for the benefits and long deployments made it more difficult to return to civilian employment (Loughran and Klerman, 2008). Some reservists also work as DoD civilian employees, which makes them "military technicians" who work under somewhat different employment terms than their civilian employee or reservist counterparts.[15] For example, a condition of their DoD civilian employment is that they maintain their membership in the Selected Reserve, although an exception may be made if they receive combat-related disability but are still able to perform their DoD civilian job.

Changes to Pay, Benefits, Programs and Services

Members of the National Guard and Reserves mobilized since 9/11 have encountered pay and allowance delays, underpayments, and overpayments that the military later sought to recoup, all due to lack of integrated pay and personnel status systems (Flores, 2009). Eligibility for benefits and services can be complicated for members of the National Guard and Reserves and their families. Exactly what they are eligible for and under what conditions varies across programs and services and can be based upon whether they are or have recently been on active duty status and whether that was under Title 32 or Title 10 orders. Perhaps most notably, reserve component families are eligible for health care benefits under TRICARE only while their service members are on active duty for more than 30 days or are mobilized for a contingency operation. Otherwise, when their service member is on reserve status or during shorter periods of active duty, the service members and their family are responsible for their own health care insurance, and the service members are responsible for ensuring that they are medically ready to deploy should they be called up.

[15]The terms are specified under Section 10216 of Title 10 in the U.S. Code.

DIVERSITY AND INCLUSION

> *As today's military community is more diverse and geographically dispersed than previous generations, the challenge becomes: How does DoD continue to address the diverse needs in the military community and foster a sense of community given ongoing shifts in demographics and the balance of the force?*—Third Quadrennial Quality of Life Review (DoD, 2017a, p. 4)

DoD has been implementing institutional policies and practices designed to reduce barriers to service and promote equitable and respectful treatment of all service members (DoD, 2017a, p. 10). According to Lutz (2013), the core training at the Defense Equal Opportunity Management Institute (DEOMI) aims to achieve total force readiness through a focus on the *American identity* of service members. This legacy of legal inclusivity has continued into the 21st century with the repeal of the so-called Don't Ask Don't Tell policy (2011), extension of family benefits with the implementation of legal same-sex marriage (2015), and most recently the lifting of blanket restrictions on the service of military women (2016). This section will highlight some examples of diversity- and inclusion-related issues, summarized in Box 4-6, but as is the case with this chapter more generally, this high-level review is by no means complete. Furthermore, it does not capture the complexity of the issues represented in the literature that a deeper dive on any one of these topics could provide.

Variability Across and Within Groups

As discussed in Chapter 2, ecological and family systems theories emphasize the embeddedness of individuals within multiple, reciprocal, and interacting contexts. As helpful as these frameworks are in identifying interactions that influence individual and family development, they do not capture systematic or structural inequity, such as race- and gender-based discrimination and attitudes, which may affect military families who are members of marginalized groups. An intersectional lens can serve as an organizing framework for understanding how overlapping social statuses, including gender, race, sexual orientation, and socioeconomic status, connect individual service member and family experiences to structural (macro) realities (Bogard et al., 2017; Bowleg, 2012).

Each military service member and each family member is positioned within a unique social location and occupies multiple social statuses, which helps to explain the tremendous diversity in individual service members' responses to what appear to be similar military and life experiences. Minority stress theory (Meyer 2003) spotlights minority group members'

BOX 4-6
Examples of Prominent Themes Associated with Diversity and Inclusion

- Pay and benefits based on equal pay for equal rank, years of service, and occupation (and not individually negotiated), and equal eligibility for allowances, special pays, and incentives
- Under-/over-representation of specific groups in some areas and across ranks resulting in some units, career fields, and rank groups being far less diverse than others
- Opportunities to interact with others from diverse backgrounds (histories, cultural traditions, perspectives, etc.)
- Individual and structural discrimination, harassment, bias, incivility, bullying, hazing, ostracism, and interpersonal violence, targeted at members based on their race, ethnicity, native language, citizenship, religion, gender, gender identity, sexual orientation, physical appearance, tenure in the organization, etc.
- Recent history of bans on military women's service in combat roles and on open service of gay, lesbian, and bisexual personnel, with cultural shifts in attitude and new policies still following
- Renewed ban on the service of transgender personnel, with exceptions for those identified during the brief period it was lifted
- Historical focus of spouse networking/support groups on women spouses of men, resulting in less inclusion of men, working spouses, partners, dual-military couples, same-sex spouses
- Concerted efforts to address race and ethnicity as they relate to equal opportunity and discrimination, but little focus on how they relate to military family well-being
- Programs and services to support family members with special needs
- Challenges managing family member special needs exacerbated by permanent change of station moves and deployments

unique experiences of chronic stresses stemming from social institutions in addition to their everyday experiences of racial bias. When applied to sexual minorities, analysis tends to focus on stresses related to heteronormative bias and anti-LGBT experiences.

Discrimination or even suspected discrimination in promotion, job assignments, assigned duties within a position,[16] opportunities for promotion and career development, and the enforcement of rules and regulations can be a detrimental stressor to the well-being of service members. Intersectionality is also a useful concept in understanding "the intersectional nature of resilience" (Santos and Toomey, 2018, p. 9), which reflects the ability

[16]For example, a women truck driver being tasked with handling the unit's administrative work, or Black or Hispanic personnel being assigned the dirty or heavy manual labor.

of military service members and their families to function well in spite of significant disadvantages, stresses, or experiences of inequity.

Taken together, ecological, life-course, and intersectional models of individual and family well-being all indicate that what is most effective at supporting military families is not a one-size-fits-all approach but rather a variety of approaches that seek to align programs with the diverse needs of service members, diverse family constellations, and local social contexts (Lerner, 2007). Of course, this is not meant to imply that a custom program must be developed for each military family. The point is that DoD and local service providers cannot make assumptions based on one or two characteristics at a given point in time (e.g., single newly enlisted service member, deployed parent, Latinx Marine) about what is most important to military personnel and military family members, what they need, or what is the best way to support them. Instead, they must take into account the perceptions, priorities, and preferences of service members and their families; provide a range of types of support from which to draw (e.g., mode of communication, military vs. nonmilitary); and ensure that the support networks contain providers with knowledge about and sensitivity to the needs of different subgroups (e.g., noncitizens and immigrants, male sexual assault victims, religious minorities).

Servicewomen in the Military

Women make up one-half of the U.S. population but only 17.5 percent of the total force (DoD, 2017c, p. 6). Notably, relatively few servicewomen occupy leadership positions at the officer ranks of colonel and admiral/general (DACOWITS, 2015). Findings from the most recent (2017) DACOWITS report indicate that women often identify different reasons for joining the military than men do, that they are more likely than men to be married to another service member (both within and across services), and that they separate from the military earlier in their careers than do men. Key factors in servicewomen's decisions to leave the military relate to the challenges of geographic separation from family, both because of deployment and inability to co-locate with a service member spouse; pressure to prioritize one's military career among dual- military service members; and difficulties with work-life-family balance. In addition, servicewomen are more likely than men to separate from the military prior to starting a family (Clever and Segal, 2013).

Globally, 74 foreign militaries allow or require women to serve, including 13 in which combat roles are open to servicewomen (DACOWITS 2017). Among militaries that have successfully integrated women, policies to support servicewomen include flexible parental leave policies, co-location and geographic stability, and comprehensive and affordable child care that can accommodate long shifts, nontraditional working hours, and care for ill children. DACOWITS (2017) presented recommendations to increase DoD's ability to attract and retain servicewomen that similarly emphasize policies supporting families with children, educational initiatives to address unhelpful perceptions related to gender roles, and protocols for appropriate physical training for women. Findings also indicate that servicewomen are disproportionately affected by findings of noncompliance with family care plans, indicating a need for more appropriate application of these protocols.

There is very little research on motherhood in the military, and almost no research on the impact on families of a military mother's deployment to war (see, e.g., Barnes et al., 2016). A series of studies of Navy mothers during the Gulf War indicated that anxiety and distress increased among the children of those who were deployed more than among children of the nondeployed (Kelley et al., 2001). Among deployed Navy mothers, length of separation from families and perceptions of social support both contributed to psychological adjustment (Kelley et al., 2002). More recent research on a sample of mothers who deployed to Iraq and Afghanistan reported that reintegrating mothers experienced more adverse past-year life events, and more depression and PTSD symptoms, than nondeployed mothers (of deployed spouses), but this research did not report worse parenting, couple functioning, or child adjustment (Gewirtz et al., 2014). More research is needed to examine the adjustment of deployed mothers, how programs and policies may affect them (Goodman et al., 2013), and other factors that may affect these mothers, such as societal norms that stigmatize a mother's leaving her children for war as "non-maternal" behavior (Gewirtz et al., 2014).

Segal and Lane (2016) bring attention to contextual factors within military culture and everyday life that likely affect servicewomen's well-being. Specifically, they identify "leadership behaviors" that set the tone for how women are treated by their male peers and commanders as well as social isolation that can result from being ostracized within a unit. As part of the 2017 DACOWITS research, focus group participants similarly indicated that servicewomen may be disadvantaged by cultural attitudes based on traditional gender roles, especially as women begin to move into previously closed combat and leadership roles. Segal and Lane (2016) bring to light gender-based sexual harassment, ranging from inappropriate behavior—such as sexual comments, jokes, offensive pictures or posters, and gestures—to criminal-level assault. Recent estimates find that servicewomen report and experience sexual harassment and sexual assault at higher rates than male service members (Davis et al., 2017; Galovski and Sanders, 2018) and that sexual trauma is likely underreported due to concerns about safety, stigma, avoidance, and shame (Galovski and Sanders, 2018). Relatedly, servicewomen are more likely than servicemen to be harassed or stalked online and through social media (DACOWITS, 2017, p. 76). The psychological impact of sexual trauma on servicewomen can be especially disruptive to fulfilling service roles, family functioning, parenting, and child outcomes (Kimerling et al., 2010; Millegan et al., 2015; Rosellini et al., 2017; Suris et al., 2013).

Segal and Lane (2016) assert that women's gynecological, contraceptive, and pregnancy-related needs are not fully and universally accessible across settings, including deployment environments. Pregnancy, new motherhood, and maternity leave can disadvantage servicewomen in several ways. Pregnancies do not always occur only and precisely when desired, and their timing can make it more difficult to manage work demands and attract harmful stigma, such as accusations of having become pregnant to avoid sea duty or deployment. Added to this, pregnancies and new motherhood can involve new physical and emotional health challenges, such as problematic pregnancies, problems at birth, difficulties breastfeeding, managing post-pregnancy physical fitness and weight requirements, and suffering from post-partum depression (Appolinio and Fingerhut, 2008).

However, the committee notes that in recent years, granting of parental leave for service members has become more common in order to increase recruitment and retention in the Armed Forces. Recent changes to military parental leave mandated in the FY 2017 National Defense Authorization Act (Section 521 of the enacted bill) authorize

> up to 12 weeks of total leave (including up to 6 weeks convalescent leave) for the primary caregiver in connection with the birth of the child. It also authorizes 6 weeks of leave for a primary caregiver in the case of an adoption of a child and up to 21 days of leave for a secondary caregiver in the case of a birth or adoption. – (Sec. 521, p. 19)[17]

More research will be needed to examine the consequences of these policy changes for service members, as well as their impact on family well-being.

Finally, with the full integration of women into combat roles, attention has turned to women's physiology and ability to meet the military's physical standards for combat and related roles. DACOWITS (2017) reports that because of physiological differences between women and men, physical training and nutritional protocols designed for men, such as "large field training" and cardio focus, may not be most efficient for women, and point to sports science and human performance approaches (pp. 55–57) to prepare all service members.

---

[17]See https://fas.org/sgp/crs/natsec/R44577.pdf, pg. 19, Sec. 521.

LGBT Status

The history of military policy related to sexual orientation, gender identity, and military service has developed in tandem with broader changes in social attitudes and evolving state and federal legislation in the post-9/11 period. Three pieces of legislation during the Obama administration represented a sea change in federal and military policy: (1) the 2009 Matthew Shepard and James Byrd Jr., Hate Crimes Prevention Act; (2) the 2011 repeal of Don't Ask Don't Tell (DADT); and (3) the 2015 legalization of same-sex marriage by the U.S. Supreme Court (*Obergefell* v. *Hodges*). Additionally, in 2016 the secretary of defense ended the ban on transgender service (although as noted in Chapter 3, those advances have been rolled back effective April 2019).

LGBT service members enlist at *higher* rates than heterosexual people and identify diverse reasons for joining (Ramirez and Bloeser, 2018) that extend beyond patriotism, altruism, and commitment to public service. For example, given the troubling rates of family rejection of LGBT youth (Zimmerman et al., 2015), some LGB service members enlist as a mechanism to escape fraught home environments (Legate et al., 2012). For some men, the hypermasculine culture of the military may be appealing, while for lesbian women, the military allows a laser focus on career and mission rather than gender-bound heteronormative roles of motherhood and marriage (Ramirez and Bloeser, 2018).

In population health research, sexual minorities have been found to be at risk for multiple health and mental health burdens when compared to heterosexuals (Hatzenbuehler, 2009). Minority stress theory (Meyer, 2003) articulates that members of sexual minorities experience excess and accumulated stress, including stigma, prejudice, and discrimination, and often expend significant energy to remain vigilant to environmental and interpersonal threats, safety, and disclosure of sexuality. In addition, for LGBT recruits, self-awareness regarding sexual orientation or the decision to live as their gender rather than birth sex and the coming out process often coincide with socialization into military culture.

Until the federal legalization of same-sex marriage, military policy and practice under DADT also interfered with lesbian, gay, and bisexual service members' family functioning and well-being (Kelty and Segal, 2013) by requiring concealment, excluding same-sex partners and children from receiving benefits, and limiting same-sex partners from participating in family roles.[18] In addition, concerns about being outed and career repercussions

---

[18]Testimony of Ashley Broadway-Mack, president of the American Military Partner Association, at *Voices from the Field*, a public information-gathering session held at the National Academies of Sciences, Engineering, and Medicine on April 24, 2018.

prevented many sexual minority service members from seeking help and support under DADT (Mount et al., 2015).

With the legalization of same-sex marriage in 2015, DoD began immediate efforts to extend benefits to spouses and children of sexual minority service members, and in 2016 new health care and service options became available for transgender service members. However, because these important policy changes are very recent, we still know little about LGBT service members, couples, parents, and families. However, some findings are emerging. A DoD systematic review indicated that active-duty lesbian, gay, and bisexual individuals may be at increased risk for sexual assault victimization (DoD, 2016c). DoD's 2015 Health Related Behaviors Survey found that LGBT personnel were as likely as other personnel to receive routine medical care and less likely to be overweight, but more likely to engage in risky behaviors such as binge drinking, cigarette smoking, unprotected sex with a new partner, and having more than one sexual partner in the past year (Meadows et al., 2018, pp. xxx–xxxi). LGBT personnel were also more likely to report moderate or severe depression, lifetime history of self-injury, lifetime suicide ideation, lifetime suicide attempt, suicide attempt in the previous 12 months, lifetime history of unwanted sexual contact, or ever being physical abused (Meadows et al., 2018, p. xxxi). Although these highlights describe LGBT people as a group, of course their needs and experiences vary. For example, "transgender" refers to a gender identity, not a sexual orientation, and a ban against transgender military service was just reinstated.

Lessons from foreign military forces in which LGBT personnel have been integrated, which date from the 1970s (in 1974 in the Netherlands), indicate that LGBT integration has had no effect on readiness or effectiveness there (Belkin and McNichol, 2000–2001, 2000). Rather, environments which are inclusive of sexual orientations and gender identities are positively linked to mental health, well-being, and productivity among LGBT individuals, which in turn benefits morale, cohesion, and recruitment and retention (Polchar et al., 2014).

A hallmark of best military personnel practices is maintaining policies that are inclusive, especially in the context of international and multinational cooperation among diverse nations (e.g., NATO, 2016, p. 45). Relevant to LGBT personnel, best practices include intentional "top-down" leadership demanding respectful conduct, and attention to deployment environments in which LGBT service members may be at greater risk because of local attitudes or local laws, including criminal statutes against same-sex relationships or sexual practices (Polchar et al., 2014, p. 13, p. 50). The most inclusive military systems, including Australia's, encourage and even require disclosure of sexual orientation within the context of national security (Polchar et al., 2014, p. 57).

The National Defense Research Institute Report (Rostker et al., 2010) concludes that the ability of LGBT persons to serve openly can increase unit trust and cohesion, enhance the well-being and performance of LGBT service members, and reduce LGBT vulnerability in out-of-country assignments and deployment environments (such as blackmail by enemy combatants), among other reasons. Common to foreign nations that have integrated LGBT service members are education and training related to fair treatment of all personnel and clear anti-discrimination policies (Azoulay et al., 2010).

Race and Ethnicity

Demographic trends in the general population indicate that the United States will become a majority-minority nation within the next generation. With only one percent of the U.S. population volunteering for military service, the current demographics of military personnel and their families do not reflect those of the population as a whole (see Chapter 3). Rather, racial and ethnic minorities, including immigrants, are more likely to consider military service than White people, and specific regions of the country, in particular several states with high percentages of Hispanics or Latinx, are over-represented (Bennett and McDonald, 2013; Council on Foreign Relations, 2015; also Elder et al., 2010). During the long wars, immigrant service members have provided critical language skills, including the roles of translator and interpreter, and offered needed cross-cultural expertise (Council on Foreign Relations, 2009; Stock, 2009).

Several scholars have concluded that the life-course impact of service for ethnic-minority families is "generally positive" and that service provides important opportunities to groups that might not have alternative pathways to socioeconomic independence and sustainability (Burland and Lundquist, 2013, p. 186). Black service members in the forces are accessing educational benefits through the GI bill at higher rates today than in earlier cohorts (Lutz, 2013, p. 75).

The scholarship on diversity and inclusion has made important contributions in the realm of exploring equal opportunity-related issues: accessions, mentors, promotions and assignments, distributions across occupations and paygrades, and discrimination and harassment (Asch et al., 2012; Booth and Segal, 2005; Lim et al., 2014; Military Leadership Diversity Commission, 2011; Parco and Levy, 2010; Rohall et al., 2017; Tick et al., 2015). All of this scholarship is important and relevant for service member and family well-being, although gaps in our understanding remain.

It is common for DoD surveys and academic studies of military family well-being to include race and ethnicity as variables and report on significant differences, but greater synthesis across the research is needed. For example, several studies indicate that racial/ethnic minority status is linked to higher self-reported rates of PTSD (Burk and Espinoza, 2012; DeVoe et al., 2017; Meadows et al., 2018) and that the positive benefits service has on families' well-being for ethnic-minority service members do not extend to combat veterans (MacLean, 2013). Other racial/ethnic differences include higher prevalence of overweight among Hispanics and non-Hispanic Blacks in the military (Reyes-Guzman et al., 2015) and various differences in health-related behaviors, such as smoking (non-Hispanic blacks were least likely to smoke) and hazardous and disordered drinking (more likely among non-Hispanic whites) (Meadows et al., 2018, p. xxxvii).

No synthesis across the literature has yet been carried out concerning how race and ethnicity relate to military family well-being. Additionally, little attention has been paid to exploring the priorities of racial and ethnic minority families to answer such questions as, What are the top problems and needs of minority service members and their families? and, Is the Military Family Readiness System addressing these problems and needs or helping minority service members and their families address them?

Families in the Exceptional Family Member Program

The Office of Special Needs was established in 2010[19] to enhance and improve DoD support for military families with special medical or educational needs. The office operates in and oversees the Exceptional Family Member Program (EFMP), the provision of services pursuant to the Individuals with Disabilities Education Act (IDEA), and a DoD Advisory Panel on Community Support for Military Families with Special Needs (Office of Special Needs, 2018).

Enrollment in the EFMP is mandatory for active component service members who have a family member with special medical or educational needs (EFMP, 2016). Approximately 133,000 military family members are enrolled in the EFMP (Office of Special Needs, 2018; GAO, 2018b). The EFMP helps families in two ways:

1. Documenting family members' special needs, so that the availability of necessary services is considered during personnel assignment decisions.
2. Identifying and accessing relevant information and military programs and services.

In a benchmark study of the EFMP (Bronfenbrenner Center for Translational Research, 2013), military families enrolled in the EFMP expressed

[19]Established in Title 10 of the U.S. Code, Sec. 1781c.

concerns regarding stigma surrounding special needs family members and military career advancement. Focus groups and interviews with service members, family members, and service providers across eight CONUS installations revealed that some families initially did not enroll in EFMP, disassociated from EFMP services, or hid their family member's needs because of embarrassment and because of fears that they would miss out on assignments important for career advancement or reenlistment opportunities. Although current policy directs that assignments should be managed to prevent adverse impact on careers (DoD, 2017d), service members may still face difficult choices. To illustrate, an officer might have to decide whether to

- turn down a key command opportunity overseas or in a domestic remote and isolated location, because the area has limited resources to support the family member,
- take the career-enhancing assignment, but serve geographically separated from the family for 2 years, leaving someone else to care for the family member with special needs, or
- take the family member along, try to compensate for the resource limitations, hope the condition does not worsen, and if on an unaccompanied tour overseas, be responsible for the cost of sending the family member back.

Within EFMP families, members with special needs are not the only ones who may need assistance. For example, deployments can present additional challenges, as the nondeployed parent can become overwhelmed managing care for EFMP family members, on top of all of the other family and household responsibilities while the service member is away from home (Bronfenbrenner Center for Translational Research, 2013). The nondeployed parent (or other caregiver) may have to quit their job or reduce their work hours to manage, which in turn can negatively impact the family's financial well-being. Especially in circumstances like these, the sole caregiver can have a dire need for respite care. Siblings may also become caregivers as well, assisting their brother or sister who, for example, has limited physical abilities or behavioral problems. While they may enjoy that role, it may also limit what else they are able to do in terms of extracurricular activities, socializing with friends, interacting with parents, or having time to themselves.

Each Service runs its own EFMP, so one of DoD's roles is to help ensure consistency and successful implementation (Office of Special Needs, 2018). However, a recent GAO report raised questions about whether there were gaps in services based on wide variation in the ratio of EFMP staff to EFMP service members, the types of program activities, and the low number of service plans given the number of enrollees and requirement that all should have plans (GAO, 2018). GAO recommended that DoD develop common performance metrics and evaluate the Services' monitoring activities, and DoD agreed and plans to do so (GAO, 2018).

A recent study of EFMP family support providers provides some insight into the types of special needs in military families (Aronson et al., 2016). The study participants were EFMP professionals who help families document the special needs and connect them to information, services, and support groups. The researchers asked whether the providers worked with families dealing with any 1 of 13 specific special health care or educational needs. Most (93 to 94%) reported working with military dependents with autism and dependents with attention-deficit hyperactivity disorder (ADHD). Each of the following types of disabilities were encountered by more than 80 percent of these family support providers: emotional/behavioral disorder, speech and language disorder, developmental delay, asthma, and mental health problems (Aronson et al., 2016).

In the same study, the providers were asked to share their impression of the impact on EFMP families of each of 12 specific challenges (including educational concerns, child behavior problems, parent stress). Of the 12 challenges, 8 were perceived to have an impact ranging on average from "moderate extent" to "great extent." Educational concerns about children were reported as the foremost issue. The next most prominent issues for families were navigating systems (e.g., school, community, or military), child behavior problems, parent mental health or stress, child care issues, and medical problems (Aronson et al., 2016).

Many of these concerns were exacerbated by the frequency of and associated stress of relocation. Lack of continuity associated with changing doctors, carrying over prescriptions, re-applying for referrals, creating new individualized education plans (IEPs), and the like can be stressful for both the families attempting to manage the care and support their loved one and the family member with special needs. Such delays leave the family member with special needs with gaps in necessary care. A recurring issue that EFMP family support providers reported, which related to their own work, was a lack of information sharing that would alert them to incoming families and their needs so that the providers could start assisting with the transition prior to the move.

Note that EFMP is not the only type of support for military family members with special needs, but it should be able to refer families to appropriate resources and help them understand their rights and protections. Figure 4-2 illustrates overlapping types of programs for children with special needs: (1) Exceptional Family Member (EFM) Program; (2) Individuals with Disabilities Education Act (IDEA) special education; and (3) school-related services or accommodation through Section 504 of the Rehabil-

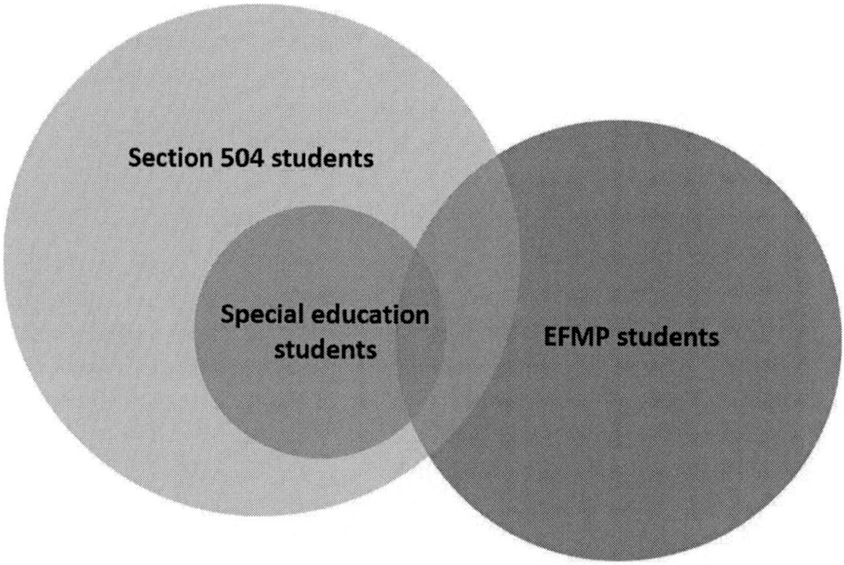

FIGURE 4-2 Overlapping eligibility for programs serving children with special needs.
SOURCE: MCEC (2005, p. 29).

itation Act of 1973 (MCEC, 2005, p. 29). Both IDEA and Section 504 aim to ensure that students with disabilities are able to receive a free and appropriate education.

Although this section tended to discuss "special needs" generally, keep in mind that this represents a great deal of variability in type, severity, and persistence of disability and variability in associated needs. It encompasses autism, blindness, deafness, learning disabilities, speech disorders, cerebral palsy, spina bifida, attention deficit hyperactivity disorder, and many other physical, mental and psychological disabilities, and of course dependents can have more than one, and families can have more than one member who has special needs.

For some families, the benefits and accommodations the military makes to support families with special needs are an incentive to remain on active duty. The advantages include medical benefits afforded to the EFMP family members and assistance coordinating with schools and other programs and services. They also include the service member having the ability to take time off of work to manage the special needs (although some supervisors might be more stringent) without worrying about getting fired or losing money the way one might in a civilian job if required to "clock out." Even if a family member with special needs is high-functioning, the service member might need to take that dependent to appointments and work with the schools on developing an Individualized Education Program (IEP).

TRANSITION OUT OF MILITARY SERVICE

Military personnel and their family members transition away from military life for a wide variety of reasons, in different life stages, and after differing levels and types of exposure to military life. Box 4-7 summarizes some key characteristics of this transition, although they are just the tip of the iceberg in terms of the post-service adjustments and post-service trajectories of veterans and their families.

BOX 4-7
Examples of Prominent Themes Associated with Transition from Military to Civilian Life

For service members:

- Transition to part-time guard/reserve status as option to ease the transition to civilian life
- Retirement benefits, including new Blended Retirement System options similar to a 401(k)
- Possible military-related impairment/disability (e.g., hearing loss, musculoskeletal, PTSD)
- Veterans Affairs health care eligibility and possible disability benefits
- Veteran hiring preference (and discrimination)
- Post-service unemployment or underemployment following end of active-duty service
- Unemployment Compensation for Ex-Servicemembers*
- Sense of loss of community
- For those in Individual Ready Reserve: Possibility of being called back to active duty after separation from service

For family members of service members:

- Family transitioning out of military life while grieving service member death
- Servicemembers' Group Life Insurance (benefit received by family after the death of their service member)
- Death gratuity payable to any person(s) the service member designates**
- Survivor benefit program (for spouses or children, or if none, any other designee)

For active component service member:

- Ability to collect retirement after only 20 years of service, begin second career

For active component and reserve component members leaving Title 10 active duty:

- Transition assistance eligibility

NOTES: *National Guard members eligible only after Title 32 active duty service; **National Guard members under certain circumstances.

Service members may die as a result of military operations, accidents, suicide, or other causes that may or may not clearly relate to their service. Such deaths can be emotionally traumatic to the family and can lead to additional challenges, such as having to leave the military community (even having to move, if they live in military housing), and losing the military pay and benefits associated with service. Post-death benefits, such as the death gratuity, are one type of military benefit for which service members can designate nonmilitary dependents to be recipients, including nonmarital partners and parents.

Service members may separate from military service voluntarily or involuntarily. Some will choose or be required to leave before their initial term of service is complete, but most will face decisions about whether to begin an additional term of service. As the size of the military expands and contracts over time, due to the changing scope of missions and congressional authorizations for personnel, periodically individuals are required or incentivized to leave military service before their current term ends. Additionally, in the event of war, the military can issue a "stop loss" to prevent service members from leaving at the end of their contracts; or, if authorized by the Presidential Reserve Callup Authority, the military can call back to active-duty individuals who had already separated or retired but had not completed their period on "Individual Ready Reserve" status (e.g., as was done to provide ground forces for deployments to Iraq and Afghanistan).

Retirement has traditionally been possible after 20 years of service, once any terms of service have been met, such as obligations after receiving additional schooling. Former spouses may be awarded a portion of a retiree's pay as a part of a divorce proceeding. As noted earlier, the new Blended Retirement System provides alternatives to this traditional system that resemble many private sector 401(k) plans.

After leaving the military, service members and their families may choose to stay in the same area as the last duty station, although those living in family housing will have to move off of the installation. Or they may move to pursue a job opportunity, live closer to relatives, live in a favorite part of the country, or live where there are other military-connected individuals and resources. The Transition to Veteran Policy Office (TVPO) is responsible for policy and implementation of the Transition Assistance Program (TAP),[20] operated by 300 Family Support Centers at military installations worldwide. TAP offers a number of services and resources including counseling, employment assistance, information on veterans' benefits, and other employment and family support. An analysis of data on the use of support services administered by transition assistance centers is underway (GAO, 2019).

---

[20] For more information, see https://www.dodtap.mil/.

Some veterans use their GI Bill benefits to attend college after they leave the service. Many are drawn to the career focus and flexibility offered by for-profit educational institutions; however, some of those schools have been found to prey upon veterans and have high dropout rates and low postgraduation employment rates (Guo et al., 2016, p. 9).

Research on recent veteran populations finds that their workforce participation rates and unemployment are similar to the rates of comparable civilians, although personnel separating at a young age (18 to 24) appear to face some employment hurdles when initially transitioning (Guo et al., 2016, p. 2). Tax credits for hiring veterans appear to be both beneficial and cost-effective: one study found that a 2007 tax credit expansion resulted in the employment of 32,000 disabled veterans in 2007 and 2009 who would have otherwise been unemployed (Guo et al., 2016, p. 4).

Multiple studies have found that both service members and veterans earn more than their comparable civilian counterparts and that service members who worked in health care, communications, or intelligence occupations saw larger earnings in their post-military careers than other veterans (Guo et al., 2016, p. 5). One study that focused on women veterans' civilian labor market earnings found that military service was even more of an advantage for racial and ethnic minority women than it was for White women veterans, so much so that it raised their earnings as high as, or in some cases higher than, White nonveterans' earnings (Padavic and Prokos, 2017).

For veterans and their family members, the transition to civilian life can be made more difficult by physical disabilities or conditions, such as chronic pain, or by mental health challenges, such as posttraumatic stress disorder or major depression (which are discussed in Chapter 5). Multiple surveys suggest that veterans who served as officers have better health than those who were enlisted (MacLean and Edwards, 2010). Women veterans appear to be more likely to have a disability or function limitation than veterans who are men (Prokos and Cabage, 2017; Wilmoth et al., 2011). As veterans move from the DoD health care system to the VA, they may find challenges to maintaining continuity of care, and not all veterans who need treatment will receive it (IOM, 2013).

Yet studies of past generations of war veterans have found that the long-term outcomes of military service are positive. The benefits of military service include not only education and economic gains but also positive coping strategies, the ability to withstand stress, and other resilience factors that can promote lifelong health and well-being (Spiro et al., 2015).

SUMMARY

Military life can offer tremendous benefits but also significant challenges. Some who enter will thrive, others will struggle or fail. Not everyone who enters will be willing or able to remain a military family member until the service members' transition to civilian life. The ongoing work for DoD, however, is to help prevent, mitigate, and respond to the negative impact of stressors to promote the well-being, readiness, effectiveness, and retention of quality service members and their families. Some of the challenges mentioned above may extend to parents, grandparents, siblings, close friends, and others in service members' personal networks, such as military separation from loved ones, concern about the safety of service members working in dangerous environments, and caring for service members' children or seriously injured service members.

Some events specifically related to military life can impact not just the service member but also other individuals in the family and subsystems within the family. Most notably, these include

- pay and in-kind benefits, such as housing and health care
- PCS moves
- assignments to installations in other countries
- deployments, sea duty, and temporary duty away from home
- combat experience and exposure
- service-related mental and physical injuries and death
- career progression (or lack thereof), and
- separation from military service and transition to civilian life.

The opportunities and challenges of military life change as the size of the military expands or contracts; as the civilian economy improves or declines; as the number, length and nature of military operations changes; and as public knowledge and attitudes toward the military change.

These types of military experiences will vary across different subgroups and regions, too. For example, military life experiences such as frequency and length of deployments, options of installation assignments, and career progression are often linked to military occupation, and military occupations vary greatly in their personnel composition (e.g., by entry requirements, race, ethnicity, gender, and concentration in the active component or National Guard or Reserves). Additionally, some military families have significantly more privileges and resources than others. The differences in pay mean senior military officers are much more likely than junior enlisted personnel to be able to afford to locate their families in neighborhoods with greater resources and better schools; to hire help with housekeeping, yardwork, or tutoring; to be able to fly other family members out to visit; to pay for their children's college education, and so on. Regardless of the resources a family may have, however, some installations are located in areas where there are few or low-quality resources, or where the resources are already overtaxed because the civilian population has great needs.

Thus, we reiterate here our call in Chapter 3 to be attentive to the ways intersectionality or overlapping statuses of numerous characteristics can shape how individual family members and families experience and interpret the events and features of military life.

It also bears repeating that we have more information on the life course of service members and military dependents than we do on partners, children who are not military dependents, and other military family members, as well as more information on historically majority subgroups in the military (e.g., men, Whites, heterosexuals).

Given finite resources and a vast array of possible challenges, the need is for DoD to find the best way to prioritize and focus its efforts to enhance the well-being of diverse military families, without compromising its ability to meet its missions. An important question to answer toward this end is: What are the most beneficial and meaningful types of interventions, guidance, and support that DoD could offer to achieve this?

CONCLUSIONS

CONCLUSION 4-1: Studies on the roles and impacts of nonmarital partners, ex-spouses, or ex-partners, parents, siblings, grandparents, and others in the personal networks of service members are scarce, despite the significant positive or negative influences those people could have or the important roles they could play in some situations, such as child custody disputes, respite child care, temporary guardianship of children during parents' deployments, and other situations.

CONCLUSION 4-2: There is a lack of understanding of how military family well-being varies by race and ethnicity, the concerns of minority families, and whether the Department of Defense is sufficiently meeting these families' needs. Scholarship on racial/ethnic diversity in the military tends to focus on equal opportunity issues for service members (such as discrimination and promotion rates), whereas findings concerning well-being are scattered widely across the literature.

CONCLUSION 4-3: The frequency of mandatory military moves and the associated stress of relocation create challenges for the continuity of care for active component military families, especially families who have members with special needs and must rely heavily upon community resources.

CONCLUSION 4-4: Since the end of the Cold War, the National Guard and Reserves have served at unprecedented levels, filling critical roles in disaster relief and homeland defense in the United States as well

as serving in military operations overseas. However, they face frequent family separations, changes in pay and benefits eligibility associated with shifting military statuses, and disruptions to civilian employment and business ownership, and they may not even live near a military community that could provide formal or informal support.

REFERENCES

Appolonio, K. K., and Fingerhut, R. (2008). Postpartum depression in a military sample. *Military Medicine, 173*(11), 1085–1991.

Aronson, K. R., Kyler, S. J., Moeller, J. D., and Perkins, D. F. (2016). Understanding military families who have dependents with special health care and/or educational needs. *Disability and Health Journal, 9*(3), 423–430.

Arthur, D. A. (2018). *Increasing Costs of the Department of Defense*. Washington, DC: Congressional Budget Office. Retrieved from https://www.cbo.gov/publication/54688.

Asch, B. J., Miller, T., and Malchiodi, A. (2012). *A New Look at Gender and Minority Differences in Officer Career Progression in the Military*. Santa Monica, CA: RAND Corporation.

Azoulay, D., Chung, J., Simcovitch, J., Sukumar, S., and Supawong, J. (2010). *Open Service and Our Allies: A Report on the Inclusion of Openly Gay and Lesbian Servicemembers in U.S. Allies' Armed Forces*. NewYork: Columbia Law School Sexuality & Gender Law Clinic.

Balderrama-Durbin, C., Cigrang, J. A., Osborne, L. J., Snyder, D. K., Talcott, G. W., Slep, A. M. S., Heyman, R. E., Tatum, J., Baker, M., Cassidy, D., and Sonnek, S., (2015). Coming home: A prospective study of family reintegration following deployment to a war zone. *Psychological Services, 12*(3), 213.

Balderrama-Durbin, C., Erbes, C. R., Polusny, M. A., and Vogt, D. (2018). Psychometric evaluation of a measure of intimate partner communication during deployment. *Journal of Family Psychology, 32*(1), 31–41.

Barnes R., Stevelink, S. A. M., Dandeker C., and Fear N. T. (2016). Military mothers. In A. Gewirtz and A. Youssef, (Eds.), *Parenting and Children's Resilience in Military Families: Risk and Resilience in Military and Veteran Families*. NewYork: Springer.

Belkin, A., and McNichol, J. (2000/2001, Winter). Homosexual personnel policy in the Canadian forces: Did lifting the gay ban undermine military performance? *International Journal*, 56, 73–88. doi:10.2307/4020353.

Belkin, A., and McNichol, J. (2000). *Effects of the 1992 Lifting of Restrictions on Gay and Lesbian Service in the Canadian Forces: Appraising the Evidence*. Santa Barbara, CA: Center for the Study of Sexual Minorities in the Military.

Bennett, P. R., and McDonald, K. B. (2013). Military service as a pathway to early socioeconomic achievement for disadvantaged groups. In J. M. Wilmoth and A. S. London (Eds.), *Life Course Perspectives on Military Service* (pp. 119–143). New York, NY: Routledge.

Bogard, K., Murry, V. M. and Alexander, C. (eds.). (2017). *Perspectives on Health Equity and Social Determinants of Health*. Washington, DC: National Academy of Medicine.

Booth, B., and Segal, D. R. (2005). Bringing the soldiers back in: Implications of inclusion of military personnel for labor market research on race, class, and gender. *Race, Gender & Class 12*(1), 34–57.

Boss, P. (2002). *Family Stress Management: A Contextual Approach* (2nd ed.). Thousand Oaks, CA: Sage.

Bowleg, L. (2012). The problem with the phrase Women and Minorities: Intersectionality—An important theoretical framework for public health. *American Journal of Public Health, 102*, 1267–1273.

Bowles, S. V., Pollock, L. D., Moore, M., Wadsworth, S. M., Cato, C., Dekle, J. W., Meyer, S. W., Shriver, A., Mueller, B., Stephens, M., and Seidler, D. A., 2015. Total force fitness: The military family fitness model. *Military Medicine, 180*(3), 246–258.

Bradshaw, C. P., Sudhinaraset, M., Mmari, K., and Blum, R. W. (2010). School transitions among military adolescents: A qualitative study of stress and coping. *School Psychology Review, 39*(1), 84–105.

Bronfenbrenner Center for Translational Research. (2013). *Department of Defense Exceptional Family Member Benchmark Study*. Ithaca, NY: Author.

Burk, J., and Espinoza, E. (2012). Race relations within the U.S. military. *Annual Review of Sociology, 38*, 401–422.

Burke, J., and Miller, A. R. (2018). The effects of job relocation on spousal careers: Evidence from military change of station moves. *Economic Inquiry, 56*(2), 1261–1277.

Burland, D., and Lundquist, J. H., (2013). The best years of our lives: Military service and family relationships—A life-course perspective. In J. M. Wilmoth and A. S. London (Eds.), *Life Course Perspectives on Military Service* (pp. 189-208). New York, NY: Routledge.

Burrell, L. M., Adams, G. A., Durand, D. B., and Castro, C. A. (2006). The impact of military lifestyle demands on well-being, army, and family outcomes. *Armed Forces & Society, 33*(1), 43–58.

Carroll, T. D., Currier, J. M., McCormick, W. H., and Drescher, K. D. (2017). Adverse childhood experiences and risk for suicidal behavior in male Iraq and Afghanistan veterans seeking PTSD treatment. *Psychological Trauma: Theory, Research, Practice, and Policy, 9*(5), 583–586.

Carter, P., Kidder, K., Schafer, A., and Swick, A. (2017). *The Future of the All-Volunteer Force*. Working paper AVF 4.0. Center for New American Security. Retrieved from https://s3.amazonaws.com/files.cnas.org/documents/AVF_WorkingPaper_FINAL.pdf?mtime=20170328111409.

Carter, S. P., and Renshaw, K. D. (2016). Spousal communication during military deployments: A review. *Journal of Family Issues, 37*(16), 2309–2332.

Chandra, A., Lara-Cinisomo, S., Jaycox, L. H., Tanielian, T., Han, B., Burns, R. M., and Ruder, T. (2011). *Views From the Homefront: The Experiences of Youth and Spouses from Military Families*. Santa Monica, CA: RAND Corporation.

Chandra, A., Martin, L. T., Hawkins, S. A. and Richardson, A. (2010). The impact of parental deployment on child social and emotional functioning: Perspectives of school staff. *Journal of Adolescent Health, 46*(3), 218–223.

Chartrand, M. M., Frank, D. A., White, L. F., and Shope, T. R. (2008). Effect of parents' wartime deployment on the behavior of young children in military families. *Archives of Pediatrics & Adolescent Medicine, 162*(11), 1009–1014.

Clever, M., and Segal, D. R. (2013). The demographics of military children and families. *The Future of Children, 23*(2), 13–39.

Commission on the National Guard and Reserves. (2008). *Transforming the National Guard and Reserves into a 21st Century Operational Force*. Arlington, VA: Commission on the National Guard and Reserves. Retrieved from https://policy.defense.gov/portals/11/Documents/hdasa/references/CNGR%20Final%20Report.pdf.

Congressional Budget Office. (2017). *Trends in the Department of Defense's Support Costs*. Washington, DC. Retrieved from https://www.cbo.gov/publication/53168.

Council on Foreign Relations (CFR). (2009). *U.S. Immigration Policy*. Independent Task Force Report No. 63. New York, NY. Retrieved from file:///C:/Users/pnalamada/Downloads/Immigration_TFR63%20(1).pdf.

Cozza, C. S. J., and Lerner, R. M. (2013). Military children and families: Introducing the issue. *The Future of Children*, 3–11.

Davis, L., Grifka, A., Williams, K., and Coffey, M. (2017). *2016 Workplace and Gender Relations Survey of Active Duty Members*. U.S. Department of Defense. Alexandria, VA. Retrieved from https://sapr.mil/public/docs/reports/FY17_Annual/FY16_Annual_Report_on_Sexual_Assault_in_the_Military_Full_Report_Part2_4.pdf.

Defense Advisory Committee on Women in the Service (DACOWITS). (2015). 1951–2015: 64 Years of DACOWITS. 2015 Report. Washington, DC: U.S. Department of Defense. Retrieved from https://dacowits.defense.gov/Portals/48/Documents/Reports/2015/Annual%20Report/2015%20DACOWITS%20Annual%20Report_Final.pdf.

Defense Advisory Committee on Women in the Service (DACOWITS). (2017). *Annual Report*. (2017). Washington, DC: U.S. Department of Defense. Retrieved from https://dacowits.defense.gov/Portals/48/Documents/Reports/2017/Annual%20Report/DACOWITS%20 2017%20Annual%20Report_FINAL.PDF?ver=2018-02-28-222504-937.

Defense Manpower Data Center. (2015). *Military Family Life Project: Active Duty Spouse Study Longitudinal Analyses 2010-2012 Project Report*. Alexandria, VA: U.S. Department of Defense. Retrieved from http://download.militaryonesource.mil/12038/MOS/Reports/MFLP-Longitudinal-Analyses-Report.pdf.

DeVoe, E. R., Paris, R., Emmert-Aronson, B., Ross, A. and Acker, M., 2017. A randomized clinical trial of a postdeployment parenting intervention for service members and their families with very young children. *Psychological Trauma: Theory, Research, Practice, and Policy, 9*(S1), 25.

Easterbrooks, M. A., Ginsburg, K., and Lerner, R. M. (2013). Resilience among military youth. *The Future of Children, 23*(2), 99–120.

Elder, G. H., Wang, L., Spence, N. J., Adkins, D. E., and Brown, T. H. (2010). Pathways to the all-volunteer military. *Social Science Quarterly 91*(2), 455–475.

Exceptional Family Member Program (EFMP). (2016) *EFMP Quick Reference Guide*. Retrieved from https://download.militaryonesource.mil/12038/MOS/ResourceGuides/EFMP-QuickReferenceGuide.pdf.

Erbes, C. R., Kramer, M., Arbisi, P. A., DeGarmo, D. and Polusny, M. A. (2017). Characterizing spouse/partner depression and alcohol problems over the course of military deployment. *Journal of Consulting and Clinical Psychology, 85*(4), 297.

Figinski, T. F. (2017). The effect of potential activations on the employment of military reservists: Evidence from a field experiment. *ILR Review, 70*(4), 1037–1056.

Flake, E. M., Davis, B. E., Johnson, P. L. and Middleton, L. S. (2009). The psychosocial effects of deployment on military children. *Journal of Developmental & Behavioral Pediatrics, 30*(4), 271–278.

Flores, N. I. (2009). *The Current Burdensome Pay Processes of the Mobilized Army National Guard Soldier: Finding Better Options*. A thesis presented to the faculty of the U.S. Army Command and General Staff College in partial fulfillment of the requirements for the Degree Master of Military Art and Science General Studies. Retrieved from https://apps.dtic.mil/dtic/tr/fulltext/u2/a512322.pdf.

Floyd L., and Phillips, D. A. (2013). Child care and other support programs. *Future of Children, 23*(2), 79–97.

Galovski, T.E. and Sanders, W. (2018). *Strengthening Support for Female Service Members Suffering from PTSD Secondary to Military-connected Sexual Trauma*. Memo prepared for the Committee on the Wellbeing of Military Families.

Gates, G. (2010). *Lesbian, Gay, and Bisexual Men and Women in the U.S. military: Updated estimates*. Los Angeles, CA: Williams Institute.

Gates, G. J., and Herman, J. (2014). *Transgender Military Service in the United States*. Los Angeles, CA: Williams Institute.

Gewirtz, A. H., DeGarmo, D. S., and Zamir, O. (2018). Testing a military family stress model. *Family Process, 57*, 415–431. doi: 10.1111/famp.12282.

Gewirtz, A. H., Erbes, C. R., Polusny, M. A., Forgatch, M. S., and DeGarmo, D. S. (2011). Helping military families through the deployment process: Strategies to support parenting. *Professional Psychology: Research and Practice, 42*(1), 56.

Gewirtz, A. H., McMorris, B. J., Hanson, S., and Davis, L. (2014). Family adjustment of deployed and nondeployed mothers in families with a parent deployed to Iraq or Afghanistan. *Professional Psychology: Research and Practice, 45*(6), 465.

Gewirtz, A. H., Polusny, M. A., DeGarmo, D. S., Khaylis, A. and Erbes, C. R. (2010). Posttraumatic stress symptoms among National Guard soldiers deployed to Iraq: Associations with parenting behaviors and couple adjustment. *Journal of Consulting and Clinical Psychology, 78*(5), 599.

Gewirtz, A. H., and Youssef, A. M., (Eds.). (2016). *Parenting and Children's Resilience in Military Families*. Switzerland: Springer.

Gibbs, D. A., Martin, S. L., Kupper, L. L. and Johnson, R. E., 2007. Child maltreatment in enlisted soldiers' families during combat-related deployments. *Journal of the American Medical Association, 298*(5), 528–535.

Gilreath, T. D., Wrabel, S. L., Sullivan, K. S., Capp, G. P., Roziner, I., Benbenishty, R. and Astor, R. A. (2016). Suicidality among military-connected adolescents in California schools. *European Child & Adolescent Psychiatry, 25*(1), 61–66.

Goodman, P., Turner, A., Agazio, J., Throop, M., Padden, D., Greiner, S., and Hillier, S. L. (2013). Deployment of military mothers: Supportive and nonsupportive military programs, processes, and policies. *Military Medicine, 178*(7), 729–734.

Guo, C., Pollak, J. and Bauman, M. (2016). *Ten Frequently Asked Questions about Veterans' Transitions: Results of a Decade of RAND Work on Veteran Life.* Santa Monica, CA: RAND Corporation.

Hatzenbuehler, M. L. (2009). How does sexual minority stigma "get under the skin"? A psychological mediation framework. *Psychological Bulletin, 135*(5), 707.

Hawkins, S. A., Condon, A., Hawkins, J. N., Liu, K., Melendrez Ramirez, Y., Nihill, M. M., and Tolins, J. (2018). *What We Know About Military Family Readiness: Evidence From 2007–2017*. Monterey, CA: Research Facilitation Laboratory.

Huebner, A. J., Mancini, J. A., Bowen, G. L. and Orthner, D. K. (2009). Shadowed by war: Building community capacity to support military families. *Family Relations, 58*(2), 216–228.

Huffman, A. H., Dunbar, N., Van Puyvelde, V., Klinefelter, Z. P., and Sullivan, K. S. (2017). Caring for children and meeting mission needs: Experiences of parents in dual-military families. *Military Behavioral Health, 6*(3), 186–197.

Institute of Medicine. (2013). *Returning Home from Iraq and Afghanistan: Assessment of Readjustment Needs of Veterans, Service Members, and Their Families*. Washington, DC: The National Academies Press. doi: 10.17226/13499.

Joint Advertising, Market Research & Studies (JAMRS). (2016). *The Target Population for Military Recruitment: Youth Eligible to Enlist Without a Waiver.* Briefing for the Defense Advisory Committee on Women in the Services. U.S. Department of Defense. Retrieved from https://dacowits.defense.gov/Portals/48/Documents/General%20Documents/RFI%20Docs/Sept2016/JAMRS%20RFI%2014.pdf?ver=2016-09-09-164855-510.

Kamarck, K. N. (2018). *Military Child Development Program: Background and Issues.* Washington, DC: Congressional Research Service.

Kelley, M. L., Hock, E., Smith, K. M., Jarvis, M. S., Bonney, J. F., and Gaffney, M. A. (2001). Internalizing and externalizing behavior of children with enlisted Navy mothers experiencing military-induced separation. *Journal of the American Academy of Child & Adolescent Psychiatry, 40*(4), 464–471.

Kelley, M. L., Hock, E., Jarvis, M. S., Smith, K. M., Gaffney, M. A., and Bonney, J. F. (2002). Psychological adjustment of Navy mothers experiencing deployment. *Military Psychology, 14*(3), 199–216.

Kelty, R., Kleykamp, M., and Segal, D. (2010). The military and the transition to adulthood. *The Future of Children, 20*(1), 181–207.

Kelty, R., and Segal, D. R. (2013). The military as a transforming influence: Integration into or isolation from normal adult roles. In J. M. Wilmoth and A. S. London (Eds.), *Life Course Perspectives on Military Service* (pp. 19–47). New York, NY: Routledge.

Kimerling, R., Street, A. E., Pavao, J., Smith, M. W., Cronkite, R. C., Holmes, T. H. and Frayne, S. M., 2010. Military-related sexual trauma among Veterans Health Administration patients returning from Afghanistan and Iraq. *American Journal of Public Health, 100*(8), 1409–1412.

Klein, D. A., Roberts, T. A., Adirim, T. A., Landis, C. A., Susi, A., Schvey, N. A., Hisle-Gorman, E. (2019). Transgender children and adolescents receiving care in the U.S. military health care system. *Journal of the American Medical Association Pediatrics, 173*(5), 491–492.

Kleykamp, M. (2013). Labor market outcomes among veterans and military spouses. In *Life Course Perspectives on Military Service* (pp. 168-188). New York, NY: Routledge.

Kleykamp, M., and Hipes, C. (2015). Coverage of veterans of the wars in Iraq and Afghanistan in the U.S. media. *Sociological Forum, 30*(2), 348–368.

Layne, C. M., Briggs, E. C., and Courtois, C. A. (2014). Introduction to the special section: Using the trauma history profile to unpack risk factor caravans and their consequences. *Psychological Trauma: Theory, Research, Practice, and Policy, 6*(1), S1–S8.

Legate, N., Ryan, R.M. and Weinstein, N. (2012). Is coming out always a "good thing"? Exploring the relations of autonomy support, outness, and wellness for lesbian, gay, and bisexual individuals. *Social Psychological and Personality Science, 3*(2), 145–152.

Lerner, R. M. (2007). Developmental science, developmental systems, and contemporary theories of human development. In W. Damon and R. Lerner (Eds.), *Handbook of Child Psychology* (6th ed., vol. 1, pp. 1–17). Hoboken, NJ: John Wiley & Sons, Inc.

Lester, P., Peterson, K., Reeves, J., Knauss, L., Glover, D., Mogil, C., Duan, N., Saltzman, W., Pynoos, R., Wilt, K., and Beardslee, W. (2010). The long war and parental combat deployment: Effects on military children and at-home spouses. *Journal of the American Academy of Child & Adolescent Psychiatry, 49*(4), 310–320.

Lim, N., Mariano, L. T., Cox, A. G., Schulker, D., and Hanser, L. M. (2014). *Improving Demographic Diversity in the U.S. Air Force Officer Corps.* Santa Monica, CA: RAND Corporation.

London, A. S., and Heflin, C. M. (2015). Supplemental Nutrition Assistance Program (SNAP) use among active-duty, military personnel, veterans and reservists. *Population Research and Policy Review, 34*(6), 805–826.

Loughran, D., and Klerman, J. (2008). *Explaining the Increase in Unemployment Compensation for Ex-Servicemembers during the Global War on Terror.* Santa Monica, CA: RAND Corporation.

Lucier-Greer, M., Arnold, A. L., Grimsley, R. N., Ford, J. L., Bryant, C., and Mancini, J. A. (2016). Parental military service and adolescent well-being: Mental health, social connections and coping among youth in the USA. *Child & Family Social Work, 21*(4), 421–432.

Lucier-Greer, M., O'Neal, C. W., Arnold, A. L., Mancini, J. A., and Wickrama, K. K. (2014). Adolescent mental health and academic functioning: Empirical support for contrasting models of risk and vulnerability. *Military Medicine, 179*(11), 1279–1287.

Lutz, A. C. (2013). Race-ethnicity and immigration status in the U.S. military. In J. M. Wilmoth and A. S. London (Eds.), *Life Course Perspectives on Military Service* (pp 68–96). New York, NY: Routledge.

Lyle, D. S. (2006). Using military deployments and job assignments to estimate the effect of parental absence and household relocations on children's academic achievement. *Journal of Labor Economics, 24*(2), 319–350.

MacLean, A. (2013). A matter of life and death: Military service and health. In J. M. Wilmoth and A. S. London (Eds.), *Life Course Perspectives on Military Service* (pp. 200–220). New York, NY: Routledge.

MacLean, A., and Edwards, R. D. (2010). The pervasive role of rank in the health of U.S. veterans. *Armed Forces & Society, 36*,(5): 765-785.

MacLean, A., and Elder, G. H. (2007). Military service in the life course. *Annual Review of Sociology, 33*, 175–196.

Maley, A. J., and Hawkins, D. N. (2018). The Southern military tradition: Sociodemographic factors, cultural legacy, and U.S. Army enlistments. *Armed Forces & Society, 44*(2), 195–218.

Mansfield, A. J., Kaufman, J. S., Engel, C. C., and Gaynes, B. N. (2011). Deployment and mental health diagnoses among children of U.S. Army personnel. *Archives of Pediatrics & Adolescent Medicine, 165*(11), 999–1005.

Masten, A. S. (2013). Afterword: What we can learn from military children and families. *The Future of Children, 23*(2), 199–212.

Masten, A. S., and Cicchetti, D. (2010). Developmental cascades. *Development and Psychopathology, 22*(3), 491–495.

McCarroll, J. E., Fan, Z., Newby, J. H., and Ursano, R. J., 2008. Trends in U.S. Army child maltreatment reports: 1990–2004. *Child Abuse Review: Journal of the British Association for the Study and Prevention of Child Abuse and Neglect, 17*(2), 108–118.

McGraw, K. (2016). Gender differences among military combatants: Does social support, ostracism, and pain perception influence psychological health? *Military Medicine, 181*(1), 80–85.

Meadows, S., Engel, C., Collins, R., Beckman, R., Cefalu, M., Hawes-Dawson, J., Doyle, M., Kress, A., Sontag-Padilla, L., Ramchand, R., and Williams, K. (2018). *2015 Department of Defense Health Related Behaviors Survey (HRBS)*. Santa Monica, CA: RAND Corporation.

Meadows, S. O., Tanielian, T., and Karney, B. R. (Eds.). (2016). *The Deployment Life Study: Longitudinal Analysis of Military Families Across the Deployment Cycle*. Santa Monica, CA: RAND Corporation.

Mesecar, D., and Soifer, D. (2018). *Getting School Districts Ready for the Military Student Identifier*. Arlington, VA: Lexington Institute. Retrieved from https://forstudentsuccess.org/wp-content/uploads/2018/09/MSI-Lex-Report_final.pdf.

Meyer, I. H. (2003). Prejudice, social stress, and mental health in lesbian, gay, and bisexual populations: Conceptual issues and research evidence. *Psychological Bulletin, 129*(5), 674.

Military Child Education Coalition (MCEC) for the United States Army Family and Morale, Welfare and Recreation Command. (2009). *What Transitioning Military Families with Children Who Have Special Needs Currently Experience: Phase II Continuity of Care within the Exceptional Family Member Program*. Harker Heights, Texas.

________. (2017). Deepening our understanding about military-connected students: A first look at one state's data. *On the Move Magazine, 11*(1).

________. (2019a). *Making the Case: Recognizing and Supporting All Military-Connected Students in Our Nation's Schools*. Harker Heights, Texas.

________. (2019b). *Frequently Asked Questions and Suggested Use for Military Student Identifier Code*. Retrieved from https://www.militarychild.org/upload/files/resources/FAQs_on_Military_Connected_Stude.2%20-%20Copy%201.pdf.

Military Interstate Children's Compact Commission. (2018). *Interstate Compact on Educational Opportunity for Military Children: Compact Rules*. Lexington, KY. Retrieved from http://www.mic3.net/assets/rules-2018-revised-9-nov--2018.pdf.

Military Leadership Diversity Commission. (2011). *From Representation to Inclusion: Diversity Leadership for the 21st Century Military*. Retrieved from https://diversity.defense.gov/Portals/51/Documents/Special%20Feature/MLDC_Final_Report.pdf.

Miller, D. P., Larson, M. J., Byrne, T. and DeVoe, E. (2016). Food insecurity in veteran households: Findings from nationally representative data. *Public Health Nutrition, 19*(10), 1731–1740.

Millegan, J., Milburn, E. K., LeardMann, C. A., Street, A. E., Williams, D., Trone, D. W., and Crum-Cianflone, N. F. (2015). Recent sexual trauma and adverse health and occupational outcomes among U.S. service women. *Journal of Traumatic Stress, 28*(4), 298–306.

Milliken, C. S., Auchterlonie, J. L. and Hoge, C. W. (2007). Longitudinal assessment of mental health problems among active and reserve component soldiers returning from the Iraq war. *Journal of the American Medical Association, 298*(18), 2141–2148.

Moeller, J. D., Culler, E. D., Hamilton, M. D., Aronson, K. R., and Perkins, D. F. (2015). The effects of military-connected parental absence on the behavioral and academic functioning of children: A literature review. *Journal of Children's Services, 10*(3), 291–306.

Mount, S. D., Steelman, S. M., and Hertlein, K. (2015). "I'm not sure I trust the system yet": Lesbian service member experiences with mental health care. *Military Psychology, 27*(2), 115–127. Retrieved from https://www.researchgate.net/publication/277580651.

Negrusa, B., and Negrusa, S. (2014). Home front: Post deployment mental health and divorce. *Demography, 51*(3), 895–916.

Negrusa, S., Negrusa, B., and Hosek, J. (2013). Going to war: Have deployments increased divorce? *Journal of Population Economics, 27*(2), 473–496.

North Atlantic Treaty Organization (NATO). (2016). *Summary of the National Reports of NATO Member and Partner Nations to the NATO Committee on Gender Perspectives 2016*. Retrieved from https://www.nato.int/nato_static_fl2014/assets/pdf/pdf_2017_11/20171122_2016_Summary_of_NRs_to_NCGP.pdf.

Office of Diversity Management and Equal Opportunity. (2017). *Hazing Prevention and Response in the Armed Forces, Annual Summary Report to Congress, Reporting Period: April 26, 2016–September 30, 2017*. Washington, DC: U.S. Department of Defense.

Office of Special Needs. (2018). *Annual Report to the Congressional Defense Committees on the Activities of the Office of Special Needs–2017*. Washington, DC: U.S. Department of Defense.

Padavic, I., and Prokos, A. (2017). Aiming high: Explaining the earnings advantage for female veterans. *Armed Forces & Society, 43*(2), 368–386.

Parco, J. E., and Levy, D. A. (Eds.). (2010). *Attitudes Aren't Free: Thinking Deeply About Diversity in the US Armed Forces*. Maxwell Air Force Base, AL: Air University Press.

Parrott, S., Albright, D. L., Dyche, C., and Steele, H. G. (2018). Hero, charity case, victim: How U.S. news media frame military veterans on Twitter. *Armed Forces & Society (1)*21.

Pew Research Center. (2018a). *Internet/Broadband Fact Sheet*. Retrieved from http://www.pewinternet.org/fact-sheet/internet-broadband.

________. (2018b). *Social Media Fact Sheet*. Retrieved from http://www.pewinternet.org/fact-sheet/social-media.

________. (2018c). *Mobile Fact Sheet*. Retrieved from http://www.pewinternet.org/fact-sheet/mobile.

Polchar, J., Sweijs, T., Marten, P., and Gladega, J. (2014). *LGBT Military Personnel: A Strategic Vision for Inclusion*. The Hague, Netherlands: The Hague Centre for Strategic Studies.

Prokos, A., and Cabage, L. N. (2017). Women military veterans, disability, and employment. *Armed Forces & Society, 43*(2), 346–367.

Ramirez, H., and Bloeser, K. (2018). Risk and resilience: A review of the health literature of veterans who identify as LGBT. In E. Ritchie, J. Wise, and B. Pyle (Eds.) *Gay Mental Healthcare Providers and Patients in the Military* (pp. 9–24). Springer, Cham.

Rentz, E. D., Marshall, S. W., Loomis, D., Martin, S. L., Casteel, C., and Gibbs, D. (2007). Effect of deployment on the occurrence of child maltreatment in military and non-military families. *American Journal of Epidemiology, 165*(10), 1199–1206.

Reyes-Guzman, C. M., Bray, R. M., Forman-Hoffman, V. L., and Williams, J. (2015). Overweight and obesity trends among active duty military personnel: A 13-year perspective. *American Journal of Preventive Medicine, 48*(2), 145–153.

Richardson, A., Chandra, A., Martin, L. T., Messan Setodji, C., Hallmark, B. W., Campbell, N. F., Hawkins, S. A., and Grady, P. (2011). *Effects of Soldiers' Deployment on Children's Academic Performance and Behavioral Health.* Santa Monica, CA: RAND Corporation.

Rohall, D., Ender, M. G., and Matthews, M. D. (Eds.). (2017). *Inclusion in the American Military: A Force for Diversity.* Lanham, MD: Lexington Books.

Rosellini, A. J., Street, A. E., Ursano, R. J., Chiu, W. T., Heeringa, S. G., Monahan, J., Naifeh, J. A., Petukhova, M. V., Reis, B. Y., Sampson, N. A. and Bliese, P. D. (2017). Sexual assault victimization and mental health treatment, suicide attempts, and career outcomes among women in the U.S. Army. *American Journal of Public Health, 107*(5), 732–739.

Rostker, B., Hosek, S. D., Winkler, J. D., Asch, B. J., Asch, S. M., Baxter, C., Bensahel, N., Berry, S. H., Brown, R. A., Werber, L. and Collins, R. L. (2010). *Sexual Orientation and U.S. Military Personnel Policy: An Update of RAND's 1993 Study.* Santa Monica, CA: RAND Corporation.

Ruff, S. B., and Keim, M. A. (2014). Revolving doors: The impact of multiple school transitions on military children. *Professional Counselor, 4*(2), 103–113.

Santos, C. E., and Toomey, R. B., (2018). Integrating an intersectionality lens in theory and research in developmental science. *New Directions for Child and Adolescent Development, 2018*(161), 7–15.

Schulte, B., and Durana, A. (2016). *The New America Care Report.* Washington, DC: New America. Retrieved from https://www.newamerica.org/better-life-lab/policy-papers/new-america-care-report/

Segal, M. W. (1986). The military and the family as greedy institutions. *Armed Forces & Society, 13*(1), 9–38.

Segal, M. W., and Lane, M. D. (2016). Conceptual model of military women's life events and well-being. *Military Medicine, 181*(suppl_1), 12–19.

Segal, M. W., Lane, M. D., and Fisher, A. G. (2015). Conceptual model of military career and family life course events, intersections, and effects on well-being. *Military Behavioral Health, 3*(2), 95–107.

Shiffer, C. O., Maury, R. V., Sonethavilay, H., Hurwitz, J. L., Lee, H. C., Linsner, R. K., and Mehta, M. S. (2017). *2017 Blue Star Families Military Family Lifestyle Survey.* Blue Star Families. Retrieved from https://www.secome.org/MFLS-ComprehensiveReport17-FINAL.pdf.

Snyder, J., Gewirtz, A. H., Schrepferman, L. P., Gird, S. R., Quattlebaum, J., Pauldine, M. R., Elish, K., Zamir, O., and Hayes, C. (2016). Parent-child relationship quality and family transmission of parent posttraumatic stress disorder symptoms and child externalizing and internalizing symptoms following fathers' exposure to combat-related trauma. *Development and Psychopathology, 28*, 947–969.

Spencer, E., Page, K., and Clark, M. G. (2016). Managing frequent relocation in families? Considering prospect theory, emotional framing, and priming. *Family and Consumer Science Research Journal, 45*(1), 77–90.

Spiro III, A., Settersten, R. A. and Aldwin, C. M. (2015). Long-term outcomes of military service in aging and the life course: A positive re-envisioning. *The Gerontologist, 56*(1), 5–13.

Stock, M. (2009). *Essential to the Fight: Immigrants in the Military Eight Years after 9/11.* Special Report. Washington, DC: Immigration Policy Center, American Immigration Council.

Substance Abuse and Mental Health Services Administration. (2013). *Strategies to Improve Media Coverage of Military Veterans with Mental Health Issues: Report of the Dialogue Meeting July 2012.* Rockville, MD. Retrieved from https://www.samhsa.gov/sites/default/files/veterans-dialogue.pdf.

Surís, A., Link-Malcolm, J., Chard, K., Ahn, C. and North, C. (2013). A randomized clinical trial of cognitive processing therapy for veterans with PTSD related to military sexual trauma. *Journal of Traumatic Stress, 26*(1), 28–37.

Task Force on Defense Personnel. (2017). *Building a F.A.S.T. Force: A Flexible Personnel System for a Modern Military: Recommendations from the Task Force on Defense Personnel.* Washington, DC: Bipartisan Policy Center.

Tick, S., Pema, E., Mehay, S., and Salas, M. (2015). *An Analysis of the Career Progression of Hispanic Military Officers.* Monterey, CA: Naval Postgraduate School.

Tong, P. K., Payne, L. A., Bond, C. A., Meadows, S. O., Lewis, J. L., Friedman, E. M., and Maksabedian Hernandez, E. J. (2018). *Enhancing Family Stability During a Permanent Change of Station: A Review of Disruptions and Policies.* Santa Monica, CA: RAND Corporation.

Trail, T. E., Martin, L. T., Burgette, L. F., Warren May, L., Mahmud, A., Nanda, N., and Chandra, A. (2017). *An Evaluation of U.S. Military Non-Medical Counseling Programs.* Santa Monica, CA: RAND Corporation.

U.S. Department of Defense (DoD). (2009). *Military Morale, Welfare, and Recreation (MWR) Programs.* DoD Instruction 1015.10). Washington, DC. Retrieved from http://www.esd.whs.mil/Portals/54/Documents/DD/issuances/dodi/101510p.pdf.

________. (2010). *DoD Housing Management. (DoD Manual 4165.63, Incorporating Change 2, August 31, 2018).* Washington, DC. Retrieved from https://www.esd.whs.mil/Portals/54/Documents/DD/issuances/dodm/416563m.pdf?ver=2018-09-20-075812-223.

________. (2015). *Memorandum for Secretaries of the Military Departments: Transgender Service Members.* Retrieved from https://dod.defense.gov/Portals/1/features/2016/0616_policy/memo-transgender-service-directive-28-July-2015.pdf.

________. (2016a). *Annual Report to the Congressional Defense Committees on the Department of Defense Policy and Plans for Military Family Readiness: Fiscal Year 2016.* Washington, DC. Retrieved from http://download.militaryonesource.mil/12038/MOS/Reports/FY2016-Report-on-DoD-Policy-and-Plans-for-MFR.pdf.

________. (2016b). *Report to the Congressional Defense Committees on Wait Times at Department of Defense Child Development Centers.* Washington, DC.

________. (2016c). *Department of Defense Annual Report on Sexual Assault in the Military: Fiscal Year 2016.* Retrieved from https://sapr.mil/public/docs/reports/FY16_Annual/FY16_SAPRO_Annual_Report.pdf.

________. (2017a). *The Third Quadrennial Quality of Life Review.* (No 17-C-0436). Washington, DC. Retrieved from http://download.militaryonesource.mil/12038/MOS/Reports/QQLR2017.pdf.

________. (2017b). *Annual Report to the Congressional Defense Committees on the Department of Defense Policy and Plans for Military Family Readiness, Fiscal Year 2016.* Washington, DC.

________. (2017c). *2017 Demographics: Profile of the Military Community.* Washington, DC. Retrieved from http://download.militaryonesource.mil/12038/MOS/Reports/2017-demographics-report.pdf.

________. (2017d). *The Exceptional Family Member Program (EFMP)*. DoD Instruction 1315.19. Washington, DC. Retrieved from https://www.esd.whs.mil/Portals/54/Documents/DD/issuances/dodi/131519p.pdf.

________. (2018). Personal communication of 2017 service member and spouse survey statistics to supplement statistics reported in *2016 Demographics: Profile of the Military Community*.

________. (2019). *Military Service by Transgender Persons and Persons With Gender Dysphoria*. Directive-type memorandum (DTM) 19-004. Retrieved from https://www.esd.whs.mil/Portals/54/Documents/DD/issuances/dtm/DTM-19-004.pdf?ver=2019-03-13-103259-670.

U.S. Department of Defense Education Activity. (2019). *About DoDEA – DoDEA Schools Worldwide*. Retrieved from https://www.dodea.edu/aboutDoDEA/today.cfm

________. (2019a). *DoDEA Educational Partnership: About Educational Partnership*. Retrieved from https://www.dodea.edu/Partnership/.

U.S. Department of Veteran Affairs. (2018). *National Center for Veterans Analysis and Statistics: Veteran Population Infographic, Veteran Population Projections 2017-2037*. Retrieved from https://www.va.gov/vetdata/docs/Demographics/New_Vetpop_Model/Vetpop_Infographic_Final31.pdf.

U.S. Departments of the Army and the Air Force. (2008). *National Guard Domestic Operations*. National Guard Regulation 500-1/Air National Guard Instruction 10-8101. Arlington, VA: National Guard Bureau.

U.S. Government Accountability Office (GAO). (2012). *Military Child Care: DoD Is Taking Actions to Address Awareness and Availability Barriers*. Washington, DC.

________. (2016). *Complete Data on Active-Duty Servicemembers' Use of Food Assistance Programs*. Washington, DC.

________. (2017). *Military Personnel: Improvements Needed in the Management of Enlistees' Medical Early Separation and Enlistment Information*. Washington, DC.

________. (2018a). *Military Readiness: Clear Policy and Reliable Data Would Help DoD Better Manage Service Members' Time Away from Home*. Washington, DC.

________. (2018b). *Military Personnel: DoD Should Improve Its Oversight of the Exceptional Family Member Program*. Washington, DC.

________. (2018c). *Military Personnel: DoD Needs to Improve Funding Process for Morale, Welfare, and Recreation Programs*. Washington, DC.

________. (2019). *Transitioning Servicemembers: Information on Military Employment Assistance Centers*. GAO-19-438R. Washington, DC. Retrieved from https://www.gao.gov/assets/700/699769.pdf.

Van Donge, N., Schvey, N. A., Roberts, T. A., Klein, D. A., (2019). Transgender dependent adolescents in the U.S. military health care system: Demographics, treatments sought, and health care service utilization. *Military Medicine, 184* (5-6), e447-e454.

Werber, L., Schaefer, A. G., Osilla, K. C., Wilke, E., Wong, A., Breslau, J., and Kitchens, K. E. (2013). *Support for the 21st-Century Reserve Force: Insights on Facilitating Successful Reintegration for Citizen Warriors and Their Families*. Santa Monica, CA: RAND Corporation.

Williams, K. D. (2007). Ostracism. *Annual Review of Psychology, 58*, 425–452.

Wilmoth, J. M., and London, A. S. (2013). *Life Course Perspectives on Military Service*. New York: Routledge.

Wilmoth, J. M., London, A. S., and Parker, W. M. (2011). Sex differences in the relationship between military service status and functional limitations and disabilities. *Population Research and Policy Review, 30*, 333–354.

Zellman, G. L., Gates, S. M., Moini, J. S., and Suttorp, M. (2009). Meeting family and military needs through military child care. *Armed Forces & Society, 35*, 437–459.

Zhao, S., and Chen, X. (2018). Maternal involvement in children's leisure activities in rural China: Relations with adjustment outcomes. *Journal of Family Psychology, 32*(1), 71–80.
Zimmerman, L., Darnell, D. A., Rhew, I. C., Lee, C. M. and Kaysen, D., 2015. Resilience in community: A social ecological development model for young adult sexual minority women. *American Journal of Community Psychology*, 55(1-2), 179–190.
Zinskie, C. D., and Rea, D. W. (2016). The Every Student Succeeds Act (ESSA): What it means for educators of students at risk. *National Youth-At-Risk Journal*, 2(1), 1.

5

Stress, Risk, and Resilience in Military Children

Almost 70 percent of children in military families are younger than age 11, and 38 percent are age 5 or younger (DoD, 2017, p. vi). For children, the early years represent a developmental stage that is particularly vulnerable to stress and a time when the characteristics of the caregiving or parenting environment are key in developing their stress-regulating capacities (Blair, 2010). The committee's charge, in part, was to provide information on children's social-emotional, physical, biochemical, and psychological development. Thus, in this chapter, the committee focuses on the impact of stressors on child development and how the developmental challenges of childhood and adolescence intersect with the unique experiences of military family life. We found no neurobiological research on military children, hence the review of the civilian literature.

Applying the concepts and definitions of *resilience* introduced in Chapters 1 and 2, we review the broader developmental literature on childhood resilience, pointing out key correlates and predictors and how they may be applied to the military child's context. Special attention is given to recent resilience research, which looks at the neurobiological, behavioral, cognitive, and emotional processes that might underpin resilience. The chapter concludes with a discussion of evidence-based interventions[1] to promote childhood resilience, highlighting prevention programs whose

[1]All interventions reviewed in this chapter are evidence-based.

caregiving or parenting interventions have demonstrated the potential to be the most relevant to military children and families.

THE IMPACT OF STRESS ON YOUTH DEVELOPMENT

Stress commonly refers to an individual's reaction to a challenge in the environment. Stress can be positive, as in the rewarding experience of rising to a challenge; it can be tolerable, as in difficult situations that are coped with in positive ways; or it can be severe, sometimes referred to as "toxic stress" (Center on the Developing Child, 2019; McEwen, 2017). In this section, the committee provides an overview of what is known about the specific effects of severe stressors on child development. Because overall development, and especially brain development, is so rapid and dynamic over the first two decades of life (Lenroot and Giedd, 2006), and because a large body of evidence has demonstrated the detrimental impact on later development of stressful early-life experiences, we focus on the impact of stress on childhood and adolescent development.

While we are aware of no research on the ways typical military family life contributes to stress and stress-related outcomes, extensive research on the development of stress regulatory systems can significantly aid in understanding how military-specific stressors affect development among children in service families. While a certain amount of stress is necessary and even optimal for healthy functioning, excessive stress has been shown to impair functioning at multiple levels—epigenetic, biological, physiological, and behavioral—and to increase risk for later pathology. However, there is significant variability across individuals in how stress is perceived, with temperamental, biological, and social factors affecting both the experiences and the expressions of stress.

Although the vast majority of stress research has been conducted with civilian families, it nevertheless demonstrates the *crucial importance of the early caregiving/parenting environment* for a child's developing ability to regulate stress. While severe stressors such as maltreatment, parental psychopathology, and violence can have profound effects on children's development, there is relatively little evidence suggesting that separations due to military deployments have these effects (Meadows et al., 2017). The effects on children of deployments and related military family transitions, such as extended occupationally related separations and relocations, are more likely mediated through their impact on parents and the caregiving system (Meadows et al., 2017). Thus, for example, when a military parent's combat exposure results in severe posttraumatic stress disorder (PTSD) or traumatic brain injury (TBI), it is the service member's compromised parenting—in concert with the child's own vulnerabilities—that may increase the child's risk for dysregulation and related difficulties. Similarly, increases in the risk of child maltreatment by the primary caregiver during a military parent's deployment would likely be what precipitates child maladjustment.

The body of literature on the impact parental deployment to war has on youths' psychosocial development has grown significantly over the past 15 years and is reviewed in Chapter 4 of this volume, but many of the details regarding *how* military family stressors affect developmental processes both "above and below the skin" (e.g., observed behavior as well as physiological and biological processes) are still lacking. However, the broader child development literature can be informative in this context, in particular the study of how development goes awry, a field known as developmental psychopathology (Cicchetti, 1989). Studies examining the impacts of separation from or loss of a primary caregiver, maltreatment, and family violence on children's developmental trajectories all provide some data applicable to the military context.

Individual Differences

In general terms, severe stressors affect youth through physiological, biological, genetic, behavioral, affective, and cognitive mechanisms. These stressors can include maltreatment, exposure to a threat of violence or death, or prolonged separation from a primary caregiver at a very young age, among others. Pre-existing risks and vulnerabilities, such as psychopathology, genetic vulnerability, or environmental risks such as poverty, may potentiate the impact of stress and trauma on development, while protective factors, such as effective caregiving, may lessen them.

Diathesis-stress and *differential susceptibility* hypotheses offer explanations for *how* individuals differ in their responsiveness to stress. Diathesis-stress models suggest that some youth are more vulnerable than others to their caregiving environments; these youth fare worse in stressful circumstances but fare as well as others in routine, low-risk environments (e.g., Walker et al., 1989). The differential susceptibility hypothesis suggests that some youth (sometimes referred to as "orchids") are more sensitive to or show more plasticity to both nurturing and high-risk caregiving environments than other youth (sometimes referred to as "dandelions"; Boyce and Ellis, 2005). Under high-risk conditions, the more sensitive "orchids" show poorer outcomes, but in enriching environments these same youth show stronger outcomes than their peers (Belsky and Pluess, 2009). More recently, scholars have suggested a third category of youth, referred to as "tulips," who are moderately sensitive and responsive to their environments (Lionetti et al., 2018). It is important to note that research suggests that these variable sensitivities to environment are likely modifiable through epigenetic processes and/or through evidence-based targeted prevention interventions (see, e.g., Bakermans-Kranenburg and van Ijzendorn, 2015).

The concepts of *multifinality* and *equifinality* (Cicchetti and Rogosch, 1996) also illustrate the complexity of understanding the impact of a particular stressor on youth. Multifinality refers to the finding that one stressor, such as physical abuse, can have many different negative effects on development. For example, it may contribute to PTSD, anxiety, behavior problems, poor academic functioning, and social challenges, and that not all individuals will experience the same negative outcomes. Equifinality refers to the obverse—that the same single outcome, such as anxiety, social challenges, or poor academic functioning, can be evident following exposure to disparate stressor events, such as prolonged parental separation, relocation, or bullying.

Providing tailored, adaptive, or personalized family-based programs, services, and supports makes it possible to respond to individual differences in risk and vulnerability (Collins and Varmus, 2015; Nahum-Shani and Militello, 2018). Chapter 8 provides examples of these adaptive interventions, including just-in-time adaptive interventions (JITAIs), that harness the potential of mobile health (mHealth) or mobile technologies to respond to individual child and family needs and preferences.

The Biology of Stress

Careful longitudinal examinations of stressful events and child/youth functioning, using data gathered through multiple methods, from multiple informants, and analyzed at multiple levels of analysis (biological, behavioral, etc.), have enabled researchers to specify with greater clarity the developmental pathways from stressor(s) to outcomes. As discussed above, there is significant variability in what is perceived as stressful and how individuals react to stressful situations, with physical, genetic, developmental, and psychosocial factors affecting these reactions (Sapolsky, 1994) as well as prior experiences (Cicchetti and Walker, 2001).

From a biological perspective, excessive stress can be seen as a threat to the body's homeostasis (its tendency to maintain internal equilibrium), a threat the body responds to by increasing autonomic nervous system activity and releasing hormone secretions to protect the body against (McEwen, 1994). The hypothalamic-pituitary-adrenal (HPA) axis is the biological system most closely linked to stress, and when individuals perceive stress it releases the hormone cortisol (Vázquez, 1998). Extensive research on the HPA axis's response to stress has demonstrated that while it is adaptive, its chronic mobilization via hyper- or hypo-secretion of glucocorticoids is damaging to other bodily systems, including the brain's structure and function (Cicchetti and Walker, 2001; Gunnar and Vazquez, 2001).

The impact of stress varies in regard to *timing* and *duration* (see Chapter 1 of this report for a discussion of these concepts). The experience of extreme stress during development likely increases vulnerability to lifetime disease, but what constitutes a sensitive period for early life stress has not yet been determined (Leneman and Gunnar, 2019). In a review highlighting the differential effects of stress across development, Lupien and colleagues (2009) describe how the effects of both chronic and acute stressors may vary depending on the areas of the brain that are developing at the time of the stress exposure. For example, prenatal stress affects the development of regions of the brain associated with the development of the HPA axis (i.e., the hippocampus, amygdala, and frontal cortex), whereas stress in early postnatal life affects the production of glucocorticoids. The hippocampus develops from birth to age two; thus, stress during infancy might increase hippocampal vulnerability (e.g. by reducing hippocampal volume). In contrast, the amygdala and frontal cortex continue to develop throughout childhood and adolescence; stress during this time period might then be associated with reductions in amygdala volume. Adolescents are very vulnerable to the impact of stress, likely because of increases in frontal cortex volume that occur at this stage, as well as protracted glucocorticoid responses that continue into emerging adulthood (Lupien et al., 2009), the period during which many youth join the military.

Although emerging and early adulthood is not the focus of this chapter, neurobiological development, particularly in the prefrontal cortex, continues into the late 20s and beyond (Giedd et al., 2015). Impulse control, self-regulation, and the ability to delay gratification all continue to develop throughout adolescence and emerging adulthood, with the capacity to plan and anticipate consequences peaking only by age 25 (Giedd et al., 2015; Steinberg et al., 2009). These findings are highly relevant for understanding and effectively serving younger service members and their families.

HOW PARENTING AFFECTS THE DEVELOPMENT OF STRESS REGULATORY CAPACITIES

The caregiving or parenting environment is key to the development of a child's stress regulatory capacities. It can result in changes in gene expression, that is, in epigenetics, the turning of genes "on" and "off" by environmental stimuli, which in turn lead to biological and behavioral changes (Romens et al., 2015; Slavich and Cole, 2013). Nowhere is this more evident than in findings regarding the impact of childhood abuse and neglect on children's development (Cicchetti et al., 2010). Extensive research on child abuse and neglect has demonstrated how child victims develop ideas of the world as a place that is dangerous and unpredictable, resulting in enhanced appraisals of threat, increasing risk for both anxiety and aggression-related psychopathology (Shackman and Pollak, 2014). For example, child maltreatment is consistently associated with disruptions in the functioning of the HPA axis (Loman et al., 2010), and this in turn has been implicated as a causal factor in a range of psychopathology (Heim et al., 2008). Additionally, a recent study of the effects of child maltreatment found epigenetic changes to the glucocorticoid receptor gene in the whole blood of 56 young adolescents (ages 11 to 14). Compared with children who had not been maltreated, those who had been exposed to physical abuse showed greater methylation within the NR3C1 promoter region[2] and the NGFI-A (nerve growth factor) binding site of the gene. This increased methylation[3] likely contributes to fewer glucocorticoid receptors in the brain and blood, disrupting the physiology of stress regulation among these youth (Romens et al., 2015).

Parenting practices and parental functioning both directly and indirectly affect children's HPA axis regulation. For example, maternal depression and anxiety (both prenatally and following birth) are associated with higher, or poorer, basal activity in children's HPA axis throughout the childhood years (O'Connor et al., 2005; Swales et al., 2018). Youth age 13 whose mothers experienced postnatal depression evidenced higher and more variable levels of morning cortisol than those whose mothers did not experience depression (Halligan et al., 2004). These cortisol differences at age 13 were associated with subsequent depression at age 16 (Halligan et al., 2007). Children living in poverty show worse psychological and physical outcomes than children in higher-SES environments, partly due to poorer HPA axis regulation (Koss and Gunnar, 2018). However, attachment status appears to buffer the detrimental impact of poverty: secure (but not insecure) attachment was associated with lower (healthier) basal cortisol in a sample of very young children (ages 12 to 22 months) attending immunization appointments (Johnson et al., 2018).

Using multiple-method and informant data to examine stress and health outcomes from childhood into adulthood, Farrell and colleagues (2017) assessed stress in children using coder-rated interviews at five developmental stages: early childhood, middle childhood, adolescence, young adulthood, and age 32. They also observed parenting quality at seven time points from birth through age 13. Early childhood, adolescent, and concurrent stress were associated with poorer physical health at age 32, but higher parenting quality (measured as maternal sensitivity) protected against these relationships (Farrell et al., 2017). In summary, effective parenting practices protect and nurture children's stress-regulatory capacities, whereas maltreatment and other severe stressors disrupt children's regulation of stress.

[2]This is also known as a glucocorticoid receptor and is the receptor to which cortisol and other glucocorticoids bind.

[3]DNA methylation is "an epigenetic mechanism that occurs by the addition of a methyl (CH_3) group to DNA, thereby often modifying the function of the genes and affecting gene expression." See https://www.whatisepigenetics.com/dna-methylation.

While severe stressors have been shown to disrupt children's ability to manage stress by interfering with development at multiple levels—epigenetic, biological, physiological, and behavioral—many of the changes in children in response to stress are not absolute or permanent. Stress research demonstrates the crucial importance of the caregiving and/or parenting environment for a child's developing ability to regulate stress. For example, the impact of prenatal stress on infants is often moderated by the quality of postnatal caregiving (Austin et al., 2017). Hypocortisolism,[4] a disorder that emerges in response to severe abuse and neglect, has been shown to be reversible with subsequent sensitive and supportive caregiving (Flannery et al., 2017). Moreover, as noted above, there is significant variability across individuals in how stress is perceived, with temperamental, biological, and social factors affecting experiences of stress. And for military families, the effects of deployments and related military family transitions are mediated through their impact on parents and the caregiving system (Creech et al., 2014).

In summary, extensive research in the civilian realm on the development of children's stress regulatory systems can significantly aid in understanding how military family stressors affect children's development. Severe stressors (e.g., parental physical injury, parental psychological trauma and maladaptive responses, parental death, or family violence) may have complex influences on child development across multiple domains, including physiological, biological, behavioral, social-emotional, and cognitive functioning. It should be noted, too, that the vast majority of the parenting literature in this area focuses on mothers, while far less research has been done on fathers and fathering (Lamb, 2004). The fact that the majority of service member parents are fathers provides an important opportunity to begin to examine the special role of military fathers in their children's development (DeGarmo, 2016).

RESILIENCE IN CHILDREN'S DEVELOPMENT

We refer the reader back to Chapters 1 and 2 for definitions of resilience and the distinctions between resilience processes/mechanisms, factors, and outcomes. In this chapter, our focus is on resilience processes/mechanisms and the factors that shape them in children and youth. Systematic, theory-driven research on resilience among youth has been ongoing since the 1970s

---

[4]Also known as adrenal insufficiency, defined by the National Institute of Diabetes and Digestive and Kidney Diseases as "a disorder that occurs when the adrenal glands don't make enough of certain hormones. These include cortisol, sometimes called the 'stress hormone,' which is essential for life." See https://www.niddk.nih.gov/health-information/endocrine-diseases/adrenal-insufficiency-addisons-disease.

and has accelerated with recent advances in prevention and intervention science as well as advances in genetics and neurobiology (see Masten [2018] for a review of the literature). Resilience researchers initially focused on variations in adaptation among children—that is, on how, among children experiencing high-risk conditions in the family and broader environment, some children fared better than their peers. In several early studies, as many as one-third of youth exposed to early stressors (e.g., parental mental illness, poverty, violence, single parenthood, and multiple children in a household) fared as well as their low-risk peers (Masten, 2001; Werner, 2012). Although this early literature suggested that resilient children were viewed as "invincible" (Werner, 1997), the research consensus today is that resilience in childhood is more appropriately viewed as what Masten (2001) has termed "ordinary magic." That is, child/youth resilience is a function of key ordinary—or typical—psychological processes that operate well, despite high-risk conditions. Youth who do as well as their low-risk peers, despite their exposure to stressful conditions in the home and the broader environment, are considered resilient.

The processes involved in childhood resilience operate across multiple domains both within and beyond the child. As such, there is no single resiliency trait (Masten and Gewirtz, 2006). In parallel, then, there is no single measure of child resilience. Rather, measurement of childhood resilient outcomes is best accomplished via multi-dimensional assessments at multiple levels of analysis, using multiple methods (e.g., self-reporting, behavioral observation, physiological measures) and multiple informants, including children, parents, and teachers. Measuring resilience in children also requires an understanding of the developmental context. For example, developmental tasks for school-age children include functioning adequately in schools or in academics; functioning well with peers (social competence); and functioning well behaviorally and emotionally.

Assessing resilience in school-age children, then, would require using reports and objective assessments of functioning, such as test scores and observations of playground behavior, across these domains, preferably based on observations from teachers, parents, children themselves, and even peers.

Key Correlates and Predictors of Childhood Resilience

Decades of resilience research has demonstrated that resilience is associated with core promotive and protective processes (see Chapter 2 of this volume for definitions); these processes galvanize positive adaptation across developmental domains. Masten and Cicchetti (2016), in their comprehensive review of childhood resilience and developmental psychopathology, outline six core correlates of resilience that have emerged from longitudinal studies. As discussed in earlier chapters, and consistent with the theoretical models outlined in this report, childhood resilience develops in multiple contexts: individual, family, school, and culture. The primary focus in this chapter is on the key correlates of childhood resilience that are most proximal, that is, those that lie within the child and the family.

First and foremost, sensitive, responsive, loving, predictable, and protective parents and caregivers help the development of a *secure attachment relationship* in infancy and early childhood (Bowlby, 1988). Throughout childhood and adolescence, effective parents help their children to understand and navigate the world by teaching prosocial skills, providing safety, limits, and routines, monitoring behavior, and helping children make meaning of life (Collins et al., 2000.) Early relationships with parents and other caregivers provide a template for how the child navigates later relationships with peers, noncaregiving adults such as teachers, and intimate partners (Feldman et al., 2013; Sroufe, 1979). Peer and other relationships, in turn, influence the child's trajectory into adolescence and beyond (Dishion and Tipsord, 2011). Caring relationships with nonparental adults also are important for youth (e.g., Perkins and Borden, 2003) and may be particularly relevant for military youth experiencing multiple transitions (Masten, 2001).

A secure attachment relationship not only provides a child with an internal working model of healthy relationships, it also provides a secure base from which a child can explore and feel effective in the outside world (Bowlby, 1988). Neurobiological and genetic research has uncovered the power of the attachment relationship; the hormone oxytocin and the oxytocin receptor gene (OXTR), among others, appear to be implicated in the core promotive and protective processes of the parent-child relationship (Feldman et al., 2014; Priel et al., 2019). For example, in a longitudinal study of children and parents exposed to ongoing political violence and war, a combination of parenting and genetic risk predicted PTSD symptoms in young children (Feldman et al., 2014).

The second key correlate of resilience is *self-regulation*, the ability to monitor and regulate one's behavior, attention, thoughts, and emotions. This is a crucial developmental task that begins to develop in early childhood and continues developing through emerging adulthood (Zelazo and Carlson, 2012). Children with effective self-regulation are at lower risk for behavioral and emotional problems and are able to be more successful in school because they can follow and comply with teacher directions. Executive functioning, a key indicator of self-regulation, predicts both concurrent and future adjustment in children (Zelazo et al., 2004). Effective self-regulation may be particularly important in high-risk settings (Duckworth, 2011; Masten and Coatsworth, 1998; Rothbart et al., 2011).

Mastery-motivation is a third key correlate of resilience (Masten et al., 1995). Effective parenting and/or caregiving likely galvanizes a child's mastery-motivation system, the adaptational system associated with the development of self-efficacy, and possibly also motivating persistence in children. Mastery-motivation refers to feelings of mastery as a consequence of successful interactions with the outside environment. For example, in observing young children learning to walk one can see that successfully standing first, and then walking, is highly motivating to a child, reinforcing more practice and ultimately further success. In middle childhood, even small successes in school, academics, sports, or social activities motivate a child to further engage in the activity, resulting in yet more success and greater activation of the mastery-motivation system. Feelings of self-efficacy likely drive this positive cycle of practice and success (Bandura, 1997).

Among a sample of military parents, for example, a parenting intervention strengthened both maternal and paternal parenting self-efficacy, leading to subsequent gains in both parent and child positive adjustment (Gewirtz et al., 2016; Piehler et al., 2016). There is a relative dearth of research on this issue, but the limited available research suggests that feelings of self-efficacy may also drive persistence or perseverance of effort (e.g., Skaalvik et al., 2015). Across early to middle childhood, persistence also appears related to sensitive or effective parenting and to self-regulation (Chang and Olson, 2016).

Across multiple studies of high-risk children, cognitive abilities, typically assessed through tests of intelligence quotient (IQ) or problem-solving capacity, appear to be significantly associated with resilience (Luthar et al., 2006; Masten, 2015). Better cognitive functioning is both promotive and protective for children and youth, and is likely related to the ability to succeed in schoolwork, in navigating novel situations, and in flexible problem-solving, as well as being protective for youth at risk of behavior problems (Lösel and Farrington, 2012; Masten and Tellegen, 2012; Werner and Smith, 1992, 2001). Cognitive skills also are associated with resources such as socioeconomic status, access to better education and more books at home, and competent parents (Masten and Cicchetti, 2016; National Academies of Sciences, Engineering, and Medicine, 2016). Conversely, highly stressful early environments ("toxic stress") such as those characterized by maltreatment, parental psychopathology, or caregiving disruptions, can impair cognitive development (Shonkoff, 2011).

Finally, hopefulness (or positive outlook) and meaning-making may also be associated with resilience, although less empirical research has been conducted on these two constructs. In both observations of resilient children after they have grown up and anecdotal accounts of resilience, hope or a positive perspective is a key theme (Maholmes, 2014; Werner and

Smith, 1992, 2001). While limited longitudinal research has been done to examine this association, one longitudinal study found that self-reported hope among children ages 10 to 18 was associated with subsequent positive life satisfaction and fewer internalizing symptoms (Valle et al., 2006).

There also is a dearth of research on the association of meaning-making with resilience in youth, although developing a narrative about life's meaning or one's own purpose in life appears to be a core theme in discussions of resilience (Masten and Cicchetti, 2016). Meaning-making is likely associated with the development of narratives about one's life, and research evidence suggests that narratives also provide an opportunity for healing after a traumatic event (Neuner et al., 2008). Both resiliency research and youth development research find that opportunities to contribute or otherwise to "matter"—meaning-making within one's context—are linked with successful outcomes in adolescents (National Research Council and Institute of Medicine, 2002; Villarruel et al., 2003). For instance, Werner and Smith (1992) examined "required helpfulness" at home and found that the key to a sense of helpfulness is for assigned work such as chores to be viewed as not just "helping out" around the house, but as necessary for the household (if not human) functioning. These acts provide youth with an opportunity to gain a sense of generosity and self-worth, as well as an opportunity to overcome the egocentric thinking so prevalent in adolescence (Perkins et al., 2018).

However, meaning-making may not always be associated with positive adjustment and prosociality, especially when meaning is found in extremism, such as in terrorism, gangs, and/or dangerous religious sects (Masten and Cicchetti, 2016). The links between meaning-making and resilience are complex and need far more longitudinal study (Park, 2011).

Resilience in Military Children

We are aware of no published longitudinal empirical studies focused on examining the correlates of resilience in military children. However, many papers have discussed or proposed frameworks for understanding resilience among military youth, with calls for more research to understand the correlates of resilience in this population (e.g., Easterbrooks et al., 2013; Masten, 2013; Park, 2011). Moreover, as Easterbrooks and colleagues (2013) note, "most military children turn out just fine" (p. 99). It is likely that the same sources of resilience found across multiple studies and described above are relevant to military children and youth. However, it is important to identify military-specific aspects of life that may help to confer resilience among children and youth in the face of stressors such as a parent's deployment, multiple moves, parental psychopathology, and family violence.

It may be the case, for example, that a parent's pride in affiliation with the military provides the children with a sense of meaning and purpose (Gewirtz and Youssef, 2016a). Similarly, the resilience-focused approaches of much military training (e.g., Bowles et al., 2015; Lester et al., 2011) may convey the importance of hope, optimism, or a positive outlook on life to parent service members, who may in turn share this outlook with their children.

Several elements of the military support system, particularly for families living on or near installations, or among other military families, may help support children's resilience. A detailed discussion of them is beyond the scope of this chapter, but they would include social and parenting support, comprehensive services, including early identification and intervention with children at-risk for poor developmental outcomes, and early child care support. For example, teachers and other caregiving adults may be particularly important for children's resilience during transitions such as moves between installations (permanent changes of station) and temporary separations from a caregiver, though there is a dearth of research on the role of extra-familial caregivers for military child resilience. These and related supports, which are embedded in the military context, are discussed in Chapters 4 and 7 of this report.

The most powerful way to identify sources of resilience is through experimental studies of preventive interventions designed to promote resilience and to prevent maladjustment in the face of risks. Because of their design, experimental intervention studies hold the promise not only to improve children's resilience but also to uncover causal factors in resilience among military children and families (Gewirtz, 2018). Unfortunately, to date few such experimental (randomized controlled) intervention studies have been conducted among military children and families.

Interventions to Promote Children's Resilience

In this section, the committee reviews the empirical literature on what has been termed the "third wave" of resilience research—aimed at addressing whether and how interventions can actually nurture and strengthen children's resilience. Over the past three decades, a large body of evidence-based preventive interventions aimed at strengthening child well-being and resilience has been developed and rigorously evaluated in randomized controlled trials (RCTs). These interventions have provided valuable information on the malleability of resilience processes in development. Although very few of these interventions have been specifically developed and tested for military children and families (see Chapter 7 for more information about the applicability of interventions to different populations), emerging evidence from RCTs funded by the National Institutes of Health and the U.S. Department of Defense has provided valuable information about malleable factors associated with resilience in military children (DeVoe et al., 2016; DiNallo et al., 2016; Youssef et al., 2016).

Interventions to promote resilience focus on strengthening protective and promotive factors empirically associated with or predictive of youth resilience. These represent a shift away from disease models of intervention and toward strengths-based and empowerment-focused positive psychology models of intervention (refer to Figure 7-1 in Chapter 7). As Masten and Cicchetti (2016) note:

> prevention research can be conceptualized as true experiments in altering the course of development, thereby providing insight into the etiology and pathogenesis of disordered outcomes and to the promotion of resilience (Cicchetti and Hinshaw, 2002; Howe, Reiss, and Yuh, 2002). The experimental nature of randomized clinical trials (RCTs) provides an unparalleled opportunity to make causal inferences in resilience research (p. 307).

Below, we briefly review selected evidence-based interventions with RCT data targeting the malleable factors associated with youth resilience described above. Because of the sizeable volume of prevention and intervention research, we highlight those interventions of most relevance to military children and families and those with data demonstrating long-term change or change at multiple levels (e.g., biological, genetic, behavioral), or both. Most of these interventions focused on parenting/caregiving and the parent-child relationship, and unsurprisingly, very few of them were developed and tested with military populations. (Chapter 7 provides detailed information on evidence-based programs evaluated with military populations).

We follow the order of the key resilience processes outlined above, with recognition that far more evidence-based prevention interventions focus on improving caregiving and parenting processes than on targeting children's resilience alone. This is likely because programs aimed at improving children's resilience have demonstrated crossover and cascading effects, improving both parental well-being and overall family well-being (e.g., Forehand et al., 2014; Gewirtz et al., 2016; Patterson et al., 2010; Sandler et al., 2011, 2015). For example, effective parents nurture their children's self-regulation skills through consistency, love, and limits; they develop their children's cognitive skills by reading to their children, modeling effective problem solving, and structuring after-school time for homework and other activities. Parents, teachers, and other key adults help children develop mastery-motivation using positive reinforcement for persistence and effort, as well as tasks well done. Finally, although meaning making, hope, and other traits associated with resilience are individual characteristics, they also may be nurtured in family interactions.

Preventive Interventions Targeting Resilience Through Parenting/Caregiving

We highlight here two research-based prevention programs demonstrating the potential of caregiving/parenting interventions to promote the resilience of diverse youth across development. Early childhood programs have targeted the parent-child attachment relationship, as well as providing parents with early childcare skills and knowledge (e.g., Fisher et al., 2006; Toth et al., 1992). For example, the *Nurse-Family Partnership* provides skills and knowledge for new parents from the second trimester of pregnancy (Olds, 2006). Tested in three RCTs with diverse low-income mothers in three cities, long-term follow-up has demonstrated reductions in child maltreatment, benefits to family socioeconomic status, and improvements across multiple domains of child and youth functioning over more than 15 years, including improved school readiness, reduced substance use and psychopathology, fewer injuries, and improved academic achievement (Eckenrode et al., 2017; Olds et al., 2010). Other RCTs of both attachment-based and behavioral early childhood interventions with maltreated youth have demonstrated both behavioral and physiological improvements as a result of improvements in parenting. These include the normalization of diurnal cortisol patterns (Fisher et al., 2007) and improvements in executive functioning (Lind et al., 2017).

Parenting interventions targeting middle childhood also have shown long-term benefits for diverse youth both "above and below the skin" (Patterson and Forgatch, 1987; Sandler et al., 2015). For example, Brody and colleagues (2009) examined the *Strong African American Families* seven-week parenting program among rural families with pre-adolescent children in the southern United States. RCT results indicated improvements on multiple child health and development indicators, including self-regulation, behavioral risks (substance use, antisocial, and risky sexual behaviors), and school attendance. A follow-up study of the youth at age 19 revealed that those who participated in the intervention showed significantly lower physical inflammation (indexing lower risk of health problems, particularly those associated with poverty) than those assigned to the control condition. Inflammatory markers were lowest in youth whose parents showed improved positive parenting and reduced coercive parenting as a result of the intervention (Miller et al., 2014).

Other studies have demonstrated that the Strong African American Families intervention was particularly beneficial for families with parents and/or youth demonstrating higher genetic risk for poor outcomes. For example, Brody and colleagues (2009) demonstrated that this program was particularly protective for youth with genetic vulnerability to risky behaviors; youth with genetic vulnerability in the intervention group were only half as likely to initiate risky behaviors as genetically vulnerable youth in the control condition.

Prevention Programs Targeting Child Self-Regulation

Programs directly targeting children's self-regulatory processes also have shown positive effects. These programs typically use school and community environments to boost the executive functioning, emotion regulation, and problem-solving skills of youth. These social-emotional learning (SEL) interventions include enrichments to Head Start and Early Head Start programs, such as Head Start REDI (Bierman et al., 2017; Sasser et al., 2017), which provided enrichment to the standard Head Start curriculum. The RCT, which followed 4-year-old children for 5 years, demonstrated improvements in children's academic outcomes by 3rd grade, and for the children lowest in baseline executive functioning skills it demonstrated significant and sustained improvements in executive functioning over 5 years.

For school-age children, SEL curricula also have demonstrated improvements to executive functioning. *Promoting Alternative Thinking Strategies*, for example, is a classroom- after-school and/or summer camp-based program aimed at reducing conflict among youth by improving outcomes such as executive functioning (Greenberg et al., 1998). Outcome analyses indicated that the program resulted in improvements to students' verbal fluency and inhibitory control after 1 year. Improvements to inhibitory control, in turn, mediated improvements in teacher reports of youths' behavioral and emotional problems after 1 year as well (Greenberg, 2006).

We are aware of no programs with RCT evaluations that target mastery-motivation, meaning-making, or hope. As noted above, these correlates of resilience typically are incorporated into broader programs.

CONCLUSIONS

CONCLUSION 5-1: Early childhood and adolescence are particularly vulnerable periods for the capacity to cope with stress because of rapid brain development during these periods. This important consideration is not fully recognized in program and policy development.

CONCLUSION 5-2: There are evidence-based practices and programs that can mitigate disruptions to children's capacity to cope with stress caused by traumatic and highly stressful events, but few interventions have been developed and tested with military populations.

CONCLUSION 5-3: Childhood resilience is multidimensional, and its measurement requires an understanding of the developmental context. Key correlates of childhood resilience include effective parenting or caregiving, self-regulation and mastery-motivation skills, strong cognitive abilities, hope/optimism, and making meaning of one's experience.

CONCLUSION 5-4: Resilience can be strengthened among youth exposed to stress or trauma. Rigorous evidence-based programs strengthening key predictors of resilience across multiple contexts (predominantly parenting/caregiving, parent-child relationship quality, and self-regulation) have demonstrated long-term improvements to children's emotional, behavioral, cognitive, physiological, and biological functioning.

REFERENCES

Austin, M. P., Christl, B., McMahon, C., Kildea, S., Reilly, N., Yin, C., Simcock, G., Elgbeili, G., Laplante, D. P., and King, S. (2017). Moderating effects of maternal emotional availability on language and cognitive development in toddlers of mothers exposed to a natural disaster in pregnancy: The QF2011 Queensland Flood Study. *Infant Behavior and Development*, *49*, 296–309.

Bakermans-Kranenburg, M. J., and van Ijzendoorn, M. H. (2015). The hidden efficacy of interventions: Gene x environment experiments from a differential susceptibility perspective. *Annual Review of Psychology*, *66*, 381–409.

Bandura, A. (1997). *Self-Efficacy: The Exercise of Control*. Macmillan.

Belsky, J., and Pluess, M. (2009). Beyond diathesis stress: differential susceptibility to environmental influences. *Psychological Bulletin*, *135*, 885–908.

Bierman, K. L., Heinrichs, B. S., Welsh, J. A., Nix, R. L., and Gest, S. D. (2017). Enriching preschool classrooms and home visits with evidence-based programming: Sustained benefits for low-income children. *Journal of Child Psychology and Psychiatry, and Allied Disciplines*, *58*, 129–137.

Blair, C. (2010). Stress and the development of self-regulation in context. *Child Development Perspectives*, *4*(3), 181–188.

Bowlby, J. (1988). *A Secure Base: Parent-Child Attachment and Healthy Human Development*. London: Routledge.

Bowles, S. V., Pollock, L. D., Moore, M., Wadsworth, S. M., Cato, C., Dekle, J. W., Meyer, S. W., Shriver, A., Mueller, B., Stephens, M. and Seidler, D. A. (2015). Total force fitness: The military family fitness model. *Military Medicine*, *180*(3), 246–258.

Boyce, W., and Ellis, B. J. (2005). Biological sensitivity to context: I. An evolutionary–developmental theory of the origins and functions of stress reactivity. *Development and Psychopathology*, *17*, 271–301.

Brody, G. H., Beach, S. R. H., Philibert, R. A., Chen, Y.-F., and Murry, V. M. (2009). Prevention effects moderate the association of 5-HTTLPR and youth risk behavior initiation: Gene x environment hypotheses tested via a randomized prevention design. *Child Development*, *80*, 645–661.

Center on the Developing Child. (2019). *Toxic Stress*. Retrieved from https://developingchild.harvard.edu/science/key-concepts/toxic-stress.

Chang, H., and Olson, S. L. (2016). Examining early behavioral persistence as a dynamic process: Correlates and consequences spanning ages 3–10 years. *Journal of Abnormal Child Psychology*, *44*, 799–810.

Cicchetti, D. (1989). Developmental psychopathology: Some thoughts on its evolution. *Development and Psychopathology*, *1*, 1–4.

Cicchetti, D., and Hinshaw, S. P. (2002). Editorial: Prevention and intervention science: Contributions to developmental theory. *Development and Psychopathology*, *14*, 667–671.

Cicchetti, D., and Rogosch, F. A. (1996). Equifinality and multifinality in developmental psychopathology. *Development and Psychopathology*, *8*, 597–600.

Cicchetti, D., Rogosch, F. A., Gunnar, M. R., and Toth, S. L. (2010). The differential impacts of early physical and sexual abuse and internalizing problems on daytime cortisol rhythm in school-aged children. *Child Development*, *81*, 252–269.

Cicchetti, D., and Walker, E. F. (2001). Editorial: Stress and development: Biological and psychological consequences. *Development and Psychopathology*, *13*, 413–418.

Collins, W. A., Maccoby, E. E., Steinberg, L., Hetherington, E. M., and Bornstein, M. H. (2000). Contemporary research on parenting: The case for nature and nurture. *American Psychologist*, *55*, 218–232.

Collins, F. S., and Varmus, H. (2015). A new initiative on precision medicine. *New England Journal of Medicine*, *372*(9), 793–795.

Creech, S. K., Hadley, W., and Borsari, B. (2014). The impact of military deployment and reintegration on children and parenting: A systematic review. *Professional Psychology, Research and Practice*, *45*, 452–464.

DeGarmo, D. S. (2016). Placing fatherhood back in the study and treatment of military fathers. In A. H. Gewirtz and A. M. Youssef (Eds.), *Parenting and Children's Resilience in Military Families* (pp. 299–306). Cham, Switzerland: Springer International.

DeVoe, E. R., Paris, R., and Acker, M. (2016). Prevention and treatment for parents of young children in military families. In A. H. Gewirtz and A. M. Youssef (Eds.), *Parenting and Children's Resilience in Military Families* (pp. 213–227). Cham, Switzerland: Springer International.

DiNallo, J., Kuhl, M., Borden, L. M., and Perkins, D. (2016). Interventions to support and strengthen parenting in military families: State of the evidence. In A. H. Gewirtz and A. M. Youssef (Eds.), *Parenting and Children's Resilience in Military Families* (pp. 195–212). Cham, Switzerland: Springer International.

Dishion, T. J., and Tipsord, J. M. (2011). Peer contagion in child and adolescent social and emotional development. *Annual Review of Psychology*, *62*, 189–214.

Duckworth, A. L. (2011). The significance of self-control. *Proceedings of the National Academy of Sciences of the United States of America*, *108*, 2639–2640.

Easterbrooks, M. A., Ginsburg, K., and Lerner, R. M. (2013). Resilience among military youth. *The Future of Children*, *23*(2), 99–120.

Eckenrode, J., Campa, M. I., Morris, P. A., Henderson, C. R., Jr, Bolger, K. E., Kitzman, H., and Olds, D. L. (2017). The prevention of child maltreatment through the nurse family partnership program: Mediating effects in a long-term follow-up study. *Child Maltreatment*, *22*, 92–99.

Farrell, A. K., Simpson, J. A., Carlson, E. A., Englund, M. M., and Sung, S. (2017). The impact of stress at different life stages on physical health and the buffering effects of maternal sensitivity. *Health Psychology*, *36*, 35–44.

Feldman, R., Bamberger, E., and Kanat-Maymon, Y. (2013). Parent-specific reciprocity from infancy to adolescence shapes children's social competence and dialogical skills. *Attachment & Human Development*, *15*, 407–423.

Feldman, R., Vengrober, A., and Ebstein, R. P. (2014). Affiliation buffers stress: Cumulative genetic risk in oxytocin–vasopressin genes combines with early caregiving to predict PTSD in war-exposed young children. *Translational Psychiatry*, *4*, e370.

Fisher, P. A., Gunnar, M. R., Dozier, M., Bruce, J., and Pears, K. C. (2006). Effects of therapeutic interventions for foster children on behavioral problems, caregiver attachment, and stress regulatory neural systems. *Annals of the New York Academy of Sciences, 1094*(1), 215–225.

Fisher, P. A., Stoolmiller, M., Gunnar, M. R., and Burraston, B. O. (2007). Effects of a therapeutic intervention for foster preschoolers on diurnal cortisol activity. *Psychoneuroendocrinology, 32*, 892–905.

Flannery, J. E., Beauchamp, K. G., and Fisher, P. A. (2017). The role of social buffering on chronic disruptions in quality of care: Evidence from caregiver-based interventions in foster children. *Social Neuroscience, 12*, 86–91.

Forehand, R., Lafko, N., Parent, J., and Burt, K. B. (2014). Is parenting the mediator of change in behavioral parent training for externalizing problems of youth? *Clinical Psychology Review, 34*, 608–619.

Gewirtz, A. H. (2018). A call for theoretically informed and empirically validated military family interventions. *Journal of Family Theory & Review, 10*, 587–601.

Gewirtz, A. H., DeGarmo, D. S., and Zamir, O. (2016). Effects of a military parenting program on parental distress and suicidal ideation: After deployment adaptive parenting tools. *Suicide & Life-Threatening Behavior, 46 Suppl 1*, S23–S31.

Gewirtz, A. H., and Youssef, A. M. (2016a). Conclusions and a research agenda for parenting in military families. In A. H. Gewirtz and A. M. Youssef (Eds.), *Parenting and Children's Resilience in Military Families* (pp. 299–306). Cham, Switzerland: Springer International.

Gewirtz, A. H., and Youssef, A. H. (Eds.) (2016b). *Parenting and Children's Resilience in Military Families*. Cham, Switzerland: Springer International Publishing.

Giedd, J. N., Raznahan, A., Alexander-Bloch, A., Schmitt, E., Gogtay, N., and Rapoport, J. L. (2015). Child psychiatry branch of the National Institute of Mental Health longitudinal structural magnetic resonance imaging study of human brain development. *Neuropsychopharmacology, 40*(1), 43.

Greenberg, M. T. (2006). Promoting resilience in children and youth: Preventive interventions and their interface with neuroscience. *Annals of the New York Academy of Sciences, 1094*, 139–150.

Greenberg, M. T., Mihalic, S. F., and Kusché, C. A. (1998). *Promoting Alternative Thinking Strategies (PATHS)*. Center for the Study and Prevention of Violence, Institute of Behavioral Science, University of Colorado Boulder.

Gunnar, M. R., and Vazquez, D. M. (2001). Low cortisol and a flattening of expected daytime rhythm: Potential indices of risk in human development. *Development and Psychopathology, 13*, 515–538.

Halligan S. L., Herbert J., Goodyer, I. M., and Murray L. (2004). Exposure to postnatal depression predicts elevated cortisol in adolescent offspring. *Biological Psychiatry, 55*, 376 –381.

_______. (2007). Disturbances in morning cortisol secretion in association with maternal postnatal depression predict subsequent depressive symptomatology in adolescents. *Biological Psychiatry, 62*, 40–46.

Heim, C., Newport, D. J., Mletzko, T., Miller, A. H., and Nemeroff, C. B. (2008). The link between childhood trauma and depression: Insights from HPA axis studies in humans. *Psychoneuroendocrinology, 33*, 693–710.

Howe, G. W., Reiss, D., and Yuh, J. (2002). Can prevention trials test theories of etiology? *Development and Psychopathology, 14*(4), 673–694.

Johnson, A. B., Mliner, S. B., Depasquale, C. E., Troy, M., and Gunnar, M. R. (2018). Attachment security buffers the HPA axis of toddlers growing up in poverty or near poverty: Assessment during pediatric well-child exams with inoculations. *Psychoneuroendocrinology, 95*, 120–127.

Koss, K. J., and Gunnar, M. R. (2018). Annual Research Review: Early adversity, the hypothalamic–pituitary–adrenocortical axis, and child psychopathology. *Journal of Child Psychology and Psychiatry*, *59*(4), 327–346.

Lamb, M. E. (Ed.). (2004). *The Role of the Father in Child Development*. Hoboken, NJ: John Wiley & Sons.

Leneman, K. B., and Gunnar, M.R. (2019). Developmental timing of stress effects on the brain. In *The Oxford Handbook of Stress and Mental Health*. Oxford, UK: Oxford University Press.

Lenroot, R. K., and Giedd, J. N. (2006). Brain development in children and adolescents: Insights from anatomical magnetic resonance imaging. *Neuroscience and Biobehavioral Reviews*, *30*, 718–729.

Lester, P. B., Harms, P. D., Herian, M. N., Krasikova, D. V., and Beal, S. J. (2011). *The Comprehensive Soldier Fitness Program Evaluation. Report 3: Longitudinal Analysis of the Impact of Master Resilience Training on Self-Reported Resilience and Psychological Health Data*. Anchorage, AK: TKC Global Solutions LLC. Retrieved from http://www.dtic.mil/docs/citations/ADA553635.

Lind, T., Raby, K. L., Caron, E. B., Roben, C. K., and Dozier, M. (2017). Enhancing executive functioning among toddlers in foster care with an attachment-based intervention. *Development and Psychopathology*, *29*(2), 575–586.

Lionetti, F., Aron, A., Aron, E. N., Burns, G. L., Jagiellowicz, J., and Pluess, M. (2018). Dandelions, tulips and orchids: Evidence for the existence of low-sensitive, medium-sensitive and high-sensitive individuals. *Translational Psychiatry*, *8*, 24.

Loman, M. M., Gunnar, M. R., and the Early Experience, Stress, and Neurobehavioral Development Center. (2010). Early experience and the development of stress reactivity and regulation in children. *Neuroscience and Biobehavioral Reviews*, *34*, 867–876.

Lösel, F., and Farrington, D. P. (2012). Direct protective and buffering protective factors in the development of youth violence. *American Journal of Preventive Medicine*, *43*(2 Suppl 1), S8–S23.

Lupien, S. J., McEwen, B. S., Gunnar, M. R., and Heim, C. (2009). Effects of stress throughout the lifespan on the brain, behaviour and cognition. *Nature Reviews: Neuroscience*, *10*, 434–445.

Luthar, S. S. (2006). Resilience in development: A synthesis of research across five decades. In D. Cicchetti and D. J. Cohen (Eds.), *Developmental Psychopathology: Risk, Disorder, and Adaptation* (vol. 3, 2nd ed.). New York: Wiley.

Maholmes, V. (2014). *Fostering Resilience and Well-being in Children and Families in Poverty: Why Hope Still Matters*. Oxford, UK: Oxford University Press.

Masten, A. S. (2001). Ordinary magic: Resilience processes in development. *The American Psychologist*, *56*, 227–238.

Masten, A. S. (2013). Competence, risk, and resilience in military families: Conceptual commentary. *Clinical Child and Family Psychology Review*, *16*, 278–281.

_______. (2015). *Ordinary Magic: Resilience in Development*. New York: Guilford.

_______. (2018). Resilience Theory and Research on Children and Families: Past, Present, and Promise. *Journal of Family Theory & Review*, *10*, 12–31.

Masten, A. S., and Cicchetti, D. (2016). Resilience in development: Progress and transformation. *Developmental Psychopathology*, *4*, 271–333.

Masten, A. S., and Coatsworth, J. D. (1998). The development of competence in favorable and unfavorable environments: Lessons from research on successful children. *American Psychologist*, *53*, 205–220.

Masten, A. S., Coatsworth, J. D., Neemann, J., Gest, S. D., Tellegen, A., and Garmezy, N. (1995). The structure and coherence of competence from childhood through adolescence. *Child Development*, *66*, 1635–1659.

Masten, A. S., and Gewirtz, A. H. (2006). Vulnerability and resilience in early child development. In K. McCartney and D. Phillips (Eds.), *Blackwell Handbook of Early Childhood Development* (pp. 22–43). Oxford, UK: Blackwell.

Masten, A. S., and Obradovic, J. (2006). Competence and resilience in development. *Annals of the New York Academy of Sciences, 1094*, 13–27.

Masten, A. S., and Tellegen, A. (2012). Resilience in developmental psychopathology: Contributions of the Project Competence Longitudinal Study. *Development and Psychopathology, 24*, 345–361.

McEwen, B. S. (1994). How do sex and stress hormones affect nerve cells? *Annals of the New York Academy of Sciences, 743*, 1–16; discussion 17–18.

McEwen, B. S. (2017). Neurobiological and systemic effects of chronic stress. *Chronic Stress, 1*, 1–11.

Meadows, S. O., Tanielian, T., Karney, B., Schell, T., Griffin, B. A., Jaycox, L. H., Friedman, E. M., Trail, T. E., Beckman, R., Ramchand, R., and Hengstebeck, N. (2017). The deployment life study: Longitudinal analysis of military families across the deployment cycle. *RAND Health Quarterly, 6*(2).

Miller, G. E., Brody, G. H., Yu, T., and Chen, E. (2014). A family-oriented psychosocial intervention reduces inflammation in low-SES African American youth. *Proceedings of the National Academy of Sciences of the United States of America, 111*, 11287–11292.

Nahum-Shani, I., and Militello, L. (2018). *Promoting Military Family Well-Being with Digitally-Supported Adaptive and Just-In-Time Adaptive Interventions: Opportunities and Challenges*. Paper commissioned by the Committee on the Well-Being of Military Families. Washington, DC: National Academies of Sciences, Engineering, and Medicine.

Neuner, F., Catani, C., Ruf, M., Schauer, E., Schauer, M., and Elbert, T. (2008). Narrative exposure therapy for the treatment of traumatized children and adolescents (KidNET): From neurocognitive theory to field intervention. *Child and Adolescent Psychiatric Clinics of North America, 17*, 641–664.

National Academies of Sciences, Engineering, and Medicine. (2016). *Parenting Matters: Supporting Parents of Children Ages 0-8*. Washington, DC: The National Academies Press.

National Research Council and Institute of Medicine (2002). *Community Programs to Promote Youth Development*. Committee on Community-Level Programs for Youth, J. Eccles and J. A. Gootman (Eds). Washington, DC: The National Academies Press.

O'Connor, T. G., Ben-Shlomo, Y., Heron, J., Golding, J., Adams, D., and Glover, V. (2005). Prenatal anxiety predicts individual differences in cortisol in pre-adolescent children. *Biological Psychiatry, 58*, 211–217.

Olds, D. L. (2006). The nurse-family partnership: An evidence-based preventive intervention. *Infant Mental Health Journal, 27*, 5–25.

Olds, D. L., Kitzman, H. J., Cole, R. E., Hanks, C. A., Arcoleo, K. J., Anson, E. A., Luckey, D. W., Knudtson, M. D., Henderson, C. R., Bondy, J. and Stevenson, A. J. (2010.) Enduring effects of prenatal and infancy home visiting by nurses on maternal life course and government spending: Follow-up of a randomized trial among children at age 12 years. *Archives of Pediatrics & Adolescent Medicine, 164*(5), 419–424.

Park, N. (2011). Military children and families: Strengths and challenges during peace and war. *The American Psychologist, 66*, 65–72.

Patterson, G. R., and Forgatch, M. (1987). *Parents and Adolescents Living Together—Part 1: The Basics*. Eugene, OR: Castalia.

Patterson, G. R., Forgatch, M. S., and Degarmo, D. S. (2010). Cascading effects following intervention. *Development and Psychopathology, 22*, 949–970.

Perkins, D. F., and Borden, L. M. (2003). Positive behaviors, problem behaviors, and resiliency in adolescence. *Handbook of Psychology, 6*, 373–394.

Perkins, D. R., Caldwell, L. L., and Witt, P.A. (2018). Resiliency, protective processes, promotion, and community youth development. In P. A. Witt and L. L. Caldwell (Eds.), *Youth Development: Principles and Practices in Out-of-School Settings* (pp. 173-192). Urbana, IL: Sagamore-Venture.

Piehler, T. F., Ausherbauer, K., Gewirtz, A., and Gliske, K. (2016). Improving child peer adjustment in military families through parent training: The mediational role of parental locus of control. *Journal of Early Adolescence*, *38*(9), 1322–1343.

Priel, A., Djalovski, A., Zagoory-Sharon, O., and Feldman, R. (2019). Maternal depression impacts child psychopathology across the first decade of life: Oxytocin and synchrony as markers of resilience. *Journal of Child Psychology and Psychiatry, and Allied Disciplines*, *60*(1), 30–42.

Romens, S. E., McDonald, J., Svaren, J., and Pollak, S. D. (2015). Associations between early life stress and gene methylation in children. *Child Development*, *86*, 303–309.

Rothbart, M. K., Sheese, B. E., Rueda, M. R., and Posner, M. I. (2011). Developing mechanisms of self-regulation in early life. *Emotion Review*, *3*, 207–213.

Sandler, I., Ingram, A., Wolchik, S., Tein, J.-Y., and Winslow, E. (2015). Long-term effects of parenting-focused preventive interventions to promote resilience of children and adolescents. *Child Development Perspectives*, *9*, 164–171.

Sandler, I. N., Schoenfelder, E. N., Wolchik, S. A., and MacKinnon, D. P. (2011). Long-term impact of prevention programs to promote effective parenting: Lasting effects but uncertain processes. *Annual Review of Psychology*, *62*, 299–329.

Sapolsky, R. M. (1994). Individual differences and the stress response. *Seminars in Neuroscience*, *6*, 261–269.

Sasser, T. R., Bierman, K. L., Heinrichs, B., and Nix, R. L. (2017). Preschool intervention can promote sustained growth in the executive-function skills of children exhibiting early deficits. *Psychological Science*, *28*, 1719–1730.

Shackman, J. E., and Pollak, S. D. (2014). Impact of physical maltreatment on the regulation of negative affect and aggression. *Development and Psychopathology*, *26*, 1021–1033.

Shonkoff, J. P. (2011). Protecting brains, not simply stimulating minds. *Science*, *333*, 982–983.

Skaalvik, E. M., Federici, R. A., and Klassen, R. M. (2015). Mathematics achievement and self-efficacy: Relations with motivation for mathematics. *International Journal of Educational Research*, *72*, 129–136.

Slavich, G. M., and Cole, S. W. (2013). The emerging field of human social genomics. *Clinical Psychological Science*, *1*, 331–348.

Sroufe, L. A. (1979). The coherence of individual development: Early care, attachment, and subsequent developmental issues. *American Psychologist*, *34*, 834.

Steinberg, L., Graham, S., O'Brien, L., Woolard, J., Cauffman, E., and Banich, M. (2009). Age differences in future orientation and delay discounting. *Child development*, *80*(1), 28–44.

Swales, D. A., Winiarski, D. A., Smith, A. K., Stowe, Z. N., Newport, D. J., and Brennan, P. A. (2018). Maternal depression and cortisol in pregnancy predict offspring emotional reactivity in the preschool period. *Developmental Psychobiology*, *60*, 557–566.

Toth, S. L., Manly, J. T., and Cicchetti, D. (1992). Child maltreatment and vulnerability to depression. *Development and Psychopathology*, *4*, 97–112.

U.S. Department of Defense (DoD). (2017). *2017 Demographics: Profile of the Military Community.* Washington, DC. Retrieved from http://download.militaryonesource.mil/12038/MOS/Reports/2017-demographics-report.pdf.

Valle, M. F., Huebner, E. S., and Suldo, S. M. (2006). An analysis of hope as a psychological strength. *Journal of School Psychology*, *44*, 393–406.

Vázquez, D. M. (1998). Stress and the developing limbic–hypothalamic–pituitary–adrenal axis. *Psychoneuroendocrinology*, *23*, 663–700.

Villarruel, F. A., Perkins, D. F., Borden, L. M. and Keith, J. G. (2003). *Community Youth Development: Practice, Policy, and Research.* Thousand Oaks, CA: Sage.

Walker, E., Downey, G., and Bergman, A. (1989). The effects of parental psychopathology and maltreatment on child behavior: A test of the diathesis-stress model. *Child Development*, *60*, 15–24.

Werner, E. E. (1997). Vulnerable but invincible: High-risk children from birth to adulthood. *Acta Paediatrica*, *86*(S422), 103–105.

_______. (2012). Children and war: Risk, resilience, and recovery. *Development and Psychopathology*, *24*, 553–558.

Werner, E. E., and Smith, R. S. (1992). *Overcoming the Odds: High Risk Children from Birth to Adulthood.* Ithaca, NY: Cornell University Press.

_______. (2001). *Journeys from Childhood to Midlife: Risk, Resilience, and Recovery.* Ithaca, NY: Cornell University Press.

Youssef, A. M., Garr, A. S., and Gewirtz, A. H. (2016). Evidence-based parenting programs for school-aged children. In A. H. Gewirtz and A. M. Youssef (Eds.), *Parenting and Children's Resilience in Military Families* (pp. 229–250). Cham, Switzerland: Springer International.

Zelazo, P. D., and Carlson, S. M. (2012). Hot and cool executive function in childhood and adolescence: Development and plasticity. *Child Development Perspectives*, *47*.

Zelazo, P. D., Craik, F. I. M., and Booth, L. (2004). Executive function across the life span. *Acta Psychologica*, *115*(2-3), 167–183.

6

High-Stress Events, Family Resilience Processes, and Military Family Well-Being

In this chapter we expand on Chapter 5's discussion of stress among military children to address high-stress events experienced by military families. We begin with a review of the literature on stress and family resilience processes (as defined in Chapter 2) to better understand the effects of stress on family well-being. The chapter then places this understanding within the military context by discussing the effects of high impact duty-related stressors, such as physical injury, psychological trauma, bereavement, family violence and child maltreatment to illustrate how stressful challenges can impact family resilience and in turn complicate family well-being. To further elaborate on military family stressors, we describe the risk processes that characterize them and then link these processes to targets for evidence-based practices.[1] We briefly highlight examples of evidence-based military family intervention programs in preparation for their more detailed examination in subsequent chapters.

As discussed in prior chapters, military children and families constitute an increasingly diverse and complex population that possesses many advantages in comparison to their civilian counterparts. As presented in Chapter 4, military families face particular experiences associated with military service, including multiple family relocations and separations that lead to transitions in residence, communities, jobs, child care, health care, and schools. These transitions can also create opportunities for new experiences,

[1]Evidence-based and evidence-informed practices are defined in Chapter 1 and discussed elsewhere (see Chapters 7 and 8); the programs discussed in this chapter are specifically evidence-based.

allow family members to access previously untested strengths, and lead to successful solutions that bring a sense of accomplishment and pride. However, some challenges, for which a family may be unprepared or ill-equipped also result in high levels of stress that are likely to disrupt access to health care or other required community resources. Certain military family challenges create levels of stress and burden that predictably overwhelm most families, if only temporarily. When highly stressful challenges related to military life overtake the capacity of individuals and families to manage, they are likely to undermine the healthy resilience processes that support family functioning, leading to cascading risk and reduction in subjective, objective, and functional well-being.

While this report addresses a broad spectrum of the experiences of military families, this chapter focuses on military families' most stressful challenges, such as combat or other duty-related mental or physical injuries and military-duty-related deaths, which can undermine family well-being by disrupting normative processes that support family resilience. Family violence and child maltreatment are additional examples of stressful challenges to families, as well as examples of maladaptive responses within overwhelmed, highly reactive, or unskilled families. This chapter underscores that all family stressors are experienced within the emerging developmental context of a family and its individual members, as well as any prior traumatic exposures or adverse childhood experiences, medical or psychiatric pre-existing conditions, the maturity and sophistication of individual family members, and other family contexts that likely moderate the effects of stress.

Unfortunately, most discussions of military family stress tend to be deficit-focused, highlighting pathology within families, an approach that only serves to further marginalize and increase their vulnerability. The present chapter parts from such historical emphases by conceptualizing how stress undermines normative and protective processes inherent to families, undermining well-being and creating risk. Employing developmental ecological and life-course models (previously described in Chapter 2), as well as the concept of "linked lives," this chapter illustrates the complex interactive effects of high-stress events among adults and children within families and highlights opportunities to activate protective pathways that promote individual and family well-being. The chapter concludes by linking malleable risk processes to evidence-based interventions shown to mitigate the effects of stress in military or civilian families.

STRESS AND FAMILY RESILIENCE PROCESSES

Consistent with conceptualizations of individual and family risk and resilience described earlier in this volume, this chapter frames stressful family experiences in a broadly ecological context (Bronfenbrenner and Morris,

2006; Sameroff, 2010). Stress can affect micro-, meso- and macro-levels of the ecological system affecting military families (see Chapter 2). Wartime stress has been shown to have varying and often negative effects on individual service members (Hoge et al., 2006; Tanielian and Jaycox, 2008), military spouses (Leroux et al., 2016; Mansfield et al., 2010), and military children (Cozza and Lerner, 2013; Siegel et al., 2013). Most importantly, an understanding of the effects of stress on family well-being requires much more than a summation of the effects of stress on individuals within the family. Individuals are affected by and can benefit from the relational processes within families that are both multifaceted and are managed across time, and it is to those effects that we now turn.

Family Stress Models

Family stress models (Conger et al., 2002; Simons et al., 2016) provide a conceptual framework for understanding how stressful contexts such as individual psychopathology, marital transitions, and socioeconomic conditions reverberate in the family and create complex effects among individuals (adults and children), in dyadic relationships (marital and parent-child), and more broadly within families. These models were first proposed to describe how socioeconomic stressors affect families (Conger et al., 2002; Elder et al., 1986), with empirical data indicating that poverty increases parental stress, adversely affecting parenting practices, ultimately impairing child functioning and adjustment (Simons et al., 2016).

Extending this model to military families, Gewirtz and colleagues (2018b) tested a Military Family Stress Model in a sample of 336 post-deployment reserve component military families. Their work revealed reciprocal paths between parental functioning (i.e., posttraumatic stress disorder [PTSD] symptoms), parenting practices, couple adjustment, and children's symptoms. Parenting practices mediated the associations between mothers' PTSD symptoms and poorer child adjustment; parenting also linked associations between couple adjustment and children's behavioral and emotional symptoms (Gewirtz et al., 2018a). In effect, family stress models posit that family stressors negatively impact family well-being by undermining distinct couple, parenting, and family-resilience processes that are necessary to effectively manage overwhelming stress. These relational processes are now discussed.

A Transactional Concept of Stress

A transactional conceptualization of stress extends beyond its effect on individuals, and describes its dyadic effects within couples. As described by Bodenmann (1997), such a conceptualization "has to take into account the dynamic interplay between both partners, the origin of the stress experienced by each individual alone or by both together, the goals of each partner or dyad as well as the coping strategies applied. . ." (p. 138). Notably, stressors tend to undermine the healthy processes within couples that are also most likely to support individuals and couples when faced with challenging experiences. Story and Bradbury (2004) summarize dyadic resilience processes that are likely to protect couples faced with stress, including *active engagement* and *protective buffering*. Active engagement refers to maximizing positive interactions through problem solving, empathic listening, expressions of caring, and constructive criticism. Protective buffering includes minimizing negative interactions through conflict avoidance and minimizing emotional distress through disengagement.

Several researchers have examined the contribution of dyadic processes to military and veteran couple health outcomes. For example, Knobloch and colleagues (2013) and Knobloch and Theiss (2011) described the contribution of *relational uncertainty* (lower degree of partner confidence in the relationship) and *interference from partners* (a disruption of partner routines that undermines goal attainment) to depressive symptoms and integration difficulties during post-deployment reunification. Another group of scientists reported that *partner accommodation* (alteration of one partner's behaviors in response to the other partner's PTSD symptoms) was associated with negative relationship satisfaction in couples (Fredman et al., 2014), but also positively contributed to treatment outcomes in couples-based therapy (Fredman et al., 2016).

Reciprocal Linkages Between Parent and Child Behaviors

Conceptualizing stress within the parenting or caregiving system informs an understanding not only of the importance of parenting for youth development and effective stress regulation, but also of the reciprocal linkages between parents and children. Effective caregiving or parenting is consistent, responsive, and sensitive and follows specific practices that vary according to the child's developmental stage.

In early childhood, the development of *a secure attachment relationship* is a key developmental task and lays the foundation for healthy child development and effective stress regulation. In middle childhood and adolescence, key developmental tasks such as effective self-regulation, social skills, and academic skills are scaffolded by parents who show warmth, teach with encouragement, set clear and consistent limits, monitor and supervise, and model effective communication, problem-solving, and emotion-regulation skills. In later adolescence and young adulthood, as youth develop autonomy and their own identity, parents shift "off the stage and into the audience," but research suggests that even in emerging adulthood authoritative parenting practices (i.e., high responsiveness with low control) are associated with fewer mental health and substance use problems in these young adults (Nelson et al., 2011).

Reciprocal linkages between parent and child behaviors intersect with individual vulnerabilities, decreasing (or increasing) the risk for psychopathology across development. For example, in a 10-year prospective longitudinal study, Brody and colleagues (2017) demonstrated reciprocal linkages from early adolescence through emerging adulthood between youth temperament, harsh parenting, genetic vulnerability, and allostatic load (a physiological indicator of the cost of stress). Teacher ratings of difficult temperament in youth at age 11 were associated with subsequent youth-reported harsh parenting at age 15; this, in turn, was associated with allostatic load at age 21 (measured by blood pressure, body mass index, cortisol, epinephrine, and norepinephrine). However, these associations were significant only for youth and parents who carried 'risky' A alleles on the oxytocin receptor (OXTR) genotype. Thus, vulnerability and protective processes at multiple levels (within and between family members) protect individuals from or render them less resilient to stress. These findings have relevance both to families in which service members are parents and to families in which the service members are emerging adults.

Patterson's (1982, 2005) social interaction learning model offers a conceptualization of *how* stress affects parenting practices. Stressed parents demonstrate higher rates of *coercive* interactions with their children, such as escalation, aversive behaviors, negative reciprocity, and negative reinforcement. Escalating conflict bouts occur that are "won" or "lost" through aversive means, such as yelling, threatening, or harsh corporal punishment. When these social interactions become the norm rather than the exception, children learn that coercion pays off and replicate coercive behaviors in the home, school, and with peers. Both experimental and passive longitudinal studies demonstrated that high rates of coercive parent-child interactions increase the risk of child maltreatment and predict an increased risk of subsequent internalizing and externalizing behaviors that extends into adulthood (Capaldi et al., 2003; Patterson et al., 1998). Fortunately, evidence-based interventions that teach effective, positive parenting behaviors reduce coercion and the risk of maltreatment and improve child adjustment and resilience (Forgatch and Gewirtz, 2017).

Walsh (1996, 2016) introduced and elaborated on naturally occurring and protective family-level resilience processes that support well-being, but that are also vulnerable to the effects of stress. The resilience processes they studied include "organizational patterns, communication and problem-solving processes, community resources, and affirming belief systems" (Walsh, 1996, p. 261). Saltzman and colleagues (2011) adapted these same principles to military families, shifting focus from identification of specific risk and resilience factors to a broad conceptualization of risk mechanisms that can undermine military family well-being when faced with stress. The latter authors highlighted five mechanisms that can undermine resilience in military families—namely, *incomplete understanding* [of military-related experiences or outcomes], *impaired family communication, impaired parenting, impaired family organization,* and *lack of guiding belief systems*—each of which can undermine health-promoting/normative family processes resulting in potential negative family outcomes. (For full description of mechanisms of risk, see Saltzman et al. [2011, p. 217, Table 1]). As a result, normative family resilience processes that are negatively impacted by military family stress can serve as points of intervention for family-centered programs designed to support well-being.

Although distinct from military family stress, disaster-related family stress shares similar family effects, and the more extensive scientific literature in this area further informs our understanding of the impact of military-related stress on family resilience processes. For example, Noffsinger and colleagues (2012) highlighted the effects of disaster-related stress on the structure, roles, boundaries, and functions (e.g., flexibility, adaptability, communication, decision making, and problem solving) within families. In turn, family mechanisms, such as family cohesion (Laor et al., 2001), family conflict (Gil-Rivas et al., 2004; Wasserstein and La Greca, 1998) and parental overprotectiveness (Bokszczanin, 2008) have all been associated with post-disaster outcomes, suggesting reciprocal mechanisms by which stress and family-level processes affect family well-being. These findings are instructive to our understanding of military families and point to additional targets of engagement for family-centered interventions to promote resilience and family well-being.

THE EFFECTS OF HIGH-STRESS EVENTS ON MILITARY FAMILIES: DUTY-RELATED ILLNESS, INJURY, AND DEATH, MILITARY FAMILY VIOLENCE, AND CHILD MALTREATMENT

As mentioned earlier, military families are affected by a range of experiences that can add both challenges and opportunities to their lives (see Chapter 4). However, certain high-stress events are more likely to be associated with negative effects within families, and this section focuses on those highly stressful experiences that have been most studied. For example, physical injury and psychological traumatic stress are important examples of defining events that can complicate a military family's well-being, lead to problems within the family, affect the functioning of marital and parenting relationships and, in turn, undermine the individual and collective well-being of adults and children. In this section, we provide examples of the potentially undermining effects of the following heightened stressors on military family well-being: service-related mental health conditions and injuries incurred in the line of duty, military-duty-related deaths, military family violence, and child maltreatment.

PTSD, Major Depressive Disorder, and Other Duty-Related Mental Health Conditions

Upon return from combat in Iraq and Afghanistan, 19 percent of service members reported symptoms consistent with the presence of a psychiatric disorder, including PTSD, depression, anxiety disorder, and substance abuse (Hoge et al., 2006). While a comprehensive review of the prevalence of mental health conditions identified that "most service members return home from war without problems and readjust successfully," that same review also found that "some have significant deployment-related mental health problems" (Tanielian and Jaycox, 2008, p. 433). Prevalence of PTSD and major depression among Operation Enduring Freedom (OEF) and Operation Iraqi Freedom (OIF) veterans was estimated to be 5 to 15 percent and 2 to 14 percent, respectively. Unfortunately, of those with probable disorders, only half were estimated to have sought help from a health care professional (Tanielian and Jaycox, 2008).

Consequently, of the 2.7 million service members who have been deployed to war zones in Iraq and Afghanistan since 2001, between 100,000 and 400,000 combat veterans have likely been affected by these disorders. Adding to these health concerns, both PTSD and major depressive disorder are known to have numerous long-term and negative effects, including functional impairment, poor physical health, neuropsychological damage, risk of comorbid substance use, and elevated risk of death among those affected (Hidalgo and Davidson, 2000; Kessler, 2000; Kessler et al., 2012).

PTSD

In addition to combat exposure, other stressors and traumatic events that occur as part of military duty may result in post-traumatic symptoms or an actual diagnosis of PTSD. For example, service members are frequently called upon in times of national or international crisis, disaster, or terrorism. In such circumstances, they may be required to function within a hostile community, serve as first responders, or otherwise be directly exposed to stressful or traumatic experiences that could put them at risk for traumatic stress responses. Body handling and other mortuary responsibilities have specifically been shown to increase risk for PTSD among military service personnel, especially in circumstances that involve exposure to gruesome human remains (Flynn et al., 2015; McCarroll et al., 1993, 1995).

In addition, a recent study describing data from the *2009-2011 National Health Study for a New Generation of U.S. Veterans* (a population-based survey of 60,000 veterans who served during OEF/OIF) found that 41 percent of female and 4 percent of male veterans reported experiencing military sexual trauma, including sexual harassment and sexual assault (Barth et al., 2016), creating additional pathways of risk. PTSD is commonly associated with military sexual trauma (Suris and Lind, 2008), adding to the mental health burden within the military community as well as among military families.

PTSD has been consistently associated with negative effects on relationships between service members and their spouses and children. Table 6-1 provides a diagrammatic summary of the effects of PTSD symptom clusters and their likely impact on familial resilience processes. Galovski and Lyons (2004) reviewed the effects of PTSD on intrafamilial relationships, describing the association of psychological symptoms and risk behaviors with poorer marital satisfaction, impaired family functioning, and greater family distress and violence. Studies of Vietnam veterans have described the relationship between PTSD and family violence (Jordan et al., 1992; Petrik et al., 1983). Other studies of combat veterans have found that the presence and severity of PTSD symptoms better account for veteran aggression than combat exposure alone (Hoge et al., 2006; Jakupcak et al., 2007; Sayers et al., 2009; Taft et al., 2007).

On a positive note, Elbogen and colleagues (2014) found that socioeconomic factors (money and stable employment), psychosocial factors (resilience, sense of control over one's life, and social support) and physical factors (adequate sleep and lack of pain) all served as protective mechanisms to decrease community violence in veterans and could potentially diminish partner aggression as well.

Some investigators have examined the impact of PTSD on marital relationship processes and found that PTSD symptoms were associated with poorer communication, marital confidence, relationship dedication, parental alliance, and relationship bonding (Allen et al., 2010). In addition, PTSD has been associated with intimate partner discord and poorer intimate relationship satisfaction, with two studies showing avoidance and numbing

TABLE 6-1 Negative Effects of PTSD Symptom Clusters on Family Resilience Processes

	Re-experiencing	Avoidance	Negative Cognitions and Mood	Arousal
Emotional Closeness	–	–	–	–
Communication		–		–
Safety and Impulse Control	–		–	–
Family Leadership		–	–	
Family Hopefulness	–		–	
Supervision of Children		–		
Authoritative Discipline of Children		–	–	–

SOURCE: Adapted from Cozza (2016).
NOTE: The minus sign indicates a negative effect.

associated with relationship dissatisfaction and hyperarousal[2] associated with marital conflict or aggression and spousal abuse (Allen et al., 2018; Monson et al., 2009). Male service members' higher experiential avoidance has been associated with poorer observed couple communication and lower perceived relationship quality in both service members and their spouses (Zamir et al., 2018). Spouses of chronically PTSD-affected service members report higher rates of distress, depression, suicidal ideation, and poorer adjustment than spouses of non-affected service members (Calhoun et al., 2002; Manguno-Mire et al., 2007).

Fredman and colleagues (2014) introduced the concept of *partner accommodation*, by which spouses appear to modify their own behavior or enable the avoidance of the PTSD-affected service member or veteran, further undermining relationships and partner health. Others have termed this process *walking on eggshells* (Snyder, 2013–2015). Recent work has summarized the effects of PTSD in affected couples, as well as outlined the importance of future research that could more broadly examine the impact of mediators and moderators on these effects, thereby suggesting additional targets of intervention (Campbell and Renshaw, 2018).

PTSD has similarly been shown to affect parenting satisfaction and parenting behaviors (Berz et al., 2008; Gewirtz et al., 2010; Samper et al., 2004), although based on observational data only mothers' PTSD symptoms (not fathers') has been found to influence couples' parenting behaviors (Gewirtz et al., 2018a). Parenting can be impaired by greater emotional reactivity, loss of cognitive capacity, greater levels of interpersonal aggression, or the increased avoidance and disconnection from loved ones that is commonplace with PTSD. For example, experiential avoidance[3] in National Guard service members moderated associations between PTSD and observed parenting behavior, such that only at high levels of avoidance were PTSD symptoms associated with impaired parenting behaviors (Brockman et al., 2016). In another report, couples' observed parenting practices mediated the associations between mothers' PTSD symptoms and poorer child adjustment, as well as the associations between couple adjustment and children's behavioral and emotional symptoms (Gewirtz et al., 2018b).

---

[2]Hyperarousal is defined by Merriam-Webster's dictionary as "an abnormal state of increased responsiveness to stimuli that is marked by various physiological and psychological symptoms (such as increased levels of alertness and anxiety and elevated heart rate and respiration)." In addition, to be diagnosed with PTSD, "a person has to have been exposed to an extreme stressor or traumatic event to which he or she responded with fear, helplessness, or horror and to have three distinct types of symptoms consisting of reexperiencing of the event, avoidance of reminders of the event, and *hyperarousal* for at least one month." (See https://www.merriam-webster.com/dictionary/hyperarousal.)

[3]Experiential avoidance is "the tendency to avoid internal, unwanted thoughts and feelings" (Kashdan et al., 2014, p. 1).

Clinical accounts describe the challenges faced by PTSD-affected couples when co-parenting (Allen et al., 2010); as a result, couples often need to renegotiate parenting responsibilities due to PTSD (Cozza, 2016).

Not unexpectedly, children are likely to be affected by the emotional and behavioral changes in a PTSD-affected parent, depending on the child's age, developmental level, temperament, and any preexisting conditions. Children of Vietnam veterans with PTSD exhibit general distress, depression, low self-esteem, aggression, impaired social relationships, and school-related difficulties (Rosenheck and Nathan, 1985). PTSD can result in greater distress or worsening of symptoms in children with pre-existing medical, developmental, behavioral, or emotional conditions. Young children may have an especially hard time understanding and coping with the parental overreaction or disengagement that can result from PTSD. Of note, family violence resulting from PTSD can further undermine child health (Galovski and Lyons, 2004). In a longitudinal study of OEF/OIF reserve component families, Snyder and colleagues (2016) demonstrated reciprocal cascades among fathers' and mothers' PTSD symptoms and their children's internalizing and externalizing symptoms.

Depression and Substance Use Disorders

Although greater attention has been paid to the impact of PTSD on intrafamilial relationships within combat veteran families, depression is also known to have serious consequences for intrafamilial relationships and, like PTSD, has been shown to be a consequence of service members' combat exposure (see Hoge et al., 2006; and Tanielian and Jaycox, 2008). Although studies within military samples are lacking, in the general population depressive disorders have been consistently associated with interpersonal negativity, communication difficulties, and interpersonal stress within affected couples and families (Gabriel, et al., 2010; Rehman et al., 2008). Not surprisingly, such effects also result in greater levels of marital dissatisfaction and discord. Relevant to military family well-being, parental depression is a known risk factor for depression and anxiety, behavioral problems, and academic and cognitive difficulties in their children (for a review, see Beardslee et al., 2011). Research examining the impact of parental depression within military families is required, especially since family-based interventions have been shown to successfully address these pathways of risk in clinical trials (Beardslee et al., 2003).

As with depressive disorders, for substance use disorders the intrafamilial effects have not been examined within military families, but studies of the general population show that they are clearly associated with marital distress (Whisman, 2007) as well as problematic parenting (Arria et al., 2012). Given that substance use disorders, like PTSD and depression, have been associated with combat deployments (Shen et al., 2012), their effects are likely present among military families, yet they remain unstudied.

Effects of Service Member Physical Injuries on Families

More than 90 percent of service members who were injured in Iraq or Afghanistan in the first 4 years of conflict survived their injuries, a testament to advances in battlefield medicine and efficiency within the aeromedical evacuation system (Goldberg, 2007). Almost 30,000 service members were wounded in action during Operation Iraqi Freedom and Operation Enduring Freedom combined (Goldberg, 2007). Describing combat wounds from 2001 to 2005, Owens and colleagues (2008) reported the following distribution by type of wound: 54 percent extremity, 11 percent abdominal, 11 percent head and neck, 10 percent facial, 6 percent thoracic, 6 percent eyes, and 3 percent ears. These injuries resulted in amputations, blindness, deafness, and other long-lasting functional impairments (Owens et al., 2008). In addition, the Defense and Veterans Brain Injury Center reports that since 2000 nearly 380,000 service members have been diagnosed with traumatic brain injury (TBI) (Defense Veterans Brain Injury Center, 2015). Although TBI may be a result of combat-related injuries, service members can also sustain such injuries from other duty-related events, such as training, operations, or deployment and from non-duty-related events, such as recreational events and motor vehicle accidents.

The burden to family members secondary to combat-related injury has been described elsewhere[4] and often includes long and stressful rounds of treatment and rehabilitation as well as changes in functioning that can require family members to assume new roles within the family, such as caregiving. A family's experience is likely to be determined by the type and severity of the injury, family composition, preexisting individual and family conditions, the ages of children, the course of required medical treatment, and whether the injured regains satisfactory functioning.

The course of recovery for the family of an injured military service member has been conceptualized as an *injury recovery trajectory* (Cozza and Guimond, 2011) consisting of four phases:

1. *Acute care*, which is initiated at the time of injury by military medics and includes care provided in combat hospitals;
2. *Medical stabilization*, which incorporates definitive medical treatment in U.S. stateside military medical centers;

---

[4]For example, in Badr et al. (2011), Cozza (2016), Cozza and Feerick (2011), Cozza and Guimond (2011), Cozza et al. (2011), and Holmes et al. (2013).

3. *Transition to outpatient care*, which often includes relocations of injured service members to treatment facilities closer to home, transition of treatment teams, and possible medical discharge from military service; and
4. *Long-term rehabilitation and recovery*, which involves the ongoing care of the service member in order to maximize treatment benefits and long-term functioning.

During each phase, families face multiple emotional and logistical challenges. For example, during medical stabilization, military spouses and children often relocate to military treatment facilities to be closer to their injured loved ones. However, depending upon circumstances, individual family members may be geographically separated, disrupting daily routines and adding stress. Transition to outpatient care involves other stressors: finding new housing, working with new health care providers, enrolling children in new schools, and possibly leaving their military friends and communities behind. These effects are long and cascading.

Depending upon the nature of the physical injury, service members may have physical, psychological, or cognitive changes that affect functioning in a variety of areas of their lives, including parenting. When injuries result in major changes to the ways in which a service member traditionally parents (e.g., when a parent can no longer walk, run, or play), this may result in a sense of loss or mourning over body changes. Cozza and colleagues (2011) described how injured service members must modify a previously held, idealized sense of themselves as parents and may need to explore new ways of playing with their children so that they can continue to relate to them. Injuries and prolonged hospitalizations or rehabilitation can also lead to conflict with spouses that can undermine marital health (Kelley et al., 1997; LeClere and Kowalewski, 1994), as well as the ability to effectively co-parent.

Effects of Traumatic Brain Injury

The neuropsychiatric consequences of TBI, including personality changes, loss of control, unexpected emotional reactions, irritability, anger, and apathy or lack of energy can be particularly problematic to interpersonal relationships (Weinstein et al., 1995). In fact, such symptoms are more distressing to family members and disruptive to family functioning than other, non-neurological physical injuries (Urbach and Culbert, 1991). In a study of nonmilitary families by Pessar and colleagues (1993), noninjured parents reported increased externalizing behaviors, as well as emotional and post-traumatic symptoms, in their children after the parental TBI. In addition, TBI correlated with compromised parenting in both injured and noninjured parents and with depression in the non-TBI parent

(Pessar et al., 1993). Children of TBI-affected parents have described feelings of loss (Butera-Prinzi and Perlesz, 2004), as well as isolation and loneliness (Charles et al., 2007), after the TBI incident. Factors that have all been associated with child outcomes include the severity of TBI symptoms, the amount of time since injury, child age and gender, preinjury family functioning, and postinjury disruptions of family organization and structure (Urbach and Culbert, 1991; Verhaeghe et al., 2005).

Given sustained neuropsychiatric impairment, TBI is likely to have a long-term impact on military families. Young families with poorer financial and social support appear to be at the greatest risk for negative outcomes (Verhaeghe et al., 2005). Financial, housing, social assistance, employment support and access to professional service are critical to the well-being of families facing the long-term effects of a TBI injury (Verhaeghe et al., 2005).

Effects on Family Caregivers

Physical and mental injuries from nearly two decades of war since 9/11 have impacted service members and veterans who rely upon family caregiving that secondarily impacts family well-being (Ramchand et al., 2014). Results of this recent RAND study indicate that there are 5.5 million military caregivers in the United States. Military caregivers are the informal network of family members, friends, or acquaintances who devote a great deal of time caring for impacted service members and veterans. Military caregivers are more likely to be nonwhite, a military veteran, and younger. They may be required to provide decades of future care for young disabled service members and older veterans and who, themselves, are less likely to be connected to support networks and describe poorer levels of personal physical health (Ramchand et al., 2014). Caregiving is provided while they attempt to maintain ongoing employment that does not uniformly support their need for flexibility. No systematic studies have examined these effects on military family well-being.

Although some medically derived interventions to support the health of military families faced with combat-related injuries or illness have been described (Smith et al., 2013), most medical systems remain committed to patient-centered rather than family-centered models of care. Not surprisingly, health care environments are often either unsuited to or unprepared for addressing these complex effects within military families.

Effects of Military-Duty-Related Death on Families and Children

Within the decade after September 11, 2001, nearly 16,000 military service members died while on active duty. These deaths were due to accidents (34%), combat (32%), suicides (15%), illnesses (15%), homicides (3%), and terrorism (less than 1%) (Cozza et al., 2017). These deceased service members left behind 9,667 dependent widowed spouses and 12,641 young dependent children whose mean age was 10.3 years (Cozza et al., 2017), as well as a difficult-to-determine number of extended relatives including parents, siblings, and cousins. A recent study examining grief responses, which examined a community sample of 1,732 first-degree family members of deceased military service members, found that 15 percent of participants reported elevated levels of grief and associated functional impairment that was consistent with a clinical disorder of impairing grief (Cozza et al., 2016). This finding should not be surprising, given that 85 percent of deaths related to military duty are sudden and violent (Cozza et al., 2016), creating greater risk for negative grief-related outcomes (Kristensen et al., 2012).

Widowed military spouses tend to be young, and many have not had the opportunity to pursue their own individual careers due to frequent moves and other requirements of military family life. Until the time of their spouses' deaths, they and their families will have lived within military communities and among other military families, accessing resources available within these communities. However, after the death of their military spouses, widowed spouses experience sudden and unanticipated transitions to life outside of the military community among civilians who often do not fully appreciate their history or their culture (Harrington-Lamorie et al., 2014). Military widows/widowers are also subject to rules that can adversely affect them if they choose to remarry. For example, if a bereaved military spouse chooses to remarry before age 55, he or she loses access to the Survivor Benefit Plan and other military-related benefits that are received after widowhood. Given the young age of bereaved military spouses, such rules can make it difficult for military widows and widowers to fully invest in their future lives (Cozza et al., 2019).

The death of a parent, particularly for young children, has been associated with anxiety, depression, and posttraumatic stress symptoms (Currier et al., 2007; Finkelstein, 1988; Reinherz et al., 2000). The loss of a parent may also lead to transitions in residence for military families, changes to financial stability, and challenges to parenting due to the resultant grief of any surviving caregiver, which can disrupt child care. In the aftermath of parental death, poorer child outcomes have been associated with poorer adult caregiver outcomes, further highlighting the linked lives within military families and potential vulnerabilities to children following parental death (Saldinger et al., 2004).

Rates of suicide have risen within the U.S. military since 2004, both among those never deployed and among prior-deployed service members (Schoenbaum et al., 2014). Suicide accounted for nearly 15 percent of military service deaths in the decade after 9/11 (Cozza et al., 2017). Suicide is a unique form of death, but like other forms of sudden and violent death it increases risk for negative grief outcomes in those who are affected

(Kristensen et al., 2012). Notably, suicide is more likely to be associated with guilt and stigmatization within families compared to other types of death (Feigelman et al., 2009), which can harm family well-being. Despite these concerns, parental suicide has not been shown to have more negative effects on children than other violent or nonviolent parental deaths (Brown et al., 2007; Cerel et al., 2000; Pfeffer et al., 2000). Historically, military suicides have not infrequently been attributed to service member misconduct or been determined to be "not within the line of duty," which can further stigmatization and result in loss of benefits to military family members. Recent efforts have attempted to reverse this practice.

Family Violence and Child Maltreatment

Family maltreatment includes physical, sexual, or emotional aggression or neglect within a family, either between adult partners (spousal abuse or intimate partner violence), between parents and children (child maltreatment), or among multiple family members (e.g., domestic violence). Any form of family maltreatment creates stressful challenges within a family, but in addition it represents maladaptive responses that undermine family well-being. In addition to posing risks to military family well-being, it poses a serious public health risk to military communities. The U.S. Department of Defense (DoD) has developed substantive prevention efforts through the Family Advocacy Program (FAP), at both DoD and military service levels. For families where maltreatment has occurred, activities in this program engage at-risk families (e.g., New Parent Support Program), identify episodes of family maltreatment (e.g., case identification), and monitor, support, and provide intervention (e.g., FAP case management).

Few studies compare rates of family maltreatment between military and civilian populations, and those that have must be cautiously interpreted due to small sample sizes and methodological limitations, including use of nonrepresentative samples. Combat deployments have been associated with small but significant increases in intimate partner violence in at least three reports (McCarroll et al., 2000, 2003; Newby et al., 2005). Additionally, depression, substance use disorders, and PTSD have each been associated with elevated levels of intimate partner violence in both active duty service members as well as veterans (Sparrow et al., 2017). In fiscal year 2017, data from the Office of the Secretary of Defense Family Advocacy Program's Central Registry, which aggregates data from each military service, indicates that the rate of reported spouse abuse per 1,000 couples was 24.5, which is a non-statistically significant 5 percent increase in the rate of reported incidents since 2016 (DoD, 2018).

Lower rates of child maltreatment have been reported in military communities as compared to civilian communities (DoD, 2018; McCarroll et al., 2003), although because these comparisons are based on the number of substantiated maltreatment cases they might not indicate actual differences in the underlying risk across communities. Regardless, child maltreatment remains a challenge to military communities and to military family well-being. In fiscal year 2017, there were 12,849 reports of suspected child abuse and neglect to the Family Advocacy Program (DoD, 2018).

Notably, child neglect comprises the most common form of family maltreatment in both military and civilian communities. Child neglect involves an act "in which a child is deprived of needed age-appropriate care by act or omission of the child's parent, guardian, or caregiver" (Fullerton et al., 2011, p. 1433). Elevated rates of military child neglect have been associated with combat activities in Iraq and Afghanistan (Gibbs et al., 2007; McCarroll et al., 2008; Rentz et al., 2007) and have continued to rise within military communities through 2014, adding concern about military family well-being even as combat deployments have decreased. Various types of child neglect—failure to provide physical needs, lack of supervision, emotional neglect—have been variably associated with deployment status (Cozza et al., 2018b) and family risk factors (Cozza et al., 2018a) in military samples, suggesting the need for tailored prevention and policy efforts.

Military family violence and child maltreatment serve as examples of maladaptive responses within highly reactive families or those that are unskilled in responding to the challenges with which they are faced. In each of the service branches, FAP currently offers the New Parent Support Program, which targets vulnerable families, including young families with newborn infants and or those challenged by deployments, mental health or substance use problems, medical or developmental disorders, or prior history of maltreatment or family violence. FAP also offers counseling for parents to discontinue harmful behaviors, manage anger, and promote positive parenting practices. Although some evaluation of existing DoD programs is underway, its scope is limited and should incorporate recommended strategies (see Chapters 7 and 8) to ensure that provided services reflect the needs of targeted populations.

Contextual Moderators

The effects of stress on families must be contextualized within preexisting levels of individual and family functioning and among multiple experiences, including prior traumas, adverse childhood experiences, acute and chronic stressors, and microaggressions. In addition, the effects of stress need to be considered within the developmental context of the family and its individual members. For example, stresses affect service members and families within the changing context of new marriages, divorces, births of children, changing medical, neurodevelopmental or educational conditions among family members, new or lost employment of military spouses, transitions from military life, or changes in extended family obligations, such as unexpected child care requirements or new responsibilities associated with aging parents. Notably, and in addition to the impact of duty-related stressors, military family well-being is likely affected by individuals' prior traumatic experiences, pre-existing mental health conditions (including personality disorders), and prior adverse childhood experiences, which have been associated with new-onset depression among service members in at least one study (Rudenstine et al., 2015).

Other factors, or contextual moderators, are likely to affect the associations between military-related adversities and family and child health and well-being. For example, families with a member on National Guard or Reserve status remain understudied. Effects on nontraditional families (including single-parent families, female service member families, dual-military families, sexual minority families, and immigrant families); families having low socioeconomic status; racial, ethnic, and religious considerations; and Exceptional Family Member Program families faced with medical or neurodevelopmental conditions have also not been examined. The greater stigmatization that families in some of those categories experience, as well as the fewer inherent resources some of them can access, their increased need for services, and their reduced access to community support are likely to add vulnerability in the face of military adversities. Community service and health care providers are less likely to be aware of and educated about the needs within these subpopulations, making it more difficult to address their needs.

OPPORTUNITIES FOR BOLSTERING RESILIENCE BY ADDRESSING RISK PATHWAYS

Of relevance to military service systems are consistent findings that the effects of severe stressors can be prevented and ameliorated with evidence-based interventions focused on strengthening the caregiving, parenting, and family environment. The risk processes that characterize the military family stresses described above can be conceptualized both as individual processes and as linked (family) processes. For example, child abuse and neglect result from ineffective regulation and skills in parental emotion and behavior, leading to an inability to inhibit physically aggressive responses to stress, poor parenting skills, preoccupation secondary to depression or substance abuse leading to neglect, impaired judgement due to cognitive limitations, and/or lack of child development knowledge. Targeting these key cognitive, emotional, and behavioral processes in parents by providing them guidance about child development, emotion regulation, and parenting skills such as effective discipline, warmth, and encouragement, reduces and prevents child maltreatment (Olds et al., 1997; Prinz, 2016). Domestic violence, which greatly overlaps child maltreatment, is associated with similar processes, that is, with cognitive, emotional, and behavioral dysregulation that is manifested in problems such as couples' poor problem solving and poor conflict resolution.

Not surprisingly, family-based prevention programs targeting these and related risk events have similar components. They are found to have generalized effects, sometimes called "crossover effects," in benefiting not simply the intervention target (parenting, the couple relationship, and/or child adjustment and development) but the entire family system through cascading positive effects that occur over time. Thus, for example, evidence-based parenting programs not only improve parenting practices but also strengthen child adjustment and parental well-being, as well as reducing PTSD, depression symptoms, and suicidality (Gewirtz et al., 2016, 2018a).

Figure 6-1 depicts targets for interventions at different levels within the family to promote resilience processes in order to support overall family well-being. The figure also provides examples of evidence-based interventions targeting individual, couple, parenting, and family-level processes. Several evidence-based military family intervention programs, which have been evaluated with randomized controlled trials, have relevance to families affected by such adversities.

Many of these programs have been developed and tested within the Department of Defense, including the Congressionally Directed Medical Research Program, and/or with research funding from the National Institutes of Health. Examples include programs targeting individual stress response, such as the Trauma Focused-Cognitive Behavioral Therapy (TF-CBT) (Cohen et al., 2012); programs targeting parenting for families with very young children, such as Strong Families Strong Forces (DeVoe et al., 2017) and Strong Military Families (Julian et al., 2018); programs targeting school-age children, such as After Deployment, Adaptive Parenting Tools/ADAPT (Gewirtz et al., 2018a); and programs targeting parenting, parent-child relationships, and family communication more broadly, such as Families OverComing Under Stress/FOCUS (Lester et al., 2013), as well as programs targeting couple functioning in particular, such as Strong Bonds (Allen et al., 2015) and Strength at Home (Taft et al., 2016). These programs are designed to support families affected by deployment and other duty-related risks through strengths-based approaches that focus on improving couple, family, and parent-child relationships by fostering family resilience processes such as such as emotion regulation, communication, problem solving, and the elements of positive parenting delineated above.

Other family-centered programs have addressed the challenges of TBI and family bereavement. For example, two programs that have been developed to support families affected by TBI—Family Focused Therapy for TBI

Military Family Stressors

Parental psychopathology: PTSD, depression, substance use

Child abuse and neglect (maltreatment)

Death of a parent

Physical injury

Intimate partner violence

Child mental health problems

Family Level	Resilience Processes Targeted for Prevention/Intervention	EBP Intervention Examples
Individual stress regulation	Individual treatment to remit symptoms and prevent deterioration that includes the family	Evidence-based individual treatments Trauma-focused Cognitive Behavioral Therapy (TF-CBT)
Parent-child relational processes	Effective parenting practices: attachment, reflective capacity, warmth, structure, encouragement, discipline, problem-solving, communication, monitoring (middle childhood and adolescence)	Family Advocacy Program, New Parents Support Program Strong Families Strong Forces Strong Military Families ADAPT FOCUS Families – Early Childhood Parent-Child Interaction Therapy (PCIT)
Couple relational processes	Effective relationships, problem solving, co-parenting	Strong Bonds Strength at Home FOCUS – Couples Cognitive-behavioral couple therapy for PTSD
Overall family processes	Family level practices Individual and interpersonal skill development: communication, emotional regulation, problem-solving, goal setting, management of trauma and loss reminders, narrative reflection/shared meaning	FOCUS – Couples and Families Family Focused Therapy for TBI Family Bereavement Program

FIGURE 6-1 Effects of military family stressors at the individual, parent-child, couple, and family-level, targets for prevention/intervention, and EBP intervention examples.

(FFT-TBI) (Dausch and Saliman, 2009) and Brain Injury Family Intervention (BIF) (Kreutzer et al., 2010)—share similar strategies to educate affected family members about TBI and improve communication within the family, as well as encourage problem solving, stress management, and family goal setting. The Family Bereavement Program (FBP) is a multimodal intervention that similarly incorporates positive parenting strategies as well as individual and relationship strengthening activities to support bereaved families (Sandler et al., 2003).

The examples provided above do not constitute an exhaustive list of family resources for military families, but instead are offered to highlight evidence-based programs that have been rigorously evaluated in a military context, as reviewed in Chapter 7. In contrast, while other military family programs may target the risk factors highlighted above, most have not yet been rigorously evaluated to determine whether they actually achieve their intended aims. In fact, all existing family programs should be evaluated (as described in Chapters 7 and 8) to ensure that they are meeting their intended goals within the context of a coherent Military Family Readiness System (as described in Chapters 7 and 8), and new programs should only be developed when unmet needs are identified as part of a process of continuous program evaluation.

Family strengthening programs are critical to a public health approach to supporting wellness at universal, selective, and indicated levels. At the universal and selective levels, family-centered prevention programs offer an opportunity to increase resilience processes, thereby reducing risk. At indicated levels, clinicians and other community support providers are obligated to identify individuals who demonstrate symptoms consistent with clinical disorders and to transition them to evidence-based treatments when indicated. Figure 6-1 provides a depiction of the impact of military family stressors at different levels within the family, and examples of EBP interventions. Although these evidence-based interventions differ in format, content, and emphasis, all share several essential family-strengthening goals, as listed in Box 6-1.

CONCLUSIONS

CONCLUSION 6-1: Military families can be adversely affected by some aspects of military life, such as deployments, illnesses, and injuries, due to their undermining of healthy intra-familial resilience processes that support family well-being and readiness. Family resilience processes (e.g., effective communication strategies, emotion regulation, problem solving, and competent parenting) serve as opportunities for promotion, prevention, and intervention in the wake of stress and trauma.

CONCLUSION 6-2: The effects of duty-related stress on families are likely to be modified by family members' prior traumas, medical or

BOX 6-1
Family-Strengthening Goals to Promote Family Resilience and Well-Being

1. ***Maintain a physically safe and structured environment***, protecting against interpersonal aggression among adults and children, and ensuring that children have adequate structure and support, have consistency in routines and rules, and are effectively monitored.
2. ***Engage required resources***, accessing instrumental and social support within and outside the family to support adults and children, dyadic relationships and the family as a whole, and teaching family members how to effectively use their support opportunities (friends, extended family, teachers, coaches, faith-based communities, etc.).
3. ***Develop and share knowledge within and outside of the family***, building shared understanding about stressors, including service members' injury or illness, as well as modeling and teaching effective communication strategies among adults and children.
4. ***Build a positive, emotionally safe, and warm family environment***, including effective stress reduction and emotional regulation strategies for parents to engage in and model for children, as well as engaging in activities that are calming and enjoyable for all.
5. ***Master and model important interpersonal skills***, including individual and relational problem solving and conflict resolution and incorporating evidence-based strategies.
6. ***Maintain a vision of hope and future optimism for the family***, engendering positive expectations among family members and creating a hope-filled family narrative.
7. ***Utilize competent and authoritative parenting***, encouraging consequence-based strategies that promote mastery and minimizing harsh disciplinary practices.
8. ***Incorporate trauma-informed approaches to care***, recognizing that families faced with stress and adversity are likely to be affected by trauma and loss experiences that uniquely impact adults and children within families, their relationships, and their development.
9. ***Promote security among adults and children***, strengthening parent-child relationships that are known to contribute to individual and relational wellness for both adults and children, and focusing on effective conflict resolution between spouses or partners.
10. ***Highlight the unique developmental needs of family members***, helping parents and other engaged adults in the family recognize and respond to their family members' needs effectively at each developmental stage.

SOURCE: Compiled by the Committee on the Well-Being of Military Families. Source for Goal #5 is Dausch and Saliman (2009); Gewirtz et al. (2018b); source for Goal # 6 is Saltzman et al. (2011).

mental health conditions, and acute or chronic family stressors, as well as by other contextual factors such as service component and single-parent or socioeconomic status.

CONCLUSION 6-3: Similar to maltreatment in civilian families, military family violence and child maltreatment indicate maladaptive responses within highly reactive families or those that are unskilled in responding to the challenges with which they are faced. Given adverse outcomes associated with family maltreatment, broadened evaluation efforts are required to examine the effectiveness of existing programs in this area.

CONCLUSION 6-4: Most health care settings are not prepared to deal with family circumstances associated with duty-related injury or illness, and would therefore benefit by being complemented with nonmedical approaches to better support family well-being.

CONCLUSION 6-5: Evidence-based programs, resources, and practices have been developed and evaluated for highly impacted military families that support normative individual and family-based resilience processes, well-being, and readiness; however, these interventions are not widely implemented in routine military family settings.

REFERENCES

Allen, E. S., Knopp, K., Rhoades, G., Stanley, S., and Markman, H. (2018). Between- and within-subject associations of PTSD symptom clusters and marital functioning in military couples. *Journal of Family Psychology 32*, 134–144.

Allen, E. S., Rhoades, G. K., Stanley, S. M., and Markman, H. J. (2010). Hitting home: Relationships between recent deployment, post-traumatic stress symptoms, and marital functioning for Army couples. *Journal of Family Psychology 24*, 280.

Allen, E. S., Stanley, S., Rhoades, G., and Markman, H. (2015). PREP for Strong Bonds: A review of outcomes from a randomized clinical trial. *Contemporary Family Therapy, 37*(3), 232–246.

Arria, A. M., Mericle, A. A., Meyers, K., and Winters, K. C. (2012). Parental substance use impairment, parenting and substance use disorder risk. *Journal of Substance Abuse Treatment 43*(1), 114–122.

Badr, H., Barker, T. M., and Milbury, K. (2011). Couples' psychosocial adaptation to combat wounds and injuries. In S. MacDermid Wadsworth and D. Riggs (Eds.), *Risk and Resilience in U.S. Military Families* (pp. 213–234). New York: Springer Science and Business Media.

Barth, S. K., Kimerling, R. E., Pavao, J., McCutcheon, S. J., Batten, S. V., Dursa, E., Peterson, M. R. and Schneiderman, A. I. (2016). Military sexual trauma among recent veterans: correlates of sexual assault and sexual harassment. *American Journal of Preventive Medicine, 50*, 77–86.

Beardslee, W. R., Gladstone, T. R., and O'Connor, E. E. (2011). Transmission and prevention of mood disorders among children of affectively ill parents: A review. *Journal of the American Academy of Child and Adolescent Psychiatry 50*(11), 1098–1109.

Beardslee, W. R., Gladstone, T. R., Wright, E. J., and Cooper, A. B. (2003). A family-based approach to the prevention of depressive symptoms in children at risk: Evidence of parental and child change. *Pediatrics 112*(2), e119–e131.

Berz, J. B., Taft, C. T., Watkins, L. E., and Monson, C. M. (2008). Associations between PTSD symptoms and parenting satisfaction in a female veteran sample. *Journal of Psychological Trauma 7*, 37–45.

Bodenmann, G. (1997). Dyadic coping-a systematic-transactional view of stress and coping among couples: Theory and empirical findings. *European Review of Applied Psychology 47*, 137–140.

Bokszczanin, A. (2008). Parental support, family conflict, and overprotectiveness: predicting PTSD symptom levels of adolescents 28 months after a natural disaster. *Anxiety, Stress, and Coping 21*, 325–335.

Brockman, C., Snyder, J., Gewirtz, A., Gird, S.R., Quattlebaum, J., Schmidt, N., Pauldine, M.R., Elish, K., Schrepferman, L., Hayes, C. and Zettle, R. (2016). Relationship of service members' deployment trauma, PTSD symptoms, and experiential avoidance to postdeployment family reengagement. *Journal of Family Psychology 30(1)*, 52–62.

Brody, G. H., Yu, T., Barton, A. W., Miller, G. E., and Chen, E. (2017). Youth temperament, harsh parenting, and variation in the oxytocin receptor gene forecast allostatic load during emerging adulthood. *Development and Psychopathology 29*, 791–803.

Bronfenbrenner, U., and Morris, P. A. (2006). The bioecological model of human development. In W. Damon, and R. M. Lerner (Eds.), *Handbook of Child Psychology* (vol. 3, pp. 793–828). Hoboken, NJ: John Wiley and Sons.

Brown, A. C., Sandler, I. N., Tein, J. Y., Liu, X., and Haine, R. A. (2007). Implications of parental suicide and violent death for promotion of resilience of parentally-bereaved children. *Death Studies 31*(4), 301–335.

Butera-Prinzi, F., and Perlesz, A. (2004). Through children's eyes: Children's experience of living with a parent with an acquired brain injury. *Brain Injury 18*, 83–101.

Calhoun, P. S., Beckham, J. C., and Bosworth, H. B. (2002). Caregiver burden and psychological distress in partners of veterans with chronic posttraumatic stress disorder. *Journal of Traumatic Stress 15*, 205–212.

Campbell, S.B., and Renshaw, K. D. (2018). Posttraumatic stress disorder and relationship functioning: A comprehensive review and organizational framework. *Clinical Psychology Review, 65*, 152-162.

Capaldi, D. M., Pears, K. C., Patterson, G. R., and Owen, L. D. (2003). Continuity of parenting practices across generations in an at-risk sample: A prospective comparison of direct and mediated associations. *Journal of Abnormal Child Psychology 31*, 127–142.

Cerel, J., Fristad, M. A., Weller, E. B., and Weller, R. A. (2000). Suicide-bereaved children and adolescents: II. Parental and family functioning. *Journal of the American Academy of Child and Adolescent Psychiatry 39*(4), 437–444.

Charles, N., Butera-Prinzi, F., and Perlesz, A. (2007). Families living with acquired brain injury: A multiple family group experience. *NeuroRehabilitation 22*, 61–76.

Cohen, J. A., Mannarino, A. P., and Deblinger, E. (Eds.). (2012). *Trauma-Focused CBT for Children and Adolescents: Treatment Applications*. New York: Guilford Press.

Conger, R. D., Wallace, L. E., Sun, Y., Simons, R. L., McLoyd, V. C., and Brody, G. H. (2002). Economic pressure in African American families: A replication and extension of the family stress model. *Developmental Psychology 38*, 179–193.

Cozza, S. J. (2016). Parenting in military families faced with combat-related injury, illness, or death. In A. H. Gewirtz and A. M. Youssef (Eds.), *Parenting and Children's Resilience in Military Families* (pp. 151–173). Cham, Switzerland: Springer International.

Cozza, S. J., Chun, R. S., and Miller, C. (2011). The children and families of combat-injured service members. In Walter Reed Army Medical Center Borden Institute, *Combat and Operational Behavioral Health* (pp. 503–534). Washington, DC: Department of the Army, The Borden Institute.

Cozza, S. J., and Feerick, M. M. (2011). The impact of parental combat injury on young military children. In J. D. Osofsky (Ed.), *Clinical Work with Traumatized Young Children* (pp. 139–154). New York: Guilford Press.

Cozza, S. J., Fisher, J. E., Mauro, C., Zhou, J., Ortiz, C. D., Skritskaya, N., Wall, M. M., Fullerton, C. S., Ursano, R. J., and Shear, M. K. (2016). Performance of DSM-5 persistent complex bereavement disorder criteria in a community sample of bereaved military family members. *American Journal of Psychiatry, 173*(9), 919–929.

Cozza, S. J., Fisher, J. E., Zhou, J., Harrington-LaMorie, J., La Flair, L., Fullerton, C. S., and Ursano, R. J. (2017). Bereaved military dependent spouses and children: Those left behind in a decade of war (2001–2011). *Military Medicine 182*, e1684–e1690.

Cozza, S. J., and Guimond, J. M. (2011). Working with combat-injured families through the recovery trajectory. In S. MacDermid Wadsworth and D. Riggs (Eds.), *Risk and Resilience in U.S. Military Families* (pp. 259–277). New York: Springer Science and Business Media.

Cozza, S. J., Harrington-Lamorie, J., and Fisher J. E. (2019). U.S. military service deaths: Bereavement in surviving families. In *American Military Life in the 21st Century: Social, Cultural, Economic Issues and Trends*. Santa Barbara: Praeger/ABC-CLIO.

Cozza, C. S. J., and Lerner, R. M. (2013). Military children and families: Introducing the issue. *The Future of Children*, *23*, 3–11.

Cozza, S. J., Ogle, C. M., Fisher, J. E., Zhou, J., Whaley, G. L., Fullerton, C. S., and Ursano, R. J. (2018a). Associations between family risk factors and child neglect types in U.S. Army communities. *Child Maltreatment*, *24*(1), 98–106.

Cozza, S. J., Whaley, G. L., Fisher, J. E., Zhou, J., Ortiz, C. D., McCarroll, J. E., Fullerton, C. S. and Ursano, R. J. (2018b). Deployment status and child neglect types in the U.S. Army. *Child Maltreatment 23*(1), 25–33.

Currier, J. M., Holland, J. M., and Neimeyer, R. A. (2007). The effectiveness of bereavement interventions with children: A meta-analytic review of controlled outcome research. *Journal of Clinical Child and Adolescent Psychology, 36*, 253–259.

Dausch, B. M., and Saliman, S. (2009). Use of family focused therapy in rehabilitation for veterans with traumatic brain injury. *Rehabilitation Psychology 54*, 279–287.

Defense Veterans Brain Injury Center. (2015). *DoD Worldwide Numbers for TBI*. Retrieved from http://dvbic.dcoe.mil/dod-worldwide-numbers-tbi.

DeVoe, E. R., Paris, R., Emmert-Aronson, B., Ross, A., and Acker, M. (2017). A randomized clinical trial of a postdeployment parenting intervention for service members and their families with very young children. *Psychological Trauma: Theory, Research, Practice and Policy*, *9*(Suppl 1), 25–34.

Elbogen, E. B., Johnson, S. C., Wagner, H. R., Sullivan, C., Taft, C. T., and Beckham, J. C. (2014). Violent behaviour and post-traumatic stress disorder in U.S. Iraq and Afghanistan veterans. *British Journal of Psychiatry 204*, 368–375.

Elder, G. H., Caspi, A., and Downey, G. (1986). Problem behavior and family relationships: Life course and intergenerational themes. *Human Development and the Life Course: Multidisciplinary Perspectives*, 293–340.

Feigelman, W., Gorman, B. S., and Jordan, J. R. (2009). Stigmatization and suicide bereavement. *Death Studies, 33*(7), 591–608.

Finkelstein, H. (1988). The long-term effects of early parent death: A review. *Journal of Clinical Psychology 44*, 3–9.

Flynn, B. W., McCarroll, J. E., and Biggs, Q. M. (2015). Stress and resilience in military mortuary workers: Care of the dead from battlefield to home. *Death Studies 39*, 92–98.

Forgatch, M. S., and Gewirtz, A. H. (2017). The evolution of the Oregon model of parent management training. In J. Weisz and A. Kazdin (Eds.), *Evidence-based Psychotherapies for Children and Adolescents Third Edition* (pp. 85–102). New York: The Guilford Press.

Fredman, S. J., Pukay-Martin, N. D., Macdonald, A., Wagner, A. C., Vorstenbosch, V., and Monson, C. M. (2016). Partner accommodation moderates treatment outcomes for couple therapy for posttraumatic stress disorder. *Journal of Consulting and Clinical Psychology 84* 79–87.

Fredman, S. J., Vorstenbosch, V., Wagner, A. C., Macdonald, A., and Monson, C. M. (2014). Partner accommodation in posttraumatic stress disorder: Initial testing of the Significant Others' Responses to Trauma Scale (SORTS). *Journal of Anxiety Disorders 28*, 372–381.

Fullerton, C. S., McCarroll, J. E., Feerick, M., McKibben, J., Cozza, S., Ursano, R. J., and Child Neglect Workgroup. (2011). Child neglect in army families: A public health perspective. *Military Medicine, 176*(12), 1432–1439.

Gabriel, B., Beach, S. R., and Bodenmann, G. (2010). Depression, marital satisfaction and communication in couples: Investigating gender differences. *Behavior Therapy 41*(3), 306–316.

Galovski, T., and Lyons, J. A. (2004). Psychological sequelae of combat violence: A review of the impact of PTSD on the veteran's family and possible interventions. *Aggression and Violent Behavior 9*, 477–501.

Gewirtz, A. H., Degarmo, D. S., and Zamir, O. (2016). Effects of a military parenting program on parental distress and suicidal ideation: After deployment adaptive parenting tools. *Suicide and Life-Threatening Behavior, 46* (Supp. 1), S23–S31.

________. (2018a). After deployment, adaptive parenting tools: 1-year outcomes of an evidence-based parenting program for military families following deployment. *Prevention Science 19*, 589–599.

________. (2018b). Testing a military family stress model. *Family Process 57*, 415–431.

Gewirtz, A. H., Polusny, M. A., DeGarmo, D. S., Khaylis, A., and Erbes, C. R. (2010). Posttraumatic stress symptoms among National Guard soldiers deployed to Iraq: Associations with parenting behaviors and couple adjustment. *Journal of Consulting and Clinical Psychology 78*, 599–610.

Gibbs, D. A., Martin, S. L., Kupper, L. L., and Johnson, R. E. (2007). Child maltreatment in enlisted soldiers' families during combat-related deployments. *Journal of the American Medical Association 298*(5), 528–535.

Gil-Rivas, V., Holman, E. A., and Silver, R. C. (2004). Adolescent vulnerability following the September 11th terrorist attacks: A study of parents and their children. *Applied Developmental Science 8*, 130–142.

Goldberg, M. S. (2007). *Projecting the Costs to Care for Veterans of U.S. Military Operations in Iraq and Afghanistan.* Washington DC: Congressional Budget Office. Retrieved from http://www.dtic.mil/docs/citations/ADA473294.

Harrington-Lamorie J., Cohen J., Cozza S. J. (2014). Caring for bereaved military family members. In S. J. Cozza, M. N. Goldenberg, and R. J. Ursano (Eds.), *Care of Military Service Members, Veterans and Their Families*. Washington, DC: American Psychiatric Press.

Hidalgo, R. B., and Davidson, J. R. (2000). Posttraumatic stress disorder: Epidemiology and health-related considerations. *Journal of Clinical Psychiatry, 61* (Supp. 7), 5–13.

Hoge, C. W., Auchterlonie, J. L., and Milliken, C. S. (2006). Mental health problems, use of mental health services, and attrition from military service after returning from deployment to Iraq or Afghanistan. *Journal of the American Medical Association 295*, 1023–1032.

Holmes, A. K., Rauch, P. K., and Cozza, S. J. (2013). When a parent is injured or killed in combat. *The Future of Children, 23*, 143–162.

Jakupcak, M., Conybeare, D., Phelps, L., Hunt, S., Holmes, H. A., Felker, B., . . . McFall, M. E. (2007). Anger, hostility, and aggression among Iraq and Afghanistan War veterans reporting PTSD and subthreshold PTSD. *Journal of Traumatic Stress, 20*, 945–954.

Jordan, B. K., Marmar, C. R., Fairbank, J. A., Schlenger, W. E., Kulka, R. A., Hough, R. L., and Weiss, D. S. (1992). Problems in families of male Vietnam veterans with post-traumatic stress disorder. *Journal of Consulting and Clinical Psychology, 60*, 916–926.

Julian, M. M., Muzik, M., Kees, M., Valenstein, M., and Rosenblum, K. L. (2018). Strong military families intervention enhances parenting reflectivity and representations in families with young children. *Infant Mental Health Journal, 39*, 106–118.

Kashdan, T. B., Goodman, F. R., Machell, K. A., Kleiman, E. M., Monfort, S. S., Ciarrochi, J., and Nezlek, J. B. (2014). A contextual approach to experiential avoidance and social anxiety: Evidence from an experimental interaction and daily interactions of people with social anxiety disorder. *Emotion, 14*(4), 769–781.

Kelley, S. D. M., Sikka, A., and Venkatesan, S. (1997). A review of research on parental disability: Implications for research and counseling practice. *Rehabilitation Counseling Bulletin, 41*(2), 105–121.

Kessler, R. C. (2000). Post-traumatic stress disorder: The burden to the individual and to society. *Journal of Clinical Psychiatry, 61* (Supp. 5), 4–12; discussion 13–14.

Kessler, R. C., Petukhova, M., Sampson, N. A., Zaslavsky, A. M., and Wittchen, H.-U. (2012). Twelve-month and lifetime prevalence and lifetime morbid risk of anxiety and mood disorders in the United States. *International Journal of Methods in Psychiatric Research, 21*, 169–184.

Knobloch, L. K., Ebata, A. T., McGlaughlin, P. C., and Ogolsky, B. (2013). Depressive symptoms, relational turbulence, and the reintegration difficulty of military couples following wartime deployment. *Health Communication, 28*, 754–766.

Knobloch, L. K., and Theiss, J. A. (2011). Relational uncertainty and relationship talk within courtship: A longitudinal actor–partner interdependence model. *Communication Monographs, 78*, 3–26.

Kreutzer, J. S., Stejskal, T. M., Godwin, E. E., Powell, V. D., and Arango-Lasprilla, J. C. (2010). A mixed methods evaluation of the Brain Injury Family Intervention. *NeuroRehabilitation, 27*, 19–29.

Kristensen, P., Weisæth, L., and Heir, T. (2012). Bereavement and mental health after sudden and violent losses: A review. *Psychiatry: Interpersonal and Biological Processes, 75*(1), 76–97.

Laor, N., Wolmer, L., and Cohen, D. J. (2001). Mothers' functioning and children's symptoms 5 years after a SCUD missile attack. *American Journal of Psychiatry, 158*, 1020–1026.

LeClere, F. B., and Kowalewski, B. M. (1994). Disability in the family: The effects on children's well-being. *Journal of Marriage and Family Counseling, 56*, 457–468.

Leroux, T. C., Kum, H. C., Dabney, A., and Wells, R. (2016). Military deployments and mental health utilization among spouses of active duty service members. *Military Medicine, 181*(10), 1269–1274.

Lester, P., Stein, J.A., Saltzman, W., Woodward, K., MacDermid, S.W., Milburn, N., Mogil, C. and Beardslee, W. (2013). Psychological health of military children: Longitudinal evaluation of a family-centered prevention program to enhance family resilience. *Military Medicine, 178*, 838–845.

Manguno-Mire, G., Sautter, F., Lyons, J., Myers, L., Perry, D., Sherman, M., Glynn, S. and Sullivan, G. (2007). Psychological distress and burden among female partners of combat veterans with PTSD. *Journal of Nervous and Mental Disease, 195*, 144–151.

Mansfield, A. J., Kaufman, J. S., Marshall, S. W., Gaynes, B. N., Morrissey, J. P., and Engel, C. C. (2010). Deployment and the use of mental health services among U.S. Army wives. *New England Journal of Medicine, 362*(2), 101–109.

McCarroll, J. E., Fan, Z., Newby, J. H., and Ursano, R. J. (2008). Trends in U.S. Army child maltreatment reports: 1990–2004. *Child Abuse Review—Journal of the British Association for the Study and Prevention of Child Abuse and Neglect, 17*(2), 108–118.

McCarroll, J. E., Thayer, L. E., Liu, X., Newby, J. H., Norwood, A. E., Fullerton, C. S., and Ursano, R. J. (2000). Spouse abuse recidivism in the U.S. Army by gender and military status. *Journal of Consulting and Clinical Psychology, 68*(3), 521.

McCarroll, J. E., Ursano, R. J., and Fullerton, C. S. (1993). Symptoms of posttraumatic stress disorder following recovery of war dead. *American Journal of Psychiatry, 150*, 1875–1877.

_______. (1995). Symptoms of PTSD following recovery of war dead: 13-15-month follow-up. *The American Journal of Psychiatry, 152*, 939–941.

McCarroll, J. E., Ursano, R. J., Newby, J. H., Liu, X., Fullerton, C. S., Norwood, A. E., and Osuch, E. A. (2003). Domestic violence and deployment in U.S. Army soldiers. *Journal of Nervous and Mental Disease, 191*(1), 3–9.

Monson, C. M., Taft, C. T., and Fredman, S. J. (2009). Military-related PTSD and intimate relationships: From description to theory-driven research and intervention development. *Clinical Psychology Review, 29*, 707–714.

Nelson, L. J., Padilla-Walker, L. M., Christensen, K. J., Evans, C. A., and Carroll, J. S. (2011). Parenting in emerging adulthood: an examination of parenting clusters and correlates. *Journal of Youth and Adolescence, 40*, 730–743.

Newby, J. H., Ursano, R. J., McCarroll, J. E., Liu, X., Fullerton, C. S., and Norwood, A. E. (2005). Postdeployment domestic violence by US Army soldiers. *Military Medicine, 170*(8), 643–647.

Noffsinger, M. A., Pfefferbaum, B., Pfefferbaum, R. L., Sherrib, K., and Norris, F. H. (2012). The burden of disaster: Part I. Challenges and opportunities within a child's social ecology. *International Journal of Emergency Mental Health, 14*, 3–13.

Olds, D. L., Eckenrode, J., Henderson, C. R., Kitzman, H., Powers, J., Cole, R., Sidora, K., Morris, P., Pettitt, L. M. and Luckey, D. (1997). Long-term effects of home visitation on maternal life course and child abuse and neglect. Fifteen-year follow-up of a randomized trial. *Journal of the American Medical Association, 278*, 637–643.

Owens, B. D., Kragh, J. F., Jr, Wenke, J. C., Macaitis, J., Wade, C. E., and Holcomb, J. B. (2008). Combat wounds in operation Iraqi Freedom and operation Enduring Freedom. *Journal of Trauma, 64*, 295–299.

Patterson, G. R. (1982). *Coercive Family Process*. Eugene, OR: Castalia.

_______. (2005). The next generation of PMTO models. *Behavior Therapist / AABT, 28*, 25–32.

Patterson, G. R., Forgatch, M. S., Yoerger, K. L., and Stoolmiller, M. (1998). Variables that initiate and maintain an early-onset trajectory for juvenile offending. *Development and Psychopathology, 10*, 531–547.

Pessar, L. F., Coad, M. L., Linn, R. T., and Willer, B. S. (1993). The effects of parental traumatic brain injury on the behaviour of parents and children. *Brain Injury, 7*, 231–240.

Petrik, N. D., Rosenberg, A. M., and Watson, C. G. (1983). Combat experience and youth: Influences on reported violence against women. *Professional Psychology, Research and Practice, 14*, 895–899.

Pfeffer, C. R., Karus, D., Siegel, K., and Jiang, H. (2000). Child survivors of parental death from cancer or suicide: Depressive and behavioral outcomes. *Psycho-Oncology: Journal of the Psychological, Social and Behavioral Dimensions of Cancer, 9*(1), 1–10.

Prinz, R. J. (2016). Parenting and family support within a broad child abuse prevention strategy: Child maltreatment prevention can benefit from public health strategies. *Child Abuse and Neglect, 51*, 400–406.

Ramchand, R.,Tanielian, T., Fisher, M. P., Vaughan, C. A., Trail, T. E., Epley, C., Voorhies, P., Robbins, M., Robinson, E., and Ghosh-Dastidar, B. (2014). *Hidden Heroes: America's Military Caregivers.* Santa, Monica, CA: RAND Corporation.

Rehman, U. S., Gollan, J., and Mortimer, A. R. (2008). The marital context of depression: Research, limitations, and new directions. *Clinical Psychology Review, 28*(2), 179–198.

Reinherz, H. Z., Giaconia, R. M., Hauf, A. M., Wasserman, M. S., and Paradis, A. D. (2000). General and specific childhood risk factors for depression and drug disorders by early adulthood. *Journal of the American Academy of Child and Adolescent Psychiatry, 39*, 223–231.

Rentz, E. D., Marshall, S. W., Loomis, D., Casteel, C., Martin, S. L., and Gibbs, D. A. (2007). Effect of deployment on the occurrence of child maltreatment in military and nonmilitary families. *American Journal of Epidemiology, 165*(10), 1199–1206.

Rosenheck, R., and Nathan, P. (1985). Secondary traumatization in children of Vietnam veterans. *Hospital and Community Psychiatry, 36*, 538–539.

Rudenstine, S., Cohen, G., Prescott, M., Sampson, L., Liberzon, I., Tamburrino, M., Calabrese, J., and Galea, S. (2015). Adverse childhood events and the risk for new-onset depression and post-traumatic stress disorder among U.S. National Guard soldiers. *Military Medicine, 180*(9), 972–978.

Saldinger, A., Porterfield, K., and Cain, A. C. (2004). Meeting the needs of parentally bereaved children: A framework for child–centered parenting. *Psychiatry: Interpersonal and Biological Processes, 67*, 331–352.

Saltzman, W. R., Lester, P., Beardslee, W. R., Layne, C. M., Woodward, K., and Nash, W. P. (2011). Mechanisms of risk and resilience in military families: Theoretical and empirical basis of a family-focused resilience enhancement program. *Clinical Child and Family Psychology Review, 14*, 213–230.

Sameroff, A. (2010). A unified theory of development: A dialectic integration of nature and nurture. *Child Development, 81*, 6–22.

Samper, R. E., Taft, C. T., King, D. W., and King, L. A. (2004). Post-traumatic stress disorder symptoms and parenting satisfaction among a national sample of male Vietnam veterans. *Journal of Traumatic Stress, 17*, 311–315.

Sandler, I. N., Ayers, T. S., Wolchik, S. A., Tein, J. Y., Kwok, O. M., Haine, R. A., Twohey-Jacobs, J., Suter, J., Lin, K., Padgett-Jones, S. and Weyer, J. L. (2003). The family bereavement program: Efficacy evaluation of a theory-based prevention program for parentally bereaved children and adolescents. *Journal of Consulting and Clinical Psychology, 71*, 587–600.

Sayers, S. L., Farrow, V. A., Ross, J., and Oslin, D. W. (2009). Family problems among recently returned military veterans referred for a mental health evaluation. *Journal of Clinical Psychiatry, 70*, 163–170.

Schoenbaum, M., Kessler, R. C., Gilman, S. E., Colpe, L. J., Heeringa, S. G., Stein, M. B., Ursano, R. J. and Cox, K. L. (2014). Predictors of suicide and accident death in the Army Study to Assess Risk and Resilience in Servicemembers (Army STARRS): Results from the Army Study to Assess Risk and Resilience in Servicemembers (Army STARRS). *Journal of the American Medical Association Psychiatry, 71*(5), 493–503.

Shen, Y. C., Arkes, J., and Williams, T. V. (2012). Effects of Iraq/Afghanistan deployments on major depression and substance use disorder: Analysis of active duty personnel in the U.S. military. *American Journal of Public Health, 102*(S1), S80–S87.

Siegel, B. S., Davis, B. E., and Committee on Psychosocial Aspects of Child and Family Health. (2013). Health and mental health needs of children in U.S. military families. *Pediatrics, 131*, 2002–2015.

Simons, L. G., Wickrama, K. A. S., Lee, T. K., Landers-Potts, M., Cutrona, C., and Conger, R. D. (2016). Testing family stress and family investment explanations for conduct problems among African American adolescents: Testing family stress and investment explanations. *Family Relations, 78*, 498–515.

Smith, R. C., Chun, R. S., Michael, R. L., and Schneider, B. J. (2013). Operation BRAVE Families: A preventive approach to lessening the impact of war on military families through preclinical engagement. *Military Medicine, 178*(2), 174–179.

Snyder, J. (2013-2015). *Preventing Military Post-Deployment Adjustment Problems: Key Family Processes*. National Institute on Drug Abuse.

Snyder, J., Gewirtz, A., Schrepferman, L., Gird, S. R., Quattlebaum, J., Pauldine, M. R., Elish, K., Zamir, O. and Hayes, C. (2016). Parent-child relationship quality and family transmission of parent post-traumatic stress disorder symptoms and child externalizing and internalizing symptoms following fathers' exposure to combat trauma. *Development and Psychopathology, 28*(4pt1), 947–969.

Sparrow, K., Kwan, J., Howard, L., Fear, N., and MacManus, D. (2017). Systematic review of mental health disorders and intimate partner violence victimisation among military populations. *Social Psychiatry and Psychiatric Epidemiology, 52*(9), 1059–1080.

Story, L. B., and Bradbury, T. N. (2004). Understanding marriage and stress: Essential questions and challenges. *Clinical Psychology Review, 23*, 1139–1162.

Suris, A., and Lind, L. (2008). Military sexual trauma: A review of prevalence and associated health consequences in veterans. *Trauma, Violence and Abuse, 9*, 250–269.

Taft, C. T., Kaloupek, D. G., Schumm, J. A., Marshall, A. D., Panuzio, J., King, D. W., and Keane, T. M. (2007). Post-traumatic stress disorder symptoms, physiological reactivity, alcohol problems, and aggression among military veterans. *Journal of Abnormal Psychology, 116*, 498–507.

Taft, C. T., Macdonald, A., Creech, S. K., Monson, C. M., and Murphy, C. M. (2016). A randomized controlled clinical trial of the Strength at Home Men's Program for Partner Violence in Military Veterans. *Journal of Clinical Psychiatry, 77*, 1168–1175.

Tanielian, T. L., and Jaycox, L. (2008). *Invisible Wounds of War: Psychological and Cognitive Injuries, Their Consequences, and Services to Assist Recovery*. Arlington, VA: RAND Corporation.

Urbach, J. R., and Culbert, J. P. (1991). Head-injured parents and their children. Psychosocial consequences of a traumatic syndrome. *Psychosomatics, 32*, 24–33.

U.S. Department of Defense (DoD). (2018). *Report on Child Abuse and Neglect and Domestic Abuse in the Military for Fiscal Year 2017*. Washington, DC: Author. Retrieved from http://download.militaryonesource.mil/12038/MOS/Reports/FAP-FY17-DoD-Report.pdf.

Verhaeghe, S., Defloor, T., and Grypdonck, M. (2005). Stress and coping among families of patients with traumatic brain injury: A review of the literature. *Journal of Clinical Nursing, 14*, 1004–1012.

Wadsworth, S. M., and Riggs, D. (Eds.). (2011). *Risk and Resilience in U.S. Military Families*. New York: Springer.

Walsh, F. (1996). The concept of family resilience: Crisis and challenge. *Family Process, 35*, 261–281.

_______. (2016). Strengthening family resilience: Overcoming serious life challenges. In P. C. Dias, A. Gonçalves, Â. Azevedo, and F. Lobo (Eds.), *Novos Desafios, Novas Competências: Contributos Atuais da Psicologia* (1st ed., pp. 11–22). Axioma - Publicações da Faculdade de Filosofia.

Wasserstein, S. B., and La Greca, A. M. (1998). Hurricane Andrew: Parent conflict as a moderator of children's adjustment. *Hispanic Journal of Behavioral Sciences, 20*, 212–224.

Weinstein, E. A., Andres, A., Salazar, M., and Franklin, D. J. (1995). Behavioral consequences of traumatic brain injury. In F. D. Jones, L. R. Sparacino, V. L. Wilcox, J. M. Rothberg, and J. W. Stokes (Eds.), *War Psychiatry,* (pp. 353–381). Washington, DC: Office of the Surgeon General.

Whisman, M. A. (2007). Marital distress and DSM-IV psychiatric disorders in a population-based national survey. *Journal of Abnormal Psychology, 116*(3), 638.

Zamir, O., Gewirtz, A. H., Labella, M., DeGarmo, D. S., and Snyder, J. (2018). Experiential avoidance, dyadic interaction and relationship quality in the lives of veterans and their partners. *Journal of Family Issues, 39*, 1191–1212.

7

The Military Family Readiness System: Present and Future

In this chapter,[1] the committee presents a framework for building a more coherent, comprehensive approach to supporting the well-being and readiness of military families. The framework draws on established models for evidence-informed assessment and interventions, such as the population health framework, and reviews of the literature on human development, psychology, prevention science, dissemination and implementation science, and social work. It also integrates emergent research on the well-being of military-connected families. The chapter provides a roadmap with actionable steps that could transform the current support infrastructure—the Military Family Readiness System (MFRS)—into a coherent, comprehensive, complex, and adaptive support system designed for military families. Chapter 8 will draw on this chapter heavily as it focuses in on the specific implementation supports needed to implement an effective system in terms of policies, programs, services, resources, and strategies.

THE STRUCTURE OF THE MILITARY'S SERVICE MEMBER AND FAMILY WELL-BEING SUPPORT SYSTEM

Military families play a critical role in the strength and readiness of our nation's military (U.S. Department of Defense [DoD], 2012). As noted in Chapter 2, the resilience, readiness, and ability of military families to thrive throughout both the expected and the unexpected challenges and

[1]This chapter draws partially on papers commissioned by the committee (Mohatt and Beehler, 2018; Thompson, 2018).

opportunities of military life impact individual service member's readiness and attentiveness to their mission. DoD implemented the MFRS to address this by establishing a comprehensive set of policies, programs, services, resources, and practices to support and promote family readiness and resilience. In short, the aim of the MFRS is to provide a support infrastructure that promotes family well-being and thereby fosters family readiness, which in turn enhances service members' readiness.

The MFRS offers a high level of support to address the demands of military service and the reliance on volunteers to serve. This level of support compares favorably to what is offered by large employers in the civilian sector. As described within this volume, the connection between "employee" and family member health is especially critical within DoD compared to other types of civilian employment, resulting in specialized emphasis on family programs. The DoD child care system is a prominent example: As stated in Chapter 4, 97 percent of DoD child development centers are nationally accredited, whereas overall only about 1 in 10 U.S. child care facilities meet this standard (DoD, 2017; Schulte and Durana, 2016, p. 6). Other notable features of the child care system include sliding subsidies, on-site trainers who work to maintain quality standards, and benefits and a career ladder for civilian federal employees. Another positive feature of existing MFRS policies, programs, services, resources, and practices is that they incorporate elements that target different needs at different life stages. In addition, an internal review and accreditation system promotes standardization and quality across military family programs.

The vast array of social supports available to service members and their families is organized and provided at various levels within the military—the DoD level, the service branch level, and in many cases the installation level. DoD-wide nonmedical counseling assistance and referrals are available to address areas of need that include the military life cycle (basic training, service, advancement, reenlistment, separation, transition/retirement), family and relationships, moving and housing, financial and legal aid, education and employment, and health and wellness. The Military OneSource website[2] serves as a clearinghouse for information on programs. It posts links to and contact information for providers and maintains a database that can be searched by the type of support provided, name of installation, or general location (in 46 states, the District of Columbia, Guam, and 20 foreign locations). Additionally, the branches have their own programs and centralized sources of information. Table 7-1 lists examples of service-specific information, resources, and referral centers available through Military OneSource.

Many installations offer their own services, which may or may not coordinate directly with their branch or DoD counterparts. These may be

[2]For more information see https://www.militaryonesource.mil.

TABLE 7-1 Examples of Service-Specific Information, Resource, and Referral Centers

Branch	Program[s]	Website[s]
Army	Army OneSource	http://www.myarmyonesource.com
	U.S. Army MWR	https://www.armymwr.com/programs-and-services/personal-assistance
Navy	Navy Fleet and Family Support Program (FFSP)	https://www.cnic.navy.mil/ffr/family_readiness/fleet_and_family_support_program.html
Marine Corps	Marine Corps Community Services (MCCS)	http://www.usmc-mccs.org/
	Marine & Family Programs	http://www.mccsmcrd.com/marine-family-programs/
Air Force	USAF Services	https://cs2.eis.af.mil/sites/10042 ***note:** unable to access; may require log-in*
	Airman and Family Readiness	https://www.afpc.af.mil/Benefits-and-Entitlements/Airman-and-Family-Readiness/
National Guard and Reserves	National Guard Family Program	https://www.jointservicessupport.org/FP/Default.aspx
	Army Reserve Family Programs	http://www.usar.army.mil/ArmyReserveResources/
	Navy Reserve Family Readiness	https://www.public.navy.mil/nrh/Pages/default.aspx [Wellness tab]
	Marine Corps Reserve Family Resources	https://www.marforres.marines.mil/Family-Resources/ https://www.marforres.marines.mil/General-Special-Staff/Marine-Corps-Community-Services/
	U.S. Air Force Reserve Airman & Family Readiness	http://www.afrc.af.mil/AboutUs/AirmanFamily.aspx

SOURCE: From Military OneSource, see https://www.militaryonesource.mil.

quite extensive and diverse, depending on the size of the garrison, the extent to which it is feasible for families to accompany service members to their posting, and the interests of garrison leadership. For example, Fort Bragg—the largest Army base in the world—maintains a website with links to 28 different community support facilities and 10 facilities and programs for child and youth services that are available to personnel and their families.[3] However, smaller and more isolated posts may offer only modest services geared toward recreation opportunities for service members. Finally, there are nonprofit organizations operating across branches, such as the National

[3]See https://bragg.armymwr.com/categories/community-support; https://bragg.armymwr.com/categories/cys-services.

Military Family Association[4] and the United Service Organization,[5] and other nonprofits focused on specific branches.[6] These nonprofits supplement all the military resources with their own sources of help and links to providers.[7] Thus, there are many sources of support and information about support.

What is unclear, though, is the extent to which service providers at the various levels of organization (i.e., DoD-wide, service branch level, installation level, and military-focused nonprofit) are aware of one another, and whether they can or do coordinate service provision. Moreover, as noted in prior Institute of Medicine reports (IOM, 2013; 2014) the vast majority of policies, programs, services, and resources they offer have not been evaluated for effectiveness. The committee did not identify any literature that directly addresses this question, although some studies do shed light on a more general, related issue: the extent to which DoD collects information on program implementation and effectiveness. Trail and colleagues (2017) note that evidence on the effectiveness of nonmedical counseling programs in the U.S. military is limited, "primarily due to the lack of coordinated monitoring and evaluation efforts" (p. 8). An earlier study focused on programs addressing psychological health and traumatic brain injury found that "no branch of service maintains a complete list of these programs, tracks the development of new programs, or has appropriate resources in place to direct service members and their families to the full array of programs that best meet their needs" (Weinick et al., 2011, p. 37). And results from a survey of 13 garrisons comprising more than 4,500 respondents suggest that coordination and communication problems are present at the installation level (Sims et al., 2018, p. 55):

> Respondents also mentioned that soldiers do not always know where to go for help with their problems. . . . Given the timing of resource seeking—namely, when a soldier or family member is experiencing a problem—this trial-and-error process may be occurring at the least opportune time. Respondents concurred that some of this bouncing around could be avoided if there were more coordination and communication among service providers, and unfortunately respondents described experiences in which resource providers were unable to direct them appropriately (e.g., "The

---

[4]See https://www.militaryfamily.org.

[5]See USO; https://www.uso.org.

[6]Army Emergency Relief [https://www.aerhq.org]; Navy-Marine Corps Relief Society [http://www.nmcrs.org]; Air Force Aid Society [https://www.afas.org].

[7]DoD funds the Penn State Clearinghouse for Military Family Readiness [http://www.militaryfamilies.psu.edu] to perform outreach, training and support of service providers, and research on the effective delivery of services. This Clearinghouse partners with DoD and the branches to help improve the quality of services and promote evidence-based decision making. While the center is oriented toward practitioners and research, its website includes information and links useful to military families, making it yet another source of support and information.

resource providers, if it is not about their program, they don't really know to tell you where to go").

Therefore, while direct evidence is lacking, available information suggests that the success of the MFRS may be hampered because programs, services, and resources are siloed, lacking mechanisms to comprehensively monitor and coordinate their contributions. The policies, programs, services, and resources that comprise the MFRS fall under the purview of the Under Secretary of Defense for Personnel and Readiness (USD P&R),[8] policies and programs are overseen by separate Assistant Secretaries of Defense, and policies are interpreted and implemented by each military branch. This division of labor and responsibilities affects the MFRS's ability to achieve a consistent, quality delivery across the system to address the needs of military families as they negotiate the military family life course. Historically, organizational limitations have also impeded full coordination between and among all of the agencies that are delivering services to individual service members and their families.

The continuing post-9/11 conflict has required the MFRS to progressively adapt in order to meet the emerging needs of military families within an ever-changing political and budgetary landscape. Parallel with the rapid evolution of military family readiness programs, services, and resources is an expansion of research on the impact of military life on families and children, as well as research on approaches developed to enhance family well-being in the context of military life stressors. As Chandra and London (2013) note, there is an increasing need to "understand military children and families—their strengths and vulnerabilities, their ability to show resilience, and the systems that support them" (p. 188), yet the lack of available data and the fragmentation of the current data infrastructure limit the advancement of a coordinated effort that could enhance supports for military families. Without a coordinated effort related to (1) the design of services and programs that include standards (i.e., SMART [specific, measurable, attainable, relevant, and time bound] goals and objectives [Ogbeiwi, 2017], a theory of change, and a logic model) and (2) data collection and analyses, the MFRS cannot ensure consistency in the current services, programs, and resources across population subgroups, service branches, and military status, nor can it respond with agility and efficiency to emergent threats to military family readiness.

The committee recognizes that Military Community and Family Policy (MC&FP) leadership is tasked with the challenge of integrating the complex support systems within DoD to address emerging needs of families and their members that develop in a rapidly evolving context, often with limited available evidence. As such, the MFRS is best conceptualized as a complex

[8]For more information, see https://prhome.defense.gov.

adaptive system, one that evolves to meet the changing needs of the population. Simply put, a complex adaptive system is a structure with many dynamic, interacting relationships among components that are greater than the sum of its parts (Ellis and Herbert, 2010; Holland, 1995; Spivey, 2018). While much remains to be accomplished to achieve a true complex adaptive support system for military family readiness, the infrastructure that has been put in place provides a sound foundation on which to build one.

Lipsitz (2012) asserts that the principles of complexity science need to be understood and applied to increase the success of a complex system, observing that nonlinear interactions in such a system can lead to an output that is greater than the sum of its parts. He writes:

> Failure to recognize this property is unfortunately one of the deficiencies of the health care system, which has established silos of care with relatively little attention to the patient transitions and communication channels between them. (p. 243)

In an analogous manner, the siloing of programs, services, resources, and practices seen in the MFRS may result in insufficient attention being paid to familial transitions and to communication channels among its many separate parts. Thus, the MFRS would benefit by better fostering shared responsibility for military families across the military branches and the various programs and services, improving inter-institutional communication, and increasing operational efficiency.

Another principle of a complex adaptive system is the establishment of feedback loops that continuously guide the system toward improvement. Feedback loops are required for emergent self-organizing behavior to be evidence-informed. We address this topic later in this chapter, describing how to strengthen a complex adaptive MFRS to be more capable of integrating and generating evidence to advance a high-quality support system for military families. Additional operational information is provided in Chapter 8.

A POPULATION-LEVEL SYSTEM PROMOTING WELL-BEING

A population-level framework for military family readiness (as defined in Chapter 2) includes a classification model for policies, programs, services, resources, and practices that promotes positive development and health, both physical and mental, and ultimately fosters well-being. Prevention includes strategies to reduce the prevalence or severity of negative development and health outcomes and foster well-being in the context of risk and adversity. Extending a version of Gordon's (1983) prevention model (i.e., universal, selective, and indicated), the committee's model (see Figure 7-1) for categorizing military family readiness policies, programs, services, and resources is consistent with three prior Institute of Medicine (IoM) reports,

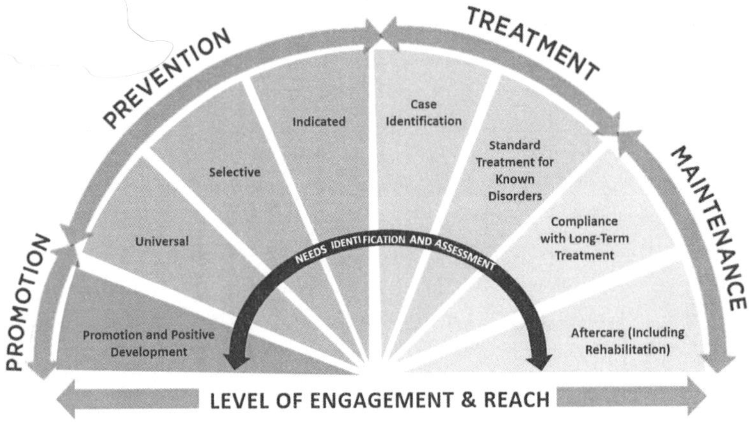

FIGURE 7-1 Continuum of coordinated support within the Military Family Readiness System.
SOURCE: Adapted from National Academies of Sciences, Engineering, and Medicine (2016, p. 180).

including a report on military and family resilience and prevention (IoM, 1994; 2014; National Research Council and Institute of Medicine, 2009). While the origin of Figure 7-1 was based on an approach to mental health (IoM, 1994), the figure has been re-envisioned as a model for a tiered continuum of support within a complex adaptive system such as the MFRS. Moreover, this adapted model has an explicit focus on promotional activities that foster competency, capacity, and skill building with individuals and families.

The concept of a tiered continuum can be seen in the graded range of policies, programs, services, resources, and practices that connects the promotion dimension of support with the prevention, treatment, and maintenance dimensions of support (Springer and Phillips, 2007). Thus, the continuum of coordinated support underlying the MFRS includes policies, programs, resources, and practices that may fall into one or more levels of this tiered continuum. The continuum underscores the importance of continuity and consistency in what is offered and tailoring to fit the unique needs of stakeholders and the contexts in which these services, programs, and resources rest.

The model highlights level of engagement and reach as critical components of a Continuum of Coordinated Support. Implementation research from the prevention science field has identified these as major road blocks to the successful scale-up of efforts (Baker, 2016; Biglan, 2015; Bumbarger and Perkins, 2008; Emshoff, 2008). The major consequence of poor participation rates and reach is that the likelihood of achieving outcomes is greatly diminished (Baker, 2016). Thus, to be effective MFRS will need to invest in multidimensional outreach efforts that include social media and partnerships with key trusted community stakeholders to actively promote engagement and increase reach.

Central to this approach is a continuous identification and assessment of needs (e.g., through screening) to support the early identification of risks within military families, especially risks to psychological health, the inclusion of selective[9] and indicated[10] preventive interventions, and treatment when warranted. The type of intervention needed is based on a staged hierarchy of interventions, known as stepped care, ranging from the least to the most intensive and matched to the individual's or family's needs. Thus, the continuum provides a guide for identifying family groups with different support needs and aligning those needs with applicable policies, programs, and practices (National Research Council and Institute of Medicine, 2009). This continuum has been specifically adapted for military personnel and families as an essential part of the proposed population level framework in the context of combat operational stress, although similar models have been variably applied across service branches (Nash et al., 2010). Table 7-2 provides definitions of the Continuum of Coordinated Support within the MFRS, with examples of programs in these domains. In order to ensure that MFRS is addressing the various slices of the Continuum of Coordinated Support, a comprehensive and systematic mapping and alignment process can be conducted that links all policies, programs, services, resources, and strategies in terms of their placement on that continuum. This effort would be conducted regularly as part of continuous quality improvement, which is discussed later in this chapter and in Chapter 8.

EVIDENCE-BASED AND EVIDENCE-INFORMED POLICIES, PROGRAMS, SERVICES, RESOURCES, AND PRACTICES

As a complex adaptive system, the MFRS and its components (policies, programs, services, resources, and practices) are dynamic and evolving, because the needs, opportunities, and challenges facing military families are continuously changing. As noted in the Continuum of Coordinated Support within the Military Family Readiness System, a comprehensive family readiness system includes strategies to promote well-being and health, reduce the prevalence or severity of negative outcomes through prevention and treatment programs, and promote positive outcomes over time. A strategy for monitoring risk and a stepped-care approach is required to link families with increased risk to appropriate programs, services, and resources.

---

[9]Selective prevention interventions are aimed at individuals or families at risk of compromised well-being (e.g., single-parent or divorced families; families experiencing multiple deployments of a parent).

[10]Indicated interventions target those already using or engaged in high-risk behaviors (e.g., substance abuse, maltreating parents).

TABLE 7-2 Definitions of the Continuum of Coordinated Support Domains and Program Examples

Promotion Domain		
Program Types	Potential Program Audience	Program Examples
Promotion and positive development services, programs, or resources	Targeted to the general military population or a specific military population (e.g., parents, spouses, children). These services, programs, and resources aim to foster children's, youth's, individuals', and families' competence and mastery, well-being, and ability to thrive in the face of adversity. In addition, these interventions are focused on increasing protective factors that have been linked to resilience.	Military and Family Support Centers; Youth Centers; Military OneSource; MWR; 4-H Program; Girls and Boys Clubs; Girl Scouts; Boy Scouts; parenting classes; child development centers; and after-school centers
Prevention Domain		
Program Types	Potential Program Audience	Program Examples
Universal prevention services, programs, or resources	Targeted to the general military population or a specific military population (e.g., single parents or children) where the intervention would be desirable to the whole group.	Military OneSource, MWR; Purple Crying Campaign; Military Family Life Counselors; Family Support Centers; Strong Bonds; FOCUS educational workshops and skills group training (Beardslee et al., 2011); After Deployment: Adaptive Parenting Tools Online program; youth centers; financial literacy programs
Selective prevention services, programs, or resources	Targeted to individuals or groups who are at increased risk for compromised functioning by virtue of exposure to a stressful context (e.g., deployment, family transitions).	New Parent Support Program; Exceptional Family Member Program; After Deployment: Adaptive Parenting Tools (Gewirtz et al., 2014); Families OverComing Under Stress (Beardslee, 2013; Lester et al., 2016); Operation Building Resilience and Valuing Empowered Families (Smith et al., 2013); Family Check-Up (Dishion et al., 2003; Fosco et al., 2013, 2016)
Indicated prevention services, programs, or resources	Targeted to individuals or groups who have clear signs or exhibiting precursor behaviors signifying a trajectory toward maladaptive behaviors or experiencing well-being issues (e.g., problematic functioning, excessive martial conflict, mental health challenges).	Strength at Home (Taft et al., 2016); Family Advocacy Program* prevention classes (anger management, relationships)

continued

TABLE 7-2 Continued

Treatment Domain		
Program Types	Potential Program Audience	Program Examples
Case management services, programs, or resources	Targeted to individuals or groups who have exhibited maladaptive behaviors (e.g., anti-social behaviors, addictive behaviors, domestic violence) or are currently experiencing well-being issues (e.g., financial stability, reintegration role problems, parenting, anxiety, depression, suicide ideation). Case management efforts are about connecting individuals to the services and resources needed. Thus, case management is a set of social service functions (e.g., assessment, planning, linkage, monitoring, and advocacy) that helps clients access the services, programs, and resources they need to recover and overcome the issue and challenges (Center for Substance Abuse Treatment, 2000).	Family Advocacy Program Case Manager; Domestic Abuse Victim Advocate
Standard treatment services, programs, or resources	Targeted to individuals or groups who have exhibited maladaptive behaviors (e.g., anti-social behaviors, additive behaviors, domestic violence), or are currently experiencing mental health issues (e.g., anxiety, depression, suicide ideation). These services and programs may involve therapy and counseling, and they are aimed at facilitating intra- and inter-personal change (Center for Substance Abuse Treatment, 2000).	Cognitive Processing Therapy (Resick et al., 2017); Prolonged Exposure Therapy (Foa et al., 2018); Adaptive Disclosure (Litz et al., 2017); Couple-based Cognitive Behavioral Therapy (CBCT)(Monson et al., 2012)
Maintenance Domain		
Program Types	Potential Program Audience	Program Examples
Compliance with long-term treatment and after-care	Targeted to individuals or groups who have successfully completed treatment to overcome a maladaptive behavior or mental health issue. The aim of these services, programs, and resources is to prevent recidivism, relapse, or reoccurrence of the behavior or issue.	Ecological Momentary Interventions (Schulte and Hser, 2015) and Mindfulness boosters (Witkiewitz et al., 2013). Annual check-ups as seen in Drinkers Check-Up, Marriage Check-Up, and Family Check-Up

SOURCE: Adapted from National Research Council and Institute of Medicine (2009).
*See https://www.militaryonesource.mil/family-relationships/family-life/preventing-abuse-neglect/the-family-advocacy-program.

Throughout this report, the committee emphasizes that MFRS programs, services, resources, and practices need to be grounded in the best available evidence. In an ideal world, there would be strong evidence of both the internal and the external validity of those components' effectiveness in supporting military family readiness, resilience, and well-being, including their effectiveness at producing the desired effects reliably and in real-world conditions. However, as noted in Chapter 1, while randomized controlled trials (RCTs) can provide strong evidence that interventions produce the desired effect for a specific context and population, there are limitations to the usefulness and appropriateness of RCTs in several contexts, depending upon the "exact question at stake, the background assumptions that can be acceptably employed, and what the costs are of different kinds of mistakes" (Deaton and Cartwright, 2018).

For this report, the committee examined publicly available evidence with a focus on building on previous knowledge, including decades of prior research on prevention science and child development, and the committee incorporated available theoretical models, observational studies, as well as experimental and quasi-experimental designs conducted with military families that allow for causal inference (Centre for Effective Services, 2011; Glasgow and Chambers, 2012; Gottfredson et al., 2015; Graczyk et al., 2003; Howse et al., 2013; Kvernbekk, 2017; Schwandt, 2014). Programs, services, resources, and practices within the MFRS need to be grounded in sound conceptual and empirical foundations and require rigorous design, implementation, and evaluation. With regard to evaluation, the system has a responsibility to conduct rigorous evaluations and ongoing monitoring for all efforts, inclusive of evidence-informed and evidence-based programming (Chambers and Norton, 2016; Glasgow et al., 2012).

Evidence-Based and Evidence-Informed

Individual *evidence-based* practices (EBPs) are typically standardized through manuals that support fidelity and enable replication. Such a manual or curriculum will provide a detailed roadmap of the program or service and its session goals, describe the approach and activities to meet those goals, and provide guidelines to deal with intervention challenges (Kendall et al., 1998). EBPs have been found to work for a wide variety of problems and issues, for demographically diverse individuals and families, for varied treatment settings, and for different intervention approaches. Nevertheless, for any given issue, setting, or population, an established specific EBP might not yet be available (see Chapter 8). EBPs are generally tested with a specific population and often in a different context from the one in which it had originally been developed, so there is often a need to engage in a systematic and culturally responsive adaptation process (detailed in

Chapter 8). In addition, implementation of EBPs or evidence-informed practices should be supported by continuous quality improvement using ongoing data collection and monitoring, which are required as part of a complex adaptive system.

The designation of *evidence-informed*, as defined in Chapter 1, describes a program, service, resource, strategy, component, practice, and/or process that (1) is developed or drawn from an integration of scientific theory, practitioner experience and expertise, and stakeholder input, using the *best available external evidence* from systematic research and a body of empirical literature; and (2) demonstrates impact on outcomes of interest through the application of scientific research (although that research achieves a lower standard of proof as it does not allow for causal inference) (Centre for Effective Services, 2011; Glasgow and Chambers, 2012; Howse et al., 2013; Kvernbekk, 2017; Schwandt, 2014). Although RCT and quasi-experimental designs are the bedrock of rigorous evaluations, mixed methods with data source triangulation, as well as public health, epidemiological, and mixed-method case-nested case studies are also useful for addressing specific questions related to program implementation.

These definitions do not set a hierarchy of standard. Rather, the use of both evidence-based and evidence-informed policies, programs, services, resources, and practices is necessary for a complex adaptive support system to achieve success. Given the fast-paced and ever-changing context of the military, the system is not in a position to conduct rigorous studies before it acts; therefore, application or implementation requires the use of promising policies, programs, services, resources, and practices grounded in the best available evidence. Thus, while adaptations or newly defined evidence-informed programs, services, resources, and practices may lack the level of scientific evidence of internal validity as EBPs have, they may nevertheless have the potential to be effective. Thus, within a complex adaptive MFRS, evidence-informed and new programs, services, and resources can be implemented using an embedded quality-monitoring process. Such a process would enable the system to test, measure, and evaluate emerging, culturally relevant, innovative practices that can then be evaluated for effectiveness in a scientifically rigorous manner, as described in Chapter 8.

To help reduce some of the barriers to the selection and utilization of EBPs, several web-based repositories of evidence-based programs have been developed, such as the School Success Best Practices Database[11] and Blueprints for Healthy Youth Development.[12] Moreover, the DoD Office of Military Community and Family Policy, in collaboration with the National Institute for Food and Agriculture, has funded the development of the

[11]See https://web.archive.org/web/20180307165748/http:/www.schoolsuccessonline.com.
[12]See https://www.blueprintsprograms.org.

Clearinghouse for Military Family Readiness[13] (hereafter, the Clearinghouse). The Clearinghouse is designed to provide professionals with tools to respond to the needs of military-dependent children, youth, and families. In addition to offering live technical assistance and support to providers concerning utilizing evidence in selecting and implementing programs, the Clearinghouse has developed a repository of information on more than 1,200 programs, and that number is growing. The programs on the Clearinghouse website cover a wide range of health and well-being issues relevant to both military and civilian families. These include, but are not limited to, parenting practices, family communication, coping and resilience, child and youth behavior, obesity intervention, prevention of alcohol and substance use, and treatment of mental health issues such as posttraumatic stress disorder (PTSD) and depression. As with other web-based repositories, the Clearinghouse reviews and places programs along a continuum of evidence derived from established criteria. Placements are rigorous, based on peer-reviewed research, and adhere to a systematized process and clearly articulated criteria. The Clearinghouse is unique in reviewing programs that are designed for and tested with service members and their families. It also reviews programs developed in nonmilitary contexts that may be relevant for military family populations. To ensure relevance and based on current research, the Clearinghouse reassesses programs on the Continuum of Evidence every 5 years.

The Clearinghouse's Continuum of Evidence was developed to provide a well-defined and useable resource to identify relevant evidence-based programs (Karre et al., 2017; Perkins et al., 2015). To be placed in this continuum, studies of programs are reviewed in accordance with specific criteria. Certain requirements determine whether each program qualifies as *Effective, Promising, Unclear,* or *Ineffective* for each individual criterion. Using the Continuum of Evidence, existing programs are reviewed and, based on the empirical evidence, each is placed into one of these categories: *Effective (RCT and Quasi); Promising; Unclear (+) with Potentially Promising Features; Unclear (Ø) With No Evaluations or Mixed Results; Unclear (–) with Potentially Ineffective Features;* or *Ineffective*. Box 7-1 describes the major criteria for these program placements on the Continuum of Evidence. As is the case with most EBP registries, the criteria emphasize research designs that demonstrate internal validity but not external validity. Many EPBs are tested in specific contexts, and thus the relevance or applicability of an individual program within diverse, rapidly evolving, and complex community contexts and delivery systems (external validity) may be challenging to establish. Given the importance of adaptability to military family readiness, these issues are addressed briefly below and in detail in Chapter 8.

[13]For more information, see https://militaryfamilies.psu.edu.

BOX 7-1
Clearinghouse for Military Family Readiness: Major Criteria for Program Placements on the Continuum of Evidence

1. ***Significant effects.*** For a program to qualify as having *Effective* or *Promising for Significant Effects*, it must demonstrate rigorous, statistically significant evidence (e.g., $p < 0.05$ in a two-tailed test). Proper statistical adjustments are made when multiple tests are conducted of a change in a highly desired outcome with no iatrogenic effects (i.e., a negative consequence of the program). To qualify as *Unclear*, the program must show mixed effects or no evidence due to a lack of peer-reviewed evaluations. To qualify as *Ineffective*, a program evaluation must fail to demonstrate a significant effect or must have an iatrogenic effect.
2. ***Sustained effects.*** For a program to qualify as *Effective,* the evaluation must demonstrate effects lasting at least two years from the beginning of the program or one year from the end. To qualify as *Promising*, the evaluation must demonstrate effects lasting at least one year from the beginning of the program or six months from the end. To qualify as *Unclear*, the maintenance of effects must not have been assessed. To qualify as *Ineffective*, a program's initial effects must diminish to nonsignificant over a specified period of time.
3. ***Successful external replication.*** For a program to qualify as *Effective for External Replication*, there must be at least two independent evaluations (at least one of which has been undertaken by a team with no connection to the program developer) that demonstrate positive results on the same outcome; both evaluations must qualify the program as *Effective* on each of the other Continuum criteria. To qualify as *Promising* or *Unclear*, a replication is not necessary. To qualify as *Ineffective*, there must be no evidence of a successful external replication.
4. ***Study design.*** For a program to qualify as *Effective* or *Ineffective*, the evaluation must be a randomized controlled trial (RCT) or a well-matched quasi-experimental design (i.e., the intervention group and the control group must be matched on demographic and pretest variables). To qualify as *Promising*, the evaluation must be at least a quasi-experimental design. To qualify as *Unclear*, the evaluation can lack a comparison group. Note that use of an RCT does not guarantee consideration of *Effective* for Study Design. If an RCT is poorly implemented, for example, or is analyzed in a manner that makes it effectively a study with no comparison group, it would not be considered *Effective* for Study Design.
5. ***Additional criteria regarding study execution.*** Currently, for a program to qualify as *Effective* or *Ineffective*, the evaluation must meet all four additional criteria. Thus, the program evaluation must have a representative sample (i.e., accurately represent the population that the program purportedly targets); modest attrition (i.e., have an acceptable level of attrition, or analyses of differential attrition are conducted); use adequate outcome measures (i.e., use reliable and valid measures); and discuss practical significance (i.e., account for the magnitude of effects). To qualify as *Promising*, a study must meet two or three additional criteria. If a study meets zero or one additional criterion, it qualifies for *Unclear*.

SOURCE: Karre et al. (2017).

Examples of Evidence-Based Programs

In this section, to highlight the use of various evidence-based and evidence-informed programs within MFRS, we present seven examples of programs for which evaluations have indicated efficacy or effectiveness. First, we summarize three research-based caregiving/parenting interventions noted in Chapter 5. Then we review an intervention relevant to the MFRS Family Advocacy Program, followed by two couple programs and one bullying prevention program. Finally, we review an example of a population-level approach, one that was tested within active-duty Air Force installations.

Strong Families Strong Forces (Strong Families) is a reflective parenting program designed to support military parents and their young children throughout the deployment cycle. In one RCT, the efficacy of Strong Families was confirmed with families of National Guard and Reserves service-member parents, who reported significantly reduced parenting stress and enhanced reflective capacity in relation to their young children (DeVoe et al., 2017). Moreover, service-member parents who endorsed higher levels of trauma symptoms also reported increased parental self-efficacy relative to waitlist control participants. Among at-home spouses, Strong Families had a positive impact on self-reported relationship satisfaction with the service member partner (Kritikos et al., 2019).[14]

Families OverComing Under Stress (FOCUS) is a family-centered preventive intervention designed to enhance resilience, which was initially adapted for military families with school-age and adolescent children from two established evidence-based preventive interventions. These interventions employed core components using a community-participatory framework and implemented at scale using a tiered public health approach (Beardslee, 2013; Beardslee et al., 2011; Lester et al., 2016; Saltzman et al., 2011, 2016). The FOCUS model has been used for early childhood (FOCUS-EC), specifically for families with a child between the ages of three and five (Mogil et al., 2010). An RCT of FOCUS-EC, delivered as an in-home tele-health preventive intervention, had several positive significant findings. Parents who participated in FOCUS-EC experienced greater reductions in PTSD symptoms compared to parents using a web-based curriculum. Primary caregivers reported significantly greater improvements in parent-child relationship quality and significant reductions in total parenting stress relative to the control group. Moreover, observed parenting and parent-child interactions were also significantly improved in the FOCUS-EC intervention group at 12 months (Lester et al., 2018).

---

[14]Note that as of this writing, a second RCT is near completion, involving a sample of active-duty Army families with very young children.

After Deployment, Adaptive Parenting Tools/ADAPT is a parenting program, based on the Parent Management Training-Oregon Model (Forgatch and Gewirtz, 2017), aimed at strengthening resilience in children ages 4 to 13 living in families in which a parent has been deployed to one of the recent conflicts. Four RCTs of ADAPT are complete or underway. Results to date from intent-to-treat analyses of a large-scale RCT with 336 military families demonstrate the program's effectiveness in strengthening children's emotional, behavioral, and social/peer functioning, and reducing youth substance use, based on parent, teacher, and child reports, from 12 to 24 months post-baseline (6 to 18 months after the end of program delivery), with these improvements mediated through strengthened observed parenting practices and improved parenting self-efficacy (Gewirtz et al., 2018; Piehler et al., 2016; Gewirtz and DeGarmo, in press). Additional findings demonstrate the program's salutary effects on parental well-being (i.e., reductions in parental depression, PTSD symptoms, and suicidality) (Gewirtz et al., 2016, 2018).

Couples Therapy for Domestic Violence: Finding Safe Solutions is a curriculum designed to provide assessment of and treatment for couples who choose to stay in a relationship after one or both individuals have been violent. Results from one RCT showed that at six months after program completion, couples in a multicouple group showed significantly lower rates of male violence recidivism, marital aggression, and acceptance of wife battering and higher rates of marital satisfaction than those in an individual couple group or a comparison group. Two years after program completion, females reported that males who participated in either the multi-couple or individual couple therapy had lower rates of recidivism than men in the comparison group (Stith et al., 2004).

Prevention & Relationship Enhancement Program (PREP) for Strong Bonds is a community-based program designed to help couples in the military strengthen their relationships and prevent or minimize marital concerns, including those that might be unique to military families. At site 1, where couples were at higher risk for relationship problems (e.g., younger, married for a shorter time, had a lower income, and had husbands with lower military rank and higher rates of deployment), there were significant positive effects in the treatment group on communication skills, confidence, bonding, and satisfaction. However, no differences were found between the treatment and control groups concerning forgiveness, dedication, or negative communication. At site 2, among lower-risk couples, there was a significant effect only on communication skills. Separate analyses found that divorce rates in the treatment group at site 1 were lower than in the control group up to two years post-intervention, and this effect was strongest for minority couples. There was no difference in divorce rates between treatment and control groups at site 2. There was no effect on overall relationship quality, communication skills, or positive bonding at either site. In addition, data from both sites combined showed an intervention effect on mitigating the risk of divorce linked to cohabitation before making a marital commitment (Allen et al., 2011; Rhoades et al., 2015; Stanley et al., 2010, 2014).

Green Dot—a violence prevention and intervention program—is designed to change social norms related to violence, increase proactive bystander behaviors, reduce acts of personal violence, and promote safe communities. Multiple evaluations by the program developers have been conducted of the high school and college versions of the Green Dot Program. Survey data from first-year students in a multiyear quasi-experimental evaluation of Green Dot on one college campus indicate that the intervention campus experienced lower rates of self-reported unwanted sexual victimization, sexual harassment, stalking, and psychological dating violence victimization and perpetration relative to two comparison campuses. However, there were no differences between intervention and comparison campuses in self-reported rates of coerced sex, physically forced sex, physical dating violence, or unwanted sexual perpetration. Results from a multiyear-cluster RCT of Green Dot in 26 high schools indicate that intervention schools experienced lower rates of self-reported sexual violence perpetration and victimization and reductions in dating violence acceptance and sexual violence acceptance relative to comparison high schools. However, these results differed by gender and were generally strongest in year 3 of program implementation, with some fading of effects in year 4 (Coker et al., 2011, 2015, 2016, 2017, 2018).

The New Orientation to Reduce Threats to Health from Secretive Problems That Affect Readiness (NORTH STAR) Program is a population-level approach to enhance the ability of base, major command, and Air Staff Integrated Delivery Systems to reduce death, injury, and degraded force readiness by (1) disseminating the prevalences of secretive problems at three levels—local (Air Force base), Major Command, and Air Force–wide; (2) providing base-level information to identify and prioritize risk and protective factors; (3) assisting bases in selecting and implementing evidence-informed and evidence-based interventions; and (4) evaluating whether prevalences were lowered (Slep and Heyman, 2008). Researchers conducted a randomized, controlled prevention trial to test the effectiveness of the NORTH STAR framework in reducing targeted risk factors; increasing targeted protective factors; and reducing base prevalences of family maltreatment, suicidality, and problematic alcohol and drug use. Twelve matched pairs of Air Force bases were randomly assigned to either (a) the NORTH STAR implementation condition or (b) the control condition (receiving comparable prevalence and risk/protective factor information but not NORTH STAR) (Heyman et al., 2011).

These programs have demonstrable albeit varied levels of effectiveness, and their use with military families provides a clear indication of their feasibility within MFRS. Nevertheless, an ongoing protocol and process for accountability is needed to ensure continuous quality improvement.

ACCOUNTABILITY AND MEASUREMENT

Accountability represents a complex adaptive system's responsibility for measuring its actions (i.e., its policies, programs, services, resources, and practices) (Patton and Blandin Foundation, 2014). Although programs, services, or resources may be effective in one context that does not necessarily mean they will work universally in all contexts. Thus, in order to be accountable, MFRS needs to assess the transportability, effectiveness, and efficiency of policies, services, programs, resources, and practices within and across the military (Damschroder et al., 2009). A critical element of accountability is demonstrating the need to adapt or tailor as well as assessing whether the benefit of tailoring would warrant the additional investment. The adaptation process is discussed below and in detail in Chapter 8.

Accurate measurement is a vital part of accountability for any complex adaptive system, like the MFRS, so that it can continuously learn and improve in its efforts to increase well-being and resilience. Measurement implies both the use of evidence-based assessment and the tracking of data outcomes essential for delivering and monitoring the effectiveness of programs, services, resources, and practices (IOM, 2013). A useful measurement frame for assessing the quality of military family readiness services is Donabedian's (2005) classic paradigm for assessing quality of care, which is based on a three-component approach focusing on structure, process, and outcome (see Figure 7-2). Donabedian's paradigm proposes that each component has a direct influence on the next, as represented by the arrows in the figure.

Structure refers to the attributes of the settings in which providers deliver programs and services, including material resources, such as service-delivery records, human resources, such as staff expertise and training, and organizational structure, for example whether the setting is a child development center, school, or community setting. The premise is that the

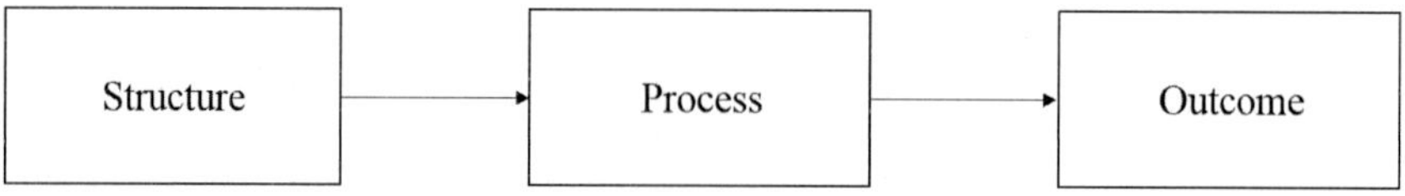

FIGURE 7-2 Donabedian paradigm.
SOURCE: IOM (2014, p. 26).

structure can be a strong determinant of service quality and that given the proper structure, good care will follow. For example, one would expect care to be of higher quality when providers and staff are trained in utilizing evidence-based programs or evidence-informed strategies and their competencies are assessed in an ongoing manner.

Process refers to the services that are delivered and received. This can include anything that is done as part of the encounter between an individual or family and the delivery system, including interpersonal processes such as providing information or resources, skill-building activities, and (or) employing evidence-informed care strategies, as well as involving individuals in decisions in a way that is consistent with their cultural backgrounds and lived experiences. Traditional process measures assess the quality of support and service that an individual or family received and the fidelity with which it was delivered (IOM, 2014).

Finally, *Outcome* refers to how an individual's or family's outcomes are affected by engagement with a program, service, or resource. There are both proximal outcomes (short-term consequences) and distal outcomes (long-term consequences). An example would be improved parenting, a proximal outcome that could eventually translate into a child's improved social-emotional functioning, a distal outcome (IOM, 2014)

Figure 7-3 is a model adapted from the IOM (2014) report to organize concepts related to the Continuum of Coordinated Support of MFRS and the measurement constructs presented in the above paragraphs, including evidence-informed and evidence-based programs, services, resources, and practices, the types of those efforts, the socio-ecological model, and performance measures. The model is not intended to capture all of the complex pathways that characterize program development and measurement but to serve as a general guide for thinking about the complex process of identifying the best metrics for assessing military family readiness services. (IOM, 2014).

Translating evidence into an effective program also requires attending to the myriad implementation processes that ensure high quality and relevance, including a balance among the fidelity, adaptation, tailoring, and cost-effectiveness of the program, service, resource, or practice. Community-engaged and participatory strategies are a key part of the implementation process (which will be addressed in detail in Chapter 8). As illustrated in Figure 7-3 by the dotted line leading to "Types of Measures," program performance can be assessed using structure, process, outcome, and cost measures (IOM, 2014). Selected measures or instruments should meet methodological standards to ensure valid and reliable measurement. In particular, attention to measurement of child well-being is central to developing an effective military family readiness system. The committee recognizes that there is no single measure of child well-being, but rather multiple subjective,

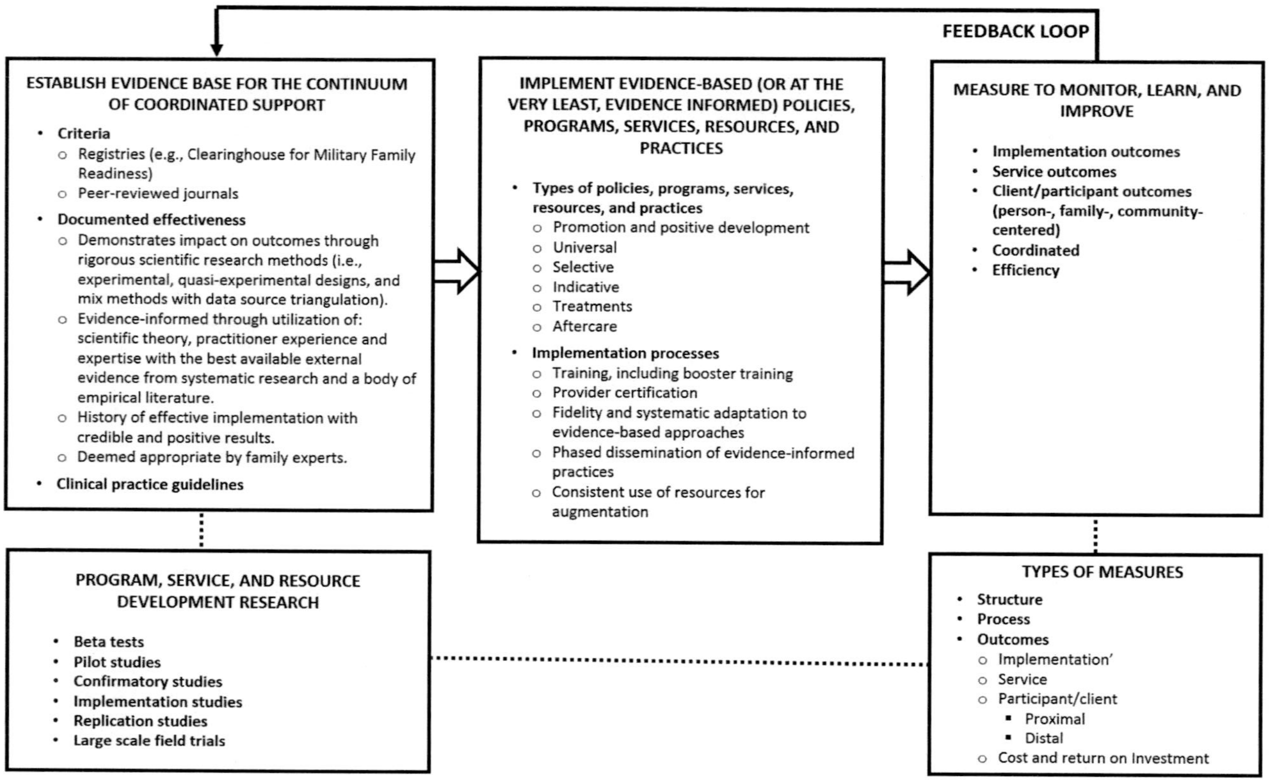

FIGURE 7-3 Model for development and measurement of coordinated support policies, programs, services, resources, and practices.
SOURCE: Adapted from IOM (2014, p. 29).

objective, and functional domains that are central to the mapping and monitoring of well-being over the trajectory of development. While a detailed review of measures of adult or child well-being and resilience is beyond the scope of this report, the committee relies on the Institute of Medicine's *Preventing Psychological Disorders in Service Members and Their Families: An Assessment of Programs* (IOM, 2014), where this is discussed in Chapter 5. The feedback loop in Figure 7-3 represents the cycle of using measurement results to continuously inform the empirical evidence and to improve program implementation and system level accountability (IOM, 2014).

Attaining a high-quality, complex adaptive MFRS depends upon the development of an integrated data infrastructure that supports population-level monitoring and mapping of family well-being, as well as effective program implementation and quality monitoring (see Figure 7-4). Ongoing evaluation of a system's policies, services, programs, and resources is essential to an embedded measurement approach to accountability and continuous quality improvement. The evaluation designs, employed to assess the effectiveness of the policy, service, program, resource, or practice in achieving outcomes, need to balance rigor and practicality with respect to both internal and external (e.g., ecological) validity (Glasgow et al., 2012).

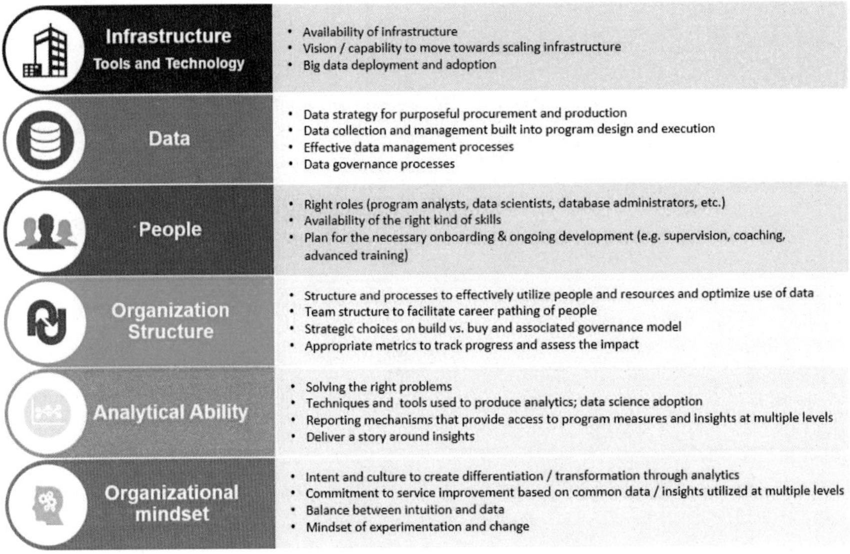

FIGURE 7-4 Integrated information infrastructure to support a complex adaptive system, such as MFRS.
SOURCE: Adapted with permission from ZS Associates, Inc., 2019.

As already noted, the measuring and ongoing tracking of outcomes at various levels is essential in order to rigorously evaluate the effectiveness and comprehensively assess the impact of a dynamic complex adaptive system. There are three major types of outcomes to be evaluated within a human service system like MFRS: implementation, service, and client/participant outcomes (see Figure 7-5) (Proctor et al., 2011). Often, the evidence-based terminology is linked to whether a program, service, resource, or practice achieves success in improving or reducing client or participant outcomes. However, simply capturing client or participant outcomes does not provide information on what part or parts of the program, service, resource, or practice worked and for whom. Thus, for more than a decade, translational research has demonstrated the importance of assessing implementation outcomes for the goal of quality scale-up (Estabrooks et al., 2018).

Central to this approach is the development of feedback processes that support the implementation and adaptation of multiple and tiered EBP and EIP interventions to support military family needs. Such data analytics infrastructure and processes are foundational to fostering learning and adaptation across the MFRS. They would support a complex adaptive system with the data and information capabilities needed to develop greater insight into monitoring and addressing system-level interactions between programs and policies and the ways that may lead to improved outcomes and, ultimately, to increased readiness across the MFRS.

As seen in Figure 7-5, implementation outcomes precede both service and client outcomes. The service outcomes noted here are drawn from the Institute of Medicine report titled, *Crossing the Quality Chasm* (IOM, 2001).

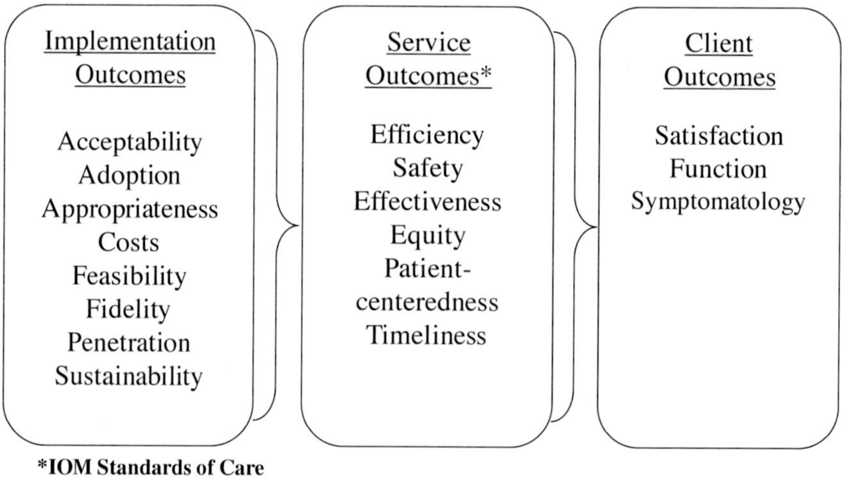

FIGURE 7-5 Types of outcomes in implementation research.
SOURCE: Proctor et al. (2011, p. 66).

Monitoring

For a system to be accountable and foster continuous quality improvements, an active monitoring protocol needs to be operationalized and implemented. Monitoring serves as the checklist for assessing implementation (Langley et al., 2009). That is, regular monitoring is required for a system to proactively identify those aspects of an implementation that need to be adapted to the new context to optimize effectiveness and lessen the potential for failure (Schwartz et al., 2015).

Monitoring should be part of a broader data-driven accountability strategy, one that involves collecting data, identifying patterns and facts from those data, and employing those facts to make inferences that influence both implementation (Knight et al., 2016) and decision making (Shen and Cooley, 2008). The broader data-driven accountability includes data drawn from monitoring, evaluation, and administrative information (e.g., budgets and staffing). Details about what should be monitored and how is discussed in Chapter 8.

The premise of ongoing monitoring is not to find fault or blame, but to promote a *culture of learning* in the system through data-driven feedback loops that support continuous quality improvement. The military's universal use of After Action Reports represents one part of a monitoring protocol. Because monitoring from quantitative measurements alone often fails to capture the cultural and contextual adaptations that would be needed to enhance implementation with diverse families, community engagement and participatory processes are useful, as they can address these gaps in data-driven feedback loops.

COMMUNITY ENGAGEMENT AND PARTICIPATORY PARTNERSHIPS

Community engagement involves identifying and collaborating with key stakeholders, including military family members, service members and veterans, all layers of military leadership across the services, and community leaders and providers. It is a multilevel continuum that begins prior to or early in program development and continues through all phases of program implementation. As described in Chapter 4, DoD does not have good visibility regarding the variety of military families, so by utilizing engagement and participatory strategies it could develop a better understanding and better identify needs among diverse family constellations.

Community engagement can also help in developing a more accurate and nuanced picture of the specific circumstances, concerns, and cultures of families within the varied local contexts, inadequate knowledge of which may be hampering access to evidence-based programming. By understanding local needs and resources, programs can develop strategies to remove barriers for families and increase program use (True et al., 2015). Furthermore, by collaborating with communities to assess barriers and opportunities, service providers can build local capacity to sustain effective outreach and engagement efforts (Huebner et al., 2009). An important challenge for the military is how to maintain the vertical command structure that is necessary for mission readiness while also empowering "horizontal" initiatives to promote local leadership, community stakeholders, and military families themselves to define their needs and influence program development, adaptation, and implementation.

A primary function of community engagement is to enhance access to and participation in programs that are known to be effective in supporting military family well-being. Improving access to care in this way may be part of the answer to the challenge of improving military family well-being. Engagement approaches are especially needed in communities where National Guard and Reserve families live and in more rural areas of the country, as well as for those who cannot access installation-centered care. The DoD service system also would benefit from the sharing of resources, successful programming, and data across the service branches to better support military families.

As is the case for civilian program efforts, a critical challenge in delivering services for military families and service members is low rates of service utilization and retention (DeVoe et al., 2012; Hoge et al., 2014; Shenberger-Trujillo and Kurinec, 2016; Steenkamp et al., 2015). Programs, services, resources, and practices cannot lead to population-level change if the target population will not engage in the opportunities being offered. As part of a quality-monitoring system, it is essential to comprehensively examine the reasons for low participation or high dropout rates (or both) among evidence-based programs and services, as these rates may illuminate poor program-community alignment. In this context, ongoing, iterative community and family engagement may be useful for improving the fit of evidence-based programs within local cultural contexts and lead to increased utilization across services. In particular, community engagement approaches can help shape effective outreach, leverage local resources, tailor services to the most pressing issues as identified by local families, and address specific barriers to services.

Detailed recommendations for tailoring evidence-based programs to different community settings (see Miller et al., 2012), cultures (see Castro et al., 2010) and populations (see Lee et al., 2008) have been published. Other areas of literature can inform the assessment of influential aspects of social settings (Tseng and Seidman, 2007) and social networks (Neal et al., 2011) to support high-quality adaptation to local circumstances. In addition, programs implemented across service settings need to carefully attend to military culture, including intersectional and military identities, behaviors, language, norms, and values, as well as the varied ways that culture may be expressed in different geographic locations. Cultural differences within military groups may be significant, for example, between U.S.-based locations and locations abroad. Cultural differences may also be significant within the United States between rural and urban settings, between the active component and the reserve component, and among settings such as health care clinics vs. employment settings, and military vs. nonmilitary environments. Even as more programs are developed specifically for military populations, it cannot be assumed that the same cultural elements will be salient across the services or across diverse settings, populations, and issues (Castro et al., 2010; Kirmayer, 2012). Community engagement strategies can support the goals of adapting programs to local contexts and increasing program uptake and implementation.

The majority of military families live in civilian communities (Whitestone and Thompson, 2016). Thus, to support and enhance military family well-being, it is essential to achieve the engagement and cooperation of organizations within the civilian settings and their collaboration with MFRS in the effort to build, adapt, and sustain relevant programming (Gil-Rivas et al., 2017). In addition, collaborative and community processes are key elements to close the significant research-to-practice gap in the integration of new evidence and evidence-based programs and to assure 'program to community alignment' (Mistry et al., 2009) in the dissemination of family programs. In the post-9/11 era, DoD, National Institutes of Health, and the U.S. Department of Veterans Affairs have all invested in the development of research-based family programs that have been found to be effective, yet many of these programs have not been implemented in routine military- or civilian-practice settings or disseminated broadly. Community engagement and participation may be critical processes with the potential to address these significant adaptation, implementation, and dissemination challenges.

Given that less than one percent of the American population serves in the all-volunteer force, many scholars and policy makers also have raised concerns about a growing military-civilian divide wherein nonmilitary communities—communities that do not have a military installation nearby—have been disconnected from the post-9/11 conflicts and the realities of military service members and their families. While there has been increased attention to building military cultural competence among civilian providers, capacity building in multiple and interconnected civilian sectors is critical to bridging this divide in support of military and veteran families (Bowen et al., 2013).

Some scholars have observed that military and civilian communities do not understand or communicate well with each other and that civilian providers may assume that military families are able to access military-specific supports (e.g., Hoshmand and Hoshmand, 2007). Since 9/11, there have

BOX 7-2
Community Engagement and Community Participatory Research

There is a growing recognition of the value of community-engaged research (CER) and community-based participatory research (CBPR) for addressing a wide range of scientific questions and with diverse communities (Blumenthal, 2011; Trickett and Espino, 2004; Trickett, 2011; Wallerstein and Duran, 2006). Over the last two decades, community-engaged research approaches have gained traction at the National Institutes of Health (NIH) as an effective approach for reducing health disparities (Wallerstein and Duran, 2006, 2010). In 2008, the National Institute of Minority Health and Development (NIMHD) launched the Community-Based Participatory Research Program to support research in which the community "is involved in the CBPR program as an equal partner with the scientists."[a] The Centers for Disease Control and Prevention (Faridi et al., 2007; IOM, 2000, 2003), and the Agency for Healthcare Research and Quality (Viswanathan et al., 2004) have both published recommendations for employing these methodologies.

[a]For more information, see https://www.nimhd.nih.gov/programs/extramural/community-based-participatory.html.

been several initiatives, such as AmericaServes[15] and the Cohen Veteran Network,[16] that leverage civilian academic, community mental health, and school systems to provide examples for advancing care (Renno and Shelton, 2017; Tanielian et al., 2017). There have likewise been initiatives to improve professional training in civilian sectors, such as the STAR Behavioral Health Providers Program[17] and PsychArmor.[18] In addition to such cross-sector collaboration, in order for the MFRS to successfully develop, implement, and sustain programs, services, and resources promoting military family well-being, a deeper understanding of specific communities and their resources is necessary, along with culturally specific knowledge of the diverse subgroups of military families (see Box 7-2).

There is emerging interest in using community engagement and participatory strategies to address and support well-being challenges in military populations (DeVoe et al., 2012; Haynes, 2015; Hoshmand and Hoshmand, 2007; Huebner et al., 2009; Shenberger-Trujillo and Kurinec, 2016). Hoshmand and Hoshmand (2007) emphasize the important role

[15]For more information, see https://americaserves.org.
[16]For more information, see https://www.cohenveteransnetwork.org.
[17]For more information, see https://www.starproviders.org.
[18]For more information, see https://psycharmor.org.

that multilevel engagement and participatory processes can play in bridging military and civilian settings that service members and their families navigate on a daily basis. Huebner and colleagues (2009) discuss how both can increase cross-sector community capacity to support military families. Shenberger-Trujillo and Kurinec (2016) identify a number of research-to-practice gaps and argue that the local knowledge and engagement developed through community engagement can help fill these gaps.

Further, there is a growing recognition that challenges facing military populations demand a public health approach to prevention and intervention. This too requires locally engaged and community-based intervention strategies in addition to clinically situated interventions (Brenner et al., 2018; Knox et al., 2010; Murphy and Fairbank, 2013; U.S. Department of Veterans Affairs, 2018).[19]

Collaborative Stance and Outreach

Institutionalized collaboration, both formal and informal, between MFRS and its programs, services and resources, community networks, researchers, and military families is essential to the well-being of military families, because each stakeholder group possesses unique knowledge and resources critical to this effort. An authentic "collaborative stance" brings in stakeholder voices and expertise to increase the likelihood that promotion, programs, resources, and services are responsive to complex and diverse military families. As Kudler and Porter (2013) conclude, "Summarizing the clinical and public health models . . . we might well say that the secret of care for military children [and their families] is creating communities that care about military children. This will require [collaborative] effort and [shared] time, but we believe it is a highly achievable goal" (Kudler and Porter, 2013, p. 182).

Successful outreach includes effective marketing of the available programs, services, and resources. Community engagement approaches also place an emphasis on the kind of outreach that is distinct from marketing—that is, going to where military families live, congregate, and interact on a daily basis (Huebner et al., 2009). In addition to reaching out to make contact with different locations and at different times and aligning with community events, outreach also includes engaging with community gatekeepers and stakeholders who maintain a high degree of authority and are trusted by military families. Collaborating with key community members, whom others look to for guidance and leadership, will improve the broader community's trust in a program (Wallerstein and Duran, 2010). Therefore, accessing local social networks to identify and conduct outreach through

[19]See Chapter 8 for a discussion of implementation science.

key network members may help spread the use of evidence-based programs and resources (Neal et al., 2011). Lastly, community engagement emphasizes that meeting service members, veterans, and their families where they are is also about assessing and understanding both the local culture and the ways military connectedness influences their lives and the services they seek (Kilpatrick et al., 2011).

Engaging community stakeholders at all phases of program, service, and resource development, delivery, and implementation increases the likelihood of the efforts' relevance and contextual soundness. Local stakeholders possess knowledge about how programs, services, and resources interrelate, including challenges in continuity of care across military settings. Yet local families and providers may not possess the authority to control or fix the system issues they identify, and military leadership with the authority to address continuity across the military may remain unaware of local issues and conditions and therefore of their possible solutions. In this regard, collaborative engagement approaches can help military leaders identify challenges and solutions that meet the needs of military families. Given communities' varying availability of resources and varying abilities to allocate existing resources, localized adaptation of the MFRS can foster both the capacity and the sustainability of programs and service provision.

Several researchers emphasize the benefits to military families of programs that take a community capacity development approach (Huebner et al. 2009; Mancini and Bowen, 2014; Mancini et al., 2018). Community capacity building through informal social networks is based on the principles of shared responsibility for family and community well-being and collective competence, which in turn reflect a community's ability to recognize and mobilize community resources to support well-being (Huebner et al., 2009, p. 219). These scholars argue that programs must be integrated into rather than set apart from the communities in which military families live, work, and play, and that effective military-civilian partnerships must involve the sharing of social capital, information and resource exchange, and orientation toward effective and relevant outcomes. Moreover, Mancini and colleagues (2018) suggest that formal policies, programs, and services need to target growing informal networks, and their success should be gauged by how well they establish a network of support for families.

At the national level, through formal collaborations, programs such as 4-H/Army Youth Development have been able to create local opportunities to expand evidence-based programming. In these examples, national military-private initiatives were set up to expand local services. Improvements in access to care, such as through transportation assistance and growth in local volunteers and clubs, emerged from these initiatives' ability to increase community capacity. In the same way, community engagement approaches build on existing community resources to embed service and program development at the local level, which increases the availability, accessibility, and relevance of programs to the daily lives of military families.

Participatory approaches rely on collaborations that involve end-users in defining their strengths, needs, and problems and contributing to (1) developing programs that target these identified needs and problems; (2) determining the conditions under which programs can be accessed and effective; and (3) identifying the extent to which programs align with and are culturally responsive to diverse military families. The Institute of Medicine and several researchers have lamented the lack of evaluation of such programs and are calling for research and evaluation processes that are more rigorous and address cultural responsiveness (Easterbrooks et al., 2013; Gewirtz, 2018; IOM, 2013). Given the diversity and complexity of contemporary military families, there is a need for caution in assuming what works, why/how, where, when, and for whom.

Collaborating with military families to clarify the well-being construct and variants across different military family subgroups and contexts may be valuable in selecting, developing or adapting evidence-based programs that can be tailored. The process of continuous quality improvement must include methods to incorporate evaluations of programs' relevance and validity for specific family types, constellations, and needs. Similarly, if existing programs have been based on intervention theories and evidence developed in civilian settings, evaluation might focus on understanding the specific context of well-being in military families and diverse communities, because mechanisms for developing family well-being may differ between military and nonmilitary families. Finally, there is a critical question about the extent to which programs, services, resources, or practices, under the best conditions, contribute to military family well-being. To be effective, they must be relevant to the population to be served. Relevance is more clearly defined as the degree to which they are *useful* to families. Thus, core elements of relevant programming require inclusiveness, adaptability, and agility in the development of programs, services, and resources to ensure relevance and enable effectiveness (Nembhard and Edmonson, 2006).

Given the tremendous diversity of military families, maintaining program relevance is a critical and never-ending process. Castro and colleagues (2004) describe a "dynamic tension" within prevention science related to a need for fidelity in the implementation of evidence-based programs balanced against the need for adaptation to ensure the relevance and fit of a program to the needs of the community (p. 41). To ensure appropriate balance, scholars suggest the development of adjustable or adaptable programs that can be tailored to the local cultural context (detailed in Chapter 8).

The Joint Responsibility of MFRS and the Community in Responding to the Dynamic and Diverse Realities of Military Families

The policies, programs, services, resources, and practices of the MFRS as well as community-based programs, services, and resources are profoundly important in providing military children and families with connections, support, and continuity. Frequent moves and changing schools add to a child's sense of uncertainty and anxiety. If a service member's child was involved in programs such as arts, clubs, or sports, there may be financial or logistical challenges to continuing these activities after the parent's discharge from the service or after a relocation. Families may need help planning for involuntary transitions, particularly during the stressful time of caring for an injured service member. Local programs, youth organizations, and activities sometimes offer connections and assistance to address these challenges (Cozza et al., 2017, p. 323). Box 7-3 includes just some of the many military family voices that acknowledge these challenges.

BOX 7-3
Military Family Voices

1. "In reality it is their self-sufficiency that determines whether they will be able to fill the gaps between what is available and how they function as a military family." (Ellyn Dunford, spouse of General Joseph F. Dunford, Chairman of the Joint Chiefs of Staff*)
2. "You want to protect your children, but you bring your family along with your career's progressions." "It hasn't been without challenges, and we have needed to look outside of just our family unit and to those who can help make a difference and help define what this new normal is." (Lieutenant Colonel Eric M. Flake, U.S. Air Force, as quoted in Military Child Education Coalition [2016, p 16]).
3. "Still, families don't just need programs . . . they need people." (Colonel Anthony Cox, Army (retired), former manager, HQDA Family Advocacy Program*)
4. "Well, I also started making friends because I got involved in a lot of the clubs and sports." (John Doe, military-connected student, as quoted in Military Child Education Coalition [2012, p. 139])
5. "Communities outside the gate are the first line of defense, especially for the families of the National Guard and Reserves." (Ellyn Dunford*)

---

*Speaker at a public information-gathering session held on April 24, 2018, at the National Academies of Sciences, Engineering, and Medicine. See Appendix B for full agenda.

The military has long been a leader and innovator in social policies and supports, including in the area of child and family readiness programming, two examples being child care supports and domestic violence prevention. A commitment to understanding how military families experience their loved ones' service and to developing more efficient and effective systems to support readiness benefits from collaborations with civilian systems of support. Strong, reciprocal collaborative relationships with civilian systems and their data monitoring agencies, such as local public education systems and child welfare and community mental health agencies, are central to creating a comprehensive continuum of support that reaches beyond installation facilities and into the communities where families live, work, and play. The challenge is that, more often than not, these collaborative efforts happen by chance, rather than by intent (Gravens and Keller, 2018).

CONCLUSIONS

CONCLUSION 7-1: The Department of Defense has developed a Military Family Readiness System that includes a number of policies, services, programs, resources, and practices. This system is complex, multifaceted, and tiered, and is to be lauded insofar as there is nothing comparable in the U.S. civilian sector.

CONCLUSION 7-2: The current Military Family Readiness System is siloed, with a diffusion in its division of labor and responsibility, and its delivery of services is fragmented in some instances. The system lacks a comprehensive, coordinated framework to support individual and population well-being, resilience, and readiness among military families. Addressing this deficit could improve quality, encourage innovation, and support effective response capabilities.

The current system also lacks the processes and structures necessary to support ongoing population-level monitoring and mapping of family well-being, including a grounding in the continuum of promotion, prevention, treatment, and maintenance dimensions and integrated data infrastructure, accompanied by validated and appropriate assessments. Finally, as noted earlier, diffusion of the division of labor and responsibilities has to do with what entity "owns" which part of the policies, programs, services, and resources that comprise the MFRS. For instance, these efforts are under the purview of the Under Secretary of Defense for Personnel and Readiness (USD P&R),[20] yet policies and programs are overseen by separate assistant secretaries of defense, and policies are interpreted and implemented by each military branch.

[20]For more information, see https://prhome.defense.gov.

CONCLUSION 7-3: Utilizing a dynamic complex adaptive support-system approach would improve the ability of the Military Family Readiness System to respond to the needs of military families. Evidence-based and/or evidence-informed practices, resources, services, programs, and policies are foundational to a complex adaptive system. A continuous quality monitoring system that utilizes solid measurements is needed to ensure a complex adaptive system that continues to progress in its effectiveness and relevance.

The Military Family Readiness System can learn from community engagement and participation examples for potential incorporation of adaptation strategies and tailoring of promotion, prevention, and intervention efforts to ensure continuous alignment, relevance, and effectiveness of programs, services, resources, policies, and practice for stakeholders with a sensitivity to local contexts.

CONCLUSION 7-4: Community engagement and meaningful collaboration with key stakeholders are critical from the beginning and throughout the implementation process to identify relevant targets for the continuum of support (i.e., promotion, prevention, and intervention efforts), ensure program alignment with diverse family needs and constellations, assure family engagement and program participation, and build community capacity to support military family well-being and readiness.

REFERENCES

Allen, E. S., Stanley, S. M., Rhoades, G. K., Markman, H. J., and Loew, B. A. (2011). Marriage education in the Army: Results of a randomized clinical trial. *Journal of Couple & Relationship Therapy: Innovations in Clinical and Educational Interventions, 10*(4), 309–326.

Baker, S. (2017). *Broadening the Reach of Evidence-Based Parenting Interventions: Evaluation of a Brief Online Version of the Triple P–Positive Parenting Program.* Thesis submitted for Doctor of Philosophy at The University of Queensland, Australia, 2016, School of Psychology.

Beardslee, W., Lester, P., Klosinski, L., Saltzman, W., Woodward, K., Nash, W., Mogil, C., Koffman, R., and Leskin, G. J. (2011). Family-centered preventive intervention for military families: Implications for implementation science. *Prevention Science, 12*(4), 339–348.

Beardslee, W. R. (2013). Military and veteran family-centered preventive interventions and care: Making meaning of experiences over time. *Clinical Child and Family Psychology Review, 16*(3), 341–343.

Biglan, A. (2015). *The Nurture Effect: How the Science of Human Behavior Can Improve Our Lives and Our World.* Oakland, CA: New Harbinger.

Blumenthal, D. S. (2011). Is community-based participatory research possible? *American Journal of Preventive Medicine 40*(3), 386.

Bowen, G. L., Martin, J. A., and Mancini, J. A. (2013). The resilience of military families: Theoretical perspectives. In M. A. Fine and F. D. Fincham (Eds.), *Family Theories: A Content-based Approach* (pp. 417–436). New York, NY: Routledge.

Brenner, L. A., Hoffmire, C., Mohatt, N. V., Forster, J. E., and the Rocky Mountain Mental Illness Research Education and Clinical Center. (2018). Commentary: Preventing suicide among veterans will require clinicians and researchers to adopt a public health approach. *FORUM: Translating Research Into Quality Healthcare for Veterans* (Spring 2018). https://www.hsrd.research.va.gov/publications/forum/spring18/default.cfm?ForumMenu=Spring18-1

Bumbarger, B. K., and Perkins, D. F. (2008). After randomized trials: Issues related to dissemination of evidence-based interventions. *Journal of Children Services, 3*, 55–64.

Castro, F. G., Barrera Jr., M., and Holleran Steiker, L. K. (2010). Issues and challenges in the design of culturally adapted evidence-based interventions. *Annual Review of Clinical Psychology*, 6, 213–239.

Castro, F. G., Barrera, M., and Martinez, C. R. (2004). The cultural adaptation of prevention interventions: Resolving tensions between fidelity and fit. *Prevention Science 5*(1), 41–45.

Center for Substance Abuse Treatment. (2000). *Comprehensive Case Management for Substance Abuse Treatment.* Treatment Improvement Protocol (TIP) Series, No. 27, HHS Publication No. (SMA) 15-4215. Rockville, MD: Author.

Centre for Effective Services. (2011). *The What Works Process: Evidence-Informed Improvement for Child and Family Services*. Dublin, Ireland: Author.

Chambers, D. A., and Norton, W. E. (2016). The adaptome: Advancing the science of intervention adaptation. *American Journal of Preventive Medicine, 51*(4), S124-S131.

Chandra, A., and London, A. S. (2013). Unlocking insights about military children and families. *The Future of Children, 23*(2), 187–198.

Coker, A. L., Bush, H. M., Brancato, C. J., Clear, E. R., and Recktenwald, E. A. (2018). Bystander program effectiveness to reduce violence acceptance: RCT in high schools. *Journal of Family Violence*, 1–12.

Coker, A. L., Bush, H. M., Cook-Craig, P. G., DeGue, S. A., Clear, E. R., Brancato, C. J., Fisher, B. S., and Recktenwald, E. A. (2017). RCT testing bystander effectiveness to reduce violence. *American Journal of Preventive Medicine 52*, 566–578.

Coker, A. L., Bush, H. M., Fisher, B. S., Swan, S. C., Williams, C. M., Clear, E. R., and DeGue, S. (2016). Multi-college bystander intervention evaluation for violence prevention. *American Journal of Preventive Medicine 50*, 295–302.

Coker, A. L., Cook-Craig, P. G., Williams, C. M., Fisher, B. S., Clear, E. R., Garcia, L. S. and Hegge, L. M. (2011). Evaluation of Green Dot: An active bystander intervention to reduce sexual violence on college campuses. *Violence Against Women, 17*(6), 777-796.

Coker, A. L., Fisher, B. S., Bush, H. M., Swan, S. C., Williams, C. M., Clear, E. R., and DeGue, S. (2015). Evaluation of the Green Dot bystander intervention to reduce interpersonal violence among college students across three campuses. *Violence Against Women, 21*, 1507–1527.

Cozza, S. J., Rauch, P., and Keller, M. (2017). Family and community support. In A. L. Kellerman and E. Elster (Eds.), *Out of the Crucible: How the U.S. Military Transformed Combat Casualty Care in Iraq and Afghanistan* (pp. 317–328). Fort Sam Houston, TX: Borden Institute.

Damschroder, L. J., Aron, D. C., Keith, R. E., Kirsh, S. R., Alexander, J. A., and Lowery, J. C. (2009). Fostering implementation of health services research findings into practice: A consolidated framework for advancing implementation science. *Implementation Science 4*(1), 50.

Deaton, A., and Cartwright, N. (2018). Understanding and misunderstanding randomized controlled trials. *Social Science & Medicine 210*, 2–21.

DeGarmo, D. S., and Gewirtz, A.H. (2018). A recovery capital and stress-buffering model for post-deployed military parents. *Frontiers in Psychology, 9*.

DeVoe, E. R., Ross, A. M., and Paris, R. (2012). Build it together and they will come: The case for community-based participatory research with military populations. *Advances in Social Work, 13*(1), 149–165.

DeVoe, E. R., Paris, R., Emmert-Aronson, B., Ross, A., and Acker, M. (2017). A randomized clinical trial of a postdeployment parenting intervention for service members and their families with very young children. *Psychological Trauma: Theory, Research, Practice and Policy*, *9*(1), 25–34.

Dishion, T. J., Nelson, S. E., and Kavanagh, K. (2003). The family check-up with high-risk young adolescents: Preventing early-onset substance use by parent monitoring. *Behavior Therapy, 34,* 553–571.

Donabedian, A. (2005). Evaluating the quality of medical care. 1966. *Milbank Quarterly, 83*(4), 691–729.

Easterbrooks, M. A., Ginsburg, K., and Lerner, R. M. (2013). Resilience among military youth. *The Future of Children, 23*(2), 99–120.

Ellis, B. S., and Herbert, S. (2010). Complex adaptive systems (CAS): An overview of key elements, characteristics and application to management theory. *Journal of Innovation in Health Informatics*, *19*(1), 33–37.

Emshoff, J. (2008). Researchers, practitioners, and funders: Using the framework to get us on the same page. *American Journal of Community Psychology*, *41*, 393–403.

Estabrooks, P. A., Brownson, R. C., and Pronk, N. P. (2018). Dissemination and implementation science for public health professionals: An overview and call to action. *Preventing Chronic Disease, 15.*

Faridi, Z., Grunbaum, J. A., Gray, B. S., Franks, A., and Simoes, E. (2007). Community-based participatory research: Necessary next steps. *Preventing Chronic Disease 4*(3).

Foa, E. B., McLean, C. P., Zang, Y., Rosenfield, D., Yadin, E., Yarvis, J. S., Mintz, J., Young-McCaughan, S., Borah, E. V., Dondanville, K. A., Fina, B. A., Hall-Clark, B. N., Lichner, T., Litz, B. T., Roache, J., Wright, E. C., and Peterson, A. L. (2018). Effect of prolonged exposure therapy delivered over 2 weeks vs 8 weeks vs present centered therapy on PTSD severity in military personnel: A randomized clinical trial. *Journal of the American Medical Association 319*(4), 354–364.

Forgatch, M. S., and Gewirtz, A. H. (2017). The evolution of the Oregon Model of parent management training: An intervention for antisocial behavior in children and adolescents. In J. R. Weiz and A. E. Kazdin (Eds.), *Evidence-based Psychotherapies for Children and Adolescents* (Third Edition). New York, NY: The Guilford Press.

Fosco, G. M., Frank, J. L., Stormshak, E. A., and Dishion, T. J. (2013). Opening the "black box": Family check-up intervention effects on self-regulation that prevents growth in problem behavior and substance use. *Journal of School Psychology 51,* 455–468.

Fosco, G. M., Van Ryzin, M. J., Connell, A. M., and Stormshak, E. A. (2016). Preventing adolescent depression with the family check-up: Examining family conflict as a mechanism of change. *Journal of Family Psychology 30,* 82–92.

Gewirtz, A. H. (2018). A call for theoretically informed and empirically validated family interventions. *Journal of Family Theory & Review, 10*(3), 587–601.

Gewirtz, A. H., DeGarmo, D. S., and Lee, S. (in press). *Effects of a Military Parenting Program on Youth Risk Behaviors: Two-Year Outcomes of After Deployment, Adaptive Parenting Tools/ADAPT.*

Gewirtz, A. H., DeGarmo, D. S., and Zamir, O. (2016). Effects of a military parenting program on parental distress and suicidal ideation: After deployment adaptive parenting tools. *Suicide and Life Threatening Behavior, 46*(1), S23–S31.

———. (2018). After deployment, adaptive parenting tools: One-year outcomes of an evidence-based parenting program for military families. *Prevention Science, 19*(4), 589–599.

Gewirtz, A. H., Pinna, K. L., Hanson, S. K., and Brockberg, D. (2014). Promoting parenting to support reintegrating military families: After deployment, adaptive parenting tools. *Psychological Services, 11*(1), 31–40.

Gil-Rivas, V., Kilmer, R. P., Larson, J. C., Armstrong, L. M. (2017). Facilitating successful reintegration: Attending to the needs of military families. *American Journal of Orthopsychiatry, 87*(2), 176–184.

Glasgow, R. E., and Chambers, D. (2012). Developing robust, sustainable implementation systems using rigorous, rapid, and relevant science. *Clinical and Translational Science, 5*(1), 48–55.

Glasgow, R. E., Vinson, C., Chambers, D., Khoury, M. J., Kaplan, R. M., and Hunter, C. (2012). National Institutes of Health approaches to dissemination and implementation science: Current and future directions. *American Journal of Public Health, 102*(7), 1274–1281.

Gordon R. (1983). An operational classification of disease prevention. *Public Health Reports, 98*, 107–109.

Gottfredson, D. C., Cook, T. D., Gardner, F. E. M., Gorman-Smith, D., Howe, G. W., Sandler, I. N., and Zafft, K. M. (2015). Standards of evidence for efficacy, effectives and scale-up research in prevention science: Next generation. *Prevention Science, 16*(7), 893–926.

Graczyk, P. A., Domitrovich, C. E., and Zins, J. E. (2003). Facilitating the implementation of evidence-based prevention and mental health promotion efforts in schools. In M. D. Weist, S. W. Evans, and N. A. Lever (Eds.), *Handbook of School Mental Health Advancing Practice and Research* (pp. 301–318). New York: Springer.

Gravens, M. L., and Keller, M. M. (2018). Nonprofit contributions: Reflections and looking forward. In L. Hughes-Kirchubel, S. MacDermid Wadsworth, and D. S. Riggs (Eds.), *A Battle Plan for Supporting Military Families* (pp. 207–222). Cham, Switzerland: Springer.

Haynes, E. N. (2015). Community-based participatory research: An overview for application in Department of Defense/Veterans Affairs Research. *Airborne Hazards Related to Deployment*, 52, 239–244.

Heyman, R. E., Slep, A. M. S., and Nelson, J. P. (2011). Empirically guided community intervention for partner abuse, child maltreatment, suicidality, and substance misuse. In S. MacDermid Wadsworth and D. Riggs (Eds.), *Risk and Resilience in U.S. Military Families* (pp. 85–110). New York: Springer.

Hoge, C. W., Grossman, S. H., Auchterlonie, J. L., Riviere, L. A., Milliken, C. S. and Wilk, J. E. (2014). PTSD treatment for soldiers after combat deployment: Low utilization of mental health care and reasons for dropout. *Psychiatric Services, 65*(8), 997–1004.

Holland, J. H. (1995). *Hidden Order: How Adaptation Builds Complexity*. Addison Wesley.

Hoshmand, L. T., and Hoshmand, A. L. (2007). Support for military families and communities. *Journal of Community Psychology, 35*(2), 171–180.

Howse, R. B., Trivette, C. M., Shindelar, L., Dunst, C. J., and The North Carolina Partnership for Children, Inc. (2013). *The Smart Start Resource Guide of Evidence-Based and Evidence-Informed Programs and Practices: A Summary of Research Evidence*. Raleigh: The North Carolina Partnership for Children, Inc.

Huebner, A. J., Mancini, J. A., Bowen, G. L. and Orthner, D. K. (2009). Shadowed by war: Building community capacity to support military families. *Family Relations 58*(2), 216–228.

Institute of Medicine (IOM). (1994). *Reducing Risks for Mental Disorders: Frontiers for Preventive Intervention Research*. Washington, DC: National Academy Press.

________. (2000). *Promoting Health: Intervention Strategies from Social and Behavioral Research*. Washington, DC: National Academy Press.

________. (2001). *Crossing the Quality Chasm: A New Health System for the 21st Century*. Washington, DC: National Academy Press.

________. (2003). *Who Will Keep the Public Healthy? Educating Public Health Professionals for the 21st Century*. Washington, DC: The National Academies Press.

———. (2013). *Returning Home from Iraq and Afghanistan: Assessment of Readjustment Needs of Veterans, Service Members, and Their Families*. Washington, DC: The National Academies Press.

———. (2014). *Preventing Psychological Disorders in Service Members and Their Families: An Assessment of Programs*. Washington, DC: The National Academies Press.

Karre, J. K., Perkins, D. F., Aronson, K. R., DiNallo, J., Kyler, S. J., Olson, J., and Mentzer, C. E. (2017). A continuum of evidence on evidence-based programs: A new resource for use in military social service delivery. *Military Behavioral Health, 5*(4), 346–355.

Kendall, P. C., Chu, B., Gifford, A., Hayes, C. and Nauta, M. (1998). Breathing life into a manual: Flexibility and creativity with manual-based treatments. *Cognitive and Behavioral Practice, 5*(2), 177–198.

Kilpatrick, D. G., Best, C. L. Smith, D. W., Kudler, H., and Cornelison-Grant, V. (2011). *Serving Those Who Have Served: Educational Needs of Health Care Providers Working With Military Members, Veterans, and Their Families*. Charleston: Medical University of South Carolina Department of Psychiatry, National Crime Victims Research & Treatment Center.

Kirmayer, L. J. (2012). Cultural competence and evidence-based practice in mental health: Epistemic communities and the politics of pluralism. *Social Science & Medicine, 75*(2), 249–256.

Knight, D., Belenko, S., Wiley, T., Robertson, A., Arrigona, N., Dennis, M., Bartkowski, J., McReynolds, L., Becan, J., Knudsen, H., and the Juvenile Justice Translational Research on Interventions for Adolescents in the Legal System Cooperative. (2016). Juvenile justice—translational research on interventions for adolescents in the legal system (JJ-TRIALS): A cluster randomized trial targeting system-wide improvement in substance use services. *Implementation Science, 11*(1), 57.

Knox, K. L., Pflanz, S., Talcott, G. W., Campise, R. L., Lavigne, J. E., Bajorska, A., Tu, X. and Caine, E. D. 2010. The U.S. Air Force Suicide Prevention Program: Implications for public health policy. *American Journal of Public Health, 100*(12), 2457–2463.

Kritikos, T. K., DeVoe, E. R., and Emmert-Aronson, B. (2019). The effect of a parenting intervention on relationship quality of recently deployed military service members and their partners. *American Journal of Orthopsychiatry, 89*(2), 170.

Kudler, H., and Porter, R. I. (2013). Building communities of care for military children and families. *The Future of Children, 23*(2), 163–185.

Kvernbekk, T. (2017). Evidence-based educational practice. *Oxford Research Encyclopedia of Education*. Oxford University Press. Retrieved from https://oxfordre.com/education/view/10.1093/acrefore/9780190264093.001.0001/acrefore-9780190264093-e-187.

Langley, G. J., Moen, R. D., Nolan, K. M., Nolan, T. W., Norman, C. L., and Provost, L. P. (2009). *The Improvement Guide: A Practical Approach to Enhancing Organizational Performance*. San Francisco, CA: John Wiley & Sons.

Lee, S. J., Altschul, I., and Mowbray, C. T. (2008). Using planned adaptation to implement evidence-based programs with new populations. *American Journal of Community Psychology, 41*(3-4), 290–303.

Lester P. (2018). *The Time Has Come: Trauma-informed Prevention and Systems of Care*. Research presentation at the 65th Annual American Academy of Child and Adolescent Psychiatry, Seattle, Washington.

Lester, P., Liang, L. J., Milburn, N., Mogil, C., Woodward, K., Nash, W., Aralis, H., Sinclair, M., Semaan, A., Klosinski, L. and Beardslee, W. (2016). Evaluation of a family-centered preventive intervention for military families: Parent and child longitudinal outcomes. *Journal of the American Academy of Child & Adolescent Psychiatry, 55*(1), 14–24.

Lipsitz, L. A. (2012). Understanding health care as a complex system: The foundation for unintended consequences. *Journal of the American Medical Association 308*(3), 243–244.

Litz, B. T., Lebowitz, L., Gray, M. J., and Nash, W. P. 2017. *Adaptive Disclosure: A New Treatment for Military Trauma, Loss, and Moral Injury*. New York: Guilford Press.

Mancini, J. A., O'Neal, C. W., Martin J. A., and Bowen, G. L. (2018). Community social organization and military families: Theoretical perspectives on transitions, contexts, and resilience. *Journal of Family Theory & Review, 10*, 550–565.

Mancini, J. A., and Bowen, G. L. (2014). *Supporting Military Service Members and Families*. Athens, and Chapel Hill: The University of Georgia and the University of North Carolina at Chapel Hill. Retrieved from https://militaryfamilieslearningnetwork.org/wp-content/uploads/2018/02/Community-capacity-building.-Supporting-military-service-members-and-families.-A-resource-manual-by-Mancini-and-Bowenl_2014.pdf.

Military Child Education Coalition. (2012). *Education of the Military Child in the 21st Century: Current Dimensions of Educational Experiences for Army Children*. A report on the research conducted by the Military Child Education Coalition for the U.S. Army. Harker Heights, TX: MCEC.

———. (2016). *On the Move*, 10(1). Harker Heights, TX: MCEC. Retrieved from https://www.militarychild.org/upload/files/OTM%20PDF/OTM_2016_Spring.pdf.

Miller, A. L., Krusky, A. M., Franzen, S., Cochran, S. and Zimmerman, M. A. (2012). Partnering to translate evidence-based programs to community settings: Bridging the gap between research and practice. *Health Promotion Practice, 13*(4), 559-566.

Mistry, J., Jacobs, F., and Jacobs, L. (2009). Cultural relevance as program-to-community alignment. *Journal of Community Psychology, 37*(4), 487–504.

Mogil, C., Paley, B., Doud, T., Havens, L., Moore-Tyson, J., Beardslee, W. R., and Lester, P. (2010). Families OverComing under Stress (FOCUS) for early childhood: Building resilience for young children in high stress families. *Zero to Three, 31*(1), 10–16.

Mohatt, N. V., and Beehler, S. (2018). *Application of Community Engaged and Community Based Participatory Research to Support Military Families*. Paper Commissioned by the Committee on the Well-Being of Military Families, Washington, DC, National Academies of Sciences, Engineering, and Medicine.

Monson, C. M., Fredman, S. J., Macdonald, A., Pukay-Martin, N. D., Resick, P. A., and Schnurr, P. P. (2012). Effect of cognitive-behavioral couple therapy for PTSD: A randomized controlled trial. *Journal of the American Medical Association 308*(7), 700–709.

Murphy, R. A., and Fairbank, J. A. (2013). Implementation and dissemination of military informed and evidence-based interventions for community dwelling military families. *Clinical Child and Family Psychology Review, 16*(4), 348–364.

Nash, W. P., Vasterling, J., Ewing-Cobbs, L., Horn, S., Gaskin, T., Golden, J., Riley, W. T., Bowles, S. V., Favret, J., and Lester, P. (2010). Consensus recommendations for common data elements for operational stress research and surveillance: Report of a federal interagency working group. *Archives of Physical Medicine and Rehabilitation, 91*(11), 1673–1683.

National Academies of Sciences, Engineering, and Medicine. (2016). *Preventing Bullying Through Science, Policy, and Practice*. Washington, DC: The National Academies Press.

National Research Council and Institute of Medicine. (2009). *Preventing Mental, Emotional, and Behavioral Disorders Among Young People: Progress and Possibilities*. Washington, DC: National Academies Press. doi: 10.17226/12480.

Neal, J. W., Neal, Z. P., Atkins, M. S., Henry, D. B., and Frazier, S. L. (2011). Channels of change: Contrasting network mechanisms in the use of interventions. *American Journal of Community Psychology, 47*(3-4), 277–286.

Nembhard, I. M., and Edmondson, A. C. (2006). Making it safe: The effects of leader inclusiveness and professional status on psychological safety and improvement efforts in health care teams. *Journal of Organizational Behavior, 27*(7), 941–966.

Ogbeiwi, O. (2017). Why written objectives need to be really SMART. *British Journal of Healthcare Management*, 23(7), 324–336.

Patton, M. Q., and Blandin Foundation. (2014). *Mountain of Accountability: Pursuing Mission Through Learning, Exploration and Development*. Grand Rapids, MN: Blandin Foundation.

Perkins, D. F., Aronson, K. R., Karre, J., Kyler, S. J., and DiNallo, J. M. (2015). Reducing barriers to evidence-based practice with military families: Clearinghouse for Military Family Readiness. *Military Behavioral Health, 4*(1), 47–57.

Piehler, T. F., Ausherbauer, K., Gewirtz, A., and Gliske, K. (2016). Improving child peer adjustment in military families through parent training: The mediational role of parental locus of control. *Journal of Early Adolescence, 38,* 1322–1343.

Proctor, E., Silmere, H., Raghavan, R., Hovmand, P., Aarons, G., Bunger, A., Griffey, R., and Hensley, M. (2011). Outcomes for implementation research: Conceptual distinctions, measurement challenges, and research agenda. *Administration and Policy in Mental Health and Mental Health Services Research, 38*(2), 65–76.

Renno, S., and Shelton, C. (2017). *Cohen Veterans Network Implementation Summit Summary, Key Messages and Challenges*. Retrieved from https://www.cohenveteransnetwork.org/wp-content/uploads/2017/03/CVN-IS-Summary.pdf.

Resick, P. A., Wachen, J. S., Dondanville, K. A., Pruiksma, K. E., Yarvis, J. S., Mintz, J., Peterson, A. L., and the STRONG STAR Consortium. (2017). Effect of group vs. individual Cognitive Processing Therapy in active-duty military seeking treatment for posttraumatic stress disorder: A randomized clinical trial. *Journal of the American Medical Association Psychiatry, 74*(1), 28–36.

Rhoades, G. K., Stanley, S. M., Markman, H. J., and Allen, E. S. (2015). Can marriage education mitigate the risks associated with premarital cohabitation? *Journal of Family Psychology, 29*, 500–506.

Saltzman, W. R., Lester, P., Beardslee, W. R., Layne, C. M., Woodward, K. and Nash, W. P. (2011). Mechanisms of risk and resilience in military families: Theoretical and empirical basis of a family-focused resilience enhancement program. *Clinical Child and Family Psychology Review, 14*(3), 213–230.

Saltzman W. R., Lester, P., Milburn, N., Woodward, K., and Stein, J. (2016). Pathways of risk and resilience: Impact of a family resilience program on active-duty military parents. *Family Process, 55*(4), 633–646.

Schulte, B., and Durana, A. (2016). *The New America Care Report*. Washington, DC: New America. Retrieved from https://www.newamerica.org/better-life-lab/policy-papers/new-america-care-report.

Schulte, M. T., and Hser, Y.-I. (2015). Developing ecological momentary intervention content for relapse prevention. *Drug and Alcohol Dependence, 146*, e92.

Schwandt, T. A. (2014). Credible evidence of effectiveness: Necessary but not sufficient. In S. I. Dondalson, C. A. Christie, M. M. Mark (Eds.), *Credible and Actionable Evidence: The Foundation for Rigorous and Influential Evaluations* (second ed., pp. 259–273). Los Angeles, CA: SAGE.

Schwartz, S. R., Clouse, K., Yende, N., Van Rie, A., Bassett, J., Ratshefola, M., and Pettifor, A. (2015). Acceptability and feasibility of a mobile phone-based case management intervention to retain mothers and infants from an option b+ program in postpartum HIV care. *Maternal and Child Health Journal, 19*(9), 2029–2037.

Shen, J., and Cooley, V. E. (2008). Critical issues in using data for decision-making. *International Journal of Leadership in Education, 11*(3), 319–329.

Shenberger-Trujillo, J. M., and Kurinec, C. A. (2016). Bridging the research to application divide: Recommendations for community-based participatory research in a military setting. *Military Behavioral Health*, 4(4), 316–324.

Sims, C. S., Trail, T. E., Chen, E. K., Meza, E., Roshan, P. and Lachman, B. E. (2018). *Assessing the Needs of Soldiers and their Families at the Garrison Level*. Santa Monica, CA: RAND Corporation. Retrieved from https://www.rand.org/content/dam/rand/pubs/research_reports/RR2100/RR2148/RAND_RR2148.pdf.

Slep, A. M. S., and Heyman, R. E. (2008). Public health approaches to family maltreatment prevention: Resetting family psychology's sights from the home to the community. *Journal of Family Psychology, 22*(4), 518–528.

Smith, R. C., Chun, R. S., Michael, R. L., and Schneider, B. J. (2013). Operation brave families: A preventive approach to lessening the impact of war on military families through preclinical engagement. *Military Medicine, 178*(2), 174–179.

Spivey, M. J. (2018). Discovery in complex adaptive systems. *Cognitive Systems Research, 51*, 40–55.

Springer, J. F., and Phillips, J. (2007). *The Institute of Medicine Framework and Its Implication for the Advancement of Prevention Policy, Programs and Practice*. Washington, DC: Department of Health and Human Services.

Stanley, S. M., Allen, E. S., Markman H. J., Rhoades, G. K., and Prentice, D. L. (2010). Decreasing divorce in U.S. Army couples: Results from a randomized controlled trial using PREP for Strong Bonds. *Journal of Couple & Relationship Therapy: Innovations in Clinical and Educational Interventions, 9*(2), 149–160.

Stanley, S. M., Rhoades, G. K., Loew, B. A., Allen, E. S., Carter, S., Osborne, L. J., Prentice, D. and Markman, H. J. (2014). A randomized controlled trial of relationship education in the U.S. Army: 2-year outcomes. *Family Relations, 63*(4), 482–495.

Steenkamp, M. M., Litz, B. T., Hoge, C. W., and Marmar, C. R. (2015). Psychotherapy for military-related PTSD: A review of randomized clinical trials. *Journal of the American Medical Association, 314*(5), 489–500.

Stith, S. M., Rosen, H., McCollum, E. E., and Thomsen, C. J. (2004). Treating intimate partner violence within intact couple relationships: Outcomes of multi-couple versus individual couple therapy. *Journal of Marital and Family Therapy, 30*, 305–318.

Taft, C. T., Creech, S. K., Gallagher, M. W., Macdonald, A., Murphy, C. M. and Monson, C. M. (2016). Strength at Home Couples program to prevent military partner violence: A randomized controlled trial. *Journal of Consulting and Clinical Psychology, 84*(11), 935.

Tanielian, T., Batka, C., and Meredith, L. S. (2017). *A New Way Forward in Veterans' Mental Health Care: How "Welcome Back Veterans" Is Making a Difference*. Santa Monica, CA: RAND Corporation. Retrieved from https://www.rand.org/pubs/research_briefs/RB9981z1.html.

Thompson, B. (2018). *Department of Defense Military Family Readiness System: Supporting Military Family Well-Being*. Paper commissioned by the Committee on the Well-Being of Military Families, Washington, DC, National Academies of Sciences, Engineering, and Medicine.

Trail, T. E., Martin, L. T., Burgette, L. F., May, L. W., Mahmud, A., Nanda, N., and Chandra, A. (2017). An evaluation of U.S. military non-medical counseling programs. *RAND Health Quarterly, 8*(2).

Trickett E. J. (2011). Community-based participatory research as worldview or instrumental strategy: Is it lost in translation(al) research? *American Journal of Public Health, 101*(8), 1353–1355.

Trickett, E. J., and Espino, S. L. R. (2004). Collaboration and social inquiry: Multiple meanings of a construct and its role in creating useful and valid knowledge. *American Journal of Community Psychology, 34*(1–2), 1–69.

True, G., Rigg, K. K., and Butler, A. (2015). Understanding barriers to mental health care for recent war veterans through photovoice. *Qualitative Health Research, 25*(10), 1443–1455.

Tseng, V., and Seidman, E. (2007). A systems framework for understanding social settings. *American Journal of Community Psychology, 39*(3-4), 217–228.

U.S. Department of Defense (DoD). (2012). *Department of Defense Instruction: Military Family Readiness.* Washington, DC. Available: http://www.esd.whs.mil/Portals/54/Documents/DD/issuances/dodi/134222p.pdf.

———. (2017). *Annual Report to the Congressional Defense Committees on the Department of Defense Policy and Plans for Military Family Readiness, Fiscal Year 2016.* Washington, DC

U.S. Department of Veterans Affairs. (2018). *National Strategy for Preventing Veteran Suicide 2018-2028.* Washington, DC. Retrieved from https://www.mentalhealth.va.gov/suicide_prevention/docs/Office-of-Mental-Health-and-Suicide-Prevention-National-Strategy-for-Preventing-Veterans-Suicide.pdf.

Viswanathan, M., Ammerman, A., Eng, E., Gartlehner, G., Lohr, K. N., Griffith, D., Rhodes, S., Samuel-Hodge, C., Maty, S., and Lux, L. (2004). Community-based participatory research: Assessing the evidence. *Evidence Report/Technology Assessment, 99*, 1–8.

Wallerstein, N. B., and Duran, B. (2006). Using community-based participatory research to address health disparities. *Health Promotion Practice, 7*(3), 312–323.

———. (2010). Community-based participatory research contributions to intervention research: The intersection of science and practice to improve health equity. *American Journal of Public Health, 100*(S1), S40–S46.

Weinick, R. M., Beckjord, E. B., Farmer, C. M., Martin, L. T., Gillen, E. M., Acosta, J., Fisher, M. P., Garnett, J., Gonzalez, G. C., Helmus, T. C., and Jaycox, L.H. (2011). Programs addressing psychological health and traumatic brain injury among U.S. military servicemembers and their families. *RAND Health Quarterly, 1*(4). Retrieved from https://www.rand.org/content/dam/rand/pubs/technical_reports/2011/RAND_TR950.pdf.

Whitestone, Y. K., and Thompson, B. A. (2016). How do military family policies influence parenting resources available to families? In A. H. Gewirtz and A. M. Youssef (Eds.), *Parenting and Children's Resilience in Military Families* (pp. 283–298). New York: Springer.

Witkiewitz, K., Bowen, S., Douglas, H., and Hsu, S. H. (2013). Mindfulness-based relapse prevention for substance craving. *Addictive Behaviors, 38*(2), 1563–1571.

8

Developing and Sustaining a Learning System to Support Military Family Readiness and Well-Being

In this chapter, the committee draws heavily from dissemination and implementation science and a learning system framework.[1] In Chapter 7, we showed why advancing military family well-being within a complex adaptive system, such as the Military Family Readiness System (MFRS), requires a comprehensive approach optimally informed by research and models from several convergent fields. The development of an *integrated information infrastructure* is needed (see Chapter 7, Figure 7-4) that can support the monitoring and delivery of data-driven programs, services, and resources to promote military family well-being and ultimately mission readiness.

Here we detail specific requirements to build a dynamic, sustainable MFRS that would lead to high quality in programs, services, and resources. Thus, this chapter presents a review of the evidence from research on translating and scaling up evidence-based and evidence-informed programs, services, and resources into larger systems, an adaptive process central to building and sustaining an effective MFRS that can be responsive to emerging and future challenges facing the U.S. Department of Defense (DoD). We also examine opportunities for utilizing advancements in big data analytics and mobile platforms/wearables to enhance the MFRS.

[1]This chapter draws partially on papers commissioned by the committee (Marmor, 2018; Nahum-Shani and Militello, 2018).

BACKGROUND ON FAMILY-BASED PROMOTION AND PREVENTION INTERVENTIONS

In developing, implementing, evaluating, and improving military family readiness policies, programs, services, and resources to promote well-being and prevent behavioral health problems, many of the challenges faced by the MFRS within DoD are similar to those found in civilian communities. These challenges are amplified by the limitations of existing research on military child and family resilience and well-being, as well as by a complex and dynamic landscape of military contexts, services, and policies. The fields of applied developmental science and prevention science can provide relevant guidance for developing policies, programs, services, resources, and practices that are guided by evidence. We examine the range of available evidence with a focus on building on previous knowledge, including decades of research on prevention science and child development, incorporating available and relevant theoretical models, observational studies, and experimental intervention design consistent with considerations of the best available evidence (as established in Chapter 1) (Deaton and Cartwright, 2018).

For example, family research in civilian populations has consistently demonstrated that couples' relationship quality, parenting, parent-child relationship quality, and other family processes (e.g., co-parenting, family conflict) influence a range of social, emotional, and behavioral outcomes over life course development (IOM, 2000; NRC and IOM, 2009b; Teubert and Pinquart, 2010). A growing body of research has documented similar influences in military families (see Chapters 5 and 6 for a review). There have been several decades of intervention research demonstrating the effectiveness of family-centered interventions in supporting child, adult, and family well-being in civilian populations across a range of adversities. In this context, family-centered interventions are those that address family members' well-being and target positive parent-child relationships, parenting practices, and other family processes (NRC and IOM, 2009a, 2009b; Siegenthaler et al., 2012).

Reviews of promotional efforts as well as universal, selective, and indicated preventive interventions show that evidence-based interventions can be effective in preventing and reducing substance use (Blitz et al., 2002; Lochman and van den Steenhoven, 2002; Spoth et al., 2008), violence and antisocial behavior (Wilson et al., 2001, 2003), and mental health problems (Durlak and Wells, 1997; Hoagwood et al., 2007), as well as in promoting positive youth development (Catalano et al, 2002; Eccles and Gootman, 2002). Indeed, findings from a meta-analytic review indicate that the results of these interventions are both statistically and practically significant, representing reductions of one-quarter to one-third in base rates in some cases (Wilson and Lipsey, 2007). There is also a growing body of evidence-based and evidence-informed practices, interventions, and programs (referred to collectively as EBPs and EIPs as defined in Chapter 1) that demonstrate the positive impact of couples/relational preventive interventions across a range of health and mental health risks (Crepaz et al., 2015; Kardan-Souraki et al., 2016; Martire et al., 2010).

A review of EIPs and EBPs consistently identifies core elements and processes across a range of contexts. For interventions designed to improve social, emotional, and behavioral outcomes in children and families at risk, core elements often include issue-specific education and developmental guidance, individual and family-level skill development (e.g., emotional regulation, problem solving, communication) and positive parenting practices (IOM, 2000; NRC and IOM, 2009a; Spoth et al., 2002). Furthermore, family-centered programs that emphasize collective processes, resilience, and strengths have been found to be more engaging and culturally acceptable than those interventions focused on addressing individual problems in other contexts (Kumpfer et al., 2002; NRC and IOM, 2009a, 2009b).

BARRIERS TO TRANSLATING EVIDENCE INTO PRACTICE

Over the last 20 years, the National Academies of Sciences, Engineering, and Medicine have convened expert committees to review research and make recommendations of prevention interventions for children and families (for summaries, see Eccles and Gootman, 2002; NRC and IOM, 2009a, 2009b). These studies have usually examined interventions designed to address specific problem areas or risk factors (e.g., parental depression) and have consistently made recommendations both for expanded prevention research and for the wider practice of prevention interventions. As noted by Rotheram-Borus and colleagues (2014), these recommendations have led to the development of hundreds of evidence-based practices (EBPs) that have typically been designed to address a specific problem and then tested within a selected population, within a geographic region, and for a specific delivery setting, such as at home, in schools, or in a community setting. Funding agencies, organizations, and researchers have invested decades of research and financial resources into the development of practices, programs, services guidelines, and interventions demonstrated through rigorous research studies to affect individual-and family-level outcomes.

Although the benefits of using EBPs to support positive developmental and well-being outcomes in children and families with a range of risk factors are solidly grounded in empirical studies,[2] the translation of this evidence

[2]Using a standard validation model for establishing evidence for each problem, context, population, and platform, programs are expected to be tested in at least one randomized trial plus an effectiveness trial to be ready for large-scale diffusion—a model that can take almost two decades to come to fruition (Hawkins et al., 1992; Olds et al., 1988). Research trials of such programs may also include testing of adaptations of EBPs using individualized delivery platforms, such as internet-based or mobile-application delivery tools.

into practice has lagged far behind, as it has for other evidence-based interventions (Bumbarger and Perkins, 2008; Glasgow and Chambers, 2012; Kazdin and Blase, 2011; NRC and IOM, 2009b). Despite the availability of hundreds of evidence-based interventions—such as the Clearinghouse for Military Family Readiness's Continuum of Evidence (Perkins et al., 2015), Blueprints for Violence Prevention,[3] and the Promising Practices Network on Children, Families, and Communities[4]—few proposed EBPs are implemented and sustained in everyday community service settings.

Research trials of EBPs also include testing adaptations of them using individualized delivery platforms, such as internet-based or mobile-application delivery tools. Using a standard biomedical validation model for establishing evidence for each problem, context, population, and platform, programs are then expected to be tested in at least one randomized trial plus an effectiveness trial to be ready for large-scale diffusion—a model that has often taken almost two decades to come to fruition (Hawkins et al., 1992; Olds et al., 1988). Despite extensive investment in randomized trials to establish the benefits of these interventions on a range of child, youth, and adult outcomes, the dissemination of existing EBPs remains quite low within most civilian settings. This well-documented "translational gap" from research to practice poses multiple obstacles within civilian settings, and those problems are only amplified within the DoD context, given its highly diverse population (e.g., diverse by service branch, geography, and family constellation) and the highly dynamic context of military service and military family readiness related to wartime service demands, emerging types of warfare, and changes in policies (e.g., Beardslee et al., 2011, 2013; Dworkin et al., 2008), as well as in highly stressful situations (as described in Chapter 6).

A growing body of research has been examining the underlying assumptions that contribute to this translational gap for both clinical and preventive interventions. This research recognizes the challenges of selecting and implementing evidence-based practices that are relevant to the needs of specific populations across different settings, as well as the limitations of an overreliance on randomized controlled trials in establishing the necessary evidence to inform both internal and external validity in real-world settings (Deaton and Cartwright, 2018; Wike et al., 2014). The research consistently identifies a range of barriers to successful implementation (Perkins et al., 2015), including the limitations of existing EBPs for emerging issues, lack of cultural relevance of the EBP for specific populations, and limitations in available resources required for rigorous implementation, including training, monitoring, infrastructure, and technical support (for a review, see Rotheram-Borus et al., 2012).

---

[3]For more information, see https://www.blueprintsprograms.org.

[4]For more information, see http://www.promisingpractices.net/programs.asp.

These challenges may emerge early, as soon as an organization or system faces the selection process for determining the best program for a specific context or problem. Criteria within some EBP registries have prioritized randomized controlled efficacy trials, which focus on *internal* validity, that is, having minimal chance of confounding variables in the study. Such trials do not commonly include evidence about a program's cultural relevance, adaptability, scalability, or sustainability relevant to *external* validity, that is, how well the results can be generalized across settings or populations. It is also the case that some registries are designed more to assist practitioners in making informed decisions in selecting a program based on their needs, situational factors, and available resources (Karre et al., 2017). An example of the challenges that face local providers and system leaders when they need to identify an EBP is evident from civilian child intervention research, which found that for a large community clinical sample of children, 86 percent of the children were not included in the 435 randomized clinical trials of EBPs when matched for age, gender, and ethnicity (Chorpita et al., 2011).

Others have noted that research on most identified EBPs largely lacks information about or inclusion of community participation or practice in the development and testing of the interventions (Weisz et al., 2006), resulting in a misalignment between the interventions and the realities of community systems. Such misalignments may be especially likely to emerge when providers' and families' voices and experiences, as well as larger system contexts, are not incorporated into the development, measurement, adaptation, and implementation of the EBP and not included as part of the criteria for inclusion into EBP registries (Burkhardt et al., 2015; Means et al., 2015; Santucci et al., 2015; Weisz et al., 2015). As Chambers and Norton (2016) note:

> There is ample documentation of mismatches among interventions, the populations they target, the communities they serve, and the service systems where they are delivered. The documented mismatch can result from multiple factors where the context and target population differ from the original intervention testing, including age, race, ethnicity, culture, organization, language, accessibility, dosage, intensity of intervention, staffing, and resource limitations. (p. S126)

However, these mismatches are often attributed to lack of organizational readiness for disseminating an intervention rather than a potential or actual misalignment between the EBP and the setting (Weisz et al., 2013).

Some researchers have proposed a paradigm shift in how evidence-based interventions are applied, expanded, and disseminated. For example, Chorpita and colleagues (2007) developed and evaluated a so-called "common elements framework" to identify, coordinate, and monitor the delivery of components from an established EBP. This framework focuses on professional training and development and supports a flexible approach to evidence-informed delivery across different settings and populations. Many researchers have advocated for an emphasis on testing core principles and elements that can be flexibly implemented rather than focusing on developing and testing new individual programs (Mohr et al., 2015), as well as an emphasis on identifying intervention "kernels" as fundamental units that underlie effective interventions (Embry and Biglan, 2008). A common elements framework allows researchers and providers first to apply empirical evidence about treatment efficacy and effectiveness, and then to incorporate local evidence and outcomes regarding individual progress through the delivery process (Becker et al., 2013; Chorpita and Daleiden, 2009; Chorpita et al., 2005; Morgan et al., 2018). This may be even more relevant in military communities, where implementations are required to address rapidly emerging requirements in wartime.

REMEDIATING THE BRIDGE FROM EVIDENCE TO PRACTICE

More than a decade ago, the field of dissemination and implementation science began to focus on understanding and improving the evidence-to-practice gap. This new approach arose primarily from failures in the adoption, implementation, and sustainability of evidence-based practices (Kelly, 2012). Dissemination and implementation science (also referred to as "implementation research") can be defined as "a multi-disciplinary set of theories, methods and evidence aimed at improving the processes of translation from research evidence to everyday practices across a wide variety of human service and policy contexts" (Kelly, 2013, p. 1). This science is devoted to rigorously studying research-to-practice gaps to identify effective ways to improve the adaptation, adoption, implementation, and sustainment of evidence-informed and evidence-based practices in routine delivery settings. It is also committed to fostering partnerships with practice organizations to accelerate the transition of interventions from research- to practice-focused settings.

A paper commissioned by the committee (Chambers and Norton, 2018, p. 5) has this to say about implementation science:

> [A]s with many relatively new scientific fields, implementation science is just one of many terms used to generally convey research focused on bridging the research-to-practice gap. Related terms and processes include dissemination, knowledge translation, diffusion, research-to-practice, discovery-to-delivery, quality improvement research, and improvement science, among others.[5]

Dissemination and implementation science includes all the components of this process, including the decision to adopt an intervention within a system, its development and engagement on it with stakeholders, workforce

[5]The authors cite work by McKibbon et al. (2010) to support this point.

skills development (i.e., training, coaching/consultation, and workforce well-being), quality monitoring (i.e., measurement selection, data collection, and quality monitoring and reporting), and administrative management. It can inform behavioral health and social service research and service delivery to guide the processes that can bridge the research-to-practice gap and lead to greater integration of EBP and evidence-informed practice (EIP) into routine service settings (Atkins et al., 2016; Durlak, 2013). While the field has advanced in recent years, Chambers and Norton (2016) assert that it has been limited by current models in which

> . . . the scientific community follows a linear, static, and simplified model of translating research into practice—one that often overlooks the complexity of pathways that better characterize research-to-practice processes. The implications of this traditional model of intervention development (i.e., the optimal path from research to practice proceeds linearly from intervention development to efficacy to effectiveness to implementation) are that the field reifies a set of assumptions that limit what is learned from implementing evidence-based approaches to prevention, and limit the degree to which the field seeks to enhance the fit between evidence-based interventions and delivery settings. (p. S125)

Within this traditional sequence, Chambers and Norton (2016) have identified a number of assumptions that may contribute to challenges in scaling EBPs, as follows. First, they include the assumption that once established, the evidence base for an intervention is stable. In fact, many of the established national registries are well populated by EBPs tested decades ago with relatively small and, in many cases, nonrepresentative convenience samples recruited in community and clinical contexts that have continuously evolved. The assumption that these established EBPs will remain efficacious when implemented at scale with diverse populations and in new contexts is also problematic. The implications of the lag between the research testing cycle and the application are highlighted by trials involving new technology platforms or mobile tools, as the tested delivery platforms may become outdated even within the duration of a single efficacy trial (Kumar et al., 2013).

A second assumption contributing to implementation challenges is that deviation from the established delivery process or manual implementation is considered an erosion of program fidelity inherently leading to reduced impact. This assumption overlooks the potential of "positive drift" that may occur as the intervention is adapted within new settings and populations. Finally, the assumption that dissemination and implementation "come after everything else" may result in a failure to develop interventions that leverage existing resources and local knowledge to improve the relevance and fit of the intervention to the context (Chambers and Norton, 2016).

As mentioned and explicated in this report, the well-documented "translational gap" from research to practice not only poses multiple obstacles within civilian settings; those problems are amplified within DoD, given the highly diverse population it embraces (e.g., service branch, geography, family constellation), the dynamic context of military service and military family readiness related to deployments, and other demands and changes in policies (Beardslee et al., 2011, 2013; Dworkin et al., 2008). The remainder of this chapter documents the committee's suggested approach to addressing this issue.

ONGOING ADAPTATION FRAMEWORK FOR A COMPLEX MILITARY FAMILY READINESS SYSTEM

Applying both the population-level and ecological models presented earlier in this report to examine military family well-being, the committee extends these to inform the continuum of military family readiness services that would be responsive to the complex and emergent needs of a complex adaptive system (see Figure 7-1 in Chapter 7). Using an ecological model to inform implementation enables providers, installation services, and leaders to comprehensively address the various levels and contexts influencing military families. As discussed in Chapter 7, the continuum of coordinated support within the Military Family Readiness System builds on local capacities, strengths, and resources and incorporates both DoD-level and local knowledge within the selection, adaptation, adoption, and implementation of support services.

As Atkins (2016, p. 215) argues, "This paradigm shift for dissemination and implementation science, away from an overemphasis on promoting program adoption, calls for fitting interventions within settings that matter most to . . . . healthy development, and utilizing and strengthening available community resources." Developing a comprehensive approach to support implementation requires the MFRS to utilize embedded assessment and monitoring in the implementation of programming and to develop an integrated information infrastructure (refer to Figure 7-4 for detailed components) that supports continuous quality improvement analogous to a learning health system, characterized here as a "learning MFRS."

Systematic, planned adaptation, often considered necessary to support the effective implementation of an EBP, can occur at multiple phases during the lifecycle of the implementation process. Note that rapid implementation, while sometimes necessary, should be avoided. At the very least, clear systematic review and data is required to assess the implementation and identify areas of needed improvement. Adaptation can be defined as the degree to which an EBP is modified by a user during adoption and implementation to suit the needs of the setting or to improve the fit to local conditions (Rabin et al., 2008; Rogers, 2010). Indeed, Chambers and colleagues (2013) have proposed that sustainability should be reconceived as the ongoing adaptation of an intervention that is supported by continuous learning and problem solving, with a focus "on fit between interventions and multi-level contexts."

The Dynamic Sustainability Framework (see Figure 8-1) illustrates how the adaptation of interventions may occur over time. It also conveys the role of continuous monitoring in supporting the integration and sustainability of interventions as they are adapted to the ever-changing context in which they are delivered, including changes occurring in the delivery setting, the target population, the evidence base, the political context, and other key variables that are known to occur over time (Chambers et al., 2013). To this end,

> adaptation should be supported—and even encouraged—during the implementation process, rather than conceptualized as something that should not occur because it leads to suboptimal levels of fidelity to intervention components, and subsequently reduces the impact of the intervention on changing behaviors or outcomes among the target population as compared to the initial or original trial testing the intervention. (Chambers and Norton, 2018, p. 15)

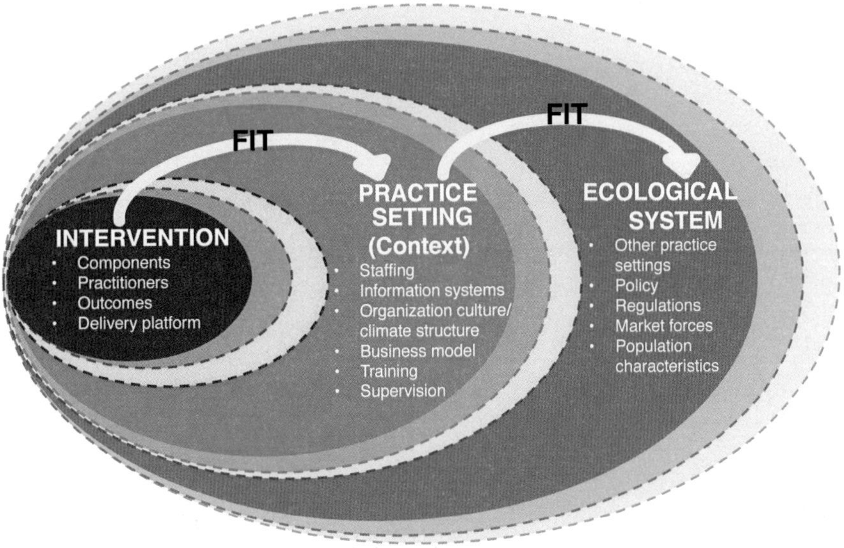

FIGURE 8-1 Dynamic sustainability framework.
SOURCE: Adapted from Chambers et al. (2013).

Planned and purposeful intervention adaptation can occur during all phases of the implementation process. Intervention adaptation can be informed by feasibility and acceptability testing, with potential end-users being asked to deliver the intervention or to define the outcomes related to well-being. Both qualitative (e.g., focus groups, interviews) and quantitative (e.g., surveys) data can be used to guide the planned adaptation of interventions, recognizing that too many significant or substantive changes to an intervention may be less desirable—and to some extent could resemble a new intervention that should then undergo its own rigorous testing before being branded as evidence-based. How much adaptation occurs before an existing EBP resembles a different intervention and should undergo separate evaluation is a significant yet unanswered question in the field. Optimally, implementers are given guidance on exercising flexibility in areas of program delivery that are not hypothesized to be directly responsible for program outcomes, while adhering to program components that are core to the EBP's theory of change. In other words, there can be "adaptation with fidelity" (Domitrovch et al., 2012; Weist and Murray, 2008).

There are many types of adaptations that can (or should) occur to an EBP. Effective interventions proposed for implementation should include parameters for fidelity monitoring that anticipate adaptation, that is, by naming which elements can and should be modified for context and culture and which are core, essential elements that cannot be modified (Bumbarger and Perkins, 2008). Stirman and colleagues (2013) proposed a framework and coding system for modifications and adaptations to EBP based on a systematic review of the literature. Their intervention adaptations were classified into five broad categories and associated subcategories (Stirman et al., 2013, Figure 2, p. 6). Their five main categories reflect five key questions about the adaptation process:

1. *By whom* are modifications made (e.g., individual, team, researcher)?
2. *What* is modified (e.g., content, context, training and evaluation)?
3. At *what level* of delivery (for whom/what) are modifications made (e.g., group level, hospital level, network level)?
4. *To what* are context modifications made (e.g., to format, to setting, to population)?
5. What is the *nature* of the content modification (e.g., tailoring, substituting, reordering)?

Building on this taxonomy, Chambers and Norton (2016) expanded the types of intervention adaptations as part of what they call the "Adaptome," a proposed set of approaches, processes, and infrastructure needed to advance the science of intervention adaptation. Sources of intervention adaptations (and example questions) include *service setting* (e.g., Who delivers the intervention? How does the proposed intervention fit with other interventions?); *target audience* (e.g., literacy, comorbid conditions, age-appropriateness), *mode of delivery* (e.g., dose of core components, number of sessions), *culture* (e.g., cultural sensitivity, use of imagery), and *core components* (e.g., mechanisms of action, core components identified through testing). See Figure 8-2.

The "Adaptome" approach to implementation provides a methodology that can support the integration of evidence—including both traditional standards of evidence and phases of EIP and EBP development and validation—while also addressing local needs. The latter aspect is important because distinctive local needs sometimes lead local providers to design and deliver their own programs ahead of evidence for effectiveness (Hallett et al., 2007). Using the Adaptome approach, and supplementing this with existing literature on the science of intervention adaptation, in the following pages we present several examples of ways in which existing EBPs can be adapted, monitored, and refined over time to meet the needs of military family resilience and well-being in the military health care and community settings in which they could be delivered. This methodology supports the integration of evidence-informed and evidence-based practice with "practice-based evidence" within a Dynamic Sustainability Framework (DSF) (Chambers and Norton, 2016).

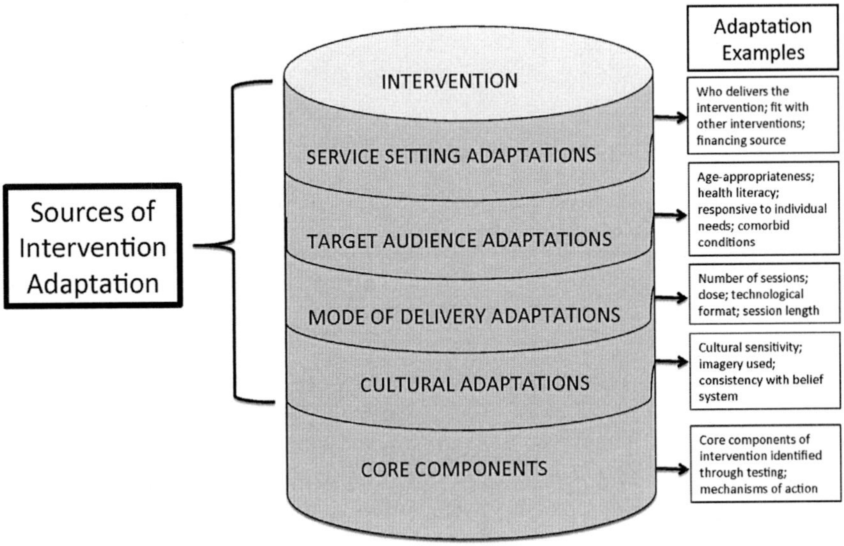

FIGURE 8-2 Sources of intervention adaptations.
SOURCE: Chambers and Norton (2016).

Adaptation to Service Settings

A well designed adaptation to a service setting will seek to better align the original evidence-based intervention with the original setting in which it is delivered. This may include changes to who delivers the intervention to military families (including active service members, children, parents, couples, caregivers, and other family members), assessment of the fit between the proposed EIP/ EBP and interventions that are already being delivered in the setting that are consistent with the organizational mission but complement other available interventions, and resources and capacity to deliver the intervention within existing systems, such as schools, early childhood programs, and primary care and community centers. Resources and capacity, in turn, include personnel, funding, organizational culture, absorptive capacity, time constraints, and competing demands.

Task-shifting is one approach commonly leveraged in low-resource settings, whereby systems with a dearth of professionally trained providers rely instead on community health workers, lay personnel, peers, or volunteers to deliver prevention programs. In this situation, it may be decided that the alternative implementers of the new prevention program need additional training and ongoing coaching or supervision, but are nonetheless able to receive that while maintaining or even improving patient-level outcomes. Regular program monitoring is required to identify any additional needs of the implementers within the system and how those needs may change over time. Such monitoring may involve tracking customer outcomes, feedback from staff, input from implementers, and practical measures of ongoing intervention adaptation. The results of the monitoring may have implications for the training of new implementers as others may transition to other responsibilities.

Target Audience Adaptations

Target audience adaptations involve adjustments to create a better fit between the intervention and the proposed target population. These adaptations may include changing the format and language used in the intervention (e.g., materials, workbooks, flyers) to better match the literacy levels of the target population. They could include use of instructional examples that are more relevant to the target population, such as having pictures included in intervention materials, or having names and locations of delivery sites, or localizing the available resources. To better achieve such matches, rapid-cycle usability testing[6] can be done on an

---

[6]A model of using small tests to accelerate improvement. See http://www.ihi.org/about/Pages/innovationscontributions.aspx.

individual basis or in a group setting. Interviews or focus groups could be employed to identify needed adaptations, such as by asking members of the target population to review intervention materials and identify aspects that they feel are relevant to them, aspects that are irrelevant, and aspects that should be modified to fit their needs. This approach could be leveraged over time to make improvements to intervention materials delivered within the same setting, or in subsequent iterations of the intervention as it is delivered to members of the target population in different geographic regions, having different literacy rates, or within different age ranges.

Delivery Adaptations

This type of adaptation focuses on changes that may be needed concerning how the intervention is delivered in terms of number of sessions (e.g., 5 vs. 10 sessions), length of sessions (e.g., 60 minutes vs. 3 hours), frequency of sessions (e.g., 4 weeks vs. 10 weeks), and mode of delivery (e.g., online vs. in-person; individual vs. group-based; clinic vs. telehealth; text messages vs. phone; active *vs.* passive telephone outreach).

For example, consider an evidence-based intervention that was originally developed in a group-based setting for 2 hours a week for 12 weeks. Although retention rates were high in the original study, this may be due in part to the participants' having received a generous incentive to complete the intervention. In fact, given the military's high operational tempo, as discussed in Chapter 2, military service members and their families may be unlikely to have time to attend all sessions along with their other responsibilities, interests, and demands. This is a common barrier in implementation and receptivity among target populations: Interventions are often designed without consideration of their viability outside the context of a highly controlled environment in a research trial, and subsequently they prove to be of no interest to the target population. This is particularly true for interventions that require a lot of time or frequent off-site visits or that rely on the participation of other group members to be effective. As an alternative, one might explore the possibility of delivering part of an intervention through private, group-based portals and reducing the number and frequency of sessions. If child-care duties are barriers to in-person participation, one may consider using barrier reduction components (Morgan et al., 2018), such as delivering the intervention in a school-based or day-care setting, to reduce impediments to participation.

Suggestions for ways to increase participation and interest in an intervention while maintaining sufficient delivery and dosage should be informed by input from the target population (as noted in Chapter 7 under "Community Engagement and Participatory Partnerships") in advance of intervention adaptations. Again, rapid-cycle evaluations can be used to inform iterations to the intervention over time as well as across geographic regions or other characteristics that may suggest the need for altered adaptations to the delivery (i.e., in dose, frequency, format, or length) as it is scaled up to other areas.

Cultural Adaptations

Cultural adaptations are essential to consider as an ongoing part of the implementation process. Often, cultural adaptations require important yet relatively subtle changes to the content of an intervention that are critical to its perceived acceptability, relevance, and credibility to the target population. Cultural adaptations go beyond minor changes to the names, locations, and lists of relevant resources and services. They include changes to culture-specific nomenclature used in intervention materials, which may vary by geographic region or by subpopulation, for example by urban versus rural; in the use of "y'all" versus "you all" for Southern versus non-Southern target populations; or by African American young adults versus African American middle-aged adults. They also include changes to culture-specific pictures (including age, gender, race/ethnicity, appearance), examples, or scenarios used in intervention materials or content, and changes that may need to occur such that the adapted intervention is consistent with the general beliefs of the target population (e.g., religiosity, stigma, social and personal attitudes, medical mistrust). Additional guidance for what types of cultural adaptations should be considered during the adaptation process are available in the literature (Bernal and Domenech Rodríguez, 2012; Cabassa and Baumann, 2013).

Core Component Adaptations

Finally, core components (also defined as core elements) are conceptualized as the "active ingredients" of an EBP, without which one would not see the intended impact on changes in behaviors and well-being outcomes among the target population (Chorpita, 2007; Embry and Biglan, 2008). The research designs to identify the exact core components of an intervention (unlike peripheral components that can be significantly changed or deleted without affecting was outcomes) are logistically challenging, costly, and impractical. Thus, alternative modes are recommended for identifying core intervention components that should be neither removed nor significantly altered during the adaptation and implementation process. This may be done, for example, through conversations with the original intervention developers and by relying on those theoretical constructs that have been demonstrated to be required for effective behavior change (i.e., skills-training and education versus education only).

An Integrated Information Infrastructure to Inform Adaptation

As noted in the Dynamic Sustainability Framework (2013) and further articulated by the Adaptome, multiple data sources and types of data are needed to inform and guide intervention adaptations for greater impact at the population level and to achieve higher quality in promotional and preventive practices for the MFRS. Within the military service context, several existing datasets could be leveraged to guide intervention adaptations, and others could be developed to inform the adaptation process consistent with learning from practice-based evidence that has been generated through local delivery in community settings such as schools and primary care. For example, better dissemination of the findings from the Status of Forces Survey of Reserve Component Members and others administered by the Office of People Analytics could be used to systematically identify the needs of different subgroups of reservists and the context in which those needs can be met. Responses could help prioritize what interventions are most needed by different types of personnel in the community (e.g., social network capacity building, alcohol prevention, spousal communication, reintegration) and the preferred delivery format (e.g., individual, group, phone, text, online). This information could be used to help guide the selection of interventions for their target populations, such as existing interventions developed for civilian populations found within the Clearinghouse for Military Family Readiness[7] (Perkins et al., 2015), an online intervention compendium.[8]

An infrastructure to support quality monitoring and integrated information is required to ensure quality service delivery. It is also required to capture local innovations by identifying emerging practices and adaptations responsive to the voices of military-connected communities and families. Additional items could be added to the Status of Forces Survey of Reserve Component Members to help monitor beliefs, attitudes, health literacy, and other characteristics that can help guide the selection of and inform initial adaptations to evidence-based interventions across various sources of intervention adaptation. This may be an efficient way to help select and initially adapt an intervention. It could be bolstered by select follow-up local surveys or group-based feedback on specific adaptations that may be needed to further enhance the fit between the intervention and the overall setting.

Additional surveys and studies—such as the Millennium Cohort Study, Military Family Life Project, Deployment Life Study, Veterans Metric Initiative, and organizational climate and community assessment surveys—can help track trends over time and indicate what additional adaptations may be needed for certain types of service members and their families. They can highlight what priorities, conditions, and contexts change over time for

[7]See https://militaryfamilies.psu.edu.

[8]See https://militaryfamilies.psu.edu/wp-content/uploads/2018/08/A-Tool-for-Assessing-Fit-and-Feasibility-9-9-17.pdf.

BOX 8-1
Applying a System-Level Approach: The Building Capacity Consortium

An example of applying a system-level approach to assess and address the needs of military-connected students is the Building Capacity Consortium (hereafter the Consortium). Designed to improve school climate and student experience, the Consortium was a partnership with eight military-connected school districts in Southern California and included 145 schools that serve roughly 117,000 students, 10.1 percent of whom are military children.

The Consortium's work was designed to be a process for systemic-regional-organizational intervention to evaluate a diverse set of outcomes, including community and school priorities and participation at every level of design. The design and methodology purposefully encouraged the use of multiple sources of data and variability across the districts and schools, and they provided qualitative and quantitative data on the multiple outcomes monitored in numerous local contexts.

Monitoring and mapping work for the Consortium was based on the assumption that schools, neighborhoods, and communities vary widely inorganizational, cultural, and economic terms and in capacity/resource issues, so that the normal classification of EBPs would likely fail and would not be sustained across local contexts. The system-level intervention utilized a monitoring infrastructure that included an existing statewide survey, the California Healthy Kids Survey (https://calschls.org), which was modified by BCC to include a military module that was optional to all California schools. The system monitoring also included local monitoring to respond to the specific needs of the Consortium districts and schools, assessing the needs and strengths of each district and every school so that programs/interventions could be selected on each of these levels and then be tailored to fit the local needs, implemented, and evaluated. Based on the findings and insights gained from this systematic monitoring, participating schools were provided with ongoing feedback for continuous improvement and summative evaluation.

different subgroups. Administrative and reporting databases can help inform intervention designers and implementers of the needs of target populations, adoption and use of evidence-informed and evidence-based interventions (e.g., guidelines delivered in clinical care), suggested adaptations, and monitoring of adaptations over time. For example, datasets in the Defense Manpower Data Center could be triangulated to identify target populations in greatest need of additional or more intense mental health treatments, based on prevalence rates of posttraumatic stress disorder, suicidality, or depression. Additional civilian datasets can be augmented with military identifiers to track military child and family needs, align policy, and monitor interventions.[9]

[9]For more information, see https://www.militarychild.org/resources/policies-initiatives?topic=36.

The system-level intervention was implemented as an evolving set of interventions designed to change the system, organization, and resource capacity of the *region* rather than the program alone, which is the more traditional evidence-based program approach. Over a nine-year period, the system intervention was monitored using multiple methods, including an intense multiyear monitoring process in the 145 schools across the eight school districts as well as control schools. The monitoring continued for three years after the end of project-supported intervention activities to assess longer-term sustainability and effectiveness. In a three-year follow up after active implementation in schools, this process done "at scale" was effective in reducing school bullying and victimization, as well as reducing incidence in several categories of substance use and gang affiliation during the intervention process—for both elementary and secondary schools. The clear majority of the 145 schools showed strong and significant reductions in these areas. When comparing outcomes one year and again three years after the intervention, it is clear that many of these reductions continue over time.

As an example highly relevant to the complex adaptive MFRS, this system-level intervention demonstrates the potential of an alternative rigorous method to advance the field beyond conventional tests of smaller-scale programs and interventions that are not sustainable and do not generalize to scaled-up implementation efforts in complex community settings such as public schools. The approach suggests that large-scale impact can be achieved through a monitoring framework that embraces the huge variations in local circumstances, needs, and preferences while providing an empirical basis that helps to select the existing evidence-based programs most appropriate for each local context, helps to implement them, and helps to evaluate their impact in the local context. Furthermore, a systemwide monitoring helps to identify promising grassroots interventions and test them in a scientifically accepted way.

SOURCES: Astor and Benbenisthy (2018), Benbenishty (2014).

Two promotional and prevention models that have used continuous quality data monitoring in civilian communities have demonstrated their success in improving youth development outcomes: the PROSPER (PROmoting School-community-university Partnerships to Enhance Resilience) model (Spoth et al., 2004, 2011) and the Communities That Care system (Hawkins et al., 1992, 2002). Each of these community-level interventions includes a data infrastructure for monitoring and mapping, as well as an infrastructure for support of innovation, analytics, training, service delivery, and technical support (coaching) that promote ongoing learning (Chilenski et al., 2016). These components are consistent with the integrated information infrastructure presented in Chapter 7 (refer to Figure 7-4). Box 8-1 provides an example of how to apply such a system-level approach.

Applying Implementation Science to the MFRS

Implementation involves a deliberate set of change strategies to integrate a program, intervention, or practice across contexts and settings (Damschroder and Hagedorn, 2011; Fixsen et al., 2005). Kelly (2013) has defined *discrete* implementation strategies as involving a single process or action, such as establishing reminders or educational meetings. By contrast, *multifaceted* implementation strategies include those that use two or more discrete strategies—such as training and technical assistance, organizational change, and external facilitation—to facilitate the adoption and integration of an evidence-based intervention into routine-care settings (Powell et al., 2012). To date, more than 60 implementation strategies have been identified from literature reviews and expert input. These strategies include planning strategies, educational strategies, financial strategies, restructuring strategies, quality management strategies, and policy context strategies (Powell et al., 2012). Generally, a combination of strategies (rather than a single strategy) is needed to effectively move an evidence-based intervention into routine practice.

To monitor an intervention or policy implementation as part of a complex adaptive system such as MFRS requires that one continually assess the implementation itself. As noted in Chapter 7, the implementation outcomes to be assessed include the program's acceptability, feasibility, appropriateness, adoption, cost, fidelity, penetration, and sustainability, as described by Proctor and colleagues (2011). Outcomes can be assessed across the phases of implementation; for example, acceptability, feasibility, and appropriateness may be best assessed at the planning phase for implementation within a specific context, whereas fidelity and penetration may be best suited for assessment during the implementation and maintenance phase. Sustainability is often assessed approximately six months to two years after the funding for the initial implementation of an evidence-based intervention has ceased (Scheirer and Dearing, 2011), so that what is assessed is essentially the extent to which the intervention can be integrated into routine delivery settings or institutionalized as standard practice. As noted in Chapter 7 and as outlined in the measurement section, qualitative and quantitative approaches can be used to assess implementation outcomes.

Dissemination and implementation science has supported the delivery of a tiered-population approach to promotion and prevention, consistent with the Spectrum of Coordinated Support presented in Chapter 7 (refer to Figure 7-1). Screening, promotion, and prevention practices can be integrated into community-, school- and family-care settings so that they are customized to suit family needs or to suit the timing, dose, provider, or platform needs. One of the most well developed and researched examples of this type of population-level approach within civilian settings is the Triple P (Positive Parenting Program), designed as a comprehensive strategy to promote skilled parenting and to prevent parenting problems early, delivering on-demand services that are standardized to include evidence-based components and tiers based on higher levels of need (Turner and Sanders, 2006).

Another example of a population-level approach, described previously in Chapter 7, is the New Orientation to Reduce Threats to Health from Secretive Problems That Affect Readiness (NORTH STAR) Program, designed to prevent substance use problems, family maltreatment, and suicide. Designed to be integrated into an existing delivery system within active-duty Air Force installations, NORTH STAR is an integrated delivery system involving commanders and providers partnered with Air Force community action and information boards at each of the 10 major commands (Heyman et al., 2011). The partners at each command selected the programs that matched their specific risk and protective factor profiles, using a guide on evidence-based programs that called for rating the programs according to evaluation outcomes and targeted risk and protective factors. The guide also includes training, implementation, and survey evaluation protocols. The use of a framework, delivery system, and guide to select prevention programs that fit a particular base's risk and protective factor profile is based on extensive community-based prevention research strategies that have been evaluated in civilian populations (Heyman and Smith Slep, 2001; Pentz, 2003; Riggs et al., 2009).

Sustainability

Sustaining effective programs and services is one of the critical goals of the MFRS. Sustainability definitions in the literature vary, but most include the continuation of the implementation of effective programs or services with the intent of maintaining positive outcomes in the served communities (Johnson et al., 2004; Scheirer, 2005; Scheirer and Dearing, 2011). The effective functioning of a complex adaptive support system, like MFRS, is designed: (1) to facilitate the high-quality implementation and ongoing management and improvement of effective programs and services; and (2) to provide capacity for the programs and services to overcome potentially disorganizing changes, such as staff turnover or shifts in funding availability (Gruen et al., 2008; Scheirer, 2005).

Multiple factors are linked to increased sustainability; however, for the complex adaptive system infrastructure two factors seem essential: a continuous quality improvement process and ongoing, proactive technical assistance (e.g., implementation coaching) (Bumbarger and Perkins, 2008; Chilenski et al., 2015, 2016; Rhoades et al., 2012; Tibbits et al., 2010). For the complex adaptive system, a continuous quality improvement process provides actionable data linked to various outcomes, such as implementation, service, and customer/participant outcomes (Procter et al., 2011). These data are employed by the system to ensure that the proactive technical assistance addresses any unwanted "reactionary drift" from protocols within programs and services, compared to planned and tested adaptations, as well as guiding specific adaptations or innovations. Moreover, identifying what programs or services need to be sustained or what components of those programs and services should be maintained (e.g., partial sustainability) demands data garnered from a continuous quality improvement (CQI) process.

To be strategic, effective, and efficient, a complex adaptive support system, like MFRS, demands a systematic formal process for determining (1) how to initiate a new program or service, (2) how to sustain an existing program or service, and (3) how and when to sunset or decommission a program or service. The evidence of effectiveness of programs and services, through rigorous evaluation, to meet real-world needs provides clear guidance as to whether those efforts should be sustained or discontinued. As newly identified family needs emerge, the system is required to engage in a service-design or program-identification process that effectively addresses those needs. Box 8-2 describes an example of how a program was sunsetted.

ADAPTATION AND CONTINUOUS QUALITY MONITORING USING A LEARNING SYSTEM FRAMEWORK

As noted earlier, an integrated approach to implementation and adaptation requires a spectrum of coordinated support and an integrated information infrastructure that supports the mapping of emerging needs as well as continuous quality monitoring (also refer to Figure 7-1 in Chapter 7).

Supporting a Learning Infrastructure

A useful model for achieving greater accountability, agility, and family/client-centered outcomes in the complex adaptive MFRS may be drawn from the "learning health system" framework, defined here as a *learning infrastructure*. The use of a learning infrastructure within a complex adaptive system helps ensure that implementation strategies are used, enhances interpretability of research findings, and bolsters the use of critical implementation strategies (Ferlie and Dopson, 2006; Pawson et al., 2005; Proctor et al., 2013).

The Institute of Medicine (IOM, now the National Academy of Medicine) defines a learning infrastructure as a structure in which "science, informatics, incentives, and culture are aligned for continuous improvement and innovation, with evidence-informed and/or promising practices seam-

BOX 8-2
Adapting a Program Sunsetting:
The Joint Family Support Assistance Program

The Joint Family Support Assistance Program (JFSAP) was developed in 2007 to address the needs of geographically separated service members and their families, especially those serving in the National Guard and Reserves as a result of their unprecedented multiple, lengthy deployments. Before the program parameters were determined, staff from Military Community and Family Policy (MC&FP) met with National Guard state program directors and headquarters staff to assess the needs that were manifesting. Utilizing the resources that MC&FP had to offer, teams were deployed to each state headquarters to support the efforts of the state family program director who is ultimately responsible for the well-being of all military personnel and their families residing in their state. A Military OneSource consultant and two Military Family Life Counselors (MFLCs), one of which could be a financial counselor, were deployed to work with the families in each state.

Over time, as deployments drew down, this program was reassessed. Although it was not curtailed, the scope of the program was shifted to become an on-demand program rather than embedding three contract employees in every state regardless of the size of the population that needed to be served. This actually broadened the availability of support throughout the states. The nomenclature of JFSAP and its embedded teams were "sunsetted," but the delivery of services continued through Military OneSource and MFLC programs.

SOURCE: Thompson (2018).

lessly embedded in the delivery process and new knowledge captured as an integral by-product of the delivery experience"[10] (IOM, 2011). The IOM has organized a continuous learning infrastructure into four foundational elements: (1) science and informatics, with real-time access to knowledge and digital capture of the service experience; (2) partnerships between providers, families, and data scientists with engaged and empowered families; (3) incentives that are aligned for value, but with full transparency; and (4) a leadership-instilled culture of continuous learning with supportive system competencies (IOM, 2013).

Big Data

Within a learning infrastructure, big data and predictive analytics have significant potential to promote military family readiness and well-being by

[10]See https://nam.edu/programs/value-science-driven-health-care/learning-health-system-series.

supporting forward-looking data-driven decisions and policies. The service delivery, provider education and training, military family and community partnerships, civilian sector partnerships, research and development, and performance improvement strategies included in the MFRS lend themselves to the development of predictive analytics. Large amounts of service delivery data and sociodemographic and socioeconomic data can be merged and harmonized in order to systematize practitioner-supported practices and to respond to emerging needs. If combined with the delivery of EIP/EBP, broad military family participation would provide extensive data points from both quantitative and qualitative data sources and would facilitate optimal service delivery, maximizing military family readiness and well-being.

Other systems using a learning infrastructure have already had a successful track record using big data to improve outcomes (Dabek and Caban, 2015; Raghupathi and Raghupathi, 2014). These could serve as models for MFRS. For instance, within the health care field, systems that harvest data across multiple service delivery systems, registries, and payers have allowed providers with real-time tools to improve the quality and value of care, allowing for a renewed focus on preventative practices (Coffron and Opelka, 2015). Private-sector initiatives that trawl through patient data to provide better care for low-income Medicaid beneficiaries (Farr, 2018) account for socioeconomic and sociodemographic differences; accounting for such differences is similarly important in military communities and for military providers, considering the diversity of trainees, active-duty members, and their families. Ultimately, the big data that are generated by military service members, their families, and networks form the backbone of the learning infrastructure within an optimized complex adaptive system for military families.

Continuous Quality Improvement

Continuous quality improvement (CQI) is a necessary component of the learning infrastructure in a complex adaptive system. CQI enables the system to be data driven with an aim of cultivating adaptations and adjustments within services, programs, and resources. Standard CQI protocol involves the systematic and constant collection of data (Langley et al., 2009) whose content should be multilevel, spanning administration, implementation, service, and customers. Being data driven within a complex adaptive system also means that all stakeholders make use of the data in their daily decision making as they implement and adapt policies, services, programs, resources, and practices. The data being collected on outcomes (i.e., implementation, service and customer/participant outcomes) provide regular feedback about adaptations and adjustments in terms of feasibility, outcomes, and impact. Client-level assessment tools can be incorporated into the routine delivery of programs for military families, with assessment occurring at program entry, program exit, and ongoing as appropriate. CQI can then be embedded in the implementation infrastructure of a complex adaptive system, which uses the continuous data to provide a practice-learning hub. The hub can use active communication feedback loops to advance the innovations among the various stakeholders (e.g., practitioners and policy analysts). To accomplish this, the MFRS needs to build a strong information systems infrastructure that can support the collection, management, storage, and analysis of these data. This could provide important evidence regarding the implementation, service, and participant outcomes.

The goal of CQI is to provide actionable data that enable the complex adaptive system to address various outcomes, such as implementation, service, and customer outcomes, through specific identifiable adaptations or innovations (Procter, 2011). Thus, the CQI process is constantly testing specific identifiable adaptations with an emphasis on substantive change, such that the "*art* of improvement is combined with the *science* of improvement" (Langley et al., 2009, p. 6). In short, CQI is embedded within learning infrastructure that involves strategic, action-planning models to develop, manage, improve, and evaluate interventions (i.e., policies, programs, services, resources, and practices) (Davidoff et al., 2008).

The Dynamic Sustainability Framework provides a strong conceptual description for system-level CQI that recognizes and accommodates the constancy of change in the use of interventions over time, the characteristics of service settings, and the broader system contexts (whether military or civilian) that determine how services are delivered and by whom (Chambers et al., 2013). A CQI process sensitive to change is critical in the military context. For example, military members and their families are highly mobile, and every summer large numbers of them receive permanent change of station (PCS) orders, requiring them to move to other jobs and/or installations. Similarly, changes to staff, new leadership, and changing military priorities can all disrupt the system's efforts. Informed by CQI data to continually improve services, programs, and resources, a complex adaptive system like MFRS acknowledges these constant changes and provides adaptive, dynamic, and fluid strategies to support the MFRS.

Centering the CQI process on the innovation, the context in which the intervention is delivered (e.g., a child development center), and the broader ecological system within which the practice operates (e.g., the Service Branches and DoD) helps ensure that the ultimate benefit of the innovation will be for family well-being and readiness outcomes within a practice setting and context. Characteristics of the setting and context include human and capital resources, organizational culture and climate, power structures, and processes for training and supervision of staff. These setting and contextual characteristics directly influence the ability of an intervention to reach the targeted population. As a result, the system's CQI process demands on-going measurement of setting and context such that strategic changes to the context and/or adaptions to the intervention can be made to resolve problems of fit. In most cases, the practice setting needs support to build its capacity for innovation and progression.

An Example of a DoD Family Readiness Program

FOCUS (Families Over-Coming Under Stress) is one example of an existing DoD military family readiness program with the potential to apply an adaptive approach to implementation consistent with a dynamic sustainability framework. Designed to strengthen family resilience, the program was adapted from the developers' evidence-based practices, which had been found through randomized control trials over longitudinal follow-up to improve parenting, family functioning, and youth and parent outcomes.

The common-core intervention elements in FOCUS were defined through expert consensus on shared contributing structures, processes, and other elements (Beardslee et al., 2003, 2007; Layne et al., 2008; Rotheram-Borus et al., 2004; for review see Lester et al., 2016). Four common core elements were defined, namely: (1) evidence-based assessment and real-time personalized guidance; (2) context-specific education, such as trauma-and resilience-informed education, positive parenting, and developmental guidance; (3) individual and family-level skill development (for such skills as emotional regulation, problem solving, communication, goal setting, managing separation/trauma reminders); and (4) the development/sharing of individual and family-level narrative communication timelines. These elements were customized, piloted, and manualized using a community participatory methodology (as reviewed in Chapter 7) with military providers, families, and leaders that informed intervention tailoring and implementation design (Beardslee et al., 2013; Lester et al., 2010; Saltzman et al., 2011).

Delivered within DoD as a suite of services based on EBP core elements, FOCUS services are delivered as a tiered continuum of prevention consistent with a population health model (National Research Council and Institute of Medicine [NRC and IOM], 2009b). These services range from universal to indicated[11] prevention services, and they use multiple platforms to support flexible engagement, screening, and intervention delivery, including educational workshops, web-based/mobile tools, skills groups, consultations, and in-person and in-home tele-prevention video-teleconferencing multi-session family interventions (Beardslee et al., 2011, 2013). Between 2008 and 2018, FOCUS services have been implemented for active

[11] *Indicated* care signifies the care designed only for those individuals showing warning signs of a problem.

duty families at 24 installations with consistently high levels of engagement and participation across the continuum of tiered services, as well as high adherence by families within the multisession models.

Follow-up evaluations of the multi-session family intervention and its adaptations have demonstrated significant and sustained individual and family-level outcomes up to six months later. In adults, these evaluations showed reductions in depression, anxiety, and PTSD symptoms; in children, they found decreased internalizing and externalizing symptoms, improved prosocial behaviors, reduced anxiety, and improved coping; and they further found improved family/couple adjustment (Lester et al., 2011, 2016; Saltzman et al., 2016). The CQI process embedded in the implementation has informed multiple adaptations of the model based on data monitoring and community participation, needs, and trends. These adaptations have included specific adaptations of FOCUS for specific family constellations (e.g. FOCUS Couples; FOCUS Early Childhood), context (e.g. FOCUS-Wounded, Ill and Injured) and platform (e.g. TeleFOCUS, FOCUS On the Go!) (Ardslee et al, 2013). As described in Chapter 7, the adaptation for early childhood delivered as an in-home telehealth platform has recently been evaluated through a randomized trial, which found that it demonstrated improvements in reported parenting stress, parent-child relationships, and observed parenting and reduced parental PSTD symptoms compared to a web-based parenting curriculum (Mogil et al., in review). Lessons from the large-scale implementation have been translated to reach military-connected couples and families in a range of settings, including school systems, international military, community mental health, and veteran-serving organizations (Garcia et al., 2015; Ijadi-Maghsoodi et al., 2017; Karnik, 2018; NATO, 2019; Tanielian et al., 2018), providing an example of the relevance of this approach across multiple systems.

How Big Data Can Support an Effective Learning System Framework

Big data, first defined in 2003, refers to the rapidly increasing volume of available data, the velocity at which data are generated, and the ways in which the data are represented (Hashem et al., 2015). Big data provides opportunities to successfully build a culture and infrastructure to support a learning MFRS that aligns with CQI monitoring as described above. To be successfully utilized for military family readiness and well-being, big data must be integrated into four major categories while also following the principles of Plan-Do-Study-Act or PDSA, (Agency for Healthcare Research and Quality, 2008; Deming, 1986) as outlined in Table 8-1.

Several important National Academies reports have outlined the benefits of using big data to improve services and health care for active service members and to provide insight into how future military members will access services. For example, in a 2014 Institute of Medicine report, the committee recommended that DoD implement comprehensive family- and patient-centered evidence-based prevention programming directed toward psychological health in military families, spouses, partners, and children (IOM, 2014). Such targeted strategies are likely to be most successful when born out of an effective learning system that incorporates the PDSA cycle outlined in Table 8-1.

Applying the Donabedian Framework in the Context of Big Data

The conceptual model shown in Figure 8-3 illustrates how collection, analysis, and dissemination of big data can use the Donabedian framework (as described in Chapter 7) to provide higher-quality services to and improve the well-being of military families. The structural elements include the infrastructure and data components from which the data points are collected, including the provider teams, active service members and their families, and service programs, schools, and community facilities, as well as population-level data for the group as a whole. As part of the process measures, the data would be transferred to a web services platform that allows for data cleaning, standardization, and visualization. Output to

TABLE 8-1 Big Data Utilization Within a Continuous Learning System Using the IOM Learning System Framework Integrated with Plan-Do-Study-Act (PDSA) Principles

Science and Informatics	Partnerships among Military Families, Providers, Leadership, And Data Scientists	Incentives	Continuous Learning Culture
Plan: Enable real-time access to knowledge and digital capture of all components of the care experience for military families in data-safe environments.	Do: Engage and empower military families in the data being captured with data-use agreements that emphasize enhanced data security.	Study: Collect meaningful data aligned with values in military families; create a fully transparent, data-safe system that avoids wasting resources and inaccurate predictions supporting poor decisions.	Act: Create a leadership-instilled culture of rigorous, continuous review of the data using algorithms supported by machine learning and driven by a multidisciplinary thought team that critically evaluates policies and preserves data safety.

SOURCE: Marmor (2018).

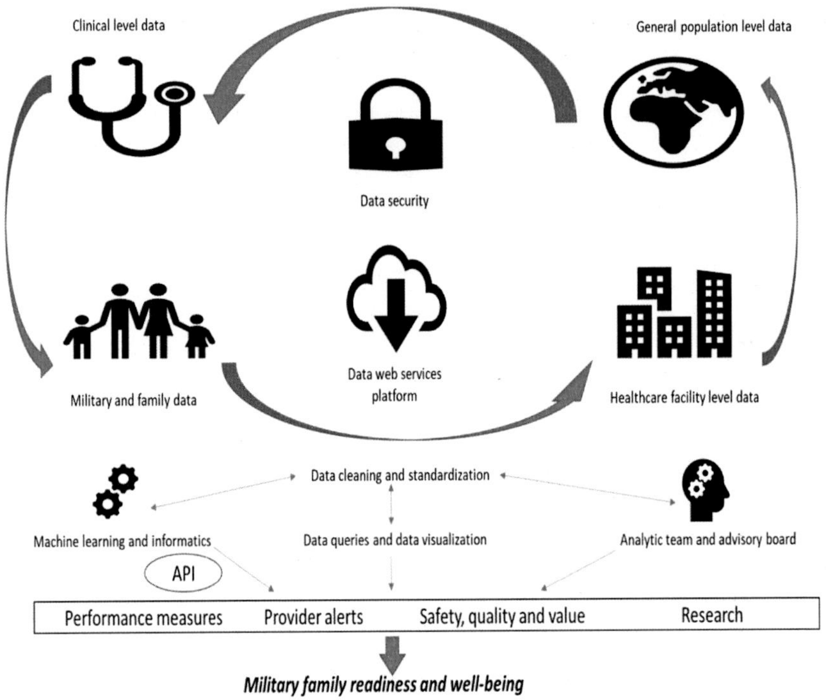

FIGURE 8-3 Conceptual model of big data collection, analysis, and dissemination to improve military family readiness and well-being.
SOURCE: Marmor (2018).

the end user is through application programing interfaces. This stack of informatics, which draws on many primary data sources, including service program and provider notes, supplies the analytics needed to give leaders, providers, researchers, families, and systems valuable, real-time information on military family well-being and needs, and provides the integrated information infrastructure to inform CQI.

This integrated information infrastructure requires operational analytics support to oversee compliance with data use agreements and data safety and to prevent misuse of data to ensure that military policy makers and end users do not misinterpret big data results and analyses. The real-time information in the outcomes portion of the model offers provider teams and families with performance measures, provider alerts, notifications on safety, quality, and value, and research data points, all of which can be used for future analyses as part of a larger monitoring effort. Military families need personalized predictions about well-being and response to interventions, as well as a deeper understanding of the complex factors and their interactions that influence well-being and readiness. Big data initiatives allow for cluster-level queries with multilevel stratifications when evidence does not exist for a decision. For example, analysis of data with learning-enhanced approaches may be used to detect mental health issues, suicidality, and other risks to family well-being, and ultimately lead to more effective methods of comparing screening and prevention options.

Meeting the challenges to developing a learning MFRS will be contingent on having sound, robust data and predictive analytics. Issues involving data inaccuracy, erroneous or ambiguous data points, missing data, and selective measurement must be addressed in designing an infrastructure. Building interoperability into the system's data infrastructure will require thoughtfulness and foresight. Currently available service record and management systems have heterogeneous architectures not always built for big data analyses and a learning system framework, and they are further limited by ways the data is entered, which may interfere with preparation for predictive analytics.

Foundational work implemented now could establish cost savings in the future as predictive analytic tools mature. This cost savings is most apparent in data safety, given the significant costs associated with the storage and necessary protections of data. Creating a learning health system in which data safety is paramount will avoid a need to spend future resources on preventing data breaches. A ground-up approach in building data systems with safety at the forefront will minimize future costs and maximize the trust and usability of the systems for the military and their families.

Cost savings can also be seen if scalable systems are built to incorporate future data sources. The advanced interconnectivity and data collection of mobile and wearable devices provides an opportunity to scale military family programming beyond traditional delivery platforms. Ensuring that the MFRS is prepared to integrate usable data from wearables would minimize future costs associated with resource expansion once data are more readily available.

Military families need personalized predictions about well-being and response to services treatments. Big data initiatives allow for cluster-level queries with multilevel stratifications when evidence does not exist for a decision. For example, analysis of data with learning-enhanced approaches may be used to detect mental health issues, suicide and family well-being, and safety problems with drugs and devices. Ultimately, this would lead to more effective methods for comparing prevention, diagnostic, and treatment options.

Although the promise of big data is enormous, the benefits gained through a big data learning MFRS include security risks that need to be addressed. Cearley and Burke (2018) note that digital ethics and privacy are critical to any technological decision that an organization may make. Consumers of technology are demanding that their personal information be protected and are concerned about how their personal data are being used. The authors observe that privacy and digital ethics are intertwined and are built on the trust of customers. The Pew Research Center (2014) surveyed more than 2,000 experts on the future of digital privacy and found that privacy and security are foundational components of the digital world. Pew's report did not find a consensus among these experts, with some of them believing that by 2025 there will not be an accepted privacy infrastructure in place and privacy concerns will worsen as individuals' wearables and other "things" will spy on them and report on their behaviors.

Others in this expert survey believed that by 2025, consumers will have increased access to tools that will give them more control over their personal information in a tiered fashion so that they can choose who to provide access to their information, such as a health care professional. Some experts predicted that a privacy system or infrastructure will be put in place that will allow individuals the ability to set their own terms and policies about who accesses their data. At any rate, experts note that a challenge will be to put in place a system that specifies standards for data protection.

Any big data learning system must strive to create safeguards that protect classified military information and have the highest levels of protection for military families. Current military regulations may need to be re-examined to maximize the benefit from data collection while simultaneously maintaining operational security and minimizing risk to service members and their families. In the wake of several data scandals involving the use of private data (e.g., Granville, 2018; Yang and Jayakumar, 2014), data use agreements must involve participants in decision-making processes, set clear standards for ethical rigor, and specify sanctions for data misuse and abuse.

The Role of Mobile Technologies and Other New Digital Technologies in Supporting a Complex Adaptive MFRS

In a recent report on the top 10 strategic technology trends for 2019 by Gartner, a technology consulting firm, several trends were identified with direct implication for the delivery of programs to military families (Cearley and Burke, 2018). For instance, one top technology trend they cite is "autonomous things" (p. 6), which can come in the form of robotics, drones, vehicles, appliances, or agents, such as virtual assistants. The MIT Media Lab is experimenting with "social robots," robots that use artificial intelligence (AI) systems to interact with people. Social robots are being used as personal health coaches, pet surrogates, companions, and more. When Breazeal and colleagues (2019) compared the use of a digital assistant versus a social robot among adults ages 50 and older, they found that older adults were more socially engaged with the robot compared to the digital assistant, and that the robots served as social catalysts and promoted human-human interaction. Social robots can also be used to foster connections with family members who are remotely located, which may be particularly applicable to spouses, partners, and children of service members.

The MIT Media Lab is also experimenting with "emotionally intelligent" virtual agents that can personalize how they interact with individuals based on their emotional state (Ghandeharioun et al., 2018). Ghandeharioun and colleagues conducted two randomized controlled trials examining different ways in which the Emotion-Aware mHealth Agent, or EMMA, improved individuals' well-being. EMMA provides wellness suggestions to participants using "micro-interventions" that use positive psychology, cognitive behavioral, meta-cognitive, or somatic psychotherapy strategies. The researchers found that EMMA was likeable but needs to be focused on more specific moods and contexts and to be less predictable in order to improve well-being. In particular, individuals who were classified as extroverts found EMMA to be likeable. In addition, the authors offered several design guidelines for emotionally intelligent virtual agents, such as "do not interrupt a good mood" and offer "short, simple, and effortless activities" (Ghandeharioun et al., 2018, pg. 23).

Integrated Mobile Technology

Another top 10 technology trend is the movement from the use of individual devices and wearables to a multichannel and multimodal experience (Cearley and Burke, 2018). In this multimodal experience, virtual reality and augmented reality will be integrated with mobile technologies and wearables. The increasing utility and acceptability of mobile platforms for the delivery of health and mental health services can be adapted to provide a special opportunity for DoD to strengthen individual and family well-being through screening and program delivery across the spectrum of coordinated support of MFRS, as described in Chapter 7 (refer to Figure 7-1). In health care settings, program components are referred to as "mHealth" when mobile or other wireless devices (e.g. smartphones, tablets, wearables[12]) have been applied to promotion and prevention contexts to support resilience and well-being (Kumar et al., 2013).

---

[12]Wearables are technological devices that are worn on the body or incorporated into clothing. These include fitness tracking devices, smart watches, and other devices that use wireless systems.

Mobile and wireless devices allow for more accessible and cost-effective interventions because: (1) their widespread use, acceptability, and convenience can help reduce certain societal and structural barriers (Amico, 2015) and (2) they offer strong capability for scaling across geographic locations (Muessig et al., 2017), including within resource-limited (Haberer et al., 2017), hard-to-reach (McInnes et al., 2014), and deployed settings (Gifford et al., 2014). Mobile devices are capable of giving round-the-clock, real-time reminders and feedback. Smartphones and tablet computers are also able to host applications (apps) with therapeutic content as well as a multitude of capabilities, such as social networking and gaming (Pellowski and Kalichman, 2012). Using these technologies to support well-being through behavioral health in a family's natural environment can mitigate the logistical burdens (e.g. scheduling conflicts, childcare, travel) associated with traditional in-person offerings of programs and services. The option to receive care outside of standard settings (e.g., in the privacy of one's own home) may be particularly appealing to service members and their families who live off-installation or who are concerned about perceived stigma associated with seeking assistance (Luxton et al., 2016).

Mobile in Stepped-care Delivery Strategies

Because mobile interventions can be disseminated conveniently and have the potential to promote behavioral change at low cost, they may have particular utility for stepped-care policies and adaptive interventions. Consistent with a spectrum of coordinated support as described in Chapter 7, stepped-care practices are evidence-based, staged systems comprising a hierarchy of interventions, from the least to the most costly/intensive, matched to the individual's needs.[13] As compared to a fixed, one-size-fits-all program, a stepped-service approach initially requires minimal support, since it starts with the least expensive and/or burdensome intervention component, and then applies more costly or more burdensome components only to those who need them the most, such as those showing early signs of nonresponse. Even less costly or less burdensome components can be offered to individuals who show adequate response to minimal support. The goal is to step up and down the intensity or cost of prevention based on early signs of progress in order to achieve a more cost-effective outcome.

Stepped-service delivery strategies are a form of adaptive intervention, an intervention design in which information about the individual's prog-

---

[13]See Australia Department of Health, *PHN Primary Mental Health Care Flexible Funding Pool Implementation Guidance, Stepped Care*, at http://www.health.gov.au/internet/main/publishing.nsf/content/2126B045A8DA90FDCA257F6500018260/$File/1PHN%20Guidance%20-%20Stepped%20Care.PDF.

ress in the course of the intervention, such as early signs of nonresponse or poor adherence, is used to modify aspects of the type, dosage, intensity, or delivery modality of an intervention. Adaptive interventions aim to address not only the unique needs but also the changing needs of individuals or families over time, so they might be uniquely suited for understanding and addressing the diversity of military family needs (Nahum-Shani and Militello, 2018). By providing appropriate interventions only to those who need them, when they need them (Carels et al., 2005, 2007), adaptive interventions can improve long-term outcomes for greater numbers of individuals, increasing the reach and impact of treatments.

Mobile in Just-in-time Delivery Strategies

Mobile tools also offer novel opportunities for delivering just-in-time adaptive interventions (JITAIs). A JITAI is a form of adaptive intervention that aims to address *in real time* the rapidly changing needs of individuals or families (Nahum-Shani, Hekler, and Spruijt-Metz, 2015; Spruijt-Metz and Nilsen, 2014). Consistent with the notion of personalized medicine, JITAIs put into practice the personalized real-time selection and delivery of intervention strategies based on real-time data (Spruijt-Metz and Nilsen, 2014). JITAIs have been developed and evaluated for a wide range of behavioral health issues, including physical activity (King et al., 2013; Thomas and Bond, 2015), alcohol use (Gustafson et al., 2014; Witkiewitz et al., 2014), mental illness (Ben-Zeev et al., 2014), and smoking cessation (Free et al., 2011; Riley et al., 2008). Most recently, they have been applied to support the well-being veterans with PTSD and their caregivers, using mobile applications, with promising initial outcomes for improving intervention engagement (Barish et al., 2014). See Box 8-3 for an example of a JITAI.

Adaptive interventions contain four key elements: (1) *decision points,* that is, points during an intervention when a decision is made about whether and what type of intervention to provide; (2) *tailoring variables*, that is, the information provided to decide whether and how to modify the intervention; (3) *intervention options*, that is, the different types of treatment, tactics, intensities, dosages, or modalities used to deliver the treatment; and (4) *decision rules*, which link information about the individual (i.e., the tailoring variable) to intervention options. The decision-making rules specify for each decision point what intervention option should be offered under various conditions.

Specific Advantages of Adaptive Interventions for Military Families

Adaptive interventions hold great potential for advancing the well-being of service members and their families in the ways they could support a complex adaptive MFRS. First, as discussed earlier, they could help

BOX 8-3
Just-In-Time Adaptive Interventions (JITAIs): An Example

Sense2Stop is a smoking-cessation JITAI (Spring, 2017). Here, we describe a simplified version of this JITAI for illustrative purposes. Sense2Stop is based on evidence suggesting that if smokers attempting to quit experience stress (a state characterized by high arousal and displeasure [Kristensen, 1996; Posner et al., 2005], these experiences likely lead to a lapse (an isolated smoking episode), which in turn likely leads to a full relapse (Lam et al., 2014). To prevent stress episodes from leading to full relapse, in Sense2Stop smokers attempting to quit wear a collection of sensors (see AutoSense [Ertin et al., 2011]) that monitor their physiology continuously. An algorithm on the mobile device uses this data to determine, for every given minute, whether or not there is sufficient evidence that the person is experiencing stress. If there is sufficient evidence that the person is experiencing stress, and the person is receptive (i.e., s/he is not driving a car and did not receive an intervention in the past 60 minutes), the mobile device prompts the individual to engage in a stress regulation exercise. Similar to AIs, JITAIs can be protocolized with decision rules. For example, the following decision rule (simplified for illustrative purposes) protocolizes Sense2Stop:

Every minute:
> If Stress and Receptivity = Yes
- Then, intervention option = [Prompt]
- Otherwise, intervention option = [Nothing].

SOURCE: Nahum-Shani and Militello (2018).

address the varying needs of military families over time, concerning both within-person variation and within-family heterogeneity. Moreover, the demands of military life, such as frequent moves, can impact continuity of care and treatment response for service members and their families (Gleason and Beck, 2017; Marshall et al., 2011). During times of transition, when traditional forms of treatment such as in-person clinical visits are not feasible, mobile monitoring and interventions can be utilized at any time and anywhere, unleashing the potential to facilitate continued access to some form of treatment.

Second, there is great fluctuation in the responses to interventions aiming to improve the health and well-being of service members and their families. As an example, consider therapies for posttraumatic stress disorder (PTSD). Although treatments such as prolonged exposure and cognitive processing therapy were found effective in reducing military-related PTSD symptoms, across a range of studies at least half of veterans still meet diagnostic criteria for PTSD following treatment (Steenkamp and Litz, 2014). This led Steenkamp and Litz (2014) to conclude that "overall, dissemination models must move beyond simple one-size-fits-all conceptualizations of treatment if they are to adequately reflect the evidence base and the complexity of PTSD in veteran populations" (p. 706). Adaptive interventions can be used to address such between-person heterogeneity by identifying individuals who show early signs of nonresponse and modifying their treatment (e.g., by providing additional support) in order to ensure that they ultimately respond.

Third, barriers to promotional and prevention services for military families include limited availability (e.g., shortage of qualified providers, long wait times), accessibility (e.g., absence of reliable transport to off-base services, limited availability of childcare), and acceptability (i.e., stigma and negative attitudes toward support services) (American Public Health Association, 2014; Verdeli et al., 2011). Using a stepped-care approach that capitalizes on mobile tools as minimal support has the potential to address these barriers. Mobile interventions may attract and retain those service members and their families who are unlikely to seek out traditional therapeutic interventions (e.g., due to burden or stigma), especially when low-intensity tools are integrated into a system of services (Monk et al., 2017).

Given the widespread use, convenience, and acceptability of mobile tools, utilizing them to deliver initial minimal support can further increase access to care. This is particularly critical in the context of military families, given that more than 70 percent of active-duty military families live off-installation (Boberiene et al., 2014; National Military Family Association, 2011; Whitestone and Thompson, 2016). Living off-installation decreases access to care due to the lack of services for military families far from military installations, and it also hinders integration into a military support network. Low-cost, low-burden, accessible mobile tools can be used to deliver to military service members and their families universal screenings and interventions and screening, that is, those designed to reach and target an entire population. Individuals or families identified as needing more than minimal support can then be linked to more costly or more intense indicated care to address their specific needs. Moreover, once the desired outcome is obtained, it is not always clinically appropriate to stop treatment completely or resume an intense treatment schedule (Borsari et al., 2011), and mobile tools can be used to "step-down" treatment instead, that is, to deliver boosters and maintain gains, such as through extended monitoring (McKay et al., 2010).

Developing Adaptive Interventions for Military Families

Although multiple evidence-based adaptive interventions exist, limited attention has been given to the systematic development and implementation of adaptive interventions for military families. First, stepped care is loosely implemented in the treatment of service members and their families, and the decision rules regarding when to step treatment up or down are not well defined. Second, current stepped-care approaches for military service members do not explicitly specify how, when, and for whom mobile tools should be used in service delivery. Finally, while mobile technology tools are natural candidates to be integrated into a stepped-care approach for military service members, these tools have not yet demonstrated evidence of effectiveness in this population (Jai et al., 2016; Miller et al., 2016; Shore et al., 2014). More evidence is needed to evaluate and optimize existing stepped-care models in military settings.

As an example of a current adaptive-intervention research effort underway for active duty families, the After Deployment, Adaptive Parenting Tools (ADAPT) Program is an intervention recently adapted to include mobile platforms to support delivery of prevention services with military families. Designed to be delivered following a parent's military deployment, ADAPT targets key parenting practices in order to strengthen children's resilience (Gewirtz et al., 2014); randomized controlled trial results have demonstrated that the program improves parenting, strengthens children's social, emotional, and behavioral functioning, and reduces parental distress (DeGarmo and Gewirtz, 2018; Gewirtz et al., 2016, 2018b; Piehler et al., 2018). The program is currently being evaluated as an adaptive intervention aimed at offering multiple formats, dosages, and sequences to deliver precision (i.e. personalized) programs for families (DeGarmo and Gewirtz, 2019). This evaluation research will inform a population-level implementation of ADAPT, which is currently planned for a large military installation and includes a universal self-directed web-based program. Following this first universal dose, parents complete an online assessment of parenting efficacy. The results of the evaluation (concerning family needs and consumer/parent preferences) determine whether and what services are subsequently offered and may include group-based and workshop programs, individual family telehealth, and face-to-face interventions.

JITAIs supported by mobile technology, including wearables, have particular applicability for military family interventions. As mentioned earlier, JITAIs are motivated by the need to address conditions that change rapidly, unexpectedly, and in the person's natural environment (Nahum-Shani et al., 2015, 2017). These conditions can represent vulnerability (high risk) or opportunity for positive changes. Use of JITAIs can also be motivated to capitalize on states of opportunity for positive changes. For example, a JITAI for promoting physical activity can use information about the person's location to identify when she or he is close to a park or a recreational facility to trigger a recommendation for the person to engage in physical activity. Here, rather than focusing on states of vulnerability to adverse outcomes the JITAI targets proximity to opportunities for engaging the individual in positive activity (refer to Box 8-3 for a detailed example.)

Stress is another example of a health risk that new advances in mobile and wireless devices can help address. Stress episodes often occur rapidly and unexpectedly. Research shows that every minute a person can transition from experiencing no-stress to experiencing stress, and it is not possible to predict exactly when a person will experience stress during the day. Stress episodes also occur in a person's natural environment, that is, while at work, due to job demands, or at home as a result of family-related demands. Identifying stress when it occurs, as soon as it occurs, and responding quickly would require the capability to continuously monitor the person's state and context as well as to deliver interventions "in the wild," that is, outside of a standard medical treatment setting. JITAIs enabled by wearable or other mobile devices may make this possible. The conditions JITAIs attempt to address are expected to emerge in the person's natural environment, where multiple demands compete for the person's time, effort and attention, and these interventions are also designed to explicitly minimize disruptions to the daily lives and routines of individuals. At the same time, this can be done only by providing an intervention only when the person is receptive, namely able and willing to capitalize on a given intervention.

Research on the behavioral health and adjustment implications of military deployments for families highlights the dynamic relationship between these military life experiences and military connected families as a source of both vulnerability and opportunity for personal growth. This dynamism has implications for the timing of preventive interventions (Najera et al., 2017). For example, empirical evidence concerning "dyadic coping"—the interplay between the stress of one partner and coping reactions of the other (MacDermid Wadsworth and Riggs, 2010)—indicates that in instances of chronic illness, such as cancer, positive or common dyadic coping (when both partners work symmetrically) is associated with improved relationship quality, self-care, and psychological functioning in both the individual coping with illness and their partners (Denham, 2002; Jones and Fiese, 2014; Monasta et al., 2010; Najera et al., 2017; Spagnola and Fiese, 2007). JITAIs have the potential to promote positive dyadic coping by providing real-time feedback and suggestions to address conditions specific to each person in the relationship, such as stress experienced by the months of service due to family separation or parenting stress experienced by the non-deployed spouse (Lara-Cinisomo et al., 2012). They may also promote positive coping by addressing dyadic conditions that arise *between* the service member and his/her partner, such as asymmetry in relational maintenance associated with communication restrictions (Merolla, 2010; Rea et al., 2015).

Military service can also impact child well-being and family functioning (Cronin et al., 2015; Gewirtz et al., 2018a; Hardy, Power, and Jaedicke, 1993; Saltzman et al., 2011). Potential sources of stress for military family children include frequent moves, often every 2 or 3 years, parental deployment(s), and/or parental injury (Chandra et al., 2010; Collins, 2015; Sogomonyan and Cooper, 2010). According to Rosenblum and Muzik (2014), although these large-scale disruptions pose challenges for parent-child relationships, meeting children's needs and addressing smaller-scale disruptions during everyday experiences are important processes by which relationships can be restored and strengthened. Additionally, resilience is the dynamic process of positive adaptation within the context of significant adversity (Collins, 2015; Cronin et al., 2015).

Critical to resilience is self-regulation (Mestre et al., 2017; Saltzman et al., 2011), namely the flexible modulation of cognition, behavior, and emotion (Nielsen et al., 2018). Empirical evidence suggests that engaging in evidence-based self-regulatory activities, such as behavioral substitution, mindful attention, relaxation techniques, and searching for strengths within common everyday experiences, can promote self-regulatory skills (Bratt et al., 2017; Elwafi et al., 2013; Goldberg et al., 2014; Padesky and Mooney, 2012). JITAIs can be used to address, in real time, parents' and children's need for hands-on strategies for managing everyday small-scale difficulties and building self-regulatory skills. Current family-based models encourage the training of parents and children to identify personal- and family-level triggers and the development of collaborative strategies for modulating their impact (Saltzman et al., 2011). Such models can be used to guide the development of JITAIs that address family needs more holistically, by detecting personal- and family-level triggers in real time and delivering commendations to engage in collaborative self-regulatory activities and supportive familial transactions.

SUMMARY

The opportunity to learn from the implementation of evidence-based interventions for military family well-being extends well beyond the specific population and service systems where military families receive services in DoD-supported systems. It includes civilian settings that are also critical to the well-being and readiness of military families, such as civilian schools and primary care settings. Learning from the implementation of evidence-based interventions in the contexts that serve military families enables the ongoing study of evidence-informed and evidence-based practice implementation, the monitoring of the impact of implementation on families, providers, and service systems, and the development of methods and measures that can serve to build tools for the field of implementation science.

There are several contributions that a functional implementation laboratory for military families' well-being can make for the field at large. First, the military context provides a rich, multilevel, multisectoral, and multiorganizational environment that is a microcosm of the ecology within which implementation science findings are applied. The constituent families must be reached across substantial geography and with a recognition of diversities in culture, socioeconomic status, access to resources, and family needs. Unlike many other settings, however, treating the MFRS as an "implementation laboratory" is an approach whose strengths could be replicated in other systems. DoD has the benefits of an integrated care system, with multiple data sources that together inform service needs, services received, and outcomes. Military families, given their diversity, have needs that can be generalized to the larger population and, thus, insights on effective implementation with military families could be generalized as well.

Second, some of the same interventions are delivered within and outside of the military context, and as such the implementation strategies to bring evidence-based interventions to military families can be simultaneously tested in external settings as well. The cross-context comparisons can help to isolate what characteristics of health care and community settings improve the adoption, implementation, and sustainability of interventions. They can also add to the field's understanding of how and why implementation strategies improve the successful integration of interventions into practice.

Third, data resources within the military context are more advanced than elsewhere, and the availability, volume, and scope of data can be leveraged to identify areas where interventions are needed for families, inform how a package of evidence-based interventions can be assembled to meet those needs, guide strategies selected to implement the set of interventions, monitor implementation progress over time, and adjust what is implemented, how it is implemented, and where it is implemented over time. This ability to study and improve understanding of intervention adaptation, intervention sustainment, and (where needed) decommissioning is generally lacking in the field. Such an effort could form the basis of a learning implementation system (IOM, 2013; Stein et al., 2016) whose benefits to our knowledge base could be immense.

Fourth, the durable, strong support of the country for its service members and their families offers an opportunity for sustained study of implementation over a longer time horizon than is typically possible in a research study. In addition, an ongoing study of implementation, adaptation, sustainment, and decommissioning that does justice to the inherent dynamism in real-world settings will require a commitment to apply the lessons learned over time, toward ongoing support-system improvement. The military context may provide one of the few examples where this commitment will persist in the coming years. Therefore, this is a natural setting in which to test innovative strategies to more effectively support implementation, adaptation, improvement, and (as appropriate) discontinuation of a variety of evidence-based practices. A significant investment in applied research that identifies core mechanisms affecting implementation processes will produce value, most directly for military families and more indirectly for the larger implementation science community.

Finally, the implementation laboratory within the collective MFRS, designed to provide support to service members and their families, allows for the investigation of a range of different research questions, a small sample of which are these:

a. What strategies and approaches to adaptation work, and how do they work?
b. How should systems optimally select and scale a combination of complementary evidence-informed and evidence-based programs?
c. Can we identify the rate at which different evidence-informed and evidence-based programs and implementation strategies can scale up across systems and communities?
d. What are the comparative effectiveness and cost-effectiveness of variable strategies to adopt, implement, adapt, sustain, or decommission interventions to promote resilience, readiness, and well-being?

Answering these and other questions can directly benefit military family well-being and ultimately contribute to the mission-readiness of the force. In addition, learning from this endeavor would greatly contribute to the larger knowledge base of implementation science. In concert with other research activities, the field can substantially improve the integration of research and practice and improve population-level well-being. The military infrastructure is uniquely positioned to both learn from and contribute to the science of intervention adaptation specifically and the field of implementation science more broadly.

CONCLUSIONS

CONCLUSION 8-1: Implementation research and models can help facilitate the integration of evidence-based and evidence-informed practices into care delivery by identifying likely barriers toward implementation and providing guidance for how best to overcome such barriers. The insights generated by the field of dissemination and implementation science can serve as a mechanism for improving the Military Family Readiness System.

CONCLUSION 8-2: A sustainable Military Family Readiness System (MFRS) requires ongoing adaptation of programs, services, resources, and practices that is supported by a continuous learning system. An effective MFRS includes, whenever possible, evidence-based and evidence-informed practices, processes, programs, and policies and uses a community participatory approach to adapt and implement within service settings and geographical contexts.

CONCLUSION 8-3: Effective implementation of military family readiness services requires an integrated information infrastructure to support the measurement, analytics, and organizational leadership infrastructure necessary for continuous quality improvement processes to inform adaptations, accountability, workforce training, and sustainability.

CONCLUSION 8-4: An effective Military Family Readiness System requires a learning system framework that is data driven and culturally responsive to family and community diversity as well as to the complex and emergent challenges of military service.

CONCLUSION 8-5: Military families and the Military Family Readiness System will benefit from the utilization of big data and predictive analytics to monitor and tailor interventions that influence well-being at the level of the individual and the family.

REFERENCES

Agency for Healthcare Research and Quality. (2008). *Plan-Do-Study-Act (PDSA) Cycle.* Retrieved from https://innovations.ahrq.gov/qualitytools/plan-do-study-act-pdsa-cycle

American Public Health Association. (2014). *Removing Barriers to Mental Health Services for Veterans.* Retrieved from https://www.apha.org/policies-and-advocacy/public-health-policy-statements/policy-database/2015/01/28/14/51/removing-barriers-to-mental-health-services-for-veterans.

Amico, K. R. (2015). Evidence for technology interventions to promote ART adherence in adult populations: A review of the literature 2012–2015. *Current HIV/AIDS Reports, 12*(4), 441–450.

Astor, R. A., and Benbenisthy, R. (2018). *Memo prepared for the Committee on the Well-being of Military Families.* Los Angeles: University of Southern California Suzanne Dworak-Peck School of Social Work.

Atkins, M. S., Rusch, D., Mehta, T. G. and Lakind, D. (2016). Future directions for dissemination and implementation science: Aligning ecological theory and public health to close the research to practice gap. *Journal of Clinical Child & Adolescent Psychology, 45*(2), 215–226.

Barish, G., Lester, P., Saltzman, W. R. and Elbogen, E. (2014). Beyond sensors: Reading patients through caregivers and context. In *Proceedings of the 2014 ACM International Joint Conference on Pervasive and Ubiquitous Computing: Adjunct Publication* (pp. 1273–1277). New York: Association for Computing Machinery.

Beardslee, W. R., Gladstone, T. R. G., Wright, E. J., and Cooper, A. B. (2003). A family-based approach to the prevention of depressive symptoms in children at risk: Evidence of parental and child change. *Pediatrics, 112*, e119-e131.

Beardslee, W. R., Klosinski, L. E., Saltzman, W., Mogil, C., Pangelinan, S., McKnight, C. P., and Lester, P. (2013). Dissemination of family-centered prevention for military and veteran families: Adaptations and adoption within community and military systems of care. *Clinical Child and Family Psychology Review, 16*(4), 394–409.

Beardslee, W., Lester, P., Klosinski, L., and Leskin, G. (2011). Family-centered preventive intervention for military families: Implications for implementation science. *Prevention Science, 12*(4), 339–348.

Beardslee, W. R., Wright, E. J., Gladstone, T. R. G., and Forbes, P. (2007). Long-term effects from a randomized trial of two public health preventive interventions for parental depression. *Journal of Family Psychology, 21*(4),703–713.

Becker, K. D., Lee, B. R., Daleiden, E. L., Lindsey, M., Brandt, N. E. and Chorpita, B. F. (2013). The common elements of engagement in children's mental health services: Which elements for which outcomes? Journal of Clinical Child & Adolescent Psychology, 44(1), 30–43.

Benbenishty, R. (2014). *Building Capacity in Military Schools: Final Technical Evaluation Report.* Los Angeles: University of Southern California School of Social Work.

Ben-Zeev, D., Brenner, C. J., Begale, M., Duffecy, J., Mohr, D. C. and Mueser, K. T. (2014). Feasibility, acceptability, and preliminary efficacy of a smartphone intervention for schizophrenia. *Schizophrenia Bulletin*, 40(6), 1244–1253.

Bernal, G. E., and Domenech Rodríguez, M. M. (2012). *Cultural Adaptations: Tools For Evidence-Based Practice With Diverse Populations.* Washington, DC: American Psychological Association.

Blitz, C. C., Arthur, M. W. and Hawkins, J. D. (2002). Preventing alcohol, tobacco, and other substance abuse. In L. A. Jason and D. S. Glenwick, (Eds.), *Innovative Strategies for Promoting Health and Mental Health Across the Life Span* (pp. 176–201). New York, NY: Springer.

Boberiene, L. V., and Hornback, B. J. (2014). How can policy strengthen community support for children in military families? *American Journal of Orthopsychiatry, 84*(5), 439.

Borsari, B., Capone, C., Mastroleo, N. R. and Monti, P. M. (2011). Clinical considerations in the treatment of substance use disorders with veterans. *Journal of Contemporary Psychotherapy, 41*(4), 247–253.

Bratt, S., Semaan, B., Britton, L., Dosono, B., and Zeno, F. (2017). Translation in personal crises: Opportunities for wearables design. In *Proceedings of the 14th International Conference on Information Systems for Crisis Response and Management– Albi, France, May 2017.*

Breazeal, C. L., Ostrowski, A. K., Singh, N., and Park, H. W. (2019). Designing social robots for older adults. *The Bridge* (National Academy of Engineering) *49*(1), 22–31.

Bumbarger, B., and Perkins, D. (2008). After randomised trials: Issues related to dissemination of evidence-based interventions. *Journal of Children's Services, 3*(2), 55–64.

Burkhardt, J. T., Schröter, D. C., Magura, S., Means, S. N. and Coryn, C. L. (2015). An overview of evidence-based program registers (EBPRs) for behavioral health. *Evaluation and Program Planning, 48*, 92–99.

Cabassa, L. J., and Baumann, A. A. (2013). A two-way street: Bridging implementation science and cultural adaptations of mental health treatments. *Implementation Science, 8*(1).

Carels, R. A., Darby, L., Cacciapaglia, H. M., Douglass, O. M., Harper, J., Kaplar, M. E., Konrad, K., Rydin, S. and Tonkin, K. (2005). Applying a stepped-care approach to the treatment of obesity. *Journal of Psychosomatic Research, 59*(6), 375–383.

Carels, R. A., Darby, L., Cacciapaglia, H. M., Konrad, K., Coit, C., Harper, J., Kaplar, M. E., Young, K., Baylen, C. A., and Versland, A. (2007). Using motivational interviewing as a supplement to obesity treatment: A stepped-care approach. *Health Psychology*, *26*(3).

Catalano, R. F., Berglund, M. L., Ryan, J. A. M., Lonczak, H. S., and Hawkins, J. D. (2002). Positive youth development in the United States: Research findings on evaluations of positive youth development programs. *Prevention & Treatment*, *5*(1).

Cearley, D., and Burke, B. (2018). *Top 10 Strategic Technology Trends for 2019*. Stamford, CT: Gartner, Inc.

Chambers, D. A., Glasgow, R. E., and Stange, K. C. (2013). The dynamic sustainability framework: Addressing the paradox of sustainment amid ongoing change. *Implementation Science*, *8*(1), 1–11.

Chambers, D. A., and Norton, W. E. (2016). The adaptome: Advancing the science of intervention adaptation. *American Journal of Preventive Medicine*, *51*(4), 124–131.

_______. (2018). *Application of Implementation Science to Population-based, Behavioral Health Prevention Continuum of Care for Military Families*. Paper commissioned for the National Academies Committee on the Well-being of Military Families.

Chandra, A., Lara-Cinisomo, S., Jaycox, L. H., Tanielian, T., Burns, R. M., Ruder, T., and Han, B. (2010). Children on the homefront: The experience of children from military families. *Pediatrics*, *125*(1), 16–25.

Chilenski, S. M., Olson, J. R., Schulte, J. A., Perkins, D. F., and Spoth, R. (2015). A multi-level examination of how the organizational context relates to readiness to implement prevention and evidence-based programming in community settings. *Evaluation and Program Planning*, *48*, 63–74.

Chilenski, S. M., Perkins, D. F., Olson, J. R. Hoffman, L., Feinberg, M. E., Greenberg, M. T., Welsh, J., Crowley, D. M., and Spoth, R. L. (2016). The power of a collaborative relationship between technical assistance providers and community prevention teams: A correlational and longitudinal study. *Evaluation and Program Planning*, *54*, 19–29.

Chorpita, B. F., Becker, K. D., Daleiden, E. L., and Hamilton, J. D. (2007). Understanding the common elements of evidence-based practice: Misconceptions and clinical examples. *Journal of the American Academy of Child & Adolescent Psychiatry*, *46*(5), 647–652.

Chorpita, B. F., Bernstein, A., and Daleiden, E. L. (2011). Empirically guided coordination of multiple evidence-based treatments: An illustration of relevance mapping in children's mental health services. *Journal of Consulting and Clinical Psychology*, *79*(4), 470.

Chorpita, B. F., and Daleiden, E. L. (2009). Mapping evidence-based treatments for children and adolescents: Application of the distillation and matching model to 615 treatments from 322 randomized trials. *Journal of Consulting and Clinical Psychology*, *77*(3), 566.

Chorpita, B. F., Daleiden, E. L., and Weisz, J. R. (2005). Identifying and selecting the common elements of evidence based interventions: A distillation and matching model. *Mental Health Services Research*, *7*(1), 5–20.

Coffron, M., and Opelka, F. (2015). Big promise and big challenges for big heath care data. *Bulletin of the American College of Surgeons*, *100*(4), 10–16.

Collins, E. (2015). Experts explain mental state of military children. *Soldiers Magazine*, May 1. Retrieved from https://www.army.mil/article/147786/experts_explain_mental_state_of_military_children.

Crepaz, N., Tungol-Ashmon, M. V., Vosburgh, H. W., Baack, B. N. and Mullins, M. M. (2015). Are couple-based interventions more effective than interventions delivered to individuals in promoting HIV protective behaviors? A meta-analysis. *AIDS Care*, *27*(11), 1361–1366.

Cronin, S., Becher, E., Christians, K. S. and Debb, S. (2015). *Parents and Stress: Understanding Experiences, Context, and Responses*. St. Paul: University of Minnesota.

Dabek, F., and Caban, J. J. (2015). Leveraging big data to model the likelihood of developing psychological conditions after a concussion. *Procedia Computer Science, 53*, 265–273.

Damschroder, L. J., and Hagedorn, H. J. (2011). A guiding framework and approach for implementation research in substance use disorders treatment. *Psychology of Addictive Behaviors*, *25*(2), 194.

Davidoff, F., Batalden, P., Stevens, D., Ogrinc, G., and Mooney, S. (2008). Publication guidelines for quality improvement in health care: Evolution of the SQUIRE project. *BMJ Quality & Safety*, *17*(1), i3-i9.

Deaton, A., and Cartwright, N. (2018). Understanding and misunderstanding randomized controlled allocation and dynamic adaptive intervention designs for family psychology trials. *Social Science & Medicine, 210*, 2–21.

DeGarmo, D. S., and Gewirtz, A. H. (2018). A recovery capital and stress-buffering model for post-deployed military parents. *Frontiers in Psychology, 9*, 1832.

________. (2019). Fixed. In B. Fiese, M. Celano, K. Deater-Deckard, E. N. Jouriles, and M. A. Whisman (Eds.), *APA Handbook of Contemporary Family Psychology: Foundations, Methods, and Contemporary Issues Across the Lifespan.* Washington, DC: American Psychological Association.

Deming, W. E. (1986). *Out of the Crisis*. Cambridge, MA: Massachusetts Institute of Technology, Center for Advanced Engineering Study.

Denham, S. A. (2002). Family routines: A structural perspective for viewing family health. *Advances in Nursing Science*, *24*(4), 60–74.

De Pedro, K. T., Astor, R. A., Gilreath, T. D., Benbenishty, R., and Berkowitz, R. (2018). School climate, deployment, and mental health among students in military-connected schools. *Youth & Society, 50*(1), 93–115.

Domitrovich, C. E., Moore, J. E., Thompson, R. A., and CASEL Preschool to Elementary School Social and Emotional Learning Assessment Workgroup. (2012). Interventions that promote social-emotional learning in young children. In Robert C. Pianta (Ed.), *Handbook of Early Childhood Education* (pp. 393-415). New York: The Guilford Press.

Durlak J. (2013). *The Importance of Quality Implementation for Research, Practice, and Policy.* ASPE Research Brief. Washington, DC: U.S. Department of Health and Human Services.

Durlak, J. A., and Wells, A. M. (1997). Primary prevention mental health programs for children and adolescents: A meta-analytic review. *American Journal of Community Psychology*, *25*(2), 115–152.

Dworkin, S. L., Pinto, R. M., Hunter, J., Rapkin, B. and Remien, R. H. (2008). Keeping the spirit of community partnerships alive in the scale-up of HIV/AIDS prevention: Critical reflections on the roll-out of DEBI (Diffusion of Effective Behavioral Interventions). *American Journal of Community Psychology*, *42*(1–2), 51–59.

Eccles, J. S., and Gootman, J. A. (2002). Features of positive developmental settings. *Community Programs to Promote Youth Development*, 86–118.

Elwafi, H. M., Witkiewitz, K., Mallik, S., Thornhill IV, T. A. and Brewer, J. A. (2013). Mindfulness training for smoking cessation: Moderation of the relationship between craving and cigarette use. *Drug and Alcohol Dependence*, *130*(1–3), 222–229.

Embry, D. D., and Biglan, A. (2008). Evidence-based kernels: Fundamental units of behavioral influence. *Clinical Child and Family Psychology Review*, *11*(3), 75–113.

Ertin, E., Stohs, N., Kumar, S., Raij, A., al'Absi, M., and Shah, S. (2011, November). AutoSense: unobtrusively wearable sensor suite for inferring the onset, causality, and consequences of stress in the field. In *Proceedings of the 9th ACM Conference on Embedded Networked Sensor Systems* (pp. 274-287). New York: Association for Computing Machinery.

Farr, C. (2018). Alphabet spinoff Cityblock raises $20 million to help low-income Americans get health care. CNBC, January 4. Retrieved from https://www.cnbc.com/2018/01/04/alphabet-spin-off-cityblock-raises-20m-for-low-income-health-care.html.

Ferlie, E., and Dopson S.(2006). Studying complex organizations in health care. In S. Dopson and L. A. Fitzgerald (Eds.), *Knowledge to Action? Evidence-Based Health Care in Context* (pp. 8-25). Oxford, UK: Oxford University Press.

Fixsen, D. L., Naoom, S. F., Blase, K. A., and Friedman, R. M. (2005). *Implementation Research: A Synthesis of the Literature.* FHMI Publication no. 231. Tampa: University of South Florida, Louis de la Parte Florida Mental Health Institute, The National Implementation Research Network.

Free, C., Knight, R., Robertson, S., Whittaker, R., Edwards, P., Zhou, W., Rodgers, A., Cairns, J., Kenward, M. G., and Roberts, I. (2011). Smoking cessation support delivered via mobile phone text messaging (txt2stop): A single-blind, randomised trial. *The Lancet, 378*(9785), 49–55.

Garcia, E., De Pedro, K. T., Astor, R. A., Lester, P., and Benbenishty, R. (2015). FOCUS school-based skill-building groups: Training and implementation. *Journal of Social Work Education, 51*(supl), 102–116.

Gewirtz, A. H., DeGarmo, D. S., and Zamir, O. (2016). Effects of a military parenting program on parental distress and suicidal ideation: After deployment adaptive parenting tools. *Suicide and Life Threatening Behavior, 46*(1), S23–S31.

________. (2018a). Testing a military family stress model. *Family Process, 57*(2), 415–431.

________. (2018b). After deployment, adaptive parenting tools: One-year outcomes of a parenting program for military families. *Prevention Science, 19,* 589k–599k.

Gewirtz, A. H., Pinna, K. L., Hanson, S. K., and Brockberg, D. (2014). Promoting parenting to support reintegrating military families: After deployment, adaptive parenting tools. *Psychological Services, 11*(1), 31–40.

Ghandeharioun, A., McDuff, D., Czerwinski, M., and Rowan, K. (2018). *EMMA: An Emotionally Intelligent Personal Assistant for Improving Wellbeing.* Cambridge, MA: MIT Media Lab.

Gifford, T., Taylor, E., Morgan, J., Nessen, S., Freedman, B., Boedeker, D., and Boedeker, B. (2014). Establishing a low-cost telecommunications method to provide tele ENT consultations from a military medical center to deployed locations. *Journal of the International Society for Telemedicine and eHealth, 2,* 50–53.

Glasgow, R. E., and Chambers, D. (2012). Developing robust, sustainable, implementation systems using rigorous, rapid and relevant science. *Clinical and Translational Science, 5*(1), 48–55.

Gleason, J. L., and Beck, K. H. (2017). Examining associations between relocation, continuity of care, and patient satisfaction in military spouses. *Military Medicine, 182*(5-6), e1657-e1664.

Goldberg, S. B., Del Re, A. C., Hoyt, W. T., and Davis, J. M. (2014). The secret ingredient in mindfulness interventions? A case for practice quality over quantity. *Journal of Counseling Psychology, 61*(3), 491.

Granville, K. (2018). Facebook and Cambridge Analytica: What you need to know as fallout widens. *The New York Times*, March 19. Retrieved from https://www.nytimes.com/2018/03/19/technology/facebook-cambridge-analytica-explained.html.

Gruen, R. L., Elliott, J. H., Nolan, M. L., Lawton, P. D., Parkhill, A., McLaren, C. J., and Lavis, J. N. (2008). Sustainability science: An integrated approach for health-programme planning. *The Lancet, 372*(9649), 1579–1589.

Gustafson, D. H., McTavish, F. M., Chih, M. Y., Atwood, A. K., Johnson, R. A., Boyle, M. G., Levy, M. S., Driscoll, H., Chisholm, S. M., Dillenburg, L. and Isham, A. (2014). A smartphone application to support recovery from alcoholism: A randomized clinical trial. *Journal of the American Medical Association Psychiatry, 71*(5), 566–572.

Haberer, J. E., Sabin, L., Amico, K. R., Orrell, C., Galárraga, O., Tsai, A. C., Vreeman, R. C., Wilson, I., Sam-Agudu, N. A., Blaschke, T. F., and Vrijens, B. (2017). Improving antiretroviral therapy adherence in resource-limited settings at scale: A discussion of interventions and recommendations. *Journal of the International AIDS Society*, *20*(1), 21371.

Hallett, T. B., White, P. J., and Garnett, G. P. (2007). Appropriate evaluation of HIV prevention interventions: From experiment to full-scale implementation. *Sexually Transmitted Infections*, *83*(suppl 1), i55–i60.

Hardy, D. F., Power, T. G., and Jaedicke, S. (1993). Examining the relation of parenting to children's coping with everyday stress. *Child Development, 64*(6), 1829–1841.

Hashem, I. A. T., Yaqoob, I., Anuar, N. B., Mokhtar, S., Gani, A. and Khan, S. U. (2015). The rise of "big data" on cloud computing: Review and open research issues. *Information Systems*, *47*, 98–115.

Hawkins, J. D., Catalano, R. F., and Arthur, M. W. (2002). Promoting science-based prevention in communities. *Addictive Behaviors, 27*, 951–976.

Hawkins, J. D., Catalano, R. F., and Miller, J. Y. (1992). Risk and protective factors for alcohol and other drug problems in adolescence and early adulthood: Implications for substance abuse prevention. *Psychological Bulletin*, *112*(1), 64.

Heyman, R. E., and Smith Slep, A. M. (2001). Risk factors for family violence: Introduction to the special series. *Aggression and Violent Behavior,* 6(2–3), 115–119.

Heyman, R. E., Smith Slep, A. M., and Nelson, J. P. (2011). Empirically guided community intervention for partner abuse, child maltreatment, suicidality, and substance misuse. In S. M. Wadsworth and D. Riggs (Eds.), *Risk and Resilience in U.S. Military Families* (pp. 85–107). New York, NY: Springer.

Hoagwood, K. E., Serene Olin, S., Kerker, B. D., Kratochwill, T. R., Crowe, M., and Saka, N., (2007). Empirically based school interventions targeted at academic and mental health functioning. *Journal of Emotional and Behavioral Disorders*, *15*(2), 66–92.

Ijadi-Maghsoodi, R., Marlotte, L., Garcia, E., Aralis, H., Lester, P., Escudero, P. and Kataoka, S., (2017). Adapting and implementing a school-based resilience-building curriculum among low-income racial and ethnic minority students. *Contemporary School Psychology*, *21*(3), 223–239.

Institute of Medicine (IOM). (2000). *From Neurons to Neighborhoods: The Science of Early Childhood Development*. Washington, DC: National Academy Press.

________. (2011). *Digital Infrastructure for the Learning Health System: The Foundation for Continuous Improvement in Health and Health Care: Workshop Series Summary.* Washington, DC: The National Academies Press.

________. (2013). *Best Care at Lower Cost: The Path to Continuously Learning Health Care in America.* Washington, DC: The National Academies Press.

________. (2014). *Preventing Psychological Disorders in Service Members and Their Families: An Assessment of Programs.* Washington, DC: The National Academies Press.

Jai, T. M., McCool, B. N., and Reed, D. B. (2016). Military parents' personal technology usage and interest in e-health information for obesity prevention. *Telemedicine and e-Health*, *22*(3), 183–190.

Johnson, K., Hays, C., Center, H., and Daley, C. (2004). Building capacity and sustainable prevention innovations: A sustainability planning model. *Evaluation Program Planning*, *27*, 135–149.

Jones, B. L., and Fiese, B. H. (2014). Parent routines, child routines, and family demographics associated with obesity in parents and preschool-aged children. *Frontiers in Psychology*, *5*, 374.

Kardan-Souraki, M., Hamzehgardeshi, Z., Asadpour, I., Mohammadpour, R. A. and Khani, S., (2016). A review of marital intimacy-enhancing interventions among married individuals. *Global Journal of Health Science*, *8*(8), 74.

Karnik, N. (2018). Memo prepared for the Committee on the Well-Being of Military Families.

Karre, J. K., Perkins, D. F., Aronson, K. R., DiNallo, J., Kyler, S. J., Olson, J., and Mentzer, C. E. (2017). A continuum of evidence on evidence-based programs: A new resource for use in military social service delivery. *Military Behavioral Health*, *5*(4), 346–355.

Kazdin, A. E., and Blase, S. L. (2011). Rebooting psychotherapy research and practice to reduce the burden of mental illness. *Perspectives on Psychological Science*, *6*(1), 21–37.

Kelly, B. (2012). Implementation science for psychology in education. In B. Kelly and D. F. Perkins (Eds.), *Handbook of Implementation Science for Psychology in Education* (pp. 3–12). London, UK: Cambridge Press.

———. (2013). Implementing implementation science: Reviewing the quest to develop methods and frameworks for effective implementation. *Journal of Neurology and Psychology, 1*.

King, A. C., Hekler, E. B., Grieco, L. A., Winter, S. J., Sheats, J. L., Buman, M. P., Banerjee, B., Robinson, T. N. and Cirimele, J. (2013). Harnessing different motivational frames via mobile phones to promote daily physical activity and reduce sedentary behavior in aging adults. *PloS one*, *8*(4), e62613.

Kristensen, T. S. (1996). Job stress and cardiovascular disease: a theoretic critical review. Journal of occupational health psychology, *1*(3), 246–260.

Kumar, S., Nilsen, W. J., Abernethy, A., Atienza, A., Patrick, K., Pavel, M., Riley, W. T., Shar, A., Spring, B., Spruijt-Metz, D., and Hedeker, D. (2013). Mobile health technology evaluation: The mHealth evidence workshop. *American Journal of Preventive Medicine*, *45*(2), 228–236.

Kumpfer, K. L., Alvarado, R., Smith, P., and Bellamy, N. (2002). Cultural sensitivity and adaptation in family-based prevention interventions. *Prevention Science, 3*(3), 241–246.

Lam, C. Y., Businelle, M. S., Aigner, C. J., McClure, J. B., Cofta-Woerpel, L., Cinciripini, P. M., and Wetter, D. W. (2014). Individual and combined effects of multiple high-risk triggers on postcessation smoking urge and lapse. *Nicotine and Tobacco Research*, *16*(5), 569–575.

Langley, G., Moen, R., Nolan, K., Nolan, T., Norman, C., and Provost, L. (2009). *The Improvement Guide: A Practical Approach to Enhancing Organizational Performance* (2nd ed.). San Francisco, CA: Jossey-Bass.

Lara-Cinisomo, S., Chandra, A., Burns, R. M., Jaycox, L. H., Tanielian, T., Ruder, T., and Han, B. (2012). A mixed-method approach to understanding the experiences of non-deployed military caregivers. *Maternal and Child Health Journal*, *16*(2), 374–384.

Layne, C. M., Saltzman, W. R., Poppleton, L., Burlingame, G. M., Pasalic, A., Durakovic, E., Music, M., and Pynoos, R. S. (2008). Effectiveness of a school-based group psychotherapy program for war-exposed adolesecents: A randomized controlled trial. *Journal of the American Academy of Child & Adolescent Psychiatry, 47*, 1048–1062.

Lester P., Liang L. J., Milburn, N., Mogil, C., Woodward, K., Nash, W., and Beardslee, W. (2016). Evaluation of a family-centered preventive intervention for military families: Parent and child longitudinal outcomes. *Journal of the American Academy of Child & Adolescent Psychiatry, 55*(1), 14–24.

Lester, P., Mogil, C., Saltzman, W., Woodward, K., Nash, W., Leskin, G., Bursch, B., Green, S., Pynoos, R., and Beardslee, W. (2011). Families overcoming under stress: Implementing family-centered prevention for military families facing wartime deployments and combat operational stress. *Military Medicine*, *176*(1), 19–25.

Lester, P., Peterson, K., Reeves, J., Knauss, L., Glover, D., Mogil, C., Duan, N., Saltzman, W., Pynoos, R., Wilt, K., and Beardslee, W. (2010). The long war and parental combat deployment: Effects on military children and at-home spouses. *Journal of the American Academy of Child & Adolescent Psychiatry*, *49*(4), 310–320.

Lochman, J. E., and van den Steenhoven, A. (2002). Family-based approaches to substance abuse prevention. *Journal of Primary Prevention*, *23*(1), 49–114.

Luxton, D. D., Pruitt, L. D., Wagner, A., Smolenski, D. J., Jenkins-Guarnieri, M. A., and Gahm, G. (2016). Home-based telebehavioral health for US military personnel and veterans with depression: A randomized controlled trial. *Journal of Consulting and Clinical Psychology, 84*(11), 923.

MacDermid Wadsworth, S., and Riggs, D. (Eds.) (2010). *Risk and Resilience in U.S. Military Families*. New York, NY: Springer Science & Business Media.

Marmor, S. (2018). *Well-being of Military Families and a Learning Health System: The Importance of Data-Driven Decision Making*. Paper commissioned by the Committee on the Well-Being of Military Families. Washington, DC: The National Academies of Sciences, Engineering, and Medicine.

Marshall, R. C., Doperak, M., Milner, M., Motsinger, C., Newton, T., Padden, M., Pastoor, S., Hughes, C. L., LeFurgy, J., and Mun, S. K. (2011). Patient-centered medical home: An emerging primary care model and the military health system. Military Medicine, 176(11), 1253-1259.

Martire, L. M., Schulz, R., Helgeson, V. S., Small, B. J., and Saghafi, E. M. (2010). Review and meta-analysis of couple-oriented interventions for chronic illness. *Annals of Behavioral Medicine*, *40*(3), 325–342.

McInnes, D. K., Sawh, L., Petrakis, B. A., Rao, S. R., Shimada, S. L., Eyrich-Garg, K. M., Gifford, A. L., Anaya, H. D., and Smelson, D. A. (2014). The potential for health-related uses of mobile phones and internet with homeless veterans: Results from a multisite survey. *Telemedicine and e-Health, 20*(9), 801–809.

McKay, J. R., Van Horn, D. H., Oslin, D. W., Lynch, K. G., Ivey, M., Ward, K., Drapkin, M. L., Becher, J. R., and Coviello, D. M. (2010). A randomized trial of extended telephone-based continuing care for alcohol dependence: Within-treatment substance use outcomes. *Journal of Consulting and Clinical Psychology*, *78*(6), 912.

McKibbon, K. A., Lokker, C., Wilczynski, N. L., Ciliska, D., Dobbins, M., Davis, D. A., Haynes, R. B., and Straus, S. E. (2010). A cross-sectional study of the number and frequency of terms used to refer to knowledge translation in a body of health literature in 2006: A Tower of Babel? *Implementation Science*, 5(1), 16.

Means, S. N., Magura, S., Burkhardt, J. T., Schröter, D. C., and Coryn, C. L. (2015). Comparing rating paradigms for evidence-based program registers in behavioral health: Evidentiary criteria and implications for assessing programs. *Evaluation and Program Planning*, *48*, 100–116.

Merolla, A. J. (2010). Relational maintenance during military deployment: Perspectives of wives of deployed U.S. soldiers. *Journal of Applied Communication Research*, *38*(1), 4–26.

Mestre, J. M., Núñez-Lozano, J. M., Gómez-Molinero, R., Zayas, A., and Guil, R. (2017). Emotion regulation ability and resilience in a sample of adolescents from a suburban area. *Frontiers in Psychology*, *8*, 1980.

Miller, C. J., McInnes, D. K., Stolzmann, K., and Bauer, M.S. (2016). Interest in use of technology for healthcare among veterans receiving treatment for mental health. *Telemedicine and e-Health*, *22*(10), 847–854.

Mogil C., Aralis, H., Paley, B., Hajal, N., Aralis, H., Milburn, N., Beardslee, W., and Lester, P. (In Review). An in-home telehealth preventive intervention for military connected families with young children: 12 month outcomes from a randomized control trial.

Mohr, D. C., Schueller, S. M., Riley, W. T., Brown, C. H., Cuijpers, P., Duan, N., Kwasny, M. J., Stiles-Shields, C., and Cheung, K. (2015). Trials of intervention principles: Evaluation methods for evolving behavioral intervention technologies. *Journal of Medical Internet Research*, *17*(7), e166.

Monasta, L., Batty, G. D., Cattaneo, A., Lutje, V., Ronfani, L., Van Lenthe, F. J., and Brug, J. (2010). Early-life determinants of overweight and obesity: A review of systematic reviews. *Obesity Reviews, 11*(10), 695–708.

Monk, J. K., Oseland, L. M., Nelson Goff, B. S., Ogolsky, B. G., and Summers, K. (2017). Integrative intensive retreats for veteran couples and families: A pilot study assessing change in relationship adjustment, posttraumatic growth, and trauma symptoms. *Journal of Marital and Family Therapy, 43*(3), 448–462.

Morgan, N. R., Davis, K. D., Richardson, C., and Perkins, D. F. (2018). Common components analysis: An adapted approach for evaluating programs. *Evaluation and Program Planning, 67*, 1–9.

Muessig, K. E., LeGrand, S., Horvath, K. J., Bauermeister, J. A., and Hightow-Weidman, L. B. (2017). Recent mobile health interventions to support medication adherence among HIV-positive MSM. *Current Opinion in HIV and AIDS, 12*(5), 432–441.

Nahum-Shani, I., Hekler, E. B., and Spruijt-Metz, D. (2015). Building health behavior models to guide the development of just-in-time adaptive interventions: A pragmatic framework. *Health Psychology, 34*(S), 1209.

Nahum-Shani, I., and Militello, L.K. (2018). *Promoting Military Family Well-Being with Digitally-Supported Adaptive and Just-In-Time Adaptive Interventions: Opportunities and Challenges.* Paper commissioned by the Committee on the Well-Being of Military Families. Washington, DC: The National Academies of Sciences, Engineering, and Medicine.

Nahum-Shani, I., Smith, S. N., Spring, B. J., Collins, L. M., Witkiewitz, K., Tewari, A., and Murphy, S. A. (2017). Just-in-time adaptive interventions (JITAIs) in mobile health: Key components and design principles for ongoing health behavior support. *Annals of Behavioral Medicine, 52*(6), 446–462.

Najera, E., Landoll, R. R., Pollock, L. D., Berman, M., Ellis, K., Knies, K. M., Seidler, D. A., Bartone, P. T., and Bowles, S. V. (2017). Stress and resilience in married military couples. In S. Bowles and P. Bartone (Eds.), *Handbook of Military Psychology* (pp. 157–175). Cham: Springer.

National Military Family Association. (2011). *Finding Common Ground: A Toolkit for Communities Supporting Military Families.* Alexandria, VA. Retrieved from https://www.militaryfamily.org/wp-content/uploads/Finding_Common_Ground__A_Toolkit_for_Communities_Serving.pdf.

National Research Council and Institute of Medicine (NRC and IOM). (2009a). *Depression in Parents, Parenting And Children: Opportunities to Improve Identification, Treatment, and Prevention Efforts.* Washington, DC: The National Academies Press.

National Research Council and Institute of Medicine (NRC and IOM). (2009b). *Preventing Mental, Emotional, and Behavioral Disorders Among Young People: Progress and Possibilities.* Washington, DC: The National Academies Press.

North Atlantic Treaty Organization. (2019). *Impact of Military Life on Children from Military Families.* Technical report STO-TR-HFM-258. S&T Organisation, NATO.

Nielsen, L., Riddle, M., King, J. W., Aklin, W. M., Chen, W., Clark, D., Collier, E., Czajkowski, S., Esposito, L., Ferrer, R. and Green, P. (2018). The NIH Science of Behavior Change Program: Transforming the science through a focus on mechanisms of change. *Behaviour Research and Therapy, 101*, 3–11.

Olds, D. L., Henderson Jr., C. R., Tatelbaum, R., and Chamberlin, R. (1988). Improving the life-course development of socially disadvantaged mothers: A randomized trial of nurse home visitation. *American Journal of Public Health, 78*(11), 1436–1445.

Padesky, C. A., and Mooney, K. A. (2012). Strengths-based cognitive-behavioural therapy: A four-step model to build resilience. *Clinical Psychology Psychotherapy, 19*(4), 283–290.

Pawson, R., Greenhalgh, T., Harvey, G., and Walshe, K. (2005). Realist review-A new method of systematic review designed for complex policy interventions. *Journal of Health Services Research & Policy, 10*(1), 21–34.

Pellowski, J. A., and Kalichman, S. C. (2012). Recent advances (2011-2012) in technology-delivered interventions for people living with HIV. *Current HIV/AIDS Reports*, 9(4), 326–334.

Pentz, M. A. (2003). Evidence-based prevention: Characteristics, impact, and future direction. *Journal of Psychoactive Drugs, 35*(1), 143–152.

Perkins, D. F., Aronson, K. R., Karre, J., Kyler, S. J., and DiNallo, J. M. (2015). Reducing barriers to evidence-based practice with military families: Clearinghouse for Military Family Readiness. *Military Behavioral Health, 4(1)*, 47–57.

Pew Research Center (2014). *The Future of Privacy*. Washington, DC.

Piehler, T. F., Ausherbauer, K., Gewirtz, A. and Gliske, K., 2018. Improving child peer adjustment in military families through parent training: The mediational role of parental locus of control. *The Journal of Early Adolescence, 38*(9), 1322–1343.

Posner, J., Russell, J. A., and Peterson, B. S. (2005). The circumplex model of affect: An integrative approach to affective neuroscience, cognitive development, and psychopathology. *Development and Psychopathology, 17*(3), 715–734.

Powell, B. J., McMillen, J. C., Proctor, E. K., Carpenter, C. R., Griffey, R. T., Bunger, A. C., Glass, J. E., and York, J. L. (2012). A compilation of strategies for implementing clinical innovations in health and mental health. *Medical Care Research and Review, 69*(2), 123–157.

Proctor, E. K., Powell, B. J., and McMillen, J. C. (2013). Implementation strategies: Recommendations for specifying and reporting. *Implementation Science, 8*(139).

Proctor, E., Silmere, H., Raghavan, R., Hovmand, P., Aarons, G., Bunger, A., Griffey, R., and Hensley, M. (2011). Outcomes for implementation research: Conceptual distinctions, measurement challenges, and research agenda. *Administration and Policy in Mental Health, 38*(2), 65–76.

Rabin, B. A., Brownson, R. C., Haire-Joshu, D., Kreuter, M. W., and Weaver, N. L. (2008). A glossary for dissemination and implementation research in health. *Journal of Public Health Management and Practice, 14*(2), 117–123.

Raghupathi, W., and Raghupathi, V. (2014). Big data analytics in healthcare: Promise and potential. *Health Information Science and Systems*, 2(1), 3.

Rea, J., Behnke, A., Huff, N., and Allen, K. (2015). The role of online communication in the lives of military spouses. *Contemporary Family Therapy*, 37(3), 329–339.

Rhoades, B. L., Bumbarger, B. K., and Moore, J. E. (2012). The role of a state-level prevention support system in promoting high-quality implementation and sustainability of evidence-based programs. *American Journal of Community Psychology*, *50*(3–4), 386–401.

Riggs, N. R., Chou, C. P., and Pentz, M. A. (2009). Preventing growth in amphetamine use: Long-term effects of the Midwestern Prevention Project (MPP) from early adolescence to early adulthood. *Addiction, 104*(10), 1691–1699.

Riley, W., Obermayer, J., and Jean-Mary, J. (2008). Internet and mobile phone text messaging intervention for college smokers. *Journal of American College Health*, 57(2), 245–248.

Rogers, E. M. (2010). *Diffusion of Innovations*. New York: Simon and Schuster.

Rosenblum, K. L., and Muzik, M. (2014). STRoNG intervention for military families with young children. *Psychiatric Services*, *65*(3), 399–399.

Rotheram-Borus, M. J., Lee, M., Lin, Y. Y., and Lester, P. (2004). Six year intervention outcomes for adolescent children of parents with HIV. *Archives of Pediatrics & Adolescent Medicine, 158*, 742–748.

Rotheram-Borus, M. J., Swendeman, D., and Becker, K. D. (2014). Adapting evidence-based interventions using a common theory, practices, and principles. *Journal of Clinical Child & Adolescent Psychology, 43*(2), 229–243.

Rotheram-Borus, M. J., Swendeman, D., and Chorpita, B. F. (2012). Disruptive innovations for designing and diffusing evidence-based interventions. *American Psychologist*, *67*(6), 463.

Saltzman, W. R., Lester, P., Beardslee, W. R., Layne, C. M., Woodward, K., Nash, W.P. (2011). Mechanisms of risk and resilience in military families: theoretical and empirical basis of a family-focused resilience enhancement program. *Clinical Child and Family Psychology Review, 14*(3), 213–230.

Saltzman, W. R., Lester, P., Milburn, N., Woodward, K., and Stein, J. (2016). Pathways of risk and resilience: Impact of a family resilience program on active-duty military parents. *Family Process, 55(4)*, 633–646.

Santucci, L. C., Thomassin, K., Petrovic, L., and Weisz, J. R. (2015). Building evidence-based interventions for the youth, providers, and contexts of real-world mental-health care. *Child Development Perspectives*, 9(2), 67–73.

Scheirer, M. A. (2005). Is sustainability possible? A review and commentary on empirical studies of program sustainability. *American Journal of Evaluation, 26*, 320–347.

Scheirer, M. A., and Dearing, J. W., (2011). An agenda for research on the sustainability of public health programs. *American Journal of Public Health, 101*(11), 2059–2067.

Shore, J. H., Aldag, M., McVeigh, F. L., Hoover, R. L., Ciulla, R., and Fisher, A. (2014). Review of mobile health technology for military mental health. *Military Medicine, 179*(8), 865–878.

Siegenthaler, E., Munder, T., and Egger, M. (2012). Effect of preventive interventions in mentally ill parents on the mental health of the offspring: Systematic review and meta-analysis. *Journal of the American Academy of Child & Adolescent Psychiatry, 51*(1), 8–17.

Sogomonyan, F., and Cooper, J. L. (2010). *Trauma Faced by Children of Military Families: What Every Policymaker Should Know.* National Center for Children in Poverty. Retrieved from http://www.nccp.org/publications/pub_938.html.

Spagnola, M., and Fiese, B. H. (2007). Family routines and rituals: A context for development in the lives of young children. *Infants & Young Children, 20*(4), 284–299.

Spoth, R., Greenberg, M., Bierman, K., and Redmond, C. (2004). PROSPER community-university partnership model for public education systems: Capacity-building for evidence-based, competence-building prevention. *Prevention Science, 5*, 31–39.

Spoth, R., Greenberg, M., and Turrisi, R. (2008). Preventive interventions addressing underage drinking: State of the evidence and steps toward public health impact. *Pediatrics, 121*(4), S311–S336.

Spoth, R. L., Kavanagh, K. A., and Dishion, T. J (2002). Family-centered preventive intervention science: Toward benefits to larger populations of children, youth, and families. *Prevention Science, 3*(3), 145–152.

Spoth, R., Redmond, C., Clair, S., Shin, C., Greenberg, M., and Feinberg, M. (2011). Preventing substance misuse through community-university partnerships: Randomized controlled trial outcomes 4(1/2) years past baseline. *American Journal of Preventive Medicine, 40*, 440–447.

Spring, B. (2017). *Sense2Stop: Mobile Sensor Data to Knowledge.* National Institutes of Health. Retrieved from https://clinicaltrials.gov/ct2/show/NCT03184389.

Spruijt-Metz, D., and Nilsen, W. (2014). Dynamic models of behavior for just-in-time adaptive interventions. *IEEE Pervasive Computing, 13*(3), 13–17.

Steenkamp, M. M., and Litz, B. T. (2014) One-size-fits-all approach to PTSD in the VA not supported by the evidence. *American Psychology, 69*(7), 706–707.

Stein, B. D., Adams, A. S., and Chambers, D. A. (2016). A learning behavioral health care system: Opportunities to enhance research. *Psychiatric Services, 67*(9), 1019–1022.

Stirman, S. W., Miller, C. J., Toder, K., and Calloway, A. (2013). Development of a framework and coding system for modifications and adaptations of evidence-based interventions. *Implementation Science, 8*, 65.

Tanielian, T., Batka, C., and Meredith, L. S. (2018). Bridging gaps in mental health care: Lessons learned from the Welcome Back Veterans Initiative. *Rand Health Quarterly, 7*(4).

Teubert, D., and Pinquart, M. (2010). The association between coparenting and child adjustment: A meta-analysis. *Parenting: Science and Practice, 10*(4), 286–307.

Thomas, J. G., and Bond, D. S. (2015). Behavioral response to a just-in-time adaptive intervention (JITAI) to reduce sedentary behavior in obese adults: Implications for JITAI optimization. *Health Psychology, 34S*, 1261–1267.

Thompson, B. (2018). *Department of Defense Military Family Readiness System: Supporting Military Family Well-Being*. Paper commissioned by the Committee on the Well-Being of Military Families, Washington, DC, The National Academies of Sciences, Engineering, and Medicine.

Tibbits, M. K., Bumbarger, B. K., Kyler, S. J., and Perkins, D. F. (2010). Sustaining evidence-based interventions under realworld conditions: Results from a large-scale diffusion project. *Prevention Science, 11*(3), 252–262

Turner, K. M., and Sanders, M. R. (2006). Dissemination of evidence-based parenting and family support strategies: Learning from the Triple P—Positive Parenting Program system approach. *Aggression and Violent Behavior, 11*(2), 176–193.

Verdeli, H., Baily, C., Vousoura, E., Belser, A., Singla, D., and Manos, G. (2011). The case for treating depression in military spouses. *Journal Family Psychology, 25*(4), 488–496.

Weist, M. D., and Murray, M (Eds.). (2008). Advances in mental health promotion. *Advances in Mental Health Promotion 1*(3). Stafford, UK: The Clifford Beers Foundation.

Weisz, J. R., Jensen-Doss, A., and Hawley, K. M. (2006). Evidence-based youth psychotherapies versus usual clinical care: A meta-analysis of direct comparisons. *American Psychologist, 61*(7), 671.

Weisz, J. R., Krumholz, L. S., Santucci, L., Thomassin, K., and Ng, M. Y. (2015). Shrinking the gap between research and practice: Tailoring and testing youth psychotherapies in clinical care contexts. *Annual Review of Clinical Psychology, 11*, 139–163.

Weisz, J. R., Ugueto, A. M., Cheron, D. M., and Herren, J. (2013). Evidence-based youth psychotherapy in the mental health ecosystem. *Journal of Clinical Child & Adolescent Psychology, 42*(2), 274–286.

Whitestone, Y. K., and Thompson, B. A. (2016). How do military family policies influence parenting resources available to families? In A. H. Gewirtz and A. M. Youssef (Eds.), *Parenting and Children's Resilience in Military Families. Risk and Resilience in Military and Veteran Families* (pp. 283–297). Cham, Switzerland: Springer.

Wike, T. L., Bledsoe, S. E., Manuel, J. I., Despard, M., Johnson, L. V., Bellamy, J. L., and Killian-Farrell, C. (2014). Evidence-based practice in social work: Challenges and opportunities for clinicians and organizations. *Clinical Social Work Journal, 42*(2), 161–170.

Wilson, D. B., Gottfredson, D. C., and Najaka, S. S. (2001). School-based prevention of problem behaviors: A meta-analysis. Journal of Quantitative Criminology, 17(3), 247–272.

Wilson, S. J., and Lipsey, M. W. (2007). School-based interventions for aggressive and disruptive behavior: Update of a meta-analysis. *American Journal of Preventive Medicine, 33*(2), S130–S143.

Wilson, S. J., Lipsey, M. W., and Derzon, J. H. (2003). The effects of school-based intervention programs on aggressive behavior: A meta-analysis. *Journal of Consulting and Clinical Psychology, 71*(1), 136.

Witkiewitz, K., Desai, S. A., Bowen, S., Leigh, B.C., Kirouac, M., and Larimer, M. E. (2014). Development and evaluation of a mobile intervention for heavy drinking and smoking among college students. *Psychology of Addictive Behaviors, 28*(3), 639–650.

Yang, J. L., and Jayakumar, A. (2014). Target says up to 70 million more customers were hit by December data breach. *Washington Post,* January 10. Retrieved from https://www.washingtonpost.com/business/economy/target-says-70-million-customers-were-hit-by-dec-data-breach-more-than-first-reported/2014/01/10/0ada1026-79fe-11e3-8963-b4b654bcc9b2_story.html.

9

Committee Recommendations

In this chapter, the committee provides its recommendations to the U.S. Department of Defense (DoD) in three major areas: (1) how to enhance DoD's ability to understand the breadth and diversity of today's service members and their families and address their needs; (2) how to improve the programs and services of the Office of Military Community Family Policy (MC&FP); and (3) how to strengthen the broader Military Family Readiness System (MFRS).

These recommendations are built on our conclusions about the evidence of what is known about family well-being in the context of military service, together with the demographic and military service characteristics of military families and the opportunities and challenges that are unique to military life, all of which was reviewed in Chapters 1 through 4 of this report. The recommendations further emerge from the committee's understanding of the impact of stressors on child development and on military families, reviewed in Chapters 5 and 6. In Chapters 7 and 8, the committee presented a framework for building a more comprehensive and coherent approach to military family well-being and readiness, relying on what research has found concerning the translation and scaling of evidence-based and evidence-informed policies, programs, services, resources, and practices into larger systems, which point the way toward an adaptive process that can help build and sustain an effective and responsive MFRS.

ENHANCE UNDERSTANDING OF TODAY'S SERVICE MEMBERS AND THEIR FAMILIES

Through its review of the evidence, the committee finds that while many of DoD's policies, programs, services, resources, and practices focus on the well-being of military families, they do not adequately address the current breadth and diversity of service members and their families and their correspondingly diverse needs. Today's military families are dynamic social systems whose diversity includes single service members, service members in committed long-term relationships with nonmarital partners, service members co-parenting with ex-spouses or partners, children and other family members with special needs, same-sex couples, and people for whom English is a second language, among others. These families have varied and ever-changing stressors and needs ranging from the commonplace to the exceptional. The following recommendations are aimed at increasing DoD's understanding of the diversity and complexity of today's military families and consequently better supporting all military families, regardless of their diversity and complexity, as they strive to fulfill their responsibilities at home and at work.

RECOMMENDATION 1: To facilitate synthesis and comparison of information across administrative and survey datasets and research studies, and to support evaluations of the effectiveness of service member and family support programs, the Department of Defense (DoD) should develop and implement a standardized, military–specific definition of "family well-being." This definition should incorporate self-definitions of family and objective, subjective, and functional perspectives. DoD should also develop and implement military-specific definitions of "family readiness" and "family resilience," as well as a set of standard indicators of family well-being, readiness, and resilience for routine use.

When concepts that matter to DoD are insufficiently defined, and countless varieties of indicators are used across analytic efforts, it becomes difficult for DoD leaders, the Congress, and the public to discern the meaning of conflicting or fluctuating findings. These operationalized definitions and indicators should utilize existing or newly developed valid and reliable measures that consider the special circumstances of families who are currently 'invisible' to DoD (e.g., co-parenting but unmarried service members and same-sex couple households) and assess exposures to and the accumulation of adversity and how these affect families.

Until such time that DoD develops its own definitions, it should consider adopting and operationalizing the following definitions:

Family: service members' own definition of their family, which could include

- people to whom service members are related by blood, marriage, or adoption, which could include spouses, children, and service members' parents or siblings;

- people for whom service members have—or have assumed—a responsibility to provide care, which could include unmarried partners and their children, dependent elders, or others; and
- people who provide significant care for service members.

Family well-being:

- *Objective* well-being refers to resources considered necessary for adequate quality of life, such as sufficient economic and educational resources, housing, health, safety, environmental quality, and social connections.
- *Subjective* well-being is the result of how individuals think and feel about their circumstances.
- *Functional* well-being focuses on the degree to which families and their members can and do successfully perform their core functions, such as caring for, supporting, and nurturing family members.

Family readiness: The *potential* capacity of families as dynamic [human] systems to adapt successfully to disturbances that threaten the function, survival, or development of these systems.[1]

Family resilience: Positive adjustment in the aftermath of adversity. Also: "the *manifested* capacity of families as dynamic [human] systems to adapt successfully to disturbances that threaten the function, survival, or development of these systems"[2]

RECOMMENDATION 2: To establish policies, procedures, and programs that will better support military family readiness, the Department of Defense should (1) take immediate steps to gain a more comprehensive understanding of the diversity of today's military families and their needs, well-being, and readiness to support service members; and (2) develop policies and procedures to continuously improve and strengthen the information it collects, analyzes, and publicly reports about service members and their families to keep pace with societal, organizational, and operational changes.

To accomplish these things, DoD should

- Stand up an Implementation Science and Evaluation Unit that specializes in the design and execution of program implementation and outcome evaluations and is able to provide programs with

[1]Adapted from Masten (2015, p. 187).
[2]Adapted from Masten (2015, p. 187).

guidance on developing recommendations for improvement. A unit dedicated to program evaluations will improve, strengthen, and more fully utilize the information DoD collects, analyzes, and publicly reports. In addition, it could provide input on the commissioning of studies (cross-sectional and longitudinal) of military-connected children, spouses, and partners to support the larger goals of tracking short-term and long-term outcomes and taking intersectional approaches to data analyses.

- Sponsor robust longitudinal studies that assist with understanding temporary versus long-term outcomes and help address cross-sectional research limitations (e.g., limitations of respondent memory and recall) by using multiple methods and informants, as noted in Chapter 5. In addition, robust longitudinal studies of military-connected children and families can better provide a clear understanding of resilience processes over time and the protective factors that these individuals and families draw on within themselves and their communities. Such information can provide direction as to the type of efforts within the Continuum of Coordinated Support (i.e., promotional and prevention efforts) that are needed.
- Sponsor a large-scale study of family members who play a major role in the care of military children, utilizing standardized measures, as well as interviews, focus groups, and other feedback channels to solicit input from nonmarital cohabitating partners of service members and primary caregivers of service members' children (e.g., service members' parents, siblings, ex-spouses, or ex-partners).
- Conduct a study focused on the well-being of racial/ethnic minority service members and their families, including minority military families to characterize their own well-being, their top concerns, and how well they feel the military family readiness system is supporting them.
- Support analyses of existing data as well as new research that better identifies the effect on stress-related outcomes of contextual moderators, including National Guard or Reserve status, membership in a nontraditional family, socioeconomic status, race and ethnicity, faith and belief systems, and families affected by medical or neurodevelopmental conditions.

These more inclusive and more refined data should be used to better understand the macro and micro segments of the military community and not be used to single out individuals. To make the most of its investments, DoD should publish and otherwise disseminate actionable information from the above recommended studies, along with other relevant demographic information, in reports and educational programs to inform service providers, program managers, community partners, and researchers. This information sharing should be multidirectional: DoD should actively collaborate with and engage stakeholders, including diverse military families, military leaders, and civilian communities, to gather their voices and lived experiences to ensure that policies, programs, services, resources, and practices are adapted to and effective with diverse military families.

> **RECOMMENDATION 3: The Department of Defense should more fully identify, analyze, and integrate existing data to longitudinally track population-based military child risk and adversity, while also ensuring the privacy of individual family member information.**

The integration of various databases will enable DoD to more accurately understand risk and resilience factors and short- and long-term outcomes of the children of service members, thereby informing the development and delivery of programs that are tailored, streamlined, and effective. More specifically, the committee recommends that DoD link data from multiple surveys and administrative data, and potentially from program participation data, as is sometimes done for service member or military spouse research. Too little is known about children in military families, too often researchers rely solely on input from parents, and data about children collected across surveys are insufficiently mined. Barriers to studying minor children can be significant, and DoD endorsement could help with both feasibility and access.

The committee notes that DoD should attend to accumulations of risk, as children's functioning may be as much due to the accumulation of risk as to any individual risk factor. This monitoring of risk could occur as a matter of course for children attending DoD schools and child development centers, through military youth programs, through the Millenium Cohort Family Study, and/or when children are seen for psychological or medical treatment. Evidence suggests that there are two primary concerns: (1) What are the accumulations that have been experienced by any individual child who is presenting a need; and (2) In the general military population, what are typical patterns of accumulation and how important are they for children's outcomes?

Regarding longitudinal studies, to date no study has been conducted that matches military and civilian children to systematically discern how they differ and how they are similar. The CDC Youth Risk Behavior Survey does collect data from both military and civilian children, but focuses only on a narrow aspect of children's outcomes, and it provides no information at all about resilience factors or the factors that predict those outcomes. Consequently, there are currently no strong available data to determine at the population level whether or how military and civilian parents behave differently. This has been of grave concern during recent conflicts, because it is impossible to determine whether military and civilian children were on "equal footing" and it is also not possible to know what was "typical" of military children.

IMPROVE MILITARY COMMUNITY AND FAMILY POLICY PROGRAMS AND SERVICES

Continuous conflict over the past two decades and associated increases in operational tempo, with an all-volunteer force, have variably impacted family well-being and resulted in support needs that are more urgent for some military families, including National Guard and Reserve families. DoD has made significant investments in supporting service member and family well-being. However, the costs of supporting and managing personnel (not just family programs and services) have become quite high (see Figure 9-1), and have led to efforts to examine spending and identify savings. Thus, we are mindful that in an era of concerted efforts to contain escalating costs, DoD will not be eager to spend even more to cover more family members (such as domestic partners) and compensate military families even further for the demands of the military lifestyle.

The military lifestyle does not *have* to include many of these stressors to the degree that it does, however. Thus, the committee considered not only how DoD could help military families cope with military stressors,

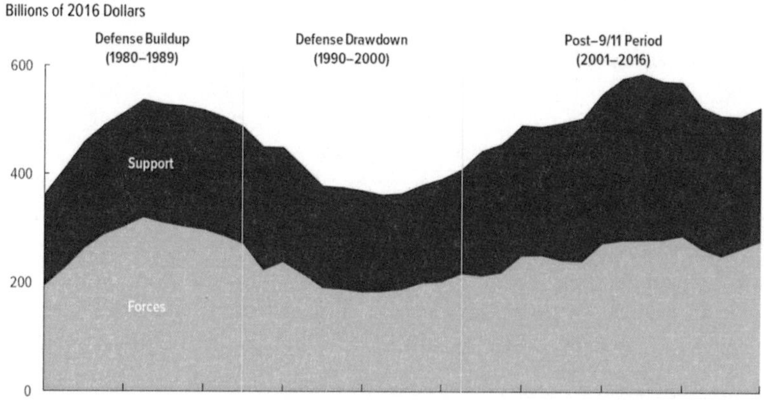

FIGURE 9-1 Trends in the Department of Defense's support costs, 1980–2016.
SOURCE: Congressional Budget Office (2017, p. 6).

but whether it could reduce some of the stressors in the first place, such as the frequency of PCS moves. For example, the FY 2019 John S. McCain National Defense Authorization Act (NDAA) authorizes (but does not require) DoD to use greater flexibility in the management of officer careers.[3] The 38-year-old one-size-fits-all up-or-out system created some of the pressures to frequently move officers so that they can obtain the diversity of assignments and experiences necessary to be promoted within a standard, limited window of time. The Services also created systems for enlisted personnel that mirrored the officer system by standardizing and limiting time to promotion in order to remain in the military. With the new NDAA, Congress allows DoD to support a wider variety of career progressions by repealing age-based officer appointment requirements, removing predetermined officer promotion timelines, allowing officers to go up for promotion multiple times, and permitting officer careers to extend to 40 years of service. Such changes could ostensibly ease work-family conflict for military personnel by reducing the need for so many military moves and corresponding family moves or separations.

In this section, the committee provides recommendations for reducing stressors and improving access to and the quality of DoD's programs and services.

RECOMMENDATION 4: The Department of Defense should review its current policies, programs, services, resources, and practices for supporting military families—as service members define families—to ensure that they recognize the wide diversity of today's military families and address the special circumstances of military life, especially with regard to major transitions such as entering military service, moving to new duty stations, deploying, shifting between active duty and reserve status, and transitioning to veteran status. This review should include, among other things, assessments of

- **the current delivery and content of relocation and other types of transition resources to determine their comprehensiveness with regard to life skills that can help families deal with these major life changes;**
- **the inclusiveness of these transition resources, such as whether the websites clarify that they are also concerned about single service members or refer only to spouses and not also partners or other family members, and whether dates or partners are made to feel**

[3]For a general summary of the NDAA, see https://www.armed-services.senate.gov/imo/media/doc/FY19%20NDAA%20Conference%20Summary1.pdf; and for a reference tool regarding laws, policies and practices in the management of military officers see http://dopma-ropma.rand.org/index.html.

welcome at military events, regardless of whether the law permits them to be military dependents; and

- **application of the new flexibilities granted by the National Defense Authorization Act for Fiscal Year 2019, which could ease the need to move personnel as frequently, allow them to move up the career ladder more slowly, and allow them to have longer military careers; these new options may benefit military family well-being by reducing turbulence and work-family conflict.**

Service members and their families rely upon DoD for assistance with major transitions. For National Guard and Reserve personnel and their families, an app, roadmap, interactive website, infographic, or other user-friendly means of conveying how their pay, allowances, benefits, and program eligibility change along with changes to military status could help reduce service access barriers and support gaps. Even when these service members are not on Title 10 active duty status, maintaining individual and family readiness among members of the reserve component is critical so that they are fully prepared when their nation needs to call on them yet again.

The committee recommends that policies, programs, services, resources, and practices incorporate the resilience factors that are more fully described in Chapter 2. These include

- developing shared belief systems;
- improving and strengthening families' organizational patterns;[4]
- strengthening communication and problem-solving skills;
- fostering social interaction in the military and nonmilitary communities in which they are embedded;
- addressing physical and psychological health concerns and needs; and
- building the effectiveness of family support systems—through both informal supports and formal resources, programs, and services.

STRENGTHEN THE BROADER MILITARY FAMILY READINESS SYSTEM

Through its review of the evidence, the committee finds that DoD recognizes the importance of families to the military performance of service members and has built an MFRS for which there is no U.S. civilian

---

[4]As stated in Chapter 2: "Organizational patterns—Family members spend time together in constructive activities, the family is organized to provide effective support to its members with a good balance of flexibility and connectedness, family members play appropriate roles, and the family has adequate social and economic resources that it manages adequately."

equivalent. In order to meet the ever-changing demands, the MFRS needs to be a flexible and adaptive system designed to keep up with the needs of families as they exist in their communities and at different points in time. The committee recognizes that Military OneSource[5] provides a valuable service in helping to match the unique needs of individual families to available DoD, Service, and certain civilian programs for which they are eligible. In addition, Military OneSource provides crisis resources and posts a wealth of military-specific information online. However, the committee finds that an even more comprehensive and coordinated approach is needed to be responsive to the diversity of families and their needs. Inconsistent attention to and utilization of empirical evidence about program alignment and implementation reduces program effectiveness. The following recommendations address ways to strengthen the broader MFRS.

RECOMMENDATION 5: To help military leaders and nonmilitary service providers in civilian communities better understand and prioritize issues specific to their local communities, the Department of Defense should provide guidance for military leaders and service providers on how to readily and reliably access and utilize information about the surrounding communities in which their personnel are situated.

DoD should task an entity with leading the charge of compiling and reporting information on a regular basis about the surrounding communities in which their personnel are situated. Military bases do not exist in isolation, and more service members and families live off military installations than on. The neighborhoods that surround military bases are not all equivalent—they can vary in social and economic conditions, which has implications for the strength of social networks to support military families, the quality and quantity of nonmilitary resources that families could tap into, job opportunities for military spouses, educational and other opportunities for military children, the personal safety of military families, and other factors. If military leaders and nonmilitary service providers know only about the characteristics of individuals on their installations, they may be blind to issues some families are facing in their neighborhoods and the extent to which community resources are already overtaxed by a civilian population with great needs that therefore cannot supplement military ones.

[5]Military OneSource is a DoD program that provides comprehensive information, referral, and assistance on aspects of military life for service members and their families. Military OneSource services are accessible via a helpline or website (https://www.militaryonesource.mil). See Chapters 4 and 7 for examples of the use of Military OneSource.

Using existing data from "outside the gate" will enable key military leaders and nonmilitary service providers to make data-driven decisions about needed policies, programs, and services. The DoD MFRS as a whole, as well as commanders on the ground, must be able to work effectively with community organizations to support military families in a well-integrated way. Aggregate statistics on local unemployment rates (U.S. Bureau of Labor Statistics), poverty levels (U.S. Census Bureau), school district data (U.S. Census Bureau), crime rates (Federal Bureau of Investigation), cost of living (DoD) and the like are free and publicly available from government websites. In addition, such statistics could be added to the DoD administrative, survey, and program databases to assist with larger-scale efforts to identify variation in needs. Supplementing survey data is especially important because it can be challenging to identify, reach, and gain sufficient response rates from military families, including nonmarital partners. There are a few published reports that illustrate that some neighborhoods around military bases are much better off than others, thus suggesting that the allocation of military base resources should take this more into account than installation population size.

RECOMMENDATION 6: The Department of Defense should build its capacity to support service members and families by promoting better civilian understanding of the strengths and needs of military-connected individuals. These efforts should particularly address misinformation, negative stereotypes, and lack of knowledge.

DoD should authorize MC&FP to partner with the Office of Communications to conduct an ongoing media relations campaign to promote the civilian community's understanding of military-connected individuals as assets. Clear informational awareness campaigns and educational efforts are needed to address misinformation, combat negative stereotypes, and promote understanding. The MC&FP-funded Military Families Learning Network is a sound example of how to increase awareness and knowledge within the military-serving practitioner and academic community. Efforts to increase civilian understanding of military-connected individuals are required to ensure that the professionals and organizations military families will encounter in communities are well prepared to serve them.

The lack of awareness and stereotypes about military families among civilians can be harmful. Ignorance and negative stereotypes can limit military families' social support networks or result in harmful, unwarranted community reactions toward them. For example, if teachers, doctors, coaches, and others do not know about how children may act or respond when a parent is deployed, they may not understand why a child is behaving in a certain manner, an appropriate way to respond, and how to potentially engage other support resources rather than berate, punish, or label the child as a "problem." As another example, civilians who hold stereotypes of veterans as possessing deficits, being unstable, mentally ill, prone to violent outbursts, or displaying other negative behaviors may be less willing to rent to them, hire them, socialize with them, and let their children socialize with veterans' children.

DoD can build its capacity to support service members and families through a social marketing information campaign and joint civilian-military events that include educational elements (e.g., educational booths, exhibits, videos, plays dispelling myths that are part of a family-friendly carnival, air show, Fourth of July celebration, or other event). School liaison officers are also very important in preparing educational systems to better serve military-connected children and their families, although they may not be present in areas where military children are uncommon.

RECOMMENDATION 7: The Department of Defense (DoD) should enable military family support providers, civilian or in uniform, who work for military systems, and consumers to access effective, evidence-based and evidence-informed[6] family strengthening programs, resources, and services. To meet the diverse and ever-changing needs of service members and their families, and address the current significant gap between research and practice, DoD should strengthen the Military Family Readiness System so that it

- **provides a comprehensive continuum of support across medical and nonmedical providers, locations, and changing benefit eligibility;**
- **facilitates adaptive and timely approaches to stepped-care[7] delivery;**
- **draws upon effective evidence-based or evidence-informed approaches;**
- **integrates routine screening and assessment tools in the delivery of family support programs;**
- **builds and employs a robust data infrastructure, for both implementation and outcome data, that supports a continuous quality improvement system; and**
- **coordinates referrals and care across military and nonmilitary resources, institutions, and communities.**

[6]See Chapter 1 for descriptions of *evidence-based* and *evidence-informed*.

[7]Stepped care models of prevention and intervention in health and behavioral health services match the type and intensity of services to family and service members' needs. Given the diverse and dynamic nature of family needs and resources, prevention and intervention services are offered along a continuum of intensity from prevention and assessment, through 'watchful waiting,' up to high intensity, targeted treatments for specific distressing or more severe conditions.

DoD should mobilize and task MC&FP and the Defense Health Agency to partner for the overall leadership, coordination, policy-making, and operationalization of the MFRS. The Services should be engaged in the tailoring of programs and services; however, the core components of those efforts must be consistent and established by MC&FP. Moreover, MC&FP should create an Implementation Science and Evaluation Unit that could lead a CQI effort involving monitoring and implementation support. It could widely promote sources of information available on evidence-based and evidence-informed programs, resources, and services. Program evaluation should be promoted, and when programs in military communities have been formally evaluated the results of these evaluations can be widely shared and promoted across DoD and the Services. The results of those evaluations should be shared in publicly accessible documentation, such as on the Military OneSource website, in the Defense Technical Information Center online (DTIC), and through other venues, including those results which show no effect or negative effects.

RECOMMENDATION 8: To support high-quality implementation, adaptation, and sustainability of policies, programs, practices, and services that are informed by a continuous quality improvement process, the Department of Defense should develop, adopt, and sustain a dynamic learning system as part of its Military Family Readiness System.

Such a dynamic learning system requires a process of tailoring and decision-making grounded in a sufficient level of evidence about screening, policies, programming, services, resources, and practices to understand and strengthen family well-being in the distinct cultural contexts of the different branches, in myriad domestic and international locations, and across ever-changing organizational and socioeconomic circumstances. By instituting ongoing accountability for system effectiveness, a high-functioning MFRS framework will incorporate assessment and the results of existing efforts, improve response capabilities, and point to the development of future resilience and readiness strategies for military families.

RECOMMENDATION 9: The Department of Defense (DoD) should continually assess the availability and effectiveness of specialized family-centered policies, programs, services, resources, and practices to support the evolving and unexpected needs of families facing exceptionally high stressors (e.g., military service related injury, illness or death), in order to implement programs targeting emerging threats to military family well-being. In particular, DoD should seek to serve highly affected families through interdisciplinary, collaborative models

in which military and nonmilitary service providers, health care providers, and other professionals, both within and outside the Military Health System, are prepared to rapidly develop and deliver family-centered services that address emerging, high-stress family challenges. Policies, programs, and services should be systematically evaluated and prepared to respond to evolving high-stress situations within the recommended Military Family Readiness Learning System.

Recent experiences have identified military families faced by illness, injury, or death as those most highly affected (see Chapter 6). However, future challenges to military families remain unknown. MC&FP[8] shares responsibility for promoting health and well-being as part of its overall leadership role in coordinating, making policy for, operationalizing, and evaluating nonmedical programs and services that comprise the MFRS. The preventive care of the most vulnerable families must remain a primary mission of MC&FP. Such an effort reflects an investment in returning all military families to full functionality and provides a significant return on investment not only for those that are most affected but for all military families who trust in the resources that will be delivered under trying conditions. Programming for highly impacted military families should be incorporated as a major function of the newly established Implementation Science and Evaluation Unit in coordination with program analysts and managers.

Candidly, the future challenges faced by military families are unknown, but are likely to include unanticipated threats, which will require the coordinated efforts of community service providers, health care providers, and others both within and outside of the military community. Currently, families turn to religious and spiritual leaders, school counselors, nonprofit organizations for war veterans, unions, city councils, first sergeants, and other resources in addition to the health care system for the issues they are facing. Future family challenges are likely to require as much if not more coordination of efforts across resources and platforms of care. We must always remember that families are not just groups of individuals, but individuals who interact as a system (see Chapter 2). Historically, this has been most relevant in military families affected by the most challenging circumstances. As a result, specialized programming targeting highly impacted families must attend to multilevel resilience pathways within families (see Chapter 6), and efforts to support them must focus on more than just the needs of individual family members. Multiple efforts, including strengthening couples, parental guidance, and programmatic counseling, as well as

[8]The committee notes that MC&FP is not a healthcare provider—that responsibility falls to the Defense Health Agency (DHA). However, this recommendation will require collaboration across DoD entities (i.e., DHA and MC&FP).

family-level efforts that target family communication, problem-solving, and conflict resolution skills all currently have evidence-based support. We must be prepared to address unforeseen high-impact stressors that are likely to affect military families in the future, requiring refinements to these existing strategies. Such refinements can be accomplished as defined by a dynamic Military Family Readiness Learning System (see Chapter 8).

RECOMMENDATION 10: To enhance the effectiveness and efficiency of the Military Family Readiness System, the Department of Defense should investigate innovations in big data and predictive analytics to improve the accessibility, engagement, personalization, and effectiveness of policies, programs, practices, and services for military families. Among other things, this should include assessment of the utility of mobile applications, virtual service delivery, and wearables for strengthening family functioning by personalizing preventive interventions and delivering them "just in time" (i.e., in real time, at the needed dose, and in the preferred formats for families).

An analysis of data with learning-enhanced approaches may be used to detect mental health issues, such as suicidality and well-being, and may lead to more effective methods of comparing intervention options. Harnessing new technologies for program delivery could broaden the range of available program options, including program intensity and dosage. Virtual service delivery and online self-directed interventions offer the user an opportunity to engage anytime, anywhere. Wearables have the potential to track individual stress points (e.g., during or just prior to a stressful event that could lead to child abuse, substance use, or other risky behavior) and consequently interrupt maladaptive behaviors, encouraging and teaching more adaptive strategies instead. Of course, DoD will need to be prudent as it evaluates the options, to manage privacy and national security concerns and other unintended consequences, as well as assess whether technologies have sufficiently evolved to be able to live up to the hype.

RECOMMENDATION 11: To facilitate the consistency and continuation of its policies regarding military family readiness and well-being across political administrations and changes of senior military leadership, the Department of Defense should update and promulgate its existing instruction that operationalizes the importance of military family well-being by incorporating the conclusions and recommendations contained in this report.

While DoD has made some commitments about *objective* family well-being, such as setting standards for housing and allowances, it has not yet committed to comprehensive standards in this regard. With regard to *subjective* family well-being, no standard has been declared, but DoD regularly monitors satisfaction with the military lifestyle. In addition, DoD has not addressed *functional* family well-being. For instance, does DoD aspire for all parents to be able to provide appropriate warmth and limits for their children? Does it aspire for all spouses or partners to effectively communicate? The committee recommends that DoD consider the research findings we have reviewed in Chapter 5 on what is required for families to be able to function effectively during service members' absences and on how to prevent maltreatment, divorce, and other family events that may prove incompatible with military service.

Policy can help clarify DoD's overarching goals and priorities in a lasting way. Because there is frequent turnover in leadership, there can be a lack of institutional memory and continued momentum after program champions have gone. Some of the committee's recommendations are for long-term action (e.g., longitudinal studies, types of data to be collected and reported). Policy can help ensure that longer-term efforts are carried through, initial steps were not wasted, and trends over time and potential causal explanations can be identified. Consistency is also important for fairness, so that service members and families in one Service are not underserved relative to service members and families in other Services. Additionally, as DoD and the Services operate with limited funds and competing demands, what is not documented in policy can be more difficult to achieve or sustain.

REFERENCES

Congressional Budget Office. (2017). *Trends in the Department of Defense's Support Costs*. Retrieved from https://www.cbo.gov/system/files/115th-congress-2017-2018reports/53168-dodsupportcosts.pdf.

Masten, A. S. (2015). Pathways to integrated resilience science. *Psychological Inquiry, 26*(2), 187–196.

Appendix A

Biosketches of Committee Members and Project Staff

COMMITTEE MEMBERS

Kenneth W. Kizer *(chair)* is a distinguished professor in the University of California, Davis, School of Medicine and the Betty Irene Moore School of Nursing, as well as director of the Institute for Population Health Improvement (IPHI) in the university's health system. An internationally respected health care leader, his multiple roles at IPHI include serving as the chief medical officer for the California Department of Managed Health Care, director of the California Cancer Reporting and Epidemiologic Surveillance Program, and chief quality improvement consultant for the Medi-Cal Quality Improvement Program. His diverse professional experience includes senior positions in the public and private sectors, in academia, and in philanthropy, including these: founding president and CEO, National Quality Forum; chairman, CEO, and president, Medsphere Systems Corporation; Under Secretary for Health, U.S. Department of Veterans Affairs, the nation's largest health care system, in which capacity he engineered the internationally acclaimed transformation of the Veterans Healthcare System in the late 1990s; director of the former California Department of Health Services; and chairman of the California Wellness Foundation. He is an honors graduate of Stanford University and the University of California–Los Angeles, the recipient of two honorary doctorates, and a fellow or distinguished fellow of 12 professional societies. He is board certified in six medical specialties and/or subspecialties, and has authored more than 500 original articles, book chapters, and other reports. He is a veteran of the U.S. Navy, a former Navy diving medical officer, and a recognized expert on medicine in wilderness and other austere environments.

David Albright currently holds the Hill Crest Foundation Endowed Chair in Mental Health at the University of Alabama, with a tenured appointment in the School of Social Work. He is a military veteran and former research fellow with both the Department of Veterans Affairs and the RAND Corporation's Center for Military Health Policy Research. Dr. Albright works to produce research that is useful for communities, health care providers, and policy makers as they work to address and improve health-related determinants and outcomes among military personnel, veterans, and their families and communities.

Stephen J. Cozza is professor of psychiatry at the Uniformed Services University, where he serves as associate director, Center for the Study of Traumatic Stress. He has served in a variety of positions of responsibility in the Department of Psychiatry at Walter Reed Army Medical Center, including chief, Child and Adolescent Psychiatry Service; program director, Child and Adolescent Psychiatry Fellowship Program; and chief, Department of Psychiatry. Dr. Cozza retired from the U.S. Army in 2006 after 25 years of military service. His professional interests have been in the areas of clinical and community response to trauma and the impact of deployment and combat injury, illness, and death on military service members, their families, and their children. Under his leadership, the Walter Reed Department of Psychiatry spearheaded the initiative to provide mental health services, support, and follow-up to the many injured service members, their families, and their children who receive medical treatment. Dr. Cozza is a diplomate of the American Board of Psychiatry and Neurology in the specialties of general psychiatry and child and adolescent psychiatry. He serves as a scientific advisor to several national organizations that focus on the needs of military children and families. He is a graduate of the U.S. Military Academy, received his medical degree from the George Washington University School of Medicine and Health Sciences, and completed his residency in general psychiatry and a fellowship in child and adolescent psychiatry at Walter Reed Army Medical Center in Washington, D.C.

Ellen DeVoe is professor and director of the doctorate program at the Boston University School of Social Work. Her early scholarship focused on sexual abuse, the impact of domestic and community violence on children and families, and intervention research. Her work has been supported by the National Institute of Mental Health (NIMH), the Centers for Disease Control and Prevention, the Robert Wood Johnson Foundation, and the Department of Defense. Since the 9/11 attacks, Dr. De Voe has been immersed in intervention research concerning parents affected by traumatic stress, including military and veteran parents and families. For the last decade, she has directed a program of research funded by the Department of Defense focused on the development of a parenting intervention program to support military parents throughout cycles of deployment and reintegration. She is currently the principal investigator of a randomized clinical trial study of deploying parents of young children at the Fort Hood Army installation, titled the Strong Families Strong Forces Prevention Project, which is evaluating the efficacy of an intervention to reduce military family distress across the military deployment cycle. She holds a B.A. from Princeton University, an M.S.W. from the University of Denver, and a Ph.D. in social work and social science from the University of Michigan and completed an NIMH postdoctoral fellowship in family-violence research training at the University of New Hampshire.

Abigail Gewirtz is the John and Nancy Lindahl Leadership professor in the Department of Family Social Science and the Institute of Child Development and director of the Institute for Translational Research in Children's Mental Health at the University of Minnesota. Her research focuses on the development, effectiveness testing, and implementation of targeted prevention programs that promote child resilience among highly stressed families, including those affected by military deployment and war. For more than a decade, her research has been funded by the National Institutes of Health, the Substance Abuse and Mental Health Services Administration, and the Department of Defense. Dr. Gewirtz is principal investigator on two current randomized controlled trials to develop and test a web-enhanced parenting program for military families with parents returning from wars in Iraq and Afghanistan. She has published and presented widely on parenting, trauma, and child adjustment, extending parent training models for populations affected by traumatic stress, and the role of community sectors of care as portals for family-based prevention. She holds a BSc. from University College London, an M.A. in psychology from Tel Aviv University, and a Ph.D. in clinical psychology from Teachers College, Columbia University. She is a licensed psychologist in Minnesota and was previously licensed in Connecticut.

Mary M. Keller serves as the president and CEO of the Military Child Education Coalition (MCEC), for which she has been the executive leader since 1998. She is one of the founders of the MCEC, the nation's only nonprofit organization that serves military children around the world as they strive to meet the challenges of frequent transitions, parental deployments, loss, and trauma. The MCEC was recognized by First Lady Laura Bush in 2004 as the Congressional Club Charity of the Year and, in 2008, was certified America's Best Charity by Independent Charities of America. Dr. Keller has also served as a teacher and school administrator in several Texas school districts for more than 21 years. She served for 8 years as assistant superintendent and area superintendent for education services for the Killeen

Independent School District, which today serves more than 20,000 military-connected children and the nation's largest military installation, Fort Hood. She holds a master's degree in education with a specialization in curriculum and instruction from Wayland Baptist University and a doctorate in educational administration from Texas Tech University. She holds professional teaching certifications in elementary as well as history, supervision, midmanagement, and superintendency. She is also trained in formal mediation and has held a certification from the Texas Bar Association.

Patricia Lester is the Nathanson Family professor of psychiatry, director of the Division of Population Behavioral Health, director of the Nathanson Family Resilience Center, and the medical director of the Family STAR (Stress, Trauma and Resilience) service, all at the University of California–Los Angeles Semel Institute for Neuroscience and Human Behavior. A board-certified child and adolescent psychiatrist, Dr. Lester's research and clinical work have been dedicated to the development, evaluation, and implementation of family-centered prevention and treatment for children and families facing adversity and trauma. She codeveloped the trauma-informed, family-centered preventive intervention FOCUS, which was designed to enhance resilience and mitigate stress in families facing adversities such as medical illness and military wartime deployment, injury, and loss. She oversees an online learning center and evaluation data management system, which utilizes web-based technologies to scale program implementation with fidelity within community, school, and health care settings. Over the past decade, she has conducted a number of research studies on the impact of parental deployment on military-connected children and families, and she is currently the principal investigator of a randomized trial of a virtually delivered family prevention intervention for military and veteran families with young children, funded by the National Institute of Child Health and Development. She is well-versed in the scientific and programmatic issues facing military-connected families and serves as an advisor on the needs of military children and families across military, university, and nonprofit agencies, including as an advisor to the Millennium Family Cohort Study. She holds an M.D. from the University of California–San Francisco School of Medicine.

Shelley MacDermid Wadsworth is professor of human development and family studies at Purdue University, where she is also director of both the Center for Families and the Military Family Research Institute and executive director of the Family Impact Institute. Her primary research interest is in the relationships between work conditions and family life. Over the past 20 years, she has studied differences between small and large workplaces, how adults grow and develop as a result of their work experiences, and how different kinds of organizational policies make it easier or more difficult for workers to be successful at work and at home. As the director of the Center for Families she conducts research and engagement activities focused on helping individuals and organizations who serve families do their work more effectively. In 2000, she began to conduct research about and for military families through the Military Family Research Institute. She has served on the Department of Defense Task Force on Mental Health, is a recipient of the Work Life Legacy Award from the Families and Work Institute, and was named a fellow of the National Council on Family Relations. She holds an M.S. and a Ph.D. in human development and family studies, as well as an M.B.A. in management, all from the Pennsylvania State University.

Laura L. Miller is a senior military sociologist at the RAND Corporation. For more than 25 years she has studied the lives of military personnel and their families through surveys, observations, discussion groups, one-on-one interviews, and analyses of military policy and personnel data. Her research topics include military culture and organization; deployment experiences; gender integration; sexual harassment and sexual assault; social problems; health and well-being; military families; military spouse education and employment; attitudes toward gays and lesbians in the military; unit cohesion and morale; and civil-military relations. To collect primary data, Dr. Miller has traveled to more than 40 stateside installations and to overseas bases and operations in Afghanistan, Bosnia, Germany, Haiti, Hungary, Korea, Kuwait, Macedonia, Qatar, the Serb Republic, and Somalia. She has served on numerous advisory boards and task forces, including as a part of the Office of the Secretary of Defense's Self-governing Review Related to Fort Hood (2009) and the Air Force Follow-On Review Related to Fort Hood (2010); as an advisor on military and sociological aspects of suicide research for the Army Science Board and the Department of the Army (2008–2009); and as a member of two commissions investigating sexual misconduct, harassment, and violence at the military service academies (2003–2005). Dr. Miller was previously an assistant professor of sociology at the University of California–Los Angeles (1997–2002) and a postdoctoral fellow at the John M. Olin Institute for Strategic Studies at Harvard University (1995–1997). She holds both an M.A. and a Ph.D. in sociology from Northwestern University and a B.A. from the University of Redlands.

Tracy Neal-Walden is senior vice president and director of the Steven A. Cohen Military Family Clinic at Easterseals, a licensed clinical psychologist, and a retired Air Force colonel with more than 25 years of experience in mental health treatment, leadership, outreach, and policy. She directs clinical, administrative, financial, and outreach operations for the clinic, which is part of the Cohen Veterans Network, providing high-quality, accessible, integrated and no-cost/low-cost mental health care to veterans, their families, and caretakers. She specializes in the cognitive-behavioral treatment of insomnia, depression, anxiety, chronic pain, and other health-related conditions in military and veteran populations. In addition, she is a clinical trainer in integrated behavioral health in primary care, and has trained, supervised, and mentored clinicians across the Air Force and Department of Defense in evidence-based treatment at both the pre- and post-doctoral levels. She serves on the American Psychological Association's Continuing Education Committee and has conducted and published research in the area of suicide prevention. She holds a Ph.D. in clinical psychology from Drexel University–Hahnemann Medical Campus and completed a 2-year postdoctoral fellowship in clinical health psychology at the Wilford Hall Medical and Surgical Center in San Antonio, Texas.

Daniel F. Perkins is a professor of family and youth resiliency and policy at the Pennsylvania State University. He is principal scientist and founder of an applied research center, the Clearinghouse for Military Family Readiness at Penn State. Dr. Perkins leads applied research projects to inform professionals who are supporting military families through high-quality program implementation and assessment activities. Dr. Perkins is also interested in hybrid evaluations of preventions and interventions, implementation science, and community-based delivery models. He has been designing and evaluating strengths-based family and youth development programs in 4-H and Cooperative Extension for more than 20 years. In addition, he is also an affiliate faculty member of the Penn State Prevention Research Center for the Promotion of Human Development. Within the field of prevention science, Dr. Perkins examines type II translational research, that is, research on transitioning evidence-based programs tested in tightly controlled environments to large-scale expansions into real-world settings. He is currently investigating the utilization of proactive technical assistance (e.g., coaching) and the role of other contextual factors (e.g., setting of the program) in contributing to the long-term implementation quality and sustainability of evidence-based programs. Dr. Perkins is also a co-principal investigator on The Veteran Metrics Initiative, leading efforts to characterize the programs veterans use as they reintegrate into civilian life and distilling the programs into their common components so that links between those components and veteran well-being can be identified. He holds a Ph.D. in family and child ecology from Michigan State University, and an M.S. in human development and family studies and a B.S. in psychology from the Pennsylvania State University.

Ashish S. Vazirani is the executive director and the chief executive officer of the National Military Family Association. He provides strategic and operational oversight of the leading nonprofit dedicated to serving the families who stand behind the uniform. Before joining NMFA, Mr. Varizani led development and programming at Armed Services YMCA. He was responsible for developing deep and lasting engagement with the donors and ensuring implementation and measurement of standardized programs serving military families. Prior to his work with the ASYMCA, Mr. Varizani spent more than 22 years as a management consultant working with leading high tech and pharmaceutical companies to improve their marketing and sales functions to deliver profitable growth. He also served as a marketing and development advisor to military services organizations such as the USO (2011–2014) and Operation Homefront (2014–2017). Before his career in consulting, and sales and marketing management, Mr. Varizani served in the U.S. Navy as a Submarine Officer from 1986 to 1993. Mr. Varizani holds a B.E. in mechanical engineering from Vanderbilt University, an M.E. from the McCormick School of Engineering at Northwestern University, and a M.B.A. from the Kellogg School of Management at Northwestern University. Mr. Varizani's family immigrated to the United States when he was 3 years old. He is the son of a combat wounded, Vietnam-era Marine and the father of a currently serving Marine; service is the family business. His priorities are faith, family and country.

Ivan C. A. Walks is the CEO of Ivan Walks & Associates, a health and human services consulting firm. He is a former chief health officer of the District of Columbia and director of the D.C. Department of Health and has served on the adjunct medical faculty at both George Washington University and Howard University. He was appointed by the governor to the State of Maryland Board of Education, which he served for 4 years. After the 9/11 terrorist attacks, Dr. Walks served on a board for the American Red Cross to oversee health recovery efforts for those impacted by the events at the Pentagon and the Twin Towers in New York. He has been honored by the American Public Health Association as a "Public Health Hero," by Mayor Anthony Williams with The Government of the District of Columbia Distinguished Public Service Award, by Leadership Greater Washington with its Founder's Award for Leadership and Community Service, and by the American Federation of Government Employees with its President's Award. He has offered testimony before both houses of Congress and was a featured presenter at the 1999 White House Conference on Mental Health. Dr. Walks has served on the American Psychiatric Association (APA) Board of Trustees; chaired the APA Committee of Residents and Fellows; and was a member of the Inaugural APA/AMA Joint Board of Trustees Meeting. He holds an M.D. from the University of California at Davis, and completed additional training at the UCLA Neuropsychiatric

Institute, the West LA Veterans Administration, the U.S. Department of Health and Human Services, and the John F. Kennedy School of Government at Harvard University.

PROJECT STAFF

Suzanne Le Menestrel (*study director*) is a senior program officer with the Board on Children, Youth, and Families at the National Academies of Sciences, Engineering, and Medicine, where her responsibilities have included directing four consensus studies focused on children and adolescents, from birth to age 21, as well as directing the Forum for Children's Well-Being. Prior to her tenure with the National Academies, Dr. Menestrel was the founding national program leader for youth development research at 4-H National Headquarters, served as research director at the Academy for Educational Development's Center for Youth Development and Policy Research, and was a research associate at Child Trends. She was a founder of the *Journal of Youth Development: Bridging Research and Practice* and chaired its Publications Committee. Dr. Le Menestrel has published in numerous refereed journals and is an invited member of several advisory groups, including a research advisory group for the American Camp Association, a Girl Scouts of the Nation's Capital STEM Strategy advisory group, and the National Leadership Steering Committee for the Cooperative Extension System–Robert Wood Johnson Foundation Culture of Health Initiative. She holds an M.S. and a Ph.D. in human development and family studies from the Pennsylvania State University, a B.S. in psychology from St. Lawrence University, and a nonprofit management executive certificate from Georgetown University.

David Butler is a scholar in the Health and Medicine Division and the director of the Office of Military and Veterans Health. Before joining the National Academies, Dr. Butler served as an analyst for the U.S. Congress Office of Technology Assessment, was a research associate in the Department of Environmental Health of the Harvard School of Public Health, and performed research at Harvard's Kennedy School of Government. He has directed several National Academies studies on environmental health and risk assessment topics, including studies examining climate change, the indoor environment, and asthma. Dr. Butler has also been lead staff officer for a number of reports on the effects of environmental exposures on the health of active-duty military personnel and veterans, including volumes of the Veterans and Agent Orange report series. He is a recipient of the Cecil Award, the highest distinction for a staff member of the Institute of Medicine (now the National Academy of Medicine). Dr. Butler holds a B.S. and an M.S. in engineering from the University of Rochester and a Ph.D. in public policy analysis from Carnegie Mellon University.

Priyanka Nalamada is an associate program officer with the Board on Children, Youth, and Families at the National Academies of Sciences, Engineering, and Medicine. Upon completing a congressional internship she joined the National Academies and worked for a number of years within the Health and Medicine Division. Her work involves research and project management in the areas of public health and education. Her past work focused on a range of global health issues including public-private partnerships in low- and middle-income countries, medical device donations in low-resource settings, and the role of multinational companies in health literacy. She holds a degree in political science from Bryn Mawr College.

Stacey Smit serves as a senior program assistant with the Board on Children, Youth, and Families at the National Academies of Sciences, Engineering, and Medicine, supporting consensus studies overseen by the board. She has more than 10 years' experience in event planning and providing administrative support and has worked at various organizations in the Washington, D.C., area. In the past, she has supported the Executive Office of the Division of Behavioral and Social Sciences and Education; the Decadal Survey of Social and Behavioral Sciences for Applications to National Security; the Committee on the Use of Economic Evidence to Inform Investments in Children, Youth, and Families; the Committee on Supporting the Parents of Young Children; the Forum on Children's Cognitive, Affective, and Behavioral Health; and the Committee on Increasing Capacity for Reducing Bullying and Its Impact on the Lifecourse of Youth Involved. She holds a B.A. in sociology from the University of Maryland, College Park.

Appendix B

Agenda for Public Information-Gathering Session

National Academy of Sciences
2101 Constitution Avenue, NW
Washington, DC

April 24, 2018

11:30am – 11:35am	**Welcome and Goals** Kenneth W. Kizer, University of California, Davis, Committee Chair
11:35am – 1:15pm	**PANEL 1: Families Underrepresented in the Research Literature** Moderator: Shelley MacDermid Wadsworth, Purdue University, Committee Member

- Ashley Broadway-Mack, President, The American Military Partner Association
- Karen Ruedisueli, Government Relations Deputy Director, National Military Family Association
- Chaplain (COL) Jimmy Nichols, Installation Command Chaplain, Fort Sill, OK
- Ed Tyner, Associate Director, Office of Family Readiness/Office of Special Needs

1:15pm – 2:55pm	**PANEL 2: Representatives of the National Guard and Reserves** Moderator: Abigail Gewirtz, University of Minnesota, Committee Member • Kelly Hokanson, spouse of National Guard Bureau Vice Chief, LTG Daniel R. Hokanson • Jill Marconi, Air Force, Director, Airman & Family Readiness • Susan Lukas, Director, Legislation & Military Policy, Reserve Officers Association • Anthony A. Wickham, J1 Program Director, National Guard Bureau
2:55pm – 3:15pm	**BREAK**
3:15pm – 4:55pm	**PANEL 3: Representatives from Military Service Branches** Moderator: Tracy Neal-Walden, The Steven A. Cohen Military Family Clinic at Easterseals, Committee Member • Col. (Ret) Anthony Cox, Army, former manager, HQDA Family Advocacy Program • Ellyn Dunford, spouse of Gen. Joseph F. Dunford, Chairman of the Joint Chiefs of Staff • Elka Giordano, Chief of Naval Operations Ombudsman-at-Large and spouse of Master Chief Petty Officer of the Navy Steven S. Giordano • Donald R. Neff, Deputy Director, Preservation of the Force and Family, United States Special Operations Command
4:55pm – 5:00pm	**Closing Remarks** Kenneth W. Kizer

Appendix C

Authors of Memos Submitted to the Committee

Individuals

Ron Avi Astor, University of Southern California, and Rami Benbenishty, Bar-Ilan University

Anthony Cox, Colonel (*retired*), U.S. Army, Brooke Army Medical Center

Glenn A. Fine, Department of Defense

Eric Flake, USUHS, Madigan Army Medical Center

Tara E. Galovski, National Center for PTSD at the VA Boston Healthcare System and Wesley Sanders Harvard Medical School

Niranjan Karnik, Rush University Medical College

Richard M. Lerner, Tufts University

Gregory Leskin, UCLA/Duke University National Center for Child Traumatic Stress

Lt. General Raymond Mason, Army Emergency Relief

Rene Robichaux, National Association of Social Workers Foundation

Margaret C. Wilmoth, University of North Carolina at Chapel Hill, and Alicia Gill Rossiter, University of South Florida

Organizations

AARP (Douglas Dickerson, State Director, AARP North Carolina)

Army Analytics Group, Research Facilitation Laboratory

Blue Star Families (Kathy Roth-Douquet, Chief Executive Officer)

Defense Advisory Committee on Women in the Services, Department of Defense

Elizabeth Dole Foundation

Military Officers Association of America

National Military Family Association

Wounded Warrior Project

Appendix D

Acronyms and Glossary of Terms

ADHD	Attention-Deficit Hyperactivity Disorder
AVF	all-volunteer force
BRAC	base realignment and closures
CBPR	community-based participatory research
CDC	Centers for Disease Control and Prevention
CPT	cognitive processing therapy
CQI	continuous quality improvement system
DACOWITS	U.S. Defense Department Advisory Committee on Women in the Services
DADT	Don't Ask, Don't Tell
DEOMI	Defense Equal Opportunity Management Institute
DMDC	Defense Manpower Data Center
DoD	Department of Defense
DoDEA	Department of Defense Education Activity
DoDI	Department of Defense Instruction
DSF	Dynamic Sustainability Framework
EBP	evidence-based practice
EFMP	Exceptional Family Member Program

FAP	Family Advocacy Program
FOCUS	Families OverComing Under Stress
FY	fiscal year
GAO	Government Accountability Office
HP2020	Healthy People 2020
HQDA	Headquarters, Department of the Army
IDEA	Individuals with Disabilities Education Act
IEP	Individual Education Plan
IOM	Institute of Medicine (now the National Academy of Medicine)
JITAI	just-in-time adaptive intervention(s)
LGB(T)	lesbian, gay, bisexual, and transgender
MAVNI	Military Accessions Vital to the National Interest
MCEC	Military Child Education Coalition
MC&FP	Military Community and Family Policy
MFFM	Military Family Fitness Model
MFLC	Military Family Life Counselor
MFRS	Military Family Readiness System
MPP	Military Personnel Policy
MWR	Morale, Welfare, and Recreation
MyCAA	My Career Advancement Account
NCO	noncommissioned officer
NDAA	National Defense Authorization Act
NIH	National Institutes of Health
NIMHD	National Institute of Minority Health and Development
NORTH STAR	New Orientation to Reduce Threats to Health from Secretive Problems That Affect Readiness Program
NRC	National Research Council
OECD	Organisation for Economic Co-operation and Development
OEF/OIF	Operation Enduring Freedom/Operation Iraqi Freedom
OMB	Office of Management and Budget
OSD	Office of Secretary of Defense
OSN	Office of Special Needs

OUSD	Office of the Under Secretary of Defense
OXTR	oxytocin receptor
PCS	permanent change of station
P-D-S-A	Plan Do Study Act
PREP	Prevention and Relationship Enhancement Program
PTSD	posttraumatic stress disorder
RCT	randomized controlled trial
ROTC	Reserve Officer Training Corps
SEL	social–emotional learning
SNAP	Supplemental Nutrition Assistance Program
TANF	Temporary Assistance for Needy Families
TBI	traumatic brain injury
TFF	Total Force Fitness
U.S.C.	United States Code
USCIS	U.S. Citizenship and Immigration Services
USD P&R	Under Secretary of Defense for Personnel and Readiness
USO	United Service Organization
VA	Department of Veterans Affairs
VHA	Veterans Health Administration
WHO	World Health Organization
WIC	Women, Infants, and Children

Glossary

"above and below the skin" – refers to observed behavior as well as physiological and biological processes that are the effect of or correlated with one's experience of an adverse event or ongoing adverse events or maltreatment

Adaptome – a proposed set of approaches, processes, and infrastructure needed to advance the science of intervention adaptation; implementation provides a methodology that can support the integration of evidence that includes both traditional standards of evidence and phases of evidence-based practice development and validation as well as addressing the need for locally acceptable prevention programs that sometimes leads local providers to design and deliver their own programs ahead of evidence for effectiveness

Affective – emotional

Agender – describes an individual whose personal identity is genderless

Amygdala – one of the four basal ganglia; part of the limbic system; key role in processing emotions

Asexual – lacking sexual feelings, associations, or behaviors

Autonomic nervous system – controls bodily functions (e.g. heartrate, respiratory rate or volume, and digestion) unconsciously; protects the body against perceived threat(s)

Bigender – describes an individual whose personal identity encompasses both male and female gender

Child maltreatment – physical, emotional, or sexual abuse or educational or health neglect of a child by an adult, often a caregiver

Chronosystem - the fifth level of Bronfenbrenner's Ecological Systems Theory; inclusive of the environmental events (e.g. sociohistorical) and transitions that impact the development or functioning of the microsystem (e.g., individual or child)

Cisgender – describes individuals whose gender identity aligns with their biological sex

Cognitive processing therapy (CPT) – an empirically based therapy for the treatment of posttraumatic stress disorder, designed for the amelioration of adverse subjective experiences of trauma; usually 12 clinical sessions (individual or group)

Compendiums – a brief collection of information or knowledge

Contextual moderators – variables, elements, or aspects of the environment, or beyond the individual or group, that impact the functioning and/or perspectives of an individual or group

Continuous quality improvement (CQI) – ongoing process(es) for proactive technical assistance for an established system or program; provides actionable data linked to various outcomes

Continuous quality improvement (CQI) system – a necessary component to ensure that programs are data-driven with a clear direction toward cultivating adaptations and adjustments within services, programs, and resources. The goal of a CQI system is to provide actionable data that enables the system to address various outcomes (i.e., implementation, service, and client or customer outcomes) through specific identifiable adaptations or innovations.

Cortisol – known as the stress hormone, a steroid hormone that regulates a range of physiological processes (i.e. metabolism, immune response, and stress response)

Cultural adaptations – changes, often subtle, to the content of an intervention that are critical for perceived acceptability, relevance, and credibility of the intervention for the target population; include changes to culture-specific nomenclature of intervention materials (or vernacular) that may vary by geographic region or sub-populations essential to the implementation process

Dating violence – physical, sexual, or psychological violence within a dating relationship

Deployment – a short- or long-term relocation of an individual or group and required resources for the purpose of a military mission (i.e. war, conflict, humanitarian effort); can be domestic or international

Developmental stage – describes the physiological, psychological, and/or emotional phase of one's growth; usually refers to children

Diathesis-stress model – a model that suggests that some youth are more vulnerable to their caregiving environments and that some youth fare worse in stressful circumstances, but do as well as others in routine, low-risk environments

Donabedian framework – a method of assessing the quality of care; includes obtaining data on performance, analyzing patterns, generating a hypothesis for the pattern analysis, taking action based upon the hypothesis, and assessing the subsequent consequences

Dynamic Sustainability Framework (DSF) – describes how the adaptation of interventions may occur over time and their role in facilitating the integration and sustainability of interventions to adapt to the ever-changing context in which they are delivered, including changes to the delivery setting, target population, evidence base, political context, and other key variables that are known to occur over time

Dynamism – vitality

Dysregulation – disrupted ability to regulate metabolic, physiological, and/or psychological processes

Ecological approach – a way of thinking that focuses on intervention from the micro (individual) to macro (population) level via direct (e.g. psychotherapy) and indirect strategies (e.g., policy development)

Ecological framework – framework for constructing practice, policy, and research based on the impact of reciprocal relational factors on human functioning, processes, and outcomes

Ecological model – a theoretical design used to inform implementation that enables providers, installation services, and leaders to build on local capacities, strengths, and resources and to incorporate the local knowledge within the selection, adaptation, adoption and implementation of support services

Epigenetic – related environmental impacts on gene expression

Epinephrine (adrenaline) – a neurotransmitter that acts on alpha and beta receptors in the arteries; epinephrine increases blood sugar levels, heart rate, and heart contractility while also relaxing smooth muscle in the airways to improve breathing

Equifinality – refers to the obverse of multifinality, namely that the same outcome (e.g., anxiety, social challenges or poor academic functioning) can be evident following exposure to disparate stressor events (i.e., prolonged parental separation, relocation, and bullying)

Etiology – cause(s) of a disease or condition

Evidence-based – in reference to knowledge, programs, or practices: derived from systematic empirical research

Evidence-based intervention – deliberate efforts (clinical or nonclinical), based on empirical research and/or literature, designed to ameliorate the effects of a maladaptive process(es), problem(s), or event(s) after occurrence

Evidence-based practice (EBP) – practice designed from empirical research and/or literature

Evidence-based program – a (human service) program designed from empirical research and/or literature

Exosystem – the third level of Bronfenbrenner's Ecological Systems Theory; inclusive of the environmental elements which impact the development or functioning of the microsystem (e.g. individual or child)

Family diversity – refers to the variety of make-ups of families (e.g., nuclear, blended, single-parent, extended, same-sex)

Family integration – the reunification and reconnection of a military family upon the return of the military member(s) from a deployment of long-term, temporary duty away from the home station; includes events and processes associated with reunification and reconnection

Family stress model – a model that provides a conceptual framework for understanding how stressful contexts such as psychopathology, marital transitions, and socioeconomic conditions reverberate in the family and create complex effects among individuals (adults and children) in dyadic relationships (marital and parent-child), and more broadly within families

Family wellness – a measure of family health that includes interpersonal interactions, bonds, trust, resiliency, and functioning

Fraternization – relationships (e.g., romantic, sexual, friendship, business) between service members, which compromise or appear to compromise the chain of command, occupational environment, and/or mission execution or success; refers to DoD and service component-level policies prohibiting such relationships

Frontal cortex – cortex of the frontal lobe of the cerebral hemisphere of the brain; associated with aggression and impulse control

Gender-fluid – describes an individual whose personal identity is not fixed to either a male or a female gender

Gender identity – one's personal sense of identity and/or gender expression or lack thereof

Glucocorticoids – used to treat conditions leading to inflammation (e.g., asthma, arthritis, allergies)

Heteronormative – describes a perspective or worldview based upon heterosexual norms

Hippocampus – brain region located in the medial temporal lobe as part of the limbic system; assists with short-term, long-term, and spatial memory

Homeostasis – the tendency towards internal equilibrium

Hyperarousal – defined by Merriam-Webster's dictionary as "an abnormal state of increased responsiveness to stimuli that is marked by various physiological and psychological symptoms (such as increased levels of alertness and anxiety and elevated heart rate and respiration)." In addition, to be diagnosed with PTSD, "a person has to have been exposed to an extreme stressor or traumatic event to which he or she responded with fear, helplessness, or horror and to have three distinct types of symptoms consisting of reexperiencing of the event, avoidance of reminders of the event, and hyperarousal for at least one month."

Hypocortisolism – acute adrenal insuffiency; also referred to adrenocortical hypofunction; symptoms include decreased stress response, fatigue, joint and/or muscle pain or weakness, hypotension, and gastrointestinal problems

Hypothalamic-pituitary-adrenal (HPA) axis – the biological system most closely linked to stress, which releases the hormone cortisol when an individual experiences stress

Intersectionality – the interconnectedness of social categorization and/or grouping (e.g., gender, socioeconomic status, race)

Intervention – deliberate efforts (clinical or nonclinical) to ameliorate the effects of a maladaptive process(es), problem(s), or event(s) after occurrence

Intrafamilial – occurring within a family system

Just-in-time adaptive interventions (JITAIs) – form of an adaptive intervention that aims to address in real time the rapidly changing needs of individuals or families

Life course – refers to the entirety of developmental and life stages throughout the duration of a life span

Life-course model – an organized concept that in the aggregate describes the cycle of developmental processes and life stages throughout the duration of a life span

Lived experience – the subjective perspective and associated functioning of an individual or group; includes contextual factors and interpersonal relations

Longitudinal – a form of scientific research (to seek knowledge through examination, observation, or inference) which studies subjects or populations over a long period of time

Macrosystem – the fifth level (cultural environment) of Bronfenbrenner's Ecological Systems Theory

Maltreatment – physical, emotional, or sexual abuse or educational, financial or health care neglect of an individual by another, usually a caregiver

Mastery-motivation – the drive to persist to achieve a difficult task or goal

Mesosystem – the second level of Bronfenbrenner's Ecological Systems Theory; inclusive of the family, peers, and surrounding community

mHealth interventions – mobile technology-based efforts, usually clinical, designed or organized to ameliorate the negative health effects of a maladaptive process(es), problem(s), or event(s) after occurrence

Microaggression – subtle overt or covert acts by an individual or group that cause distress to another individual or group

Microsystem – the first level (individual level) of Bronfenbrenner's Ecological Systems Theory

Military dependent – a family member for whom a military service member is financially responsible and who is a recipient of military benefits (e.g., health care, base access, and services)

Military Family Fitness Model (MFFM) – a comprehensive model aimed at enhancing family fitness and resilience across the life span. The MFFM has three core components: (1) family demands, (2) resources (including individual resources, family resources, and external resources), and (3) family outcomes (including related metrics)

Military family readiness – the capacity of a family to manage military lifestyle and functions (e.g., deployment, relocation, military trauma and/or strain)

Military Family Readiness System (MFRS) – the network of programs, services, people and agencies, and the collaboration among them, that promotes the readiness and quality of life of service members and their families

Minority stress theory – a theory that describes minority group members' unique experiences of chronic stresses stemming from social institutions in addition to everyday experiences of racial bias. When applied to sexual minorities, analysis tends to focus on stresses related to heteronormative bias and anti-LGBT experiences

Multifinality – refers to the finding that one stressor (e.g., physical abuse) can have many different negative effects on neurodevelopmental conditions – intellectual and/or psychological conditions that develop in early childhood (e.g., autism, learning disabilities)

Norepinephrine – a neurotransmitter that acts on alpha receptors in the arteries; increases blood sugar levels, heart rate, and heart contractility

Operational tempo – the pace of military operations and/missions; descriptive of the demands on personnel to achieve operational or/or mission objectives

Oxytocin – a neurotransmitter (hormone) produced by the hypothalamus and secreted by the pituitary gland

Oxytocin receptor (OXTR) – a protein that acts as a receptor for the neurotransmitter (hormone) oxytocin; can buffer the adverse impacts of social environments, events, or processes

Pathogenesis – the development of events leading to a disease or pattern of disease

Permanent change of station (PCS) – permanent relocation of a military member and/or family from one military installation to another

Personnel tempo (*perstempo*) – refers to the amount of time individuals serve away from their home duty station, whether for deployments, sea duty, exercises, unit training or individual training.

Population health framework – a conceptual, practice, or policy framework in which health, disease, and/or health risks are examined, treated, or mitigated based upon community or group health trends and needs

Prolonged exposure (PE) – an empirically-based therapy for the treatment of posttraumatic stress disorder, designed for the amelioration of adverse subjective experiences of trauma; focuses on guided and graduated exposure to trauma-related events, details, fears, and/or avoided triggers

Prosociality – the quality of prosocial behavior (e.g., donating, sharing, helping, caregiving, cooperating)

Psychopathology – the study or presence of mental health disorder(s)

Questioning – may refer to the status of an individual who questions his/her/their own gender status and/or sexual orientation

Readiness – state of preparedness for military-related actions or defense (e.g. deployment, antiterrorism, installation defense)

Resilience – the capacity of an individual or group to endure and/or overcome adversity; functions of intra-individual characteristics and associated with characteristics of the outside environment

Self-efficacy – one's personal sense of competence in general or in a given area

Self-regulation – an individual's ability to manage emotions, behaviors, and interactions for optimal functioning

Sexual violence – the use of physical force to compel a person to witness or engage in a sexual act against his or her will. Sexual violence includes attempted or completed nonconsensual sex, unwanted sexual contact, and sexual harassment.

Stress regulatory systems – most commonly the nervous system and endocrine system

Systems principle of homeostasis – principle of Bronfenbrenner's Ecological Systems Theory; idea that the whole system, inclusive of five levels, remains relative stable and/or seeks equilibrium upon disruption

Taxonomy – classification or organization of individuals or groups

Third gender – describes an individual whose personal identity is neither male nor female, not both male and female, and not any combination of male and female

Total Force Fitness – a holistic concept for building and maintaining health, readiness, and optimal performance of the U.S. Armed Forces using the connection between mind, body, spirit, environment, and relationships (see https://www.hprc-online.org/page/total-force-fitness)

Transgender – describes individuals whose gender expression or identity does not match or is not limited to their biological sex

Trauma-informed – health care, programs, or practices developed from and responsive to all types of trauma (e.g. military-related trauma, domestic or interpersonal violence, health crisis, threat to life or well-being)

BOARD ON CHILDREN, YOUTH, AND FAMILIES

The Board on Children, Youth, and Families (BCYF) is a nongovernmental, scientific body within the National Academies of Sciences, Engineering, and Medicine that advances the health, learning, development, resilience, and well-being of all children, youth, and families. The board convenes top experts from multiple disciplines to analyze the best available evidence on critical issues facing children, youth, and families. Our ability to evaluate research simultaneously from the perspectives of the biological, behavioral, health, and social sciences allows us to shed light on innovative and influential solutions to inform the nation. Our range of methods—from rapidly convened workshops to consensus reports and forum activities—allows us to respond with the timeliness and depth required to make the largest possible impact on the health and well-being of children, youth, and their families throughout the entire lifecycle. BCYF publications provide independent analyses of the science and go through a rigorous external peer-review process.